Violence against Girls and Women

Recent Titles in
Women's Psychology

"Intimate" Violence against Women: When Spouses, Partners, or Lovers Attack
Paula K. Lundberg-Love and Shelly L. Marmion, editors

Daughters of Madness: Growing Up and Older with a Mentally Ill Mother
Susan Nathiel

Psychology of Women: Handbook of Issues and Theories, Second Edition
Florence L. Denmark and Michele Paludi, editors

WomanSoul: The Inner Life of Women's Spirituality
Carole A. Rayburn and Lillian Comas-Diaz, editors

The Psychology of Women at Work: Challenges and Solutions for Our Female Workforce
Michele A. Paludi, editor

Feminism and Women's Rights Worldwide, Three Volumes
Michele A. Paludi, editor

Single Mother in Charge: How to Successfully Pursue Happiness
Sandy Chalkoun

Women and Mental Disorders, Four Volumes
Paula K. Lundberg-Love, Kevin L. Nadal, and Michele A. Paludi, editors

Reproductive Justice: A Global Concern
Joan C. Chrisler, editor

The Psychology of Love, Four Volumes
Michele A. Paludi, editor

An Essential Handbook of Women's Sexuality, Two Volumes
Donna Castañeda, editor

Psychological Health of Women of Color: Intersections, Challenges, and Opportunities
Lillian Comas-Díaz and Beverly Greene, editors

Violence against Girls and Women

International Perspectives

Janet A. Sigal and
Florence L. Denmark, Editors
Foreword by Joan C. Chrisler

Volume 1

In Childhood, Adolescence, and Young Adulthood

Praeger Perspectives
Women's Psychology
Michele A. Paludi, Series Editor

An Imprint of ABC-CLIO, LLC
Santa Barbara, California • Denver, Colorado • Oxford, England

Library of Congress Cataloging-in-Publication Data

Violence against girls and women : international perspectives / Janet A. Sigal and Florence L. Denmark, editors ; foreword by Joan C. Chrisler.
volumes cm. — (Women's psychology)
Includes bibliographical references and index.
ISBN 978-1-4408-0335-2 (hardcover : alk. paper) — ISBN 978-1-4408-0336-9 (ebook)
1. Girls—Violence against. 2. Girls—Crimes against. 3. Women—Violence against. 4. Women—Crimes against. I. Sigal, Janet. II. Denmark, Florence.
HV6250.4.G57V558 2013
362.88—dc23 2013002150

ISBN: 978-1-4408-0335-2
EISBN: 978-1-4408-0336-9

17 16 15 14 13 1 2 3 4 5

This book is also available on the World Wide Web as an eBook.
Visit www.abc-clio.com for details.

Praeger
An Imprint of ABC-CLIO, LLC

ABC-CLIO, LLC
130 Cremona Drive, P.O. Box 1911
Santa Barbara, California 93116-1911

This book is printed on acid-free paper ♾
Manufactured in the United States of America

This book is dedicated to Malala Yousafzai, a young girl from Pakistan who was attacked by the Taliban for advocating education for girls. We also dedicate this book to all the brave individuals around the world who fight to protect girls and women from violence.

"If the new generation is not given pens they will be given guns by the terrorists. We must raise our voice."
—Malala Yousafzai (*Newsweek,* October 29, 2012, p. 43)

Contents

Series Foreword

> Because women's work is never done and is underpaid or unpaid or boring or repetitious and we're the first to get fired and what we look like is more important than what we do and if we get raped it's our fault and if we get beaten we must have provoked it and if we raise our voices we're nagging bitches and if we enjoy sex we're nymphos and if we don't we're frigid and if we love women it's because we can't get a "real" man and if we ask our doctor too many questions we're neurotic and/or pushy and if we expect childcare we're selfish and if we stand up for our rights we're aggressive and "unfeminine" and if we don't we're typical weak females and if we want to get married we're out to trap a man and if we don't we're unnatural and because we still can't get an adequate safe contraceptive but men can walk on the moon and if we can't cope or don't want a pregnancy we're made to feel guilty about abortion and . . . for lots of other reasons we are part of the women's liberation movement.
>
> —Author unknown, quoted in *The Torch*
> September 14, 1987

The sentiment in this excerpt outlines the major goals of Praeger's book series, Women's Psychology:

1. Valuing women. The books in this series value women by valuing children and working for affordable child care; valuing women by respecting all physiques, not just placing value on slender women;

valuing women by acknowledging older women's wisdom, beauty, aging; valuing women who have been sexually victimized and viewing them as survivors; valuing women who work inside and outside of the home; and valuing women by respecting their choices of careers, of whom they mentor, of their reproductive rights, their spirituality and their sexuality.
2. Treating women as the norm. Thus the books in this series make up for women's issues typically being omitted, trivialized, or dismissed from other books on psychology.
3. Taking a non-Eurocentric view of women's experiences. The books in this series integrate the scholarship on race and ethnicity into women's psychology, thus providing a psychology of *all* women. Women typically have been described collectively, but we are diverse.
4. Facilitating connections between readers' experiences and psychological theories and empirical research. The books in this series offer readers opportunities to challenge their views about women, feminism, sexual victimization, gender role socialization, education, and equal rights. These texts thus encourage women readers to value themselves and others. The accounts of women's experiences as reflected through research and personal stories in the texts in this series have been included for readers to derive strength from the efforts of others who have worked for social change on the interpersonal, organizational, and societal levels.

A student in one of my courses on the psychology of women once stated:

> I learned so much about women. Women face many issues: discrimination, sexism, prejudices . . . by society. Women need to work together to change how society views us. I learned so much and talked about much of the issues brought up in class to my friends and family. My attitudes have changed toward a lot of things. I got to look at myself, my life, and what I see for the future. (Paludi, 2002, p. 378)

It is my hope that readers of the books in this series also reflect on the topics and look at themselves, their own lives, and what they see for the future.

Dr. Janet Sigal and Dr. Florence Denmark have honored the goals of this series on women's psychology by placing violence in its cultural context. Sigal and Denmark aptly note that gender-based hate crimes are the most prevalent type of hate crimes committed by and experienced by children, adolescents, and adults throughout the world. Contributors to these volumes have addressed that violence against women is shaped by gender roles and status in society. Furthermore, with respect to the impact of violence to children, adolescents, and adults, including rape, intimate partner violence, sexual harassment, and bullying, several reports have documented the high cost of various forms of violence within three major perspectives: (a) psychological health, (b) physiological, and (c) education and work. Responses by individuals to violence include headaches, sleep disturbances, disordered eating, gastrointestinal disorders, nausea, crying spells, scars, bruising, broken bones, absenteeism from school or work, decreased morale, decreased life satisfaction, performance decrements, damage to interpersonal relationships at school or work, and posttraumatic stress disorder. In addition, girls and women think about violence to themselves through self-injury (e.g., cutting) as well as suicide. Furthermore, individuals who have not had anyone intervene on their behalf to stop the violence learn to keep silent about future abuse because they believe no one will ever help them.

Sigal and Denmark's texts teach us that gendered violence is a major public health, human rights, and global health issue that requires a coordinated response from parents, teachers, legislators, counselors, and providers in the individual's community. Sigal and Denmark also encourage us to be advocates in guiding institutional and social policy change in work and educational institutions and in lobbying state and federal legislators on issues related to international violence against women.

These texts support United Nations Secretary-General Ban Ki-moon's message for the International Day for the Elimination of Violence against Women (November 25, 2011; UN News Center, 2011):

> Violence against women and girls takes many forms and is widespread throughout the globe. . . . On this International Day, I urge governments and partners around the world to harness the energy, ideas and leadership of young people to help us to end this pandemic of violence. Only then will we have a more just, peaceful and equitable world.

Sigal and Denmark's texts provide us with the frameworks for accomplishing this goal.

Michele A. Paludi

REFERENCES

Paludi, M. (2002). *The psychology of women* (2nd ed.). Upper Saddle River, NJ: Prentice Hall.

UN News Center. (2011). Top UN officials highlight youth leadership in ending violence against women. Retrieved from http://www.un.org/apps/news/story.asp?NewsID=40494#.UTpLRKXQ2s1

Foreword

> A dog, a wife, and a cherry tree, the more ye beat them the better they be.
>
> —Anonymous (as cited by Stahly, 2008, p. 359)

> In a culture of domination, preoccupation with victimage is inevitable.
>
> —bell hooks (1992)

Feminist activists and scholars who work to expose and oppose violence against women are often derided in the media as "victim feminists" who prefer to ignore women's progress and wallow in the dark side of human nature (e.g., http://fathersforlife.org/feminism/victim_feminism.htm; http://victimfeministcentral.blogspot.com). Such derision is intended to minimize and marginalize the real and present dangers to women and girls around the world whose lives have been marred, scarred, or lost due to violence and to those who are at risk of similar experiences. Like all feminists, I delight in celebrating women's progress and success, but I remain aware that I cannot avert my eyes from the pain and suffering of those who have been harmed, both physically and mentally, by the misogyny, domination, and abusive tactics that are too frequently deployed to prevent further progress and success. The brightness of the light side must not be allowed to blind us to the presence of the dark side until all of us are standing in the light.

Why is there so much violence in the world, and why is so much of it directed at women? These are not easy questions to answer. Psychologists have suggested a number of possible reasons that derive from evolutionary, emotional, and social learning theories (Franzoi, 2009). First, evolutionary pressures, such as efforts to protect resources (e.g., territory, mates) that enable survival and reproduction (i.e., passing on one's genes), are frequently assumed to be underlying causes of violence. Wars over territory and control of natural resources are examples that support this perspective, as is intimate partner violence aimed at controlling women's behavior and ensuring that one's mate is not "poached" by another man. Second, the frustration-aggression hypothesis suggests that negative emotions can trigger violence, especially under conditions of traumatic stress or deprivation or when individuals do not have sufficient resources to cope with their emotions. Intimate partner violence, rape (including war-related sexual assaults), and elder abuse could be considered examples that support this theory. Third, social learning theory indicates that most violence is learned from watching other people act aggressively and abusively. If people see others rewarded (or at least not punished) for violent behavior, they will be more inclined to act violently themselves. This is likely to be especially true when cultural and social norms condone violence. The United States, for example, has been described as a rape-prone culture (Rozee, 1995) that celebrates aggression and domination. Violence is a frequent theme in American films, television shows, pornography, video games, comic books, and popular songs (Chrisler & Ferguson, 2006), and we export our cultural products all over the world. Of course, other cultures throughout history also have had reputations for violent behavior and cultural images, and they also have exported their norms, albeit less quickly than is possible today with the help of the Internet. Every type of violence against women and girls is showcased in popular culture, and thus taught and "condoned" (at least to some extent).

Regardless of the cause of any particular act of violence, these theories all suggest that women and girls are especially likely to suffer because of their lower social status (e.g., they are often objectified and considered "belongings" of men), lesser physical strength and social power to defend themselves, tradition or other social norms that condone or fail to punish transgressions against women and girls consistently, and the ubiquity of images of women as victims in cultural products of many kinds. Violence against women and girls takes a huge toll on individuals, families, and societies. Victims suffer a myriad of physical injuries, which are often followed by deficits in mental health and well-being that can last for a long time. Victims may be unable to work for short or long periods of time after the violence, which results in economic loss to the family that can damage the well-being of those (e.g., children, elders) who depend on the woman's income or labor. Societies must pay for health care for victims and deal with other aftereffects of violence, such as the loss of human capital (e.g., unnecessary deaths, loss of women's labor in the home and the workplace, family disintegration). Thus, it is in everyone's best interest that public policy support interventions (e.g., risk reduction, screening for experience of violence, support for coping and recovery from violence) designed to ameliorate the damage violence causes the world's women and girls.

In 1985, U.S. Surgeon-General C. Everett Koop declared violence against women a public health crisis (Chrisler & Ferguson, 2006). Despite efforts in many countries to provide victim services and undertake prevention efforts, the situation worldwide remains bleak, and new forms of violence (e.g., cyberbullying, trafficking, elder abuse) have arisen and been exposed since that time. UN Secretary-General Ban Ki-moon (2009) recently described violence against women as a pandemic "abomination" that should be considered an attack on "the foundation of our civilization" and "against everything in the United Nations Charter." Documentation and recognition of the extent of the problem is the first step in solving it. Drs. Janet Sigal and Florence Denmark are advancing those efforts by providing a broad-based and international perspective on violence against women and girls. This two-volume work is unusual in that it combines and presents topics that are rarely considered together as part of the same public health crisis (e.g., cyberbullying, genital cutting, workplace violence, elder abuse). The decision to take such a broad view will offer readers ample opportunity to consider the ways that disparate types of violence and abuse converge and diverge, and this opportunity will, perhaps, allow us to determine better prevention measures. A particular strength of these books is the editors' instruction to each author to discuss intervention efforts and public policy initiatives that have been, or could be, effective.

It is not easy for authors, editors, or readers to confront descriptions of pain and suffering like those found in this work. I advise readers to take it one chapter at a time, with a pause between chapters to reflect and refocus, rather than reading the books straight through, which could be overwhelming. Furthermore, I encourage readers to admire the resilience, as well as sympathize with the suffering, of survivors of violence. As we read, we must focus on the authors' practical suggestions for changing policy and practice in ways that could ultimately reduce violence, and then we must participate actively in the hard work of making change that will promote peace and social justice. The health and well-being of the world's women and girls depend on our efforts. It is a matter of life or death.

Joan C. Chrisler

REFERENCES

Ban, K. (2009, March 5). Violence against women "cannot be tolerated" in any circumstance, by any political leader or government, says secretary-general, at

New York observance. Retrieved from http://www.un.org/News/Press/docs/2009/sgsm12127.doc.htm

Chrisler, J. C., & Ferguson, S. (2006). Violence against women as a public health issue. *Annals of the New York Academy of Sciences, 1087*, 235–249.

Franzoi, S. L. (2009). *Social psychology* (5th ed.). New York, NY: McGraw-Hill.

Hooks, B. (1992). Agent of change: An interview with bell hooks. *Tricycle.* Retrieved from http://www.tricycle.com/special-section/agent-change-an-interview-with-bell-hooks

Rozee, P. (1993). Forbidden or forgiven: Rape in cross-cultural perspective. *Psychology of Women Quarterly, 17*, 499–514.

Stahly, G. B. (2008). Battered women: Why don't they just leave? In J. C. Chrisler, C. Golden, & P. D. Rozee (Eds.), *Lectures on the psychology of women* (4th ed., pp. 356–375). New York, NY: McGraw-Hill.

Acknowledgments

We want to thank all our wonderful colleagues who have contributed chapters to our books. We are grateful for their knowledge, expertise, sensitivity, and alacrity in responding quickly to our requests. We have learned so much about violence against girls and women from their chapters, many of which included students as coauthors. Throughout our careers, students have inspired us because of their concern for those girls and women who have confronted violence.

We are most indebted to the NGO community at the UN in New York for increasing our awareness of the scope and magnitude of this global problem.

Our thanks also to our colleagues in the International Social and Behavioral Research Alliance for their encouragement and support throughout this process.

Michele Paludi has been particularly helpful with both her suggestions and her enthusiasm for this project.

Emily Dow has provided us with essential technical assistance, and Deborah Williams and Amy Nadel have assisted us in many small but significant tasks throughout this endeavor.

Finally, our thanks to Debbie Carvalko, who has guided us through this intensive and complex process.

Chapter 1

Introduction

Janet A. Sigal and Florence L. Denmark

The world is a dangerous place for women and girls. They are subjected to violent attacks in the home, schools, and the workplace and are victims of sexual assault in their communities.

At times, a violent act against girls or women is so graphic and appalling it captures the attention of the global community. Recently, Malala Yousafzai, a 15-year-old girl from the Swat Valley in Pakistan, was shot in the head as she rode on a bus. She was attacked because "she had become a symbol of resistance against the Taliban, advocating access to education for girls in an area that has been one of the Taliban's main strongholds in Pakistan" (*New York Times,* October 27, 2012, p. A9). Condemnation of this vicious act and sympathy for her plight came from all over the world after the attack.

Although this type of extreme and horrific incident is sometimes universally condemned, continuing acts of violence in global settings often are not known or reported. As an example, the Human Rights Watch report (2012) on Afghanistan indicating that 87% of women in that country experience some type of violence in their lives was not widely disseminated.

In fact, it took a near-death attack for the world to be aware of the horror of Malala's situation. Expressing the hopelessness that many girls in Afghanistan and other countries feel, 17-year-old student Pashtuna said, "I dream, but I fear to dream" because she knows that when she awakens from the dream her hopes of a better life will be crushed and she will be devastated (S. Maier, personal communication, October 27, 2012).

After hearing about violent attacks all over the world, and because we are both part of Psychology NGOs at the UN in New York, we decided to edit these books on violence against girls and women. Through our work on NGO committees, including the Committee on the Status of Women, the Committee on Ageing, the Committee on the Family, and the Committee on Mental Health, we have become energized and hopeful but, at the same time, discouraged. We are hopeful because the UN, other organizations such as the World Health Organization (WHO), and NGOs around the world have made eliminating violence a priority in their attempts to create a safer world for girls and women. However, it is also discouraging because despite these efforts, girls and women of all ages still live in a hostile world in many societies. Even in nations that have laws prohibiting violence against women and girls, these laws often are not effectively implemented or have been criticized and attacked. In the United States, for example, the Violence Against Women Act (VAWA) was reauthorized by Congress and then signed by President Barrack Obama on March 7, 2013, after a long delay because of an inability to reconcile the Senate and House of Representatives Bill. In addition, during the 2012 presidential and congressional election campaigns, there were attacks on women's reproductive rights, with some candidates suggesting that women who have been victims of "legitimate" rape cannot get pregnant! Thus, even in Westernized nations, women are being forced to fight battles again that they thought were won.

It is important to offer statistics illustrating the pattern of various types of violence, even though these statistics are difficult to obtain because of underreporting. The following numbers partially illuminate the magnitude of this global problem:

1. Domestic violence ranges from about 15% to 71% globally (WHO, 2005).
2. Approximately 1 in 5 women have experienced sexual abuse as young girls (WHO, 2005).
3. Sex trafficking of women and girls is one of the most lucrative criminal enterprises in the world (see the chapter by Sidun and Rubin in Volume 2 of this text).

In this two-volume publication, we begin with a historical context of violence against girls and women and a description of how violence in families may be cyclical. We then conceptualize violence against girls and women on a developmental continuum that is illustrated by the scope of our chapters. Violence begins prebirth, through sex selection and forced abortions, continues through childhood, and extends into adolescence and early adulthood. In adulthood through older age, women are subjected to sexual harassment, domestic violence, sexual assault, sex trafficking, and elder abuse. Our two volumes are separated into Volume 1: In Childhood, Adolescence, and Young Adulthood, and Volume 2: In Adulthood, Midlife, and Older Age.

Many of our authors are members of the NGO community at the UN or members of international organizations that are concerned with this global problem. Each chapter describes examples and information about violence against girls and women throughout the world. Each of our authors emphasize cultural factors and the need for culturally sensitive intervention programs. Working through local NGOs or "boots on the ground" is the preferred approach, and there is agreement that one size (or approach) will not fit in all situations.

The importance of changing the status of women globally, reducing gender inequality, and increasing respect for women is advocated in several chapters. In this regard, several of our coauthors address the issue of adverse effects of patriarchal attitudes on women and girls. Education and empowerment often are recommendations in the chapters to combat this global violence.

Violence against females of all ages is a human rights violation that prevents women from leading fulfilling lives. However, there are some encouraging signs. Referring to our earlier example of Malala Yousafzai, despite the patriarchal culture of the Taliban and death threats, her father and her family continue to support all her efforts. Her father spoke emotionally from England where she is being treated and said: "They wanted to kill her . . . but she fell temporarily. She will rise again. She will stand again" (*New York Times,* October 20, 2012, p. A9).

If women are given their rightful place in society, without fear of violence, not only women, but all people and societies, will benefit.

REFERENCES

Cowell, A. (2012, October 26). Pakistani activist, 15, recovering at "encouraging speed," father says. *New York Times.* Retrieved from http://www.nytimes.com/2012/10/27/world/asia/malala-yousafzai-is-recoving-at-encouraging-speed-father-says.html?_r=0

Human Rights Watch. (2012). *World report 2012: Violence and discrimination against women and girls.* Downloaded at http://www.hrw.org/world-report-2012/world-report-2012-afghanistan

World Health Organization. (2005). *WHO multi-country study on women's health and domestic violence against women: Summary report of initial results on prevalence, health outcomes, and women's responses.* Geneva, Switzerland: Author. Retrieved from http://www.who.int/gender/violence/who_multicountry_study/en

Chapter 2

From Social Purity to Women's Liberation: A History of Violence against Women in the United States

Alexandra Rutherford and Jenna MacKay

Violence, or the threat of violence, has been an omnipresent part of women's lives throughout history. Yet as many scholars have pointed out, from the early 1900s until the 1970s, there was a notable absence of public discussion about violence against women in the United States. This silence created the perception, held by many Americans during that time, that rape, incest, and domestic violence rarely happened (Breines & Gordon, 1983; F. Davis, 1991; Pleck, 2004). As one historian has noted, "There were virtually no public discussions of wife-beating from the turn of the century until the mid-1970s" (Pleck, 2004, p. 182). When domestic violence was discussed during this time, it was cast by police as "domestic disturbance" or by counselors or caseworkers as "family maladjustment." Rape too went largely undefined and undiscussed as a social problem from the early 1900s until the speak-outs of the early 1970s. One catalyst for mass public awareness at this time was the publication of feminist writer Susan Griffin's article "Rape—The All-American Crime" in *Ramparts* magazine (Griffin, 1971). This was followed a few years later by Susan Brownmiller's classic work *Against Our Will: Men, Women, and Rape* in 1975. One reviewer of this work wrote at the time that rape was a topic "hitherto as well known to conventional scholars as the dark side of the moon" (Shorter, 1977, p. 471).

Thus, despite the undeniable reality of many forms of violence in American women's lives, violence against women as a *public reality*, as something named, talked about, and identified as a social problem, emerged briefly in the mid- to late-1800s, then receded until the 1970s. Once it resurfaced due to the efforts of second-wave feminists, it became a potential topic for social scientific inquiry (Rutherford, 2011). In this chapter we outline in broad brushstrokes how, in the United States, violence against women emerged, receded, and reemerged in public discourse from the late 1800s to the 1970s. This ebb and flow was intimately tied to social, political, moral, and legal shifts in how "the family" has been defined, to the changing legal rights and status of children and women in American society, and to the ebb and flow of feminism itself. We then briefly outline and contextualize some of the pioneering research on violence against women conducted by social scientists, focusing particularly on the research that emerged in the early 1970s. We leave discussion of more contemporary work to other chapter authors who are themselves research experts on violence against women.

It is important to note at the outset that the history of violence against women in the United States is deeply imbued with race and class issues, a complexity that we hint at but do not fully develop in this short chapter. Additionally, in confining ourselves to the American context, we clearly restrict the geographic, cultural, and sociopolitical scope of our analysis. However, to even attempt to sample the extensive literature on the history of violence against women in other parts of the world would result in a highly superficial pastiche of this important work, which must itself be understood within its own historical and cultural contexts. Finally, although violence against women takes many forms (e.g., verbal, physical, emotional, sexual) and occurs at both individual and societal levels, we focus our discussion around male violence against women (formerly referred to as "wife-beating") and rape, acknowledging that these intersect with other forms of violence.

VIOLENCE AS VICE: FIRST-WAVE FEMINISM AND THE SOCIAL PURITY MOVEMENT

The late-1800s marked both the height of the Social Purity movement in the United States and a period of intense activity by first-wave feminists; the two were not unrelated. The goal of the Social Purity movement was to root out prostitution, pornography, and male sexual vice. The campaign for social purity focused both on regulating male sexuality and rescuing wayward girls and prostitutes with the aim of abolishing prostitution entirely (we use the historically appropriate term *prostitution* here, but acknowledge that the term *sex work* is preferred in the contemporary context). It was allied with other social reform movements such as the Temperance movement. Many first-wave feminists, such as Elizabeth Cady Stanton and Susan B. Anthony, identified with one or both of these movements. Indeed, in casting women as naturally moral and virtuous, the "purer sex," many women's rights activists hoped to convince the general public of women's right to vote and make other important decisions.

In this context, specific concern about male violence focused initially on the issue of child welfare, temperance, and social purity and only indirectly on violence against wives and mothers. As Linda Gordon has noted: "The issue of wife-beating was influential throughout the nineteenth-century women's rights movement, but it was addressed primarily indirectly, through temperance, child welfare, and social purity campaigns, and only marginally through direct lobbying for legislative or judicial reforms" (Gordon, 1988, p. 254). Prohibitionists tied family violence to male drunkenness; social purity reformers saw unchecked male sexual desire as one cause of male violence, including what we would now call marital rape. Indeed, the first social agencies devoted to family violence arose in the 1870s and were called Societies for the Prevention of Cruelty to Children (SPCCs), which themselves had been preceded by Societies for the Protection of Cruelty to Animals. With the establishment of SPCCs, however, it quickly became clear that child abuse often occurred in tandem with wife abuse. Even so, women's rights activists—especially those who were less radical in their methods—were reluctant to make wife-beating itself the centerpiece of their campaigns. Demanding too much power for women, such as the right to divorce an abusive husband or legally take away his children, was regarded as sufficiently radical as to pose a threat to their overall cause. The long-suffering, devoted wife—in a system where victimization signaled virtue—was a more valuable political symbol than the rebellious wife who rejected her violent husband. There were divorce rights activists, to be sure (including Stanton, Anthony, and Amelia Bloomer), but even they tended to focus more on the issue of marital rape than on wife-beating (see Pleck, 1983). Infused with the eugenic concern that women who had to submit sexually to their drunken husbands might bear children who would inherit his degenerate propensities, they called on women and lawmakers to support the right to divorce.

Despite the common misconception that husbands had the right to beat their wives in the 19th century, by the 1880s, it was effectively illegal to beat one's wife in most states. In 1850 and 1857, Tennessee and Georgia, respectively, passed laws making wife-beating a misdemeanor (Pleck, 1979). Maryland became the first state, in 1882, to pass a law that made wife-beating a criminal offence. The enforcement of the law was slower in coming. Informal tolerance of wife-beating was reflected in the prevalent notion of the "rule of thumb." This rule indicated that a husband must not use a stick thicker than his thumb to beat his wife. Furthermore, public discussion of wife-beating was still deemed unseemly, or as Gordon (1988) has put it, "Although wife-beating was not widely considered legitimate, neither was public discussion of it" (p. 255). In some respects, this tolerance of wife-beating reflected a general social and state reluctance to intervene in the "private" affairs of the family—at least those affairs concerning two adults. Notably, the protection of *children* became a national movement that "swept aside the fear of outside intervention in the family" (Pleck, 2004, p. 69). This may have helped women's rights activists, who used this newly overcome reluctance to renew their cause of fighting cruelty in the home, including cruelty toward wives.

In 1885, a group of affluent women members of Chicago's Moral Education Society set up the Protective Agency for Women and Children. The establishment of the Protective Agency was catalyzed in part by social purity concerns heightened by widespread publicity over sex crimes, especially against children. Referred to by one historian as "the most significant organizational effort to aid female victims of violence in nineteenth-century America" (Pleck, 2004, p. 95), the agency provided both legal aid and temporary shelter to assaulted wives and rape victims. It was the first and only 19th-century agency of its kind in the United States (Pleck, 1983). As agency members stepped up their work and the number of cases increased, it became clear to them that women's inability to leave violent marriages was a major obstacle to progress and reform. They began to help women obtain legal separations and divorces and to force men to assume child support. These actions led to the perception that the agency was antifamily and provoked public scorn, but the work continued.

The fate of the Protective Agency for Women and Children is telling. Although the agency proposed the idea of a network of other agencies across the country to the National Council of Women, no action was taken to form such a network and no new agencies were founded. Instead, the Protective Agency merged in 1896 with the Bureau of Justice, a predominantly male organization, in part to leverage the resources of a much larger bureaucracy. For a number of years, the Protection Agency maintained control over its own jurisdiction—namely, cases affecting women and children. Members continued to help women secure divorces in cases of abuse. In 1905, the Bureau of Justice merged with the Legal Aid Society of Chicago, and the Protective Agency continued to maintain its autonomy within this merger. However, by 1912, reports of the agency's work dropped from the annual reports, and by 1920, Chicago Legal Aid adopted an official policy of discouraging divorce in all cases (Pleck, 2004). By this time, feminism in general was on the decline, and public attention to crimes against women had become virtually nonexistent.

SOCIAL PURITY, RACE, AND RAPE: FEMINISTS DIVIDED

The links between racism and first-wave feminism have been well documented (A. Y. Davis, 1981; Giddings, 1984; Lerner, 1979). Many White women's rights activists shrunk from including allied Black reformers in the fight for (or even cause of) suffrage, and many—such as Charlotte Perkins Gilman—were outright racist and eugenicist (see Gilman, 1908, 1914). Nowhere did these tensions play out more prominently than in the relationship between Frances Willard, the head of the Women's Christian Temperance Union, and Ida B. Wells, prominent antiracist activist, feminist, and antilynching campaigner.

Wells, a well-known African American journalist and coeditor of Memphis' Black weekly newspaper *Free Speech,* turned her considerable intellect and energy to the antilynching cause after a particularly brutal incident in Memphis, Tennessee, in 1892. In this horrifying case, three prominent Black businessmen were dragged from prison where they were awaiting trial for attempted murder and were savagely tortured and shot by a White mob. Earlier, gun-toting White intruders (actually sheriffs in plainclothes who had been hired by the White owner of a competing business) had entered the store owned by the Black businessmen, who responded to the intrusion by shooting in self-defense. Thus "tricked," the men were put in jail to await trial, when four days later they were dragged out of their cells and murdered. Wells knew one of the men well and was aghast not only at the viciousness of the killings but also at the callousness with which the White press reported the incident. From that moment on, she devoted herself tirelessly to the antilynching campaign, as well as to eradicating the myth of the "Negro" rapist (see Bederman, 1995).

As Wells began to research and report on the crime of lynching, she quickly discovered that the rape of White women by Black men was frequently used by Whites as the unassailable justification for lynching, even though evidence for the crime was usually nonexistent. In a short anonymous editorial published in *Free Speech* in May of 1892, Wells outlined her concerns. She also intimated that if one looked hard and long at the issue of Black men's relationships with White women, the women might be more complicit in the "crime" than their morally virtuous reputations would suggest.

Reaction to Wells's editorial was swift and virulent, complete with death threats. She was out of town when the editorial appeared, and her friends and neighbors urged her to stay away lest her authorship of the editorial become known and her life endangered. Wells reestablished herself in Chicago and did not set foot south of the Mason-Dixon line again until 1922. She traveled and campaigned extensively in England, hoping to generate political pressure on the United States to prohibit the barbaric act of lynching. Her British audiences wanted to know how other American activists responded to the problem, and here a likely ally was Frances Willard. Willard was well known in England as an ardent follower of social purity principles and a leader of the American Temperance movement. Although Willard publicly denounced lynching, she could not—and did not—endorse Wells's campaign. In short, Wells's suggestion that White women were in part responsible for seducing Black men, thus challenging the myth of the "Negro" rapist, threatened Willard's social purity stance that White women were morally virtuous victims. Although both Wells and Willard were vehemently pro-temperance and agreed on many important issues, Willard had built her campaign around the notion that White women were inherently pure and needed to be protected from corrupt men, especially those who drank, both Black and White. Willard could not reconcile the notion that Wells proposed—that White women could be sexual seductresses—with her stance.

The Wells–Willard relationship, as one historical snapshot among many, is important because it highlights the cracks and fissures in the feminist movement along race lines where "crimes against women" were a wedge that forced open the fissure. It provides important historical context for later social science research that has acknowledged the complex history in which the contemporary antirape movement is embedded, especially for Black feminists. In psychology, African American feminist psychologists Gail Wyatt and Aaronette White, for example, have both called attention to the need for Black feminist models of antirape advocacy that acknowledge this history of racism, sexism, and class dynamics (White, 1999; White, Strube, & Fisher, 1998; Wyatt, 1992).

As the 19th century turned into the early 20th, cultural attitudes toward public discussion of rape, incest, and other sexual crimes became more negative. Changing demographics in the women's movement after about 1890 also marked a declining interest in highlighting "crimes against women." As Pleck (1983) has noted,

> Older leaders of the women's movement who had been interested in the issue died, and younger women and Black women of all ages found it an unappealing, somewhat dated cause. Black suffragists, for example, who formed their own woman's clubs in this decade, associated crimes against women with the lynching of Black males for alleged rape of [W]hite women. They believed concern for the protection of women to be largely a subterfuge for racism. (p. 469)

Additionally, inasmuch as protection campaigns had been taken up most enthusiastically by social purity and temperance reformers, as the character of these movements changed, so did concern with the issue. The very idea of women's purity became somewhat dated as the Progressive

Era unfolded and the "new woman" asserted her social, professional, and political presence. Women's rights activists, social reformers, and social scientists turned their attention to the social conditions that caused crime, violence, drunkenness, and poverty, rather than emphasizing the protection or vulnerability of women per se. Furthermore, as a new class of professionals emerged to take care of the problem of family violence, including social welfare case workers, psychologists, and psychiatrists, public interest and corresponding moral and emotional outrage waned:

> With the disappearance of rhetoric about "evil beasts" and social purity, the emotional outrage required to generate a public campaign was gone. Only after another 80 years would feminists renew their sisterhood with victims of crimes against women, to refute once again popular stereotypes and to challenge the conspiracy of silence. (Pleck, 1983, p. 470)

RECESSION AND REEMERGENCE: THE PERSONAL AGAIN BECOMES POLITICAL

In 1930, psychoanalyst Helene Deutsch published "The Significance of Masochism in the Mental Life of Women" in which she argued for a theory of female masochism that became the dominant psychiatric explanation for why women stayed in abusive relationships (Deutsch, 1930). According to Deutsch and her adherents, women secretly enjoyed the pain inflicted on them by their abusers. She argued that women derived sexual gratification from being beaten and humiliated, and she urged therapists to help women accept their masochistic impulses to connect with the deepest part of their feminine selves. In the history of violence against women, the seeds were sown for what later feminists would call a rape myth: that women secretly enjoy being raped. This idea was actively pursued in the midcentury psychological literature on rape. During the 1940s and 1950s, any published research on rape that appeared in this literature (there was very little; see Rutherford, 2011), was written by psychoanalysts influenced by this point of view (e.g., Devereux, 1957; Factor, 1954; Fodor, 1948; Grotjahn, 1949; von Hentig, 1940). It was not until the 1980s that feminist psychologists explicitly challenged the myth of female masochism that Deutsch's work had perpetrated and began analyzing abused women's reluctance to leave the perpetrators of abuse in social, structural, and political terms. In 1985, Paula Caplan published *The Myth of Women's Masochism* in which she rejected the psychoanalytic explanations to which she had been exposed in her clinical psychology training and put forth the position that no one is inherently masochistic: One must look to the environments in which abuse occurs to understand why some women stay with their abusers. Neither rape nor male violence against women reentered public consciousness, however, until they were taken up by second-wave feminists as major causes in the fight for women's liberation.

SPEAKING OUT ABOUT RAPE

In January of 1971, the New York Radical Feminists (NYRF) held the first public event in the United States at which women spoke about their experiences of being raped. The speak-out was organized by NYRF at the suggestion of Susan Brownmiller, whose experience in her own consciousness-raising group convinced her that *public* consciousness-raising was needed (Bevacqua, 2000). A committee was struck to plan the event and the speak-out was held in a small Episcopal church in midtown Manhattan. The church filled with 300 women, 40 of whom spoke publicly about their experiences of being raped, both at the hands of the rapist and then again in their interactions with the justice system (Bevacqua, 2000; F. Davis, 1991). The *Village Voice* and *New York* magazine covered the proceedings. In April, a conference was held, including another speak-out as well as the presentation of research papers (see Connell & Wilson, 1974, for reprints of these papers), and this time, the *New York Times* sent a reporter. Particular concern again focused on the way the legal system was biased in favor of those accused of rape, and much ensuing feminist activism centered on challenging and changing rape laws. In 1971, Susan Griffin published her widely read article titled "Rape: The All-American Crime" in *Rampart* magazine. In this article, she asserted that no less than the dismantling of patriarchy and the complete reorganization of gender roles would eliminate rape.

It is notable that despite the long "private" history of rape and the efforts of some first-wave feminists to bring attention to the problem, never before had a feminist analysis of rape been put so forcefully—and successfully—on the public agenda (Bevacqua, 2000; Gavey, 2005). Although late-19th- and early-20th-century feminists had campaigned for women's sexual rights and awareness of "crimes against women," their activities were constrained by the parameters of the social purity movement and, as we have shown, lost steam by the 1890s. It would take the support of 1970s consciousness-raising groups to give victims/survivors the courage to speak out about rape and the powerful "grassroots praxis" of the women's liberation movement to amplify the issue so it could not be ignored (Gavey, 2005, p. 26). The result was the Antirape movement, which in addition to undertaking legal reform, also focused on setting up rape crisis centers and hotlines, forming antirape coalitions, and staging public demonstrations, early precursors to the now-familiar "Take Back the Night" events.

Concurrent with this groundswell of antirape activism in the 1970s and 1980s came writings and critiques from Black feminists who argued that Black women's experiences of rape were fundamentally different from White women's and had been ignored by the almost exclusively White antirape movement. These writers (e.g., A. Y. Davis, 1981; Giddings, 1984) pointed out that rape charges against Black men and the rape experiences of Black women were deeply entwined with racism throughout U.S. history. Furthermore, many worried that changes to rape laws would make Black men even more vulnerable to false charges in a system operating under the long-held myth of the Black rapist. It was well documented that despite a system traditionally arranged to discredit the accuser and exonerate those accused of rape, the one reliable exception to this rule was the case of a White woman accusing a Black man of rape (LaFree, 1980). Despite these deeply rooted, raced and gendered problems that White feminists often ignored, feminists of color actively participated in the antirape movement. By 1973, rape had, according to Bevacqua (2000, p. 42), "also become a cause for feminists of color."

Rape was thus transformed from a personal and private experience to a political and public one during this time period. Feminist social scientists also took up the cause. In 1975, sociologist Diana Russell published *The Politics of Rape: The Victim's Perspective,* a groundbreaking work not only for its methodological sophistication but because it included women's voices in each of its 22 chapters (Russell, 1975). In part, these testimonials helped support antirape ideology, a movement to combat rape myths and rape acceptance, in what was increasingly characterized as a "rape culture" by radical feminists. The aforementioned myth of the Black rapist was just one of many myths that surrounded rape, most of which had to do with justifying or explaining rape using both sexist and racist stereotypes and beliefs, such as "Women secretly enjoy being raped," "Only bad girls get raped," "Women ask for it by dressing seductively," "Anyone who fights hard enough can resist rape," "Women cry rape when they want to get even or have something to hide," "Unattractive women don't get raped," "Most rapists are poor Black men," and "Rapists are sex-starved maniacs." These examples are just a few of the rape myths challenged by antirape ideology (for reviews, see Burt, 1980; Lonsway & Fitzgerald, 1994), but the task of dislodging rape myths is a frustratingly ongoing one.

In this newly politicized arena, feminist social scientists also sought to break the silence and bring their expertise to a deeper understanding of rape. As Gavey (2005) observed, "Before feminism called public attention to the issue of rape as a social problem, the social sciences had largely been quiet about the subject" (p. 28). The theories and empirical studies that did exist were, many argued, highly problematic. For example, Albin (1977), in her critique of psychology's treatment of rape, argued that existing studies were inadequate because they (a) typically regarded rape as victim-precipitated, (b) insisted that it was a crime perpetrated only by deranged sexual psychopaths, and/or (c) had little real-world validity. A new generation of feminist researchers would change this state of affairs. In the 1980s, for example, psychologist Mary Koss named the "hidden" rape victim and identified acquaintance rape as an extremely prevalent phenomenon (see Koss, 2011), and psychologist Irene Frieze wrote about the causes and consequences of marital rape (Frieze, 1983).

SCREAM LOUDLY: EMERGENCE OF THE BATTERED WOMEN'S MOVEMENT

The battered women's movement emerged alongside antirape organizing in local communities, with both developing through feminist consciousness-raising groups (Schechter, 1982; Thomas, 1988). In the early 1970s, there was no specific language to name male violence against women, and the issue was identified by the terms *wife beating, wife assault, wife abuse, battered women,* and *battered wives* interchangeably, although later feminist reflection recognized some terminology as problematic (G. Walker, 1990). Early organizing focused on physical violence, but the definition quickly expanded to include emotional abuse, financial abuse, isolation, threats, and coercion (Miller, 2010). During the 1960s and 1970s, survivors increasingly sought support from local women's centers when they were in crisis situations and in need of alternative housing. Because battered women's shelters did not yet exist, women's "choices" were to "remain in the home where there was at least food and shelter or to risk homelessness or survival in substandard accommodation in order to stay alive" (Thomas, 1988, p. 10). Given the lack of adequate social services and resources, sheltering became a pragmatic focus of the movement, along with the goal of eradicating male violence against women and children. Particularly, the movement aimed to shift attitudes that regarded male violence against women as a private family issue that was precipitated by the victim. Dominant understandings of male violence against women blamed the victim and shaped unresponsive and inappropriate responses from legal, health, and mental health institutions and social services (Panzer, Philip, & Hayward, 2000).

Shelters for abused women were organized at the local level without in-depth knowledge of women's organizing in other geographical regions (G. Walker, 1990). The concept of a shelter was not new; many North American communities had previously established shelters to support various disenfranchised groups such as the homeless, alcoholics, the mentally ill, and runaways (Thomas, 1988). Early battered women's shelters were established by neighborhood women, religious groups, social service professionals, and feminist activists (Schechter, 1982).

In general, there were two types of feminist shelters: conventional social service agencies that were staffed by professionals and egalitarian collectives that were survivor-driven (Rodriguez, 1988). P. Y. Martin (1990) described these differences as arising from divergent feminist ideologies, in which liberal feminism framed conventional social service agencies and socialist, radical, and lesbian feminisms framed grassroots collectives.

There are conflicting accounts of the "first" American women's shelter. Chiswick Women's Aid opened in London, England, in 1971 and is generally recognized as the model for shelters in North America (Riger et al., 2002). For instance, in 1974 the founder, Erin Pizzey wrote *Scream Quietly or the Neighbors Will Hear,* a first-person account that chronicled the development of Britain's first shelter, providing guidance for shelters internationally. However some American shelters preceded this British model. Haven House, established in 1964 in Pasadena, California, and a shelter in St. Paul, Minnesota, founded by the Women's Advocates in 1973 have both been regarded as America's first shelter (Murray, 1988). However, before the establishment of many officially recognized shelters, individual women opened their homes as "safe houses" in their communities (Rebick, 2005; Schechter, 1982). The movement quickly grew. Whereas in 1975 there were "a mere half dozen" emergency shelters in the United States (Panzer et al., 2000, p. 341), by 1982 there were more than 300, with a shelter in each state (Schechter, 1982). Early shelters were not seen as places to change women and their behaviors but as safe places in which women could feel protected and live away from their abusers. It was thought that this time and space would enable a woman to engage in self-reflection and make her own choices about her future (Thomas, 1988). The women who worked at the collectivist shelters often drew on their own experiences of abuse and regarded women using the shelter as "sisters in struggle," encouraging them to become involved in the movement (Morgan, 1981). The growth of the movement included 24-hour hotlines, coalitions, and national organizations such as the National Coalition Against Domestic Violence (Miller, 2010).

In the early 1970s woman abuse and its prevalence was invisible in part because police, hospitals, and courts failed to record relevant statistics (Miller, 2010). The National Organization for Women conducted one study that is regarded as the entry point for further North American research (Pagelow, 1984, as cited in Miller, 2010, p. 6). This study highlighted that the "prevalence and severity of wife abuse was far greater than expected" (p. 6) and was the catalyst for a National Taskforce on Battered Women/Household Violence in 1973. With the growing visibility of violence against women scholars began focusing their research on the topic in an effort to formulate more adequate social responses to what was becoming recognized as a serious social issue.

This growth of research on male violence against women included sociological and psychological theories, including two dominant theories of woman abuse developed by Straus (1978) and Gelles (1974). These psychosocial theories aimed to understand family interactions as embedded within social cultural norms that condoned violence. Straus focused on social learning, where both the perpetrator and victim/survivor learn violence in their family of origin, repeat violence in intimate relations, and transmit said violence generationally, also called the *cycle of violence*. Gelles also emphasized learned behavior, along with economic stressors, suggesting violence was more prevalent in low-income households given the increased stress and lack of resources. These theories have been critiqued for not adequately addressing the gendered context of violence and for focusing on the safety of the children at the expense of the woman's safety. For example, Straus and Gelles collaborated in the development and use of a survey that decontextualized violence and found that men and women experience equivalent amounts of violence (G. Walker, 1990). This survey is problematic because it does not account for who the primary aggressor is, the proportionality of violence, and acts of self-defense. Furthermore when applied in family therapy, these theories suggest that couples learn new methods of communication and ways to reduce anger, which situates the woman as partially responsible and at increased risk. Feminist critiques of these psychosocial theories developed more slowly than those of psychoanalytic-psychodynamic understanding of violence (i.e., women's masochism), as they provided some political utility in coordinating social services (G. Walker, 1990).

In contrast, feminist research has understood patriarchal power and the historical contextualization of women's subordination as the root of male violence against women (e.g., Dobash & Dobash, 1979; D. Martin, 1976; Schechter, 1982). Much of this research was outside of the academic mainstream, and although Pizzey's (1974) text was not academic, it provided an important foundation (Miller, 2010). Del Martin (1976) and Lenore Walker's (1979) work was significant because it used existing knowledge and research methods to incorporate a feminist analysis into social science discourse.

In 1976, Del Martin published the influential study *Battered Wives* in which she noted the relative absence of public interest in domestic violence compared with rape, despite its alarming prevalence. Martin was also an activist who had contributed to establishing an early shelter in San Francisco (Miller, 2010). *Battered Wives* articulated a radical analysis that was informed by the movement; however, it also put forth professional aims. Specifically, Martin argued that "Lasting solutions to this complex problem should come from the collective thinking of researchers in government and social service agencies, the institutional religions and political action groups" (p. 8).

In 1979, psychologist Lenore Walker published *The Battered Woman,* which was unique in including reports of women's lived experiences in an academic forum. Using interview data *The Battered Woman* debunked myths and illuminated abusers' "coercive techniques," which were commonly cited in women's subjective reports of their experiences of violence. On the basis of these interviews, Walker outlined *battered woman syndrome,* a psychological construct that theorizes two aspects of the dynamics of abuse: (a) the cycle of abuse and (b) learned helplessness. The cyclical nature of abuse was hypothesized to have three phases. The first phase was a tension-building phase, during which abuse is relatively minimal but the threat of future violence is increasing. The second phase is an outburst, in which the perpetrator batters his partner, often triggered by a seemingly trivial event. The final phase is the honeymoon, in which the abuser was loving and usually promised never to hurt his partner again. The construct of learned helplessness explained how the survivor of violence developed low self-esteem, guilt, and feelings of being helpless about her situation, therefore making it difficult for her to leave. Walker's theory was widely disseminated and quickly absorbed into the mainstream, elevating her to expert status in legal trials to explain why some survivors murder their abusers (L. E. Walker, 1984, 2002).

CONCLUSION

The second-wave women's movement is generally regarded as naming male violence against women. Although feminist organizing of the 1970s was instrumental in developing a language and analysis of such violence and was unprecedented in its social impact, women had previously drawn attention to the issue of violence in their lives. How society has (or has not) addressed the issue of male violence against women is historically located, informed, and constrained by social, political, moral, and legal contexts. In the late-19th century, first-wave activists were constrained by rigid notions of femininity and the family, as well as moral and legal discourse. In contrast, following the 1960s decade of social change, second-wave feminists were able to question gender roles and the family, allowing for private family matters to be framed as political and social issues.

Making male violence against women visible, as a public issue, was important for several reasons. By naming male violence against women as a social issue, second-wave feminist activism opened the door for mainstream and feminist researchers to develop an understanding of the prevalence of violence and develop explanatory theories. Additionally, institutions and community organizations recognized their role in responding to this social issue and aimed to develop ways of working with survivors. The chapters in this book are indebted to antiviolence feminists who have opened the door for social scientists to address the significant and all-too-common issue of male violence in women's lives. It is also important to remember that although the second-wave women's movement produced incredible social gains for survivors of violence, it is possible that once again male violence against women will retreat from its visibility in public and legal discourse. Indeed, *feminist* understandings of male violence against women are increasingly marginalized, and silence and victim-blaming myths remain deeply embedded in American culture. Furthermore, in the increasingly neoliberal tenor of our times, we need to be aware of our history and remain vigilant to the tendency to decontextualize and individualize violence and to focus on managing or treating the issue rather than seeking social solutions to prevent and eradicate violence against women.

REFERENCES

Albin, R. S. (1977). Psychological studies of rape. *Signs: A Journal of Women in Culture and Society, 3,* 423–435.

Bederman, G. (1995). *Manliness and civilization: A cultural history of gender and race in the United States, 1880–1917.* Chicago: University of Chicago Press.

Bevacqua, M. (2000). *Rape on the public agenda: Feminism and the politics of sexual assault.* Boston, MA: Northeastern University Press.

Breines, W., & Gordon, L. (1983). The new scholarship on family violence. *Signs, 8,* 490–531.

Brownmiller, S. (1975). *Against our will: Men, women, and rape.* New York, NY: Simon & Schuster.

Burt, M. R. (1980). Cultural myths and supports for rape. *Journal of Personality and Social Psychology, 38,* 217–230.

Caplan, P. J. (1985). *The myth of women's masochism.* New York, NY: New American Library.

Connell, N. & Wilson, C. (Eds.). (1974). *Rape: The first sourcebook for women.* New York, NY: A Plume Book.

Davis, A. Y. (1981). *Women, race, and class.* New York: Vintage.

Davis, F. (1991). *Moving the mountain: The women's movement in America since 1960.* New York, NY: Simon & Schuster.

Deutsch, H. (1930). Significance of masochism in the mental life of women. *International Journal of Psychoanalysis, 2,* 48–60.

Devereux, G. (1957). The awarding of a penis as compensation for rape: A demonstration of the clinical relevance of the psycho-analytic study of cultural data. *The International Journal of Psychoanalysis, 38,* 398–401.

Dobash, R. E., & Dobash, R. (1979). *Violence against wives.* New York, NY: Free Press.

Factor, M. (1954). A woman's psychological reaction to attempted rape. *The Psychoanalytic Quarterly, 23,* 243–244.

Fodor, N. (1948). The role of the mother in the fear of rape. *American Imago, 5,* 317–334.

Frieze, I. (1983). Investigating the causes and consequences of marital rape. *Signs, 8,* 532–553.
Gavey, N. (2005). *Just sex? The cultural scaffolding of rape.* East Sussex, England: Routledge.
Gelles, R. (1976). Abused wives: Why do they stay? *Journal of Marriage and Family, 3,* 659–668.
Giddings, P. (1984). *When and where I enter: The impact of black women on race and sex in America.* New York, NY: Bantam.
Gilman, C. P. (1908). A suggestion on the Negro problem. *American Journal of Sociology, 1,* 78–85.
Gilman, C. P. (1914, May). Immigration, importation, and our fathers. *Forerunner, 5,* 117–119.
Gordon, L. (1988). *Heroes of their own lives: The politics and history of family violence.* New York, NY: Viking.
Griffin, S. (1971). Rape: The all-American crime. *Ramparts, 10,* 26–35.
Grotjahn, M. (1949). The primal crime and the unconscious. In K. Eissler (Ed.), *Searchlights on delinquency: New psychoanalytic studies* (pp. 306–314). Oxford, England: International Universities Press.
Koss, M. P. (2011). Hidden, unacknowledged acquaintance rape: Looking back, looking forward. *Psychology of Women Quarterly, 35,* 348–354.
LaFree, G. D. (1980). The effect of sexual stratification by race on official reactions to rape. *American Sociological Review, 45,* 842–854.
Lerner, G. (1979). Black and white women in interaction and confrontation. In *The majority finds its past: Placing women in history* (pp. 94–111). New York, NY: Oxford.
Lonsway, K. A. & Fitzgerald, L. F. (1994). Rape myths: A review. *Psychology of Women Quarterly, 18,* 133–164.
Martin, D. (1976). *Battered wives.* San Francisco, CA: Glide.
Martin, P. Y. (1990). Rethinking feminist organizations. *Gender and Society, 4,* 182–206.
Miller, E. B. A. (2010). Moving to the head of the river: The early years of the U.S. battered women's movement. Unpublished doctoral dissertation, University of Kansas, Lawrence.
Morgan, P. (1981). From battered wife to program client: The state's shaping of social problems. *Kapitalistate, 9,* 17–39.
Murray, S. B. (1988). The unhappy marriage of theory and practice: An analysis of a battered women's shelter. *NWSA Journal, 1,* 75–92.
Panzer, P. G., Philip, M. B., & Hayward, R. A. (2000). Trends in domestic violence service and leadership: Implications for an integrated shelter model. *Administration and Policy in Mental Health, 27,* 339–352.
Pizzey, E. (1974). *Scream quietly or the neighbours will hear.* London, England: Penguin.
Pleck, E. (2004). *Domestic tyranny: The making of American social policy against family violence from the colonial times to the present.* New York, NY: Oxford University Press.
Pleck, E. (1983). Feminist responses to "crimes against women," 1868–1896. *Signs, 8,* 451–470.

Pleck, E. (1979). Wife-beating in 19th-century America. *Victimology, 4,* 62–74.

Rebick, J. (2005). *Ten thousand roses: The making of a feminist revolution.* Toronto, Canada: Penguin Canada.

Riger, S., Bennett, L., Wasco, S. M., Schewe, P. A., Frohmann, L., Camacho, J. M., & Campbell, C. (2002). *Evaluating services for survivors of domestic violence and sexual assault.* Thousand Oaks, CA: Sage.

Rodriguez, N. M. (1988). Transcending bureaucracy: Feminist politics and a shelter for battered women. *Gender and Society, 2,* 214–227.

Russell, D. E. H. (1975). *The politics of rape: The victim's perspective.* New York, NY: Stein and Day.

Rutherford, A. (2011). Sexual violence against women: Putting rape research in context. *Psychology of Women Quarterly, 35,* 342–347.

Schechter, S. (1982). *Women and male violence: The visions and struggles of the battered women's movement.* Boston: South End Press.

Shorter, E. (1977). On writing the history of rape. *Signs: Journal of Women in Culture and Society, 3,* 471–482.

Straus, M. (1978). Wife beating: How common and why? *Victimology International Journal, 2,* 443–458.

Thomas G. S. (1988). A history of the sheltering movement for battered women in Canada. *Canadian Journal of Community Mental Health, 7*(2), 9–21.

von Hentig, H. (1940). Some remarks on the interaction of perpetrator and victim. *Journal of Criminal Law and Criminology, 31,* 303–309.

Walker, L. E. (2002). Politics, psychology and the battered women's movement. *Journal of Trauma Practice, 1,* 81–103.

Walker, L. E. A. (1984). Battered women, psychology, and public policy. *American Psychologist, 39,* 1178–1182.

Walker, L. E. (1979). *The battered woman.* New York, NY: Viking Press.

Walker, G. (1990). *Family violence and the women's movement: The conceptual politics of struggle.* Toronto, Canada: University of Toronto Press.

White, A. M. (1999). Talking feminist, talking Black—Micromobilization processes in a collective protest against rape. *Gender & Society, 13,* 77–100.

White, A. M., Strube, M. J., & Fisher, S. (1998). A Black feminist model of rape myth acceptance: Implications for research and anti-rape advocacy in Black communities. *Psychology of Women Quarterly, 22,* 157–175.

Wyatt, G. E. (1992). The sociocultural context of African American and White American women's rape. *Journal of Social Issues, 48,* 77–91.

Chapter 3

The Cycle of Violence

Florence L. Denmark and Deborah A. Williams

Family violence is a topic that is difficult to study. When familial violence does occur, survivors of the abuse are reluctant to contact authorities or those who may offer protective resources. It is often a secret a family keeps, only to transmit violence to the next generation. The intergenerational transmission of violence is a topic that has been discussed and dissected over the past 40 years, and this topic has led to one conclusion: Violence begets violence; the cycle is continuous. Abused children and children who witness abuse are more likely to become abusers themselves as adults. Their children then experience the same effects, as do their children, and so on and so forth. This cycle is detrimental to parents, children, neighbors, and whole sections of modern society. Because this topic is also extremely taboo for both the abusers and abused to discuss, the exploration and striving for an end to the cycle is that much harder. Indeed, the question of how to end the cycle has plagued researchers and policy makers for much of the past 40 years.

When children are abused or neglected, it raises the likelihood that they will themselves become abusers; in fact, this is the number one indicator of those adults who will abuse or neglect their own children. Child physical abuse often co-occurs with other violent behaviors, such as domestic partner abuse or child verbal abuse. In this chapter, abuse is categorized into four domains: physical abuse, verbal abuse, sexual abuse, and neglect.

Much of this chapter focuses on how the patterns of abuse affect the approximately 1.3 million women who are abused each year (National Coalition Against Domestic Violence, 2007). However, men are also frequently victims of domestic violence: From 80,000 to 800,000 men report being physically or sexually assaulted by an intimate partner every year (Tjaden & Thoennes, 2000). Although women are not the sole recipients of abuse, it is our goal to focus on females who are neglected or abused physically, verbally, and sexually and examine the outcomes of their lives as survivors of abuse. We examine the likely outcomes for women who have experienced childhood abuse or neglect. In addition, the topic of exposure to abuse as a child and the outcomes of this exposure are examined. Later, the topic of elderly abuse is examined to investigate whether the cycle comes full circle.

This chapter ends with a discussion of those who have ended the cycle of violence. The traits that these individuals possess, along with an examination of familial violence prevention programs that have been successful, are vetted. It is our belief that there truly is a way out of the cycle of violence.

THE CYCLE OF VIOLENCE: A HISTORY

The cycle of violence did not become a widely used term until the 1960s when awareness of family and intimate partner violence (IPV) increased. With this increased awareness and longitudinal studies of victims of child abuse came the empirically supported fact that violence can be intergenerationally transmitted. Although this is true for nearly all cultures, research focused on American families. Throughout American history, women have had fewer legal rights and career opportunities than men; therefore, it was harder for women to leave an abusive husband, especially when there were children present. During the 1960s, several federal laws improving the economic status of women were passed. The Equal Pay Act of 1963 required equal wages for men and women doing equal work. The Civil Rights Act of 1964 prohibited discrimination against women by any company with 25 or more employees. A Presidential Executive Order in 1967 prohibited bias against women in hiring by federal government contractors. Women began to have more career opportunities and the financial ability to leave their abusive homes with their children, but many did not. Researchers were puzzled as to why, when given the opportunity, more victims of abuse (both women and men) did not escape the abuse.

An influential study conducted by Cathy Spatz Widom (1989a) gave researchers a glimpse into understanding whether violence truly begets violence and if simply witnessing violence has an impact on a child's violent behaviors. She found that abused and neglected children have a higher likelihood of arrests for delinquency, adult criminality, and violent criminal behavior than their nonabused or neglected peers. She concluded that not only is there a transmission of violent behavior, but that it is pervasive, extending beyond the home. More studies followed this, examining community violence and familial violence, as well as the intersectionality of race, poverty, and violence, in an effort to break the cycle.

In addition, Widom (1989b) also conducted a literature review that looked at the cycle of violence and found that physical aggression may be learned from generation to generation, much like cultural or family attitudes are learned. She discovered that abuse and neglect differ, with different sequelae and overt symptoms. Boys and girls are affected by abuse and neglect differently, and the long-term effects of this abuse are reflected in their adult lives. Most important, she made a point to state that not all children who are survivors of abuse or neglect will go on to abuse their children, giving hope to a way out of the cycle.

Currently, researchers are still attempting to find ways to break the cycle of violence. Many studies focus on when children become violent adolescents and what would be the best intervention when trying to prevent the intergeneration transmission of abuse (ITA). Studies focusing on violence and the intersectionality of sex, race, and poverty have documented which children are at increased risk for being victims of child abuse; however, there is not yet an intervention plan to examine how to prevent child abuse. Prevention of the continuation of violence is the focus of current research

According to the National Coalition Against Domestic Violence (NCADV, 2007), one in four women will experience domestic violence at some point in her life. In addition, it is expected 1.3 million women are victims of a physical assault by an intimate partner each year. Almost one third of female homicide victims that are reported in police records are killed by an intimate partner. These are shocking statistics. When considering the fact that witnessing violence between one's parents or caretakers is the strongest risk factor of transmitting violent behavior from one generation to the next, these statistics are even more shocking.

Violence Begets Violence

Researchers have estimated the rate of intergenerational transmission of child abuse (ITCA) to be seven times higher than in a randomized community sample (Dinwiddle & Bucholz, 1993). In 2007, approximately 794,000 children were determined by state and local child protective services agencies to be victims of child abuse or neglect. This study also found that an estimated 1,760 children younger than 18 years old died as a result of this maltreatment (U.S. Department of Health and Human Services [DHHS], 2009). That is nearly 800,000 children who are seven times more likely to engage in abuse of their own children one day. It is imperative that intervention and prevention techniques are developed to aid these victims and ensure the next generation has less victims of childhood abuse.

The Cycle and Women

Women experience the cycle differently from men. Girls are more likely than boys to be victims of sexual abuse, which then increases their risk for being victims of sexual assault and repeated sexual abuse later in life (Noll, Horowitz, Bonanno, Trickett, & Putnam, 2003). In addition, women make up 85% of domestic violence victims (NCADV, 2007). However, most cases of domestic violence are not reported to police, suggesting the women who come forward may have different protective factors that could break the cycle than other women who do not report abuse. There are numerous resources available to victims of domestic violence, especially to women and women with children. However, women must first break the cycle of violence by leaving their abusive partner to take advantage of these resources, and that is not so simple.

HOW THE CYCLE WORKS

The cycle of violence, or ITA, is the transmission of learned violent behavior across generations. Children who witness intimate partner violence (IPV) between their parents have been shown to be significantly more likely to become perpetrators or victims themselves when they are involved in their own intimate relationships (NCADV, 2007). Children who are victims of childhood abuse are significantly more likely to abuse their own children. This abuse has been shown to be type-specific—that is, parents who were physically abused are more likely to physically abuse their children than engage in another type of abuse. Family and spousal abuse have been shown to be cyclical and repetitive, passed down from generation to generation.

Learned Behavior

Alfred Bandura's Social Learning Theory

Abuse is often described as a learned behavior, which is how the cycle of violence can continue from generation to generation, despite the tremendous amount of pain it causes victims. Bandura's social learning theory describes learned behavior as learning by observing others' behaviors and attitudes, as well as the outcomes of behaviors. "Most human behavior is learned observationally through modeling: from observing others, one forms an idea of how new behaviors are performed, and on later occasions this coded information serves as a guide for action" (Bandura, 1977, p. 22). For social learning to occur successfully, the one observing the behavior (in the case of ITA a child) must be paying attention, be able to retain the image of the action, be able to reproduce the image, and have motivation to imitate the action. In ITA, all of these occur repeatedly; if a child witnesses IPV between his parents, or abuse of themselves or siblings, he or she learns that this is the behavior that occurs among family members and is more likely to engage in this behavior as a spouse and parent.

Martin Seligman's Theory of Learned Helplessness

Another popular theory that helps to explain the continuation of abuse is Seligman's theory of learned helplessness (Seligman, 1975). Seligman's theory sought to explain certain forms of psychological paralysis by using social learning and cognitive-motivational theoretical principles. By conducting experiments on dogs that could and could not control shocks given by performing tasks, Seligman found that those dogs that could not control the shocks did not attempt to escape shocks later on when they were easily avoidable. These distorted perceptions, according to Seligman, resulted from an inability to predict the efficacy of one's actions. Seligman then drew comparisons between the behavior of the animals in the study and certain forms of human depression.

INTIMATE PARTNER VIOLENCE

IPV is a complex relationship that occurs when one person abuses, physically, emotionally, or sexually, a person with whom he or she is in a sexual relationship. The abuse does not need to occur more than once, although it often does. Men do not need to be the perpetrator of the abuse, although they often are. IPV can occur in all types of relationships: gay, straight, rich, poor, Black, White, married, dating. A central chord of theories of domestic partner violence centers around the idea of the abuser and abused both containing beliefs and expectations that justify interpersonal aggression (Riggs & O'Leary, 1996; Wolfe et al., 2003). For example, the abuser and victim may both believe that the victim transgressed in such a way to deserve the abuse.

Lenore Walker first coined the term *battered woman syndrome* to describe a set of distinct psychological and behavioral symptoms that result from prolonged exposure to situations of IPV. She hypothesized that this abuse happened in a cyclical manner, with the severity of transgressions changing throughout the cycle. The three stages—tension building, the acute battering incident, and loving contribution (i.e., the honeymoon phase)—would all occur repeatedly and contribute to the learned helplessness that prevents the abuse from ending (Walker, 1984). In the first stage, tension rises as the perpetrator of the violence engages in demeaning verbal and/or emotional interactions. The woman then may attempt to pacify their abuser using techniques that have been effective in the past. Although this technique may work, the woman's passivity encourages the partner's behavior to escalate until physical abuse occurs. The severity of the abuse may vary, but the woman is acutely aware of the danger in the relationship during this stage. In the third stage, the partner is remorseful and promises to change his behavior. With time, the cycle begins again.

Walker drew from Seligman's learned helplessness theory to hypothesize that women with continual exposure to domestic violence would not be able to trust that their actions would have any efficacy and would not be able to make the same cognitive and behavioral choices that a woman who had never been abused would make. The abused woman would be less able to see a practical way of escaping her situation.

Poverty and the Cycle

Children who grow up in impoverished neighborhoods and families are more likely than their middle-income counterparts to witness and experience violence. IPV, child maltreatment, and youth violence are more likely to occur in families characterized by social and economic disadvantage—that is, economically poor families; families dealing with parental separation or divorce; and families living in disadvantaged neighborhoods (Fang & Corso, 2007). Women living in neighborhoods with very low median household income had at least twice the IPV-related death, hospitalization, and emergency department visit rates compared with women living in higher income neighborhoods (Stayton et al., 2008). These confounding variables suggest that prevention and intervention attempts should be aimed at those living in high-risk areas as well as in disadvantaged neighborhoods and schools.

Protective Factors

Although children who are victims of abuse are at an increased risk for being perpetrators of abuse as an adult, this by no means suggests that every child who is a victim of abuse will become a violent adult. There are protective factors that exist that may help stop the cycle. Protective factors are conditions or attributes in individuals, families, communities, or the larger society that mitigate or eliminate risk in families and communities and increase the health and well-being of children and families. These factors include having another adult present who provides a supportive, safe, nurturing environment to the child. This may be a person at school, a grandparent, or a neighbor (U.S. DHHS, 2012). Children themselves may contain their own protective factors or resiliency that cannot be easily defined. It is still not clear why some children become abusers and victims and others do not. This topic is discussed further in "Breaking the Cycle" later in the chapter.

VIOLENCE AGAINST WOMEN

Violence against women is recognized as a serious public health problem worldwide (World Health Organization [WHO], 2011a). Because violence tends to co-occur, meaning that victims of violence are likely to experience more than one type of violence during their lifetime (Cavanaugh et al., 2012), examining violence against women is necessary when describing the cycle of violence. It is difficult for women to break the cycle because, once abused, they are at increased risk for repeated violence. By examining the role that women play as victims of violence, better preventative measures can be put in place.

Exposure to IPV

Although women are assaulted and raped by strangers, the majority of acts of violence against women are perpetrated by someone the woman knows. In 2003 to 2005, nearly half of the fatal violence against women was a result of IPV (Stayton et al., 2008).

Compared with teens and older women, women aged between 20 and 29 years were twice as likely to be killed by an intimate partner, to be treated at the hospital, or to visit an emergency department for an IPV-related assault. Likewise, Black and Hispanic women were more than twice as likely as women of other racial-ethnic groups to be killed or injured by an intimate partner (Stayton et al., 2008).

Girls who have been exposed to violence in the home through IPV are more likely to take part in the intergenerational transmission of violence, often becoming victims of IPV in adulthood (Dankoski et al., 2006). In the United States, it is estimated that 10 million children annually witness the punching, kicking, and beating of a parent, most commonly their mother (Humphreys, 1997). This is a large number of children who are at risk for long-term effects of exposure to IPV including weight gain, anxiety, difficulty sleeping, and depression, to name just a few physiological and psychological distresses that occur (McFarlane, Groff, O'Brien, & Watson, 2005). As adults, women who fear IPV have higher levels of asthma and psychological distress, as well as increased amounts of binge drinking (Stayton et al., 2008).

As was discussed earlier, women who are in abusive relationships tend to experience the symptoms of the battered woman syndrome. They are often unable to see the escape path of their situation, eventually coming to believe that they are helpless, with some victims even believing that they deserve this treatment. These relationships often lack successful problem-solving skills. For example, communication and successful interpersonal skills have been shown to be at a deficit in violent husbands. An example of this deficit is that these men tend to attribute hostile intent to their wives neutral actions (Holtzworth-Munroe & Smutzer, 1996).

Adolescent Dating Violence

Adolescent dating violence appears to be on the rise; one report from New York City revealed that since 1999, physical dating violence reported by public high school girls has risen almost 50%. Adolescent dating violence comes with its own set of side effects. The public high school girls who reported dating violence were three times more likely to attempt suicide than those who did not report dating violence (Stayton et al., 2008).

It is important to examine adolescent dating violence because it is a gateway to IPV. In particular, adolescent dating violence reveals some basic differences from adult partner violence. The latter is characterized by a predominance of men directing harm, especially physical harm, toward women. However, adolescents often display mutually abusive relationships in which both members of the relationship execute and incur physical and verbal damage (Spencer & Bryant, 2000), and in some studies, girls have reported a higher amount of perpetrating dating violence than boys. Wolfe et al. (2003) suggested that midadolescent dating violence may be a time when teens are experimenting with early patterns of abuse, trying to understand their own childhood abuse and make sense of the types of relationship they wish to have as adults. Teens may continue on the path of partner violence if they are not shown healthy models of problem solving and conflict resolution.

In a longitudinal study conducted by Fang and Corso (2007), the authors examined nearly 1,000 children who were victims of abuse (sexual and physical abuse, neglect). This study examined two relationships, the first is the relationship among child abuse, youth violence perpetration, and IPV perpetration. The second is the relationship among child abuse, youth violence victimization, and IPV victimization. The authors wanted to determine whether risk factors such as family background and community had an impact on the abused child becoming either a perpetrator or victim of abuse and when this change occurred. The findings suggested that a larger percentage of women and girls reported both IPV perpetration and victimization than men. Men in the study reported higher rates of youth violence perpetration and victimization. This study also found that childhood physical abuse and neglect were significant predictors of youth violence perpetration for both genders. The findings of increased violence in adolescence suggest that children who have been maltreated, especially girls who are victims of physical abuse and/or neglect, may be good candidates for IPV prevention. This intervention should occur much earlier than the age most programs currently target to prevent dating violence and other adolescent violence.

SIBLING ABUSE

Considerable efforts have been made in public policy to detect, prevent, and intervene in child abuse and domestic partner abuse. However, a type of family abuse often overlooked is sibling abuse. Wiehe (1997) estimated that as many as 53 of every 100 children are perpetrators of sibling abuse. Sibling abuse may be physical, emotional, or sexual, just like the other types of familial abuse. Often this type of abuse occurs within the home, with parents nearby (who may or may not have knowledge of the abuse). Parents often do not take the reports of abuse as valid, wanting to believe that their child could not be a perpetrator of violence or believing that this type of abuse is simply a normal part of growing up with siblings. This leads to sibling abuse being over looked for long periods of time. Generally, abuse between siblings does not come to the attention of the courts "unless a parent or victim is willing to file assault charges against the perpetrating sibling" (Wiehe, 1997, p. 4), which is a rare occurrence.

Sibling abuse is also overlooked when it is categorized as "kids will be kids." Parents, teachers, physicians, and those in the mental health field have brushed off reports of sibling abuse as "normal" and a "stage of development." It is the responsibility of adults to take claims of sibling abuse as seriously as one would take reports of child abuse. The duration, intent, severity, and repeated occurrence of the abuse should be questioned to open an investigation and proceed in protecting the child.

Kiselica and Morrill-Richards (2007) suggested that sibling abuse may occur because of maladaptive parental behavior and dysfunctional family structures that play key roles in the genesis of sibling abuse. How parents treat each other and their children serves as a template for how children treat each other. If the family values power imbalances, rigid gender roles, and differential treatment of siblings, there is an increased risk for sibling abuse. In addition, perpetrators of sibling abuse are likely to be victims of child abuse, witness spousal abuse, or see their sibling be abused by a parent.

Although this form of abuse is not the type of abuse most professionals are aware of, the long-term sequelae is similar to those of other types of child abuse. As adults, survivors of sibling abuse are more likely to have problems with drugs and alcohol, be less able to trust others, and have low self-esteem and to be at increased risk for subsequent abuses (Wiehe, 1997). Likewise, those who are victims of the abuse tend to have similar characteristics, including being dependent on the abusive sibling and having cognitive deficits or developmental delays; they may also have a history of being victimized by other people in the family or outside of the family. Often they have no social supports, and girls are more likely to be the victim of sexual sibling abuse than boys (Kiselica & Morrill-Richards, 2007).

CHILD ABUSE AND THE CYCLE

In 1962, Henry Kempe and his colleagues published an article called "The Battered-Child Syndrome," giving a name to the clinical condition of children who have been the victims of long-term physical abuse and neglect. It was instrumental in creating mandated reporting laws for physicians, teachers, and mental health practitioners who work with children. The syndrome was characterized as a spectrum of mild trauma, in which abuse is often unsuspected and unidentified, to those abuses that have caused bone and soft tissue damage. This article gave a name to the long seen physical evidence of abuse. Although this was the first time child abuse was given a name and identifying features, this does not mean it was the first time child abuse had occurred. This article brought awareness to general physicians that child abuse can occur in any social economic status, with members of any race, and in any neighborhood.

Although Kempe et al. (1962) brought forward the occurrence and instant signs of child abuse, the long-term effects of abuse are still being discovered. The sequelae of childhood trauma, including abuse, are different for each survivor. These long-term effects include persisting posttraumatic stress disorder, pathological dissociation, psychiatric and substance-abuse disorders, sexual distortion, early sexual initiation, obesity, poor health, teen pregnancy, and self-harm, to name but a few. Just as the long-term effects of abuse are different for each person, the manifestations of these symptoms occur at different points as well (Noll, 2005). The negative effects of child abuse have been well documented. In the United States among victims of child abuse, 78% suffered neglect, 18% were physically abused, 9% were sexually abused, 8% were psychologically maltreated, and an estimated 2% were medically neglected. In addition, about 10% of victims experienced "other" types of maltreatment such as "abandonment," "threats of harm to the child," and "congenital drug addiction" (U.S. DHHS, 2009).

Type-specific patterns of ITCA may influence the type of abuse passed on or whether the perpetration or victimization occurs. For example, childhood sexual abuse has been shown to significantly increase the risk of subsequent sexual and physical victimization (Noll et al., 2003). Other studies have found that the type of abuse experienced as a child has an impact on IPV perpetration and victimization differently. This is further affected by the gender of the child (Fang & Corso, 2007). Understanding type-specific patterns of ITCA could help prevention and intervention techniques look at abuse in a more practical light to target specific interventions.

Not all children who are abused, or who witness abuse, become abusers. Not all children who are survivors of abuse become victims. However, there are increased risk factors for children who fall into these distinct categories, which are discussed in the following subsections.

Child Grows Up and Becomes Aggressor to Partner

Previous research has suggested that children, especially boys, who witness abuse but are not themselves victims of abuse are more likely to transmit physical violence across generations, becoming abusers themselves (Dankoski et al., 2006). This suggests that boys who have witnessed IPV may benefit from interventions that help them understand affect regulation, open communication, and successful problem-solving skills for anger management.

Women also engage in partner perpetration; however, there are far less reported cases of women perpetrators. Significant direct predictors of IPV perpetration for women include youth violence perpetration, childhood physical abuse, and childhood neglect (Fang & Corso, 2007).

Child Grows Up and Becomes Aggressor to Child

A common occurrence with children who are abused is to then become an abusive parent themselves. This often results from a psychological defense known as *identification with the aggressor*. Children who experience emotional trauma that threatens their lives form a bond with the abuser to protect their own fragile ego and physical self. Being abused challenges the child's feelings of self-worth and ultimately leaves them feeling powerless to protect themselves. Because the child loves his or her abusive parent and sees the parent as a powerful being, worthy of love, the child then identifies with the abuser, wanting to be like him or her—worthy of love and a powerful being.

A study conducted by Kim (2009) sought to examine the relationship between type of child abuse and ITCA. He found that parents who did not experience any childhood abuse were the least likely to report abuse or neglect of their own children. In addition, he found that parents who reported the most severe childhood victimization pattern (experiencing neglect and physical and sexual abuse) were the most likely to report either neglect or physical abuse of their children; 42% of these parents reported abusing their children. It was also found that 30% of parents who were both neglected and physically abused as a child reported neglectful or physically abusive parenting actions. Parents who had experienced physical abuse as children were significantly more likely to report physically abusing their own children than parents who were not physically abused as children. The parents who had been physically abused, however, were not more likely to neglect their children, suggesting a type specific transmission of violence. Although this study shows that ITCA is still prevalent, the discovery of type-specific transmission suggests that type-specific interventions may be better suited for a majority of victims of childhood abuse to prevent further abuse. It may be more beneficial than a general intervention.

Child Grows Up and Becomes the Victim

Becoming a victim of abuse as an adult after experiencing forms of abuse as a child is different for men and women, usually based on the type of abuse experienced as well as the protective factors that the child has. For example, childhood neglect has been shown to be a significant predictor of youth violence victimization for men; likewise, in men, youth violence victimization is significantly predicative of IPV victimization. This has not been shown to be true for women, however (Fang & Corso, 2007). However, being married significantly increases a woman's risk for being a victim of IPV, whereas higher levels of education significantly decrease a woman's risk for IPV victimization (Fang & Corso, 2007).

It is worthwhile to note that in some domestic violence relationships, it is possible for the abuser to also be the victim. Often couples in violent relationships form a codependent partnership in which each partner takes a turn being the perpetrator and victim. Much as in sibling abuse, this form of abuse is reminiscent of childhood abuse in which the child is used to being a victim of violence but also gains feelings of power from being the abuser. Couples in codependent relationships exhibit this struggle to feel powerful and also experience love in a familiar way. Typical attributes of those engaged in a codependent relationship include low self-worth, a self-identity based largely on external validation, unrealistic expectations of themselves or others, and a high tolerance for inappropriate behavior (Collins, 1993).

THE CYCLE CONTINUES: A LOOK AT ELDER ABUSE

Elder abuse is a social, political, and economic issue that is not limited to one country or culture but is prevalent in developed and developing countries worldwide (Podnieks, Anetzberg, Wilson, Teaster, & Wangmo, 2010). Elder abuse is defined by the WHO as "a single, or repeated act, or lack of appropriate action, occurring within any relationship where there is an expectation of trust which causes harm or distress to an older person" (WHO, 2011b, p. 126). The abuse may be physical, sexual, psychological, or emotional; neglectful; or it may involve financial or other material exploitation (WHO, 2011b). As populations in both developing and developed countries live longer, concerns regarding elder abuse are raised. According to a United Nations projection, the global population for those over 60 years of age will more than double by 2025. Elder abuse is a global issue that is underreported in most cultures (Podnieks et al., 2010). Additionally what constitutes elder abuse changes from culture to culture. Therefore, it makes it difficult to perceive a clear picture of elder abuse and how often it occurs. In the United States, it is estimated that 2.1 million older adults are abused each year, and most abuse and neglect takes place at the elder's home, not in an institution (American Psychological Association, 2011). This abuse is often perpetrated by their children.

Researchers have been examining elder abuse in relation to the intergenerational transmission of violence. Elderly victims are not likely to come forward and report the abuse due to feelings of dependency on the abuser, fear of being institutionalized, or feelings of love and responsibility for the abusive family member (Schiamberg & Gans, 2000). There are a number of risk factors associated with elder abuse, including female gender, being married, advanced age, deteriorating health, dementia, disruptive behavior, substance abuse, depression, and social isolation. Some characteristics of adult children who abuse their elderly parents are those who are under financial pressure, those who abuse alcohol or other drugs, those who are experiencing mental or emotional illness, lack of caregiving experience, and a lack of social support (Schiamberg & Gans, 2000). Not surprisingly, elder abuse is more common in families with established lifelong patterns of violent behavior; however, intergenerational transmission of family violence is more useful in explaining child abuse by parents than aging parent abuse by adult offspring (Korbin, Anetzberger, & Austin, 1995).

Acknowledging risk factors may lead to more thorough prevention programs to be put in place for adult children who become caregivers for their parents. In 1987, the Older American Act added a provision titled "Elder Abuse Prevention Activities." This provision mandated that states develop public education and outreach to identify abuse, neglect, and exploitation, these preventative programs appear to be more effective than laws that reduce family privacy and control (Hudson, 1986). Preventative measures include preplacement screening, which may occur with a social worker or when a frail elderly adult is placed with their family through the court. Being able to identify risk factors within the family before placing an elderly parent with the family means that the family can then have access to programs that can teach the caregivers successful strategies to care for their parent without feeling undo stress.

IT TAKES A VILLAGE: THE CYCLE AND COMMUNITIES

Violence is not limited to the family structure. It is passed on through generations and is also dispersed into neighborhoods. As stated earlier, communities can have an impact on the degree of violent behaviors exhibited by adolescents and young adults. ITA has been reported for criminal convictions, serious violent offending, and criminal careers (Frisell, Lichtenstein, & Långström, 2011).

Early experiences of familial violence have been linked with violence perpetrated outside the family as a juvenile or adult (Dankoski et al., 2006). This is a primary reason communities should work to create preventative measures that target survivors of abuse or those children who have been exposed to IPV in the home. As a community, people can work together to create services and supports for their most vulnerable members. A decrease in familial violence would, in theory, create safer neighborhoods. Research has shown that areas with higher levels of poverty are at a higher risk for community and familial violence; therefore, lower SES communities with high levels of community crime would be an excellent place to put abuse prevention programs into effect.

BREAKING THE CYCLE

Compounding effects of repeated abuse make "breaking the cycle" extremely difficult. Rarely are there survivors of one instance of abuse without comorbid occurrences of violence or occurrences of mental health disorders, such as anxiety, depression, or substance abuse. Because there are so many forms of familial abuse, as well as so many forms of side effects of the abuse, targeting treatment programs to those who have been abused cannot come in a "one size fits all" format. Adult women who have been in an abusive intimate relationship may need more practical support and application than children who have been abused. In addition, these women may have children who have witnessed IPV in the home and who thus may need an intervention that helps them to understand what they have witnessed and their feelings in regard to this. However, some survivors of abuse may not be ready for an immediate intervention and need time to process the trauma that has occurred. For example, some clinicians believe that treatment of childhood sexual abuse should either continue throughout development or be revisited when issues about the abuse become developmentally salient (Noll, 2005). Most researchers and clinicians agree that there is no simple answer to the questions of how to break the cycle of violence. This section briefly examines the possible strategies and interventions for breaking the cycle.

Strategies and Interventions

One overarching strategy for breaking the cycle of violence is to attempt to remove the stigma that comes along with being both a victim and a victimizer. As Beverly Engel stated, "No one consciously sets out to be an abusive person. Neither does anyone set out to become a victim" (Engel, 2005, pp. 20). The stigma of abuse is one people internalize for much of their lives; unfortunately, they are also likely to experience external shame, blame, and degradation due to abuse. Clinicians can help to reduce this stigma by reinforcing that it is not the survivor's fault; with victimizers, clinicians can examine the trauma that is most likely present in their past that has influenced their behavior.

Educating the general public as to what qualifies as abuse and how to get help is an essential step in trying to reduce the occurrence of violence within the home. Too often women who are victims of IPV are not aware that unwanted sexual intercourse is abuse or that physical abuse without a weapon is still considered abuse. Those who are aware of what constitutes abuse may not be aware of the programs that exist to protect them and their children. Public service announcements and easy access (without endless lines and red tape) to shelters, counseling centers, and protective agencies should be made readily available to women who are victims of abuse.

Children also need to be educated on what constitutes abuse, what to do when it is happening to them, and what to do if they see it going on. When physical, emotional, and sexual abuse against children occurs, children are often confused about what is happening to them or to others in their household. Schools are an opportune place to educate children on what constitutes abusive behavior and who they can talk to when it occurs.

Identifying risk factors within a population may help to break the cycle. As stated in the previous section, communities that have a lower socioeconomic status and higher crime rates are more likely to experience familial violence. Children who have witnessed IPV or have been victims of abuse are more likely to abuse their children than are their nonabused counterparts. Interventions that prevent the continuation of abuse can be made in these communities or these homes.

Acknowledging protective factors is also essential when creating an intervention to break the cycle. Researchers Susuki, Geffner, and Bucky (2008) found that adults who were exposed to IPV as children but did not go on to become an abusive partner shared certain protective factors. When interviewing 10 participants about their experiences and perceptions of resilience, the participants responded that they believed being goal-oriented, obtaining academic success, having an internal locus of control, being able to successfully regulate their emotions, and having a generally positive perception of themselves helped these people avoid abusive relationships. These participants also discussed being close with one member in their family of origin and obtaining physical distance from and accepting the imperfections within their family of origin. Perhaps the most significant protective factor was that all participants addressed the importance of having a social support system. In addition, most of the participants reported having the presence of a positive adult figure in childhood outside of their parents. By identifying these protective factors, clinicians who work with abused populations may be able to identify one of these factors in an abused child and create a supportive environment that centers around a protective factor. Early intervention is important in these cases.

CONCLUSION

Research has shown time and again that violence begets violence: Families pass down violence from generation to generation through learned behavior and learned helplessness. However, research has also shown that it is not a sure bet children who were abused will continue on into abusive relationships. There are risk factors that increase a child's odds of continuing the cycle, but the more that is learned about protective factors, the better chance these children have of escaping violence.

It is still unclear why certain children develop long-lasting negative effects and others do not. In addition, certain children are at risk for repeated instances of abuse but others are not. Further research should set out to examine why some survivors of childhood abuse are at considerable risk for recurrent abuse while others successfully avoid it (Noll, 2005).

Awareness is key. Interventions that target women who have experienced IPV should be easily accessible and should address the myriad symptoms that come with battered woman syndrome. Parent and clinician awareness of sibling abuse will help to curb this underaddressed problem. Speaking to children regarding what constitutes abuse and how to get help will aid in the prevention of the continuation of violence.

There is much to learn about the effect of the cycle of violence and how it affects women, but there is also much hope in how society can target survivors of abuse so that the cycle can be broken. Going forward, we must do more as a society to protect those most vulnerable and offer them a way out.

REFERENCES

American Psychological Association. (2011). *Elder abuse and neglect: In search of solutions.* Retrieved from http://www.apa.org/pi/aging/resources/guides/elder-abuse.aspx

Bandura, A. (1977). *Social learning theory*. New York: General Learning Press.

Cavanaugh, C. E., Messing, J. T., Petras, H., Fowler, B., La Flair, L., Kub, J., & Campbell, J. C. (2012). Patterns of violence against women: A latent class analysis. *Psychological Trauma: Theory, Research, Practice, and Policy, 4,* 169–176.

Collins, B. G. (1993). Reconstructing codependency using self-in-relation theory: A feminist perspective. *Social Work, 38,* 470–476.

Dankoski, M. E., Keiley, M. K., Thomas, V., Choice, P., Lloyd, S. A., & Seery, B. L. (2006). Affect regulation and the cycle of violence against women: New directions for understanding the process. *Journal of Family Violence, 21,* 327–339.

Dinwiddie, S. H., & Bucholz, K. K. (1993). Psychiatric diagnoses of self-reported child abusers. *Child Abuse & Neglect, 17,* 465–476.

Engel, B. (2005). *Breaking the cycle of abuse: How to move beyond your past and create an abuse-free future.* Hoboken, NJ: Wiley.

Fang, X., & Corso, P. S. (2007). Child maltreatment, youth violence, and intimate partner violence: Developmental relationships. *American Journal of Preventive Medicine, 33,* 281–290.

Frisell, T. T., Lichtenstein, P. P., & Långström, N. N. (2011). Violent crime runs in families: A total population study of 12.5 million individuals. *Psychological Medicine, 41,* 97–105.

Holtzworth-Munroe, A., & Smutzler, N. (1996). Comparing the emotional reactions and behavioral intentions of violent and nonviolent husbands to aggressive, distressed, and other wife behaviors. *Violence and Victims, 11,* 319–339.

Hudson, M. F. (1986). Elder mistreatment: Current research. In K. A. Pillemer & R. S. Wolf (Eds.), *Elder abuse: Conflict in the family* (pp. 125–165). Dover, MA: Auburn House.

Humphreys, J. (1997). Nursing care of children of battered women. *Pediatric Nursing, 23,* 122–128.

Kempe, C. H., Silverman, F. N., Steele, B. F., Droegemueller, W., & Silver, H. K. (1962). The battered-child syndrome. *Journal of the American Medical Association, 181,* 17–24.

Kim, J. (2009). Type-specific intergenerational transmission of neglectful and physically abusive parenting behaviors among young parents. *Children and Youth Services Review, 31,* 761–767.

Kiselica, M. S., & Morrill-Richards, M. (2007). Sibling maltreatment: The forgotten abuse. *Journal of Counseling & Development, 85,* 148–160.

Korbin, J. E., Anetzberger, G., & Austin, C. (1995). Intergenerational cycle of violence in child and elder abuse. *Journal of Elder Abuse and Neglect, 7,* 1–15.

McFarlane, J. M., Groff, J. Y., O'Brien, J. A., & Watson, K. (2005). Behaviors of children exposed to intimate partner violence before and 1 year after a treatment program for their mother. *Applied Nursing Research, 18,* 7–12.

National Coalition Against Domestic Violence. (2007). *Domestic violence facts.* Retrieved from http://www.ncadv.org/files/DomesticViolenceFactSheet(National).pdf

Noll, J. G. (2005). Does childhood sexual abuse set in motion a cycle of violence against women?: What We Know and What We Need to Learn. *Journal of Interpersonal Violence, 20,* 455–462.

Noll, J. G., Horowitz, L. A., Bonanno, G. A., Trickett, P. K., & Putnam, F. W. (2003). Revictimization and self-harm in females who experienced childhood sexual abuse: Results from a prospective study. *Journal of Interpersonal Violence, 18,* 1452–1471.

Podnieks, E., Anetzberger, G. J., Wilson, S. J., Teaster, P. B., & Wangmo, T. (2010). Worldview environmental scan on elder abuse. *Journal of Elder Abuse & Neglect, 22,* 164–179.

Riggs, D. S., & O'Leary, K. (1996). Aggression between heterosexual dating partners: An examination of a causal model of courtship aggression. *Journal of Interpersonal Violence, 11,* 519–540.

Schiamberg, L. B., & Gans, D. (2000). Elder abuse by adult children: An applied ecological framework for understanding contextual risk factors and the intergenerational character of quality of life. *The International Journal Of Aging & Human Development, 50,* 329–359.

Seligman, M. E. P. (1975). *Helplessness: On Depression, Development, and Death.* San Francisco, CA: W. H. Freeman

Spencer, G. A., & Bryant, S. A. (2000). Dating violence: A comparison of rural, suburban, and urban teens. *Journal of Adolescent Health, 27,* 302–305.

Stayton, C., Olson, C., Thorpe, L., Kerker, B., Henning, K., & Wilt, S. (2008). *Intimate partner violence against women in New York City. Report from the New York City Department of Health and Mental Hygiene.* Retrieved from http://www.nyc.gov/html/doh/downloads/pdf/public/ipv-08.pdf

Susuki, S. L., Geffner, R., & Bucky, S. F. (2008). The experiences of adults exposed to intimate partner violence as children: An exploratory qualitative study of resilience and protective factors. *Journal of Emotional Abuse, 8,* 103–121.

Thoennes, N., & Tjaden, P. G. (1990). The extent, nature, and validity of sexual abuse allegations in custody/visitation disputes. *Child Abuse & Neglect, 14,* 151–163.

U.S. Department of Health & Human Services. (2009). *Child maltreatment 2007.* Washington, DC: Government Printing Office.

U.S. Department of Health & Human Services. (2012). *Preventing child maltreatment and promoting well-being: A network for action.* Retrieved from http://www.childwelfare.gov/pubs/guide2012/guide.pdf

Walker, L. E. (1984). *The battered woman syndrome.* New York, NY: Springer Publishing Company.

Widom, C. S. (1989a). The cycle of violence. *Science, 244,* 160–166.

Widom, C. S. (1989b). Does violence beget violence? A critical examination of the literature. *Psychological Bulletin, 106,* 3–28.

Wiehe, V. R. (1997). *Sibling abuse: Hidden physical, emotional and sexual trauma.* Thousand Oaks, CA: Sage.

Wolfe, D. A., Wekerle, C., Scott, K., Straatman, A., Grasley, C., & Reitzel-Jaffe, D. (2003). Dating violence prevention with at-risk youth: A controlled outcome evaluation. *Journal of Consulting And Clinical Psychology, 71,* 279–291.

World Health Organization. (2011a). *Gender-based violence.* Retrieved from http://www.who.int/gender/violence/en/

World Health Organization. (2011b). Abuse of the Elder. In *World Report on Violence and Health* (pp. 125–145). Geneva, Switzerland: Author.

Chapter 4

Gendered Violence and Reproductive Issues

Nancy Felipe Russo, Lisa Rubin, Kathryn Becker-Blease, and Emily Breitkopf

INTRODUCTION

Gendered violence encompasses a wide variety of abusive and violent behaviors that are likely to result "in physical, sexual, or psychological harm or suffering to women, including threats of such acts, coercion or arbitrary deprivation of liberty, whether occurring in public or private life" (United Nations, 1995, Platform for Action D.112). Gendered violence is manifested in many forms over the life cycle, including sex-selective feticide and infanticide, childhood physical and sexual abuse, sexual coercion, rape, and intimate partner violence (IPV), among others (Russo, 2006). An estimated 1 in 5 women will experience gendered violence in her lifetime, making it "one of the most pervasive violations of human rights in all societies" (Amnesty International, 2004; World Health Organization [WHO], 2005, p. 9).

Gender-based violence both reflects and perpetuates gender inequalities that undermine social and economic development and have negative health and social consequences for women, their families, and society

(WHO, 2005). Multiple conditions converge to devalue and disempower women, construct gendered inequalities, foster gendered violence, and undermine maternal and child health. Consequently, findings based on cross-national comparisons should be applied to a specific culture with caution. Although we can spotlight some variance and commonalities of conditions transnationally, complexity, and synergism among converging conditions need to be examined within specified cultural contexts. An illustration of the complexity that can be involved is found in Wall's (1998) vivid description of the plight of "dead mothers and injured wives" in northern Nigeria resulting from the convergence of

> an Islamic culture that undervalues women; a perceived social need for women's reproductive capacities to be under strict male control; the practice of purdah (wife seclusion), which restricts women's access to medical care; almost universal female illiteracy; marriage at an early age and pregnancy often occurring before maternal pelvic growth is complete; a high rate of obstructed labor; directly harmful traditional medical beliefs and practices; inadequate facilities to deal with obstetric emergencies; a deteriorating economy; and a political culture marked by rampant corruption and inefficiency. (Wall, 1998, p. 341)

These are just some of the conditions that can shape the dynamics and outcomes of gendered violence in a specific cultural context.

Keeping this caveat in mind, in this chapter, we consider negative health and social outcomes of gendered violence in the context of pregnancy and childbearing. The dynamics of gendered violence have special significance for reproductive issues and outcomes (WHO, 2010). Throughout history, the sex difference in reproduction has been a primary basis for the construction of gender roles. This sex difference has influenced the organization of societal institutions as well as cultural mores that confer and legitimize power and control of men over women and justify gendered violence. The resulting gender inequalities in entitlements, power, and control—in society and interpersonally—play a central role in the dynamics of gendered violence and the shaping of pregnancy and childbearing outcomes.

PATRIARCHY, SOCIAL CONTROL, AND REPRODUCTIVE COERCION

Women's power in society as well as in intimate relationships is profoundly affected by patriarchal systems of gendered inequality, privilege, and entitlement in the larger society and culture. Across cultures and throughout time, women have been expected to become wives and mothers. Although the norms, rights, and obligations of these gendered family roles vary substantially across cultures, patriarchy is the rule rather than the exception. In many cultures, motherhood continues to define whether a female is a "real" woman, and "barren" women are diminished in social status. Furthermore, in many societies the mother-son relationship continues to be a crucial definer of women's status, and sons are preferred by both men and women (Mahalingam & Wachman, 2012).

Women's "motherhood mandate" (Russo, 1976) has been enforced in a variety of violent and coercive ways at societal and interpersonal levels, and gendered violence has profound implications for reproductive justice (Russo & Steinberg, 2012). Although power and control are not the only factors that contribute to higher risk of gendered violence against women, we believe they play a starring role in the context of pregnancy and childbearing because they are the means for achieving male reproductive goals, goals that reflect and reinforce patriarchal social and cultural values and traditional gender roles.

In patriarchal societies, women have less sexual reproductive autonomy, and a married woman may not be allowed to refuse sex, use contraception, or have the "choice" of continuing a pregnancy that is unwanted by her husband. In Tamil Nadu, India, for example, nearly 1 of 10 women who had an abortion reported being compelled to do so by husbands or in-laws (Ravindran & Balasubramanian, 2004). However, even in highly developed countries where violence is socially disapproved and that are known for their egalitarianism, such as Norway and Sweden, women may still feel a need to defer to their partner's preference and can be found identifying partner wishes as the most important reason for seeking abortion (Broen, 2005).

When women's sexual and reproductive autonomy are viewed as threatening to the patriarchal social order, coercion and violence have been used to suppress efforts to attain reproductive rights (Amnesty International, 2011). Women's reproductive autonomy is also violated by rape during armed conflict, which has occurred in numerous countries, sometimes on a massive scale. Genocidal rape aimed at "cleansing" bloodlines by impregnating women is a severe example of violence as a form of social control (Amnesty International, 2004; Human Rights Watch, 2011). At the interpersonal level, intimate relationships of women and girls reflect patriarchal assumptions of male power, entitlement, and privilege. These assumptions shape normative gendered role expectations for both women and men, including male authority for husbands and female obedience for wives.

In some cultures, women as well as men may believe a husband is justified in using violence to punish a wife who violates her gender role expectations. For example, the landmark *WHO Multi-country Study on Women's Health and Domestic Violence against Women* (WHO, 2005) identified a variety of role violations women considered as justifying partner violence. The WHO investigators found wide variation in the proportion of women who believed there were some behaviors that justified IPV. Female infidelity was most widely accepted as a justification for violence, ranging from 6% agreement in Serbia to 80% in Ethiopia. Disobeying a husband was the second most widely accepted reason, followed by failure to complete housework. Combining all reasons, women with histories of violence were more likely to view IPV as justified than other women (WHO, 2005).

At the interpersonal level, gendered violence and coercion function as a form of social control that perpetuates women's subordinate social and political status at large. Around the world, men who are physically and/or sexually violent with their partners are more likely to exhibit controlling behaviors than men who are not violent (Kishor & Johnson, 2004; WHO, 2005). Furthermore, men who connect masculinity with being able to control and dominate their partners are more likely to be violent (Goodrum, Umberson, & Anderson, 2001). There is cross-cultural evidence to suggest sexual coercive control provides a primary link between controlling behaviors and IPV (see Tanha et al., 2010).

Having a child provides an additional point of leverage for male control via threats to harm the child and can be used to entrap women in a violent relationship (Ptacek, 1997). Controlling behavior that is consistently associated with gendered violence internationally is found to be linked to pregnancy and childbearing outcomes. For example, in a study of nine developing countries (Cambodia, Colombia, Dominican Republic, Egypt, Haiti, India, Nicaragua, Peru, and Zambia), Kishor and Johnson (2004) reported a strong association between a partner's controlling behaviors and partner violence that was in turn associated with both a higher unmet need for contraception and a greater likelihood of having a birth unwanted by the woman.

Although this finding underscores a possible link between male control and pregnancy outcomes, the direct association was not examined in these studies. Furthermore, the controlling behaviors studied (e.g., keeping the woman from seeing friends and family, always knowing where she is, accusing her of infidelity) were not specifically defined in relation to pregnancy outcomes. Subsequent work, focusing on controlling behavior in the context of pregnancy, has revealed forced sex and sexual coercion are used to exert male control over women's reproduction. Before pregnancy, this reproductive coercion is on getting the woman pregnant: Men's attempts at reproductive coercion at this time include verbal threats and pressure to become pregnant as well as birth control sabotage. Birth control sabotage can involve direct interference with contraceptive use or involve the use of threats of violence if she broaches the use or tries to use contraception. During pregnancy, reproductive coercion encompasses controlling, abusive, and violent behaviors aimed at either terminating or continuing the pregnancy, including interference with pregnancy-related health care (Miller et al., 2007; Miller & Silverman, 2010).

Reproductive coercion has been linked to risk for unintended pregnancy among women experiencing other forms of gender violence (Miller et al., 2010; Moore, Frohwirth, & Miller, 2010). For example, in a large study of 1,463 participants, women experiencing IPV were more likely to report their partners wanted them to get pregnant or didn't want to use birth control and made it difficult for the women to use birth control (Gee, Mitra, Wan, Chavkin, & Long, 2009). In this context, it is not surprising that experiencing prepregnancy violence has linked to higher pregnancy and birth rates, particularly for women with unwanted pregnancies and births (WHO, 2005; Secretariat of the Pacific Community for Ministry of Internal and Social Affairs, 2010). For example, a U.S. study based on 12,612 women found that 70% of new mothers with a history of physical IPV in the year before giving birth reported their pregnancy was unintended (Gazmararian et al., 1995). Subsequent research based on 39,348 women replicated these findings (Goodwin et al., 2000).

Surprisingly, both studies found that the association between IPV and unintended pregnancy was weaker for women with fewer social advantages—that is, weaker for the women who would be expected to lack the resources to leave the relationship. The explanation for this paradoxical finding may be found in the fact that these findings are based on new mothers—living women who had unplanned pregnancies ending in birth, which raises an important methodological concern for research on the relation of violence in pregnancy to reproductive outcomes. In other words, these findings are based only on pregnancies resulting in birth and are not representative of all pregnancies.

Women who experience the most severe forms of violence in pregnancy may be more likely to have their pregnancies terminated by miscarriage, abortion, or maternal death. When the goal of reproductive coercion and violence is to promote pregnancy, pregnancy may well be protective and bring a drop in violence when it occurs. However, the most severe forms of violence and reproductive coercion may occur in pregnancies that are not wanted by male partners, increasing the likelihood a woman may miscarry or seek an abortion (Russo & Denious, 2001; Steinberg & Russo, 2008). If the IPV in this context is extreme, the outcome may be maternal death. Women who experience violence in pregnancy are at higher risk for homicide by their partner, particularly if the paternity of the child is in question (Chambliss, 2008). In one study, a comparison of IPV homicide victims compared with living controls found that 26% of the homicide group had a history of being abused during pregnancy compared to 7% of the control group (Campbell et al., 2003). Consequently, studies of gendered violence and pregnancy outcomes that do not take into account men's pregnancy goals or focus on new mothers or living women do not present a full and accurate picture of the violence experienced by pregnant women.

VIOLENCE, PREGNANCY, AND CHILDBEARING

Precursors of Violence in Pregnancy

A substantial body of work suggests that women typically experience more than one form of gendered violence before becoming pregnant. The synergistic and cumulative effects of childhood physical and sexual abuse, rape, reproductive coercion, and IPV before pregnancy deserve special attention in any analysis of the relation of gendered violence to pregnancy and childbearing outcomes (Steinberg & Russo, 2008). Women's childhood exposure and experience with multiple forms of gendered violence have profound and long-lasting effects on their reproductive health and social behaviors over the life cycle.

Childhood sexual abuse (CSA) is an international problem, although the specific definitions of what constitutes abuse vary cross-nationally. The WHO Multi-Country Study (2005) found that anonymously reported sexual abuse (sexual touching or making a child do something sexual they did not want to do) below the age of 15 varied widely across settings, from a high of 21.3% in urban Namibia to a low of 4% Serbia/Montenegro City (Bangladesh women were not included in these analyses because of women's reluctance to mark a piece of paper anonymously without their husband's permission). In addition, substantial numbers of women reported their first experience of sexual intercourse as forced, with percentages ranging from 30% in rural Bangladesh to .4% in urban Japan (WHO, 2005). Note that a large number of studies in the field define CSA as "contact or noncontact sexual experiences between a person younger than 18 years of age and an adult or other person at least 5 years older or sexual experiences resulting from coercion, regardless of the age of the other person" (Lalor & McElvaney, 2010, p. 162), so that comparing rates and outcomes across studies with different definitions of abuse should be made with caution.

Methodological issues notwithstanding, it can be concluded that CSA survivors around the world are more likely to experience a range of problems that interfere with healthy pregnancy. Negative outcomes include psychiatric diagnoses, substance dependence, and other kinds of violence and revictimization, including sexual assault and exploitation, having multiple sex partners, and having a pregnancy in adolescence (Lalor & McElvaney, 2010; Noll, Trickett, Harris, & Putnam, 2009). CSA is strongly associated with experiencing other adverse childhood experiences, including physical abuse and neglect, witnessing partner violence, and other types of household dysfunction (Dong, Anda, Dube, Giles, & Felitti, 2003). Exposure to intimate partner violence in childhood is associated with greater likelihood of sexual risk taking behavior, having a sexually transmitted disease, first intercourse at less than 15 years of age, having more than 30 lifetime sexual partners, having an adolescent pregnancy, and having an unintended adult pregnancy (Bair-Merritt, Blackstone, & Feudtner, 2006).

The greater the number of adverse experiences, the greater the likelihood of behaviors or conditions that negatively affect maternal and fetal health, including alcoholism, illicit drug use, smoking, and depression (Felitti et al., 1998). For example, smoking in pregnancy is associated with greater likelihood of women having a posttraumatic stress disorder and reporting abuse as their worst lifetime trauma (Lopez, Konrath, & Seng, 2011). As the number of adverse childhood experiences increases, so does risk for negative behaviors that directly affect sexual and reproductive health: early initiation of sexual activity, multiple sexual partners, sexually transmitted diseases (including HIV/AIDS), adolescent pregnancy, unintended pregnancy, fetal death, and IPV (Bair-Merritt, Blackstone, & Feudtner, 2006; Centers for Disease Control and Prevention, 2013; Felitti et al., 1998). This relationship appears to hold across culture. For example, Ramiro, Madrid, and Brown (2010) found a strong relationship between risky behaviors and number of adverse childhood experiences in a Philippines sample.

Prepregnancy IPV has been found to be consistently associated with sexual risk taking, partner "nonmonogamy," inconsistent condom use, and having a sexually transmitted infection (including HIV/AIDS), sexual dysfunction (particularly chronic pelvic pain), unwanted pregnancy, and induced abortion (Coker, 2007). Damage to reproductive organs from physical and sexual violence includes vaginal bleeding, vaginal discharge, painful menstruation, sexual dysfunction, decreased sexual desire, and pelvic inflammatory disease (Akyüz, Yavan, Şahiner, & Kılıç, 2009). It has also been associated with fetal loss and recurrent fetal loss (Alio, Nana, & Salihu, 2009).

More needs to be learned about how the biological, psychological, and social outcomes of gendered violence in childhood interact in ways that directly and indirectly increase risk for negative sexual and reproductive health outcomes. For example, sufficient physical maturation for fecundity is a necessary condition for pregnancy. Girls and women who have been sexually abused have an earlier age of menarche than do those who have not experienced abuse (Boynton-Jarrett et al., 2012; Foster, Hagan, & Brooks-Gunn, 2008; Zabin, Emerson, & Rowland, 2005). Child physical abuse is also associated with both early menarche (Boynton-Jarrett et al., 2012; Foster et al., 2008) and late menarche (after age 15; Boynton-Jarrett et al., 2012), albeit to a lesser extent.

Risk of early menarche is associated with abuse severity in a dose-response fashion. Boynton-Jarrett et al. (2012) reported that forced sexual activity was associated with higher risk of menarche before age 11 compared with sexual touching, which in turn was associated with higher risk than no sexual abuse. Zabin et al. (2005) did not find increased risk associated with increased "invasiveness" of sexual abuse (i.e., touching, penetration), but they did find a strong effect for perpetrator relationship. Girls who were sexually abused by close perpetrators (e.g., someone in the home or a father) had earlier ages of menarche than other girls. In fact, girls abused by their fathers, on average, reached menarche almost a full year before girls who were sexually abused by strangers.

Suggested mechanisms through which child abuse leads to early menarche differ. One biological explanation is that stress of many kinds leads to accelerated aging (Foster et al., 2008). Nutrition, social context, other kinds of victimization and stress all likely play a role as well (e.g., Zabin et al., 2005). Early maturation may then draw the attention of predatory males or male relatives who feel entitled to have female members of their household sexually service them, increasing risk for unintended pregnancy.

Violence in Pregnancy

Given the ubiquity of gendered violence in childhood and adolescence, it is no surprise that violence in pregnancy is a common phenomenon around the world (Devries et al., 2010). An estimated 1 in 4 women experiences physical or sexual violence during pregnancy, 90% at the hands of an intimate partner (Campbell, García-Moreno, & Sharps, 2004; WHO, 2005). Adolescents may be at even higher risk for IPV than adult women (Chambliss, 2008). The relation of childhood violence to early marriage and adolescent pregnancy is of substantial concern because complications of pregnancy and maternal death are among the leading causes of death globally for girls 15 to 19 years of age. Maternal mortality in adolescence is five times higher than in adulthood (Rowbottom 2007). In particular, sexually abused mothers are more likely than other mothers to have given birth during their teenage years and to experience a range of problems that interfere with healthy pregnancy including psychiatric diagnoses, substance dependence, and other kinds of violence and revictimization (Noll, Trickett, Harris, & Putnam, 2009).

Although pregnancy has been characterized as conferring protection against violence, protective effects are not found to be consistent across cultures (Pallitto, Campbell, &, O'Campo, 2005). As noted earlier, the protective effects that are found may reflect methodologic shortcomings of the research rather than an accurate picture of pregnancy violence prevalence.

Findings from WHO's multicountry study of women's health and partner violence shed some light on similarities and differences in the dynamics of violence in pregnancy cross-nationally. The WHO investigators found that the majority of women experiencing violence in pregnancy had experienced violence before becoming pregnant (WHO, 2005). Nonetheless, from 3% (Ethiopia) to approximately 50% (urban Brazil, Serbia, and Montenegro) of these women reported being beaten for the first time after becoming pregnant, providing some evidence that something about the context of the pregnancy may have triggered the pregnancy violence (WHO, 2005).

It is difficult to distinguish men who beat wives who happen to be pregnant from men who beat their wives because they are pregnant. However, it is possible to identify men who kick or punch their pregnant partners in the abdomen. The WHO investigators found that across settings, approximately a quarter to a half of the women reporting violence during pregnancy reported being kicked or punched in the abdomen (WHO, 2005, Figure 12, p. 17). It is not surprising that women experiencing violence in pregnancy are more likely to have had a miscarriage or induced abortion (WHO, 2005) or have a child who died (Secretariat of the Pacific Community for Ministry of Internal and Social Affairs, 2010).

GENDERED VIOLENCE AND REPRODUCTIVE OUTCOMES

Around the world, gendered violence has been found to have multiple, indirect, and rippling effects on women's reproductive and sexual health outcomes, including adverse health outcomes for the woman, the pregnancy, and the newborn (Akyüz et al., 2012). The most direct and extreme outcomes of violence in pregnancy are risk of death for the woman and fetus (Campbell, 2002). Pregnancy-associated death (deaths occurring during or within 1 year of pregnancy) is a leading cause of maternal mortality; pregnant women have 2 to 3 times higher risk for homicide compared with nonpregnant women (Campbell et al., 2007). Violence in pregnancy is also associated with greater risk for late fetal and perinatal death (Coker, Sanderson, & Dong, 2004).

For surviving women, negative outcomes include reduced sexual autonomy and higher perinatal death and morbidity (Sharps, Laughon, & Giangrande, 2007). Such morbidity includes edema, diabetes, hypertension, severe nausea and vomiting, dehydration, chronic pelvic pain, vaginal bleeding, placental problems, infections of the urinary tract or kidneys, and premature rupture of membranes. Other negative outcomes include higher risk for risky behaviors such as smoking or illicit drug use, sexually transmitted diseases (including HIV/AIDS), premature labor, miscarriage, unintended pregnancy, unwanted births, and multiple abortions (Campbell, 2002; Chambliss, 2008; Sarkar, 2008; Sharps et al., 2007). Outcomes are moderated by women's pregnancy intentions: Mistimed versus unwanted births differ, with a greater likelihood of adverse outcomes more often found for unwanted births (D'Angelo et al., 2004). The relation between gendered violence and unwanted pregnancy and its outcomes is discussed later in the chapter.

Infants of survivors are more likely to experience premature delivery, low birth weight, and neonatal morbidity and death (Rosen, Seng, Tolman, & Mallinger, 2007). Controlling behavior and IPV are associated with risk for higher mortality among infants and young children. For example, researchers in Ethiopia found that controlling behaviors in marriage and experiencing psychological, physical, or sexual violence were associated with higher rates of under-five child mortality (Garoma, Fantahum, & Worku, 2012).

Pregnancy-related violence has implications for the relation between mother and child. Survivors of pregnancy violence are less likely to obtain prenatal care or breast feed their babies (Campbell, 2002; Chambliss, 2008; Salihu, 2004; Sarkar, 2008; Sharps et al., 2007). They are more likely to be identified as insecurely attached to their infant than are women who have not experienced IPV (Huth-Bocks, Levendosky, Theran, & Bogat, 2004; Zeanah et al., 1999).

IPV during pregnancy continues in the postpartum period, and as documented in our description of precursors to violence in pregnancy, children raised in violent homes have both immediate and long-term adverse health outcomes as a result of their exposure to gendered violence. Violence in pregnancy has been prospectively associated with higher risk for subsequent maternal child abuse and neglect (Chan et al., 2012). In particular, unwanted children are at higher risk for experiencing violence. Furthermore, children whose paternity is uncertain may be at higher risk for physical abuse by fathers (Alexandre et al., 2011). And the cycle of violence continues (Denmark & Williams, Chapter 3 of this volume).

UNINTENDED PREGNANCY, BIRTH, AND ABORTION

Around the world, unintended pregnancy is found to be a common outcome of gendered violence, with profound implications for the health and well-being of women, their families, and society. In 2008, an estimated 41% of the world's pregnancies were unintended; 39% ended in unintended birth; 49% and 12% ended in abortion and miscarriage, respectively (Singh, Wulf, Hussain, Bankole, & Sedgh, 2009). Although the role that gendered violence plays in increasing risk for unintended pregn ancy varies transnationally, the interconnection is undeniable (Amnesty

International, 2011; Pallitto, Campbell, & O'Campo, 2005; Sarkar, 2008). In countries as diverse as Azerbaijan, Bangladesh, Brazil, Colombia, Ethiopia, India, Moldova, Namibia, Peru, Tanzania, Thailand, Ukraine, and the United States, women experiencing physical or sexual IPV have been found to be more likely to have an unintended pregnancy compared with other women (Cripe et al., 2008; Dietz et al., 2000; Martin et al., 1999; Pallitto et al., 2012; Pallitto & O'Campo, 2004; Silverman, Gupta, Decker, & Kapur, 2007).

The impact of gendered violence on unintended pregnancy and abortion around the world is substantial. Analyses on WHO Multi-Country Study data found women reporting physical and/or sexual partner violence had almost twice the odds of having an unintended pregnancy. The percentage of unintended pregnancy attributable to IPV averaged 15% across the 14 study locations with applicable data ranged from a low of 3.4% in "Brazil city" to a high of 35.1% in "Thailand city." An even stronger association was found for abortion: Women experiencing physical and/or sexual partner violence had nearly 3 times the odds of having an abortion. An average of 29.8% of abortions were attributable to IPV across the 15 sites of the study, figures ranging from a low of 9.2% in Thailand city to a high of 79.1% in Ethiopia. On the basis of these findings, the study investigators estimated that reducing IPV by 50% could potentially result in lowering unintended pregnancy by 2% to 18% and abortion by 4.5% to 40% according to population-attributable risk estimates. (Pallitto et al., 2012).

These findings are congruent with other evidence that suggests that higher rates of violence are found in the lives of pregnant women who resolve their pregnancies through abortion rather than delivery (Russo & Denious, 2001; Steinberg & Russo, 2008). For example, a comparison of U.S. women who terminated versus delivered their first pregnancy found that 39% of women in the abortion group experienced some type of violence compared with 27% of women in the birth group. In particular, women in the abortion group had significantly higher rates of rape (15.1% vs. 7.5%) and molestation (18.3% vs. 11.6%), respectively. Furthermore, 41% of women who reported multiple abortions (an indicator of repeat unwanted pregnancy) experienced some form of violence (Steinberg & Russo, 2007). Given that unintended pregnancies can lead to unsafe abortions in countries where abortion is illegal the compounding of health risks of gendered violence with those of unsafe abortion is of serious concern. These concerns are compounded in countries where women's status is devalued, there is widespread preference for having sons, reproductive coercion in the service of male reproductive goals is socially approved, and women carrying female fetuses are forced to terminate their pregnancies by unsafe abortion (Bankole, 1998).

Female Infanticide and Sex Selection

A preference for male children, common in many countries around the globe, carries important implications for the intersection of gendered violence and reproductive issues. In some cultures, this preference for sons has been resulted in female infanticide: the abandonment, neglect, or killing of a female child within the first year of life. Son preference has long been recognized as contributing to high female mortality rates as well as severe neglect and poor access to health care for women and girls (Hesketh & Xing, 2006; Tandon & Sharma, 2006). Reasons for female infanticide vary across cultures. Some reasons may have to do with unwanted obligations associated with raising daughters, such as the need to pay a dowry or the increased risk to family honor that women bring to the family setting. In others, the cost of having daughters may be less important than the benefits and need to have sons. Both types of motives converge to result in son preference, which has resulted in violence against girls and women through the abandonment, neglect, and infanticide of female infants. Such behaviors are "as old as many cultures" and have been most documented in Asian countries, including China, India, and Korea (Mahalingam & Wachman, 2012, p. 251). Access to sex-selective practices means that families can achieve their goal of having a male child (Lee & Paik, 2006; Loo et al., 2012; Wertz & Fletcher, 1993).

For more than four decades, individuals have used reproductive technologies—before and/or during pregnancy—throughout the world to selectively give birth to male children. Advancements in reproductive technology have created new contexts and intersections between gendered violence and pregnancy outcomes. In the United States and other Global North countries, sex selection is framed as "family balancing," and couples use sex selection to have female children to ensure "a boy for me and a girl for you" (Kalfoglou, Scott, & Hudson, 2008; Missmer & Jain, 2007). Nonetheless, use of sex-selection procedures to prevent birth of daughters is increasingly common around the world. For example, in India, where advances in sex-selection technology began to be applied in 1974, female infanticide decreased as son preference became increasingly attained via sex selection (Garlough, 2008).

Although sex-selective practices may lower the demand for female infanticide, both reflect a devalued status for women, exacerbate and result from gender inequities, and have interpersonal as well as societal consequences that perpetuate a cycle of violence against women across the life span. Outcomes of son preference reflect the larger context of objectification and devaluation of women, current ongoing assaults on reproductive freedom, and the globalization of reproductive technologies.

Son Preference: Outcomes and Issues

The context of son preference means that ready access to sex-selective practices combined with female child mortality due to infanticide and neglect can have an enormous impact on the sex ratio of a country's population. Countries such as China, Taiwan, South Korea, India, Pakistan, and some sub-Saharan African countries have had sex ratios of men to women that are higher than would be expected under normal conditions. For example, in China a reported ratio was 120 men for every 100 women; similarly, in India a reported ratio was 106 men to every 100 women (Loo et al., 2010; Wertz & Fletcher, 1993). These skewed sex ratios have inspired scholars such as Amartya Sen (2003) to call attention to the phenomenon of "missing girls" across the world, particularly in India and China. Sen has sought to estimate the number of missing girls across the world, as Klasen and Wink (2003) described, to "assess the cumulative impact of gender bias in mortality" (p. 264).

Unbalanced sex ratios both reflect women's devaluation as well as help perpetuate further devaluation through objectification and commodification of women's bodies. For example, China has witnessed a rise in sex work, sexually transmitted infections, and the kidnapping of girls and women from other countries for marriage. In rural Punjab, fraternal polyandry (where younger brothers have sex with the older brother's wife) is becoming more common (Mahalingam & Wachman, 2012). Meanwhile, there is a dearth of women to perform elder care, which is traditionally a cultural role performed by women (Ebenstein & Sharygin, 2009; Mahalingam & Wachman, 2012).

Such structural and cultural factors work together to produce the "simultaneous entanglement [of reproductive issues] with gender and generational relations, kinship, religious, and governmental regulation at both the local and the international level" (Rapp, 2011, p. 696). Although a comprehensive analysis of the implication of gendered violence for these entanglements beyond the scope of this paper, we highlight several key ways a variety of practices have been found to motivate son preference and encourage female infanticide and neglect of girls (Mahalingam & Wachman, 2012).

Across Asia, reasons for son preference include carrying on the family name, serving as a source of economic support for the family, and the desire to avoid costly dowries and economic dependence associated with daughters. Country-specific reasons can be identified as well: for example, in South Korea, son preference increased during the year of the horse (a South Korean symbol of masculinity); China's "one-child policy" means that families have only one opportunity to have a son.

Loo, Li, and Tan (2010) examined the relationship between a family's son preference and pregnant women's prenatal anxiety in the context of

China's one-child policy. They found that the anxiety and depression typically expected given the psychosocial stresses of childbearing could be exacerbated by pressure to bear a male child. In both China and India, women report experiencing such pressure as an indicator of their social, maternal, and female empowerment (Garlough, 2008; Loo et al., 2010). If women are able to produce a male child who can carry on the family name, it can be empowering when it is seen as benefiting the larger family as well as enhancing their own identity as mothers (Wertz & Fletcher, 1993). However, some women fear abandonment if they were to challenge the wishes of their family or husband (Mahalingam & Wachman, 2012). Women may be put in a no-win situation: They may be pressured to terminate a female fetus against their wishes and then be criticized and shamed after the procedure (Garlough, 2008). In this context, a woman who bears a female child may experience reproductive coercion, violence, and abuse if she does not violate the wishes of the state and seek to bear a son (Anagnost, 1988).

Sex Selection and Assisted Reproductive Technologies

Sex selection practices include prenatal ultrasound or genetic screening followed by induced abortion, as well the more advanced assisted reproductive technologies (ARTS) of prefertilization strategies (e.g., "sperm sorting") and postfertilization technologies used before pregnancy through preimplantation genetic diagnosis (PGD). ARTs include "sperm sorting" or flow cytometry during prefertilization to separate X- and Y-chromosome-bearing sperm (WHO, 2012). Chromosomally selected sperm matching sex preferences are then used to fertilize the egg, either through artificial insemination or in vitro fertilization (IVF). Another technology, PGD, involves biopsy and testing of embryos created through IVF to identify X- or Y-bearing chromosomes, with only sex-selected embryos transferred to a woman's uterus for implantation.

The controversies and issues associated with these different technologies vary across societies. Although abortion is a common practice globally, it is often illegal and unsafe (Russo & Steinberg, 2012). Thus, using abortion as a method of sex selection potentially contributes to the unacceptably high rates of unsafe abortion around the world. Furthermore, forced abortion for any reason, including elimination of female fetuses in the service of son preference, is a form of reproductive coercion that undermines women's reproductive autonomy.

Ironically, preventing forced abortion has been used as an argument to justify further undermining of women's reproductive autonomy by banning abortion for all reasons and in all cases, even when the abortion is desired by the woman and needed to preserve her physical and/or mental health. Also, a paradoxical situation is created when a woman who wants to have a male child seeks to have a voluntary abortion to eliminate a female fetus, thereby exercising her reproductive autonomy by using a practice that leads to imbalanced sex ratios and related conditions that in turn further devalue the position of girls and women in society and undermine their reproductive autonomy.

In contrast to sex-selective abortion, more "advanced" ARTs occur before pregnancy and do not involve elimination of female fetuses. ARTs may be considered more acceptable than using sex-selective abortion in countries like the United States where personhood for zygotes is promoted in conservative political discourse. A downside of these practices, however, is that they create a context for what Colen (1995) has described as a "transnational, highly stratified system of reproduction" (p. 78).

Stratified Reproduction in a Global Economy

Stratified reproduction refers to the ways in which

> physical and social reproductive tasks are accomplished differently according to the inequalities that are based on hierarchies of class, race, ethnicity, gender, place in a global economy, and migration status, and that are structured by social, economic, and political forces. (Colen, 1995)

ARTs are extremely expensive and accessible to a select few even within the wealthier global North. Use of ARTs correlates with class privilege, whereas abortion is more economically accessible and widespread (Abrevaya, 2009). Sex selection technologies are largely unregulated in the United States, where sex selection is actively promoted and marketed, sometimes through highly gendered pink and blue pamphlets (Center for Genetics and Society, n.d.).

A number of countries have developed legislation prohibiting "social" sex selection, without interfering with abortion rights. For instance, in the early 1990s the Pre-Natal Diagnostic Techniques (Regulation and Prevention of Misuse) Act (PNDT) was passed in India to ban sex determination while maintaining women's right to abortion (Bumgarner, 2007). This legislation responded to concerns about an imbalanced societal sex ratio while being supportive of women's reproductive autonomy. Yet Indian families have continued sex selection through various sources, including ordering tests on the Internet and sending them to labs in the United States, thereby demonstrating how far-reaching and effective the global market for sex selection can be (Garlough, 2008). In this context, laws and policies enacted to outlaw prenatal screening only serve to create a health disparity as those who have economic means will have such screening conducted in other parts of the world where testing is allowed.

Ironically, the use of sex selection to have a child who will be expected to take on male gender roles is an imperfect system. As de Melo-Martin points out, "biology is not determinative of gender characteristics" (p. 14). The practice of sex selection through medical technologies helps to "legitimize false ideas that selection of sex is sufficient to determine gender" (p. 14), perpetuating the harmful conflation of the two and reinforcing the essentialization of gender roles which underlies gender inequities (Mahalingam, Haritatos, & Jackson, 2007).

Danis (1995) pointed out that the "transhistorical quest for male children undoubtedly reflects the prevalence of societies in which maleness has been a form of social, political, and economic entitlement" (p. 2). This connection is reflected in the various forms of sex selection and their growing effects on sex ratio imbalance in many countries. Structural and cultural norms inform the ways sex is interpreted as gender. This drives the devaluation of female gender roles and idealization of male roles, which help maintain gender inequities across the globe. The specific act of male preference is part of a cycle of violence across women's lives; it is neither a beginning nor an end. The specific act of sex selection cannot be simply reduced to being seen as a form of gendered violence because it remains part of a larger system of "reproductive entanglements" through which structural and cultural forces drive the cycle of violence against women over the life span.

GENDERED VIOLENCE, PREGNANCY, AND HEALTH PROFESSIONALS

Given the magnitude of the problem and the relative paucity of resources, prevention and intervention from a public health perspective must be a priority. WHO continues to be a global leader on this issue and provides a public health model for preventing physical and sexual violence against women (WHO, 2010). There are many challenges ahead, including the complexity of the interconnections that need to be addressed and the difficulties in conducting culturally sensitive research and evaluation that can inform effective program development (WHO, 2010). However, the strong association between gendered violence over the life cycle and women's sexual and reproductive health outcomes means that health professionals have essential roles to play—as researchers, clinicians, educators, program developers, administrators, advocates, and leaders—in violence intervention and prevention efforts as well as ameliorating negative outcomes (WHO, 2002, 2005, 2010).

Although much has been done, the need for sensitization and education of health and other service providers in their respective fields continues. Adequately training current and future health professionals, particularly in specialties focused on maternal and child health, as well as other future health care providers, about the nature, pervasiveness, and outcomes of gendered violence will require the development of guidelines for practice as well as curriculum change around the world. The research findings presented in this chapter underscore the need for such efforts to pay special attention to information on the intersections of gendered violence, reproductive coercion, and sexual and reproductive health. The curriculum change efforts and guidelines developed by the American College of Obstetricians and Gynecologists are an example of such efforts (Chamberlain & Levenson, 2012).

Health care practitioners, particularly those who provide services to pregnant women, are in a unique position to identify women who are at high risk for experiencing gendered violence. The impact of gendered violence on health during pregnancy and the perinatal period means that, in addition to family practitioners and emergency room personnel, midwives, obstetricians, gynecologists, pediatricians, pediatric nurses, social workers, family planning practitioners, and pregnancy and abortion counselors are all in a position to identify at-risk women and help them obtain the services they need to prevent gendered violence and ameliorate its effects. In addition to physician's offices and emergency rooms, potential settings for identification and intervention include family planning clinics, prenatal care programs, sexually transmitted infection and HIV clinics and prevention programs, adolescent health clinics and service providers, and individual or group practice settings that offer reproductive health services (Chamberlain & Levenson, 2012).

Addressing multiple outcomes of violence and the needs of survivors requires a multipronged response. Health professionals may be the only people an abused woman can speak with privately and may be uniquely positioned to observe physical signs of abuse. For these reasons, screening and referrals through health care practitioners are important. Health professionals need plans for how to identify at-risk women and to direct them to sources of assistance. There are two important caveats. First, an insufficient or unsupportive response could be more damaging than not asking at all (Ullman & Filipas, 2001). Therefore sufficient training, time, and resources to assist women must be available for screening to be helpful. Health care professionals should work with advocates to ensure that there are services available to help women identified in the screening process. Second, some women consciously choose not to tell their health care providers about abuse for a variety of reasons. Many previously abused women have successfully coped, recovered, and perhaps even experienced growth after their abuse. These women prefer health care providers who will work with them as a collaborator and ally, not as an authority figure whose role is to redirect them to support services (Seng, Sparbel, Low, & Killion, 2002). When asking women to disclose abuse, it is important to validate both real concerns for safety and well-being with appreciation for the coping and recovery some women have brought about for themselves (Ullman & Filipas, 2001).

Although few researchers have examined the varying needs of violence survivors transnationally, it is clear that, just as we cannot assume all women have the same beliefs, knowledge, and desires about reproductive issues, we cannot assume that violence survivors are a homogenous group. For example, Seng, Sparbel, Low, and Killion (2002) found three distinct groups of violence survivors in one area of the United States. Survivors who had successfully processed and significantly recovered from the violence were interested in childbirth attendants who would be collaborative and supportive. Those who were less far along in recovery, including those currently in abusive relationships, preferred providers who were more authoritative and provided referrals for additional services. A third group was not willing or ready to disclose a violence history and were less open to either discussing or receiving referrals; members of this group may respond to mentoring to begin to deal with the violence. Thus, it is clear that a one-size-fits-all approach will not lead to healthier pregnancies or babies. Rather, culturally sensitive interventions must be tailored to meet diverse needs and, in addition to other aspects of the cultural context, respect women's needs at different points in recovery from violence in their lives.

CONCLUSION

Gender-based violence takes multiple forms and is rooted in patriarchal social structures and cultural roles of women and men, including the gendered family roles of wife–husband and mother–son. Such violence has widespread and enduring physical, mental, and behavioral health effects on women and men, their families, and society. Gendered violence—before, during, and after pregnancy—affects sexual and reproductive health outcomes in multiple and profound ways around the world. In particular, adverse childhood experiences, reproductive coercion, and violence in pregnancy have multiple and severe effects on the health of women and children. These effects are compounded by strong association of gendered violence with maternal death, miscarriage, unintended and unwanted pregnancy, unsafe abortion, and sex selection—conditions that themselves have a severe and negative impact on women. As a consequence, gendered violence results in enormous and rippling social and economic costs to society. These costs have yet to be fully included when evaluating the economic and social impact of gendered violence (García-Moreno & Watts, 2011).

Although it is clear that legal and policies changes are needed, the key to eliminating sexual and reproductive violence and ameliorating its effects lies in changing traditional attitudes and practices that underlie women's unequal, subordinate status in the family and society, legitimize violence as a means for enforcing male status and entitlement, do not respect women's reproductive autonomy, devalue female children and make women and girls "fair game" for physical and sexual abuse, and increase risk for unwanted pregnancy and childbearing. Prevention and intervention programs that challenge patriarchal values and attitudes and teach males of all ages to value women as equal partners in the family and society are a necessary condition for gender-based violence to be truly eliminated and not merely suppressed.

REFERENCES

Abrevaya, J. (2009). Are there missing girls in the United States? Evidence from birth data. *American Economic Journal: Applied Economics, 1,* 1–34.

Akyüz, A., Yavan, T., Şahiner, G., & Kılıç, A. (2012). Domestic violence and woman's reproductive health: A review of the literature. *Aggression and Violent Behavior, 17,* 514–518.

Alexandre, G. C., Nadanovsky, P. Wilson, M., Daly, M., Moraes, C. L., & Reichenheim, M. (2011). Cues of paternal uncertainty and father to child physical abuse as reported by mothers in Rio de Janeiro, Brazil. *Child Abuse & Neglect 35,* 567–573

Alio, A. P., Nana, P. N., & Salihu, H. M. (2009). Spousal violence and potentially preventable single and recurrent spontaneous fetal loss in an African setting: Cross-sectional study. *Lancet, 373,* 318–324.

Amnesty International. (2004). *It's in our hands: Stop violence against women.* Oxford, England: Alden Press.

Anagnost, A. S. (1988). Family violence and magical violence: The woman as victim in China's one-child family policy. *Women and Language,11*(2), 16–22.

Bair-Merritt, M. H., Blackstone, M., & Feudtner, C. (2006). Physical health outcomes of childhood exposure to intimate partner violence: A systematic review. *Pediatrics, 117,* 278–290. doi: 10.1542/peds. –1473

Bankole, A. (1998). Reasons why women have induced abortions: Evidence from 27 countries. *International Family Planning Perspectives, 24,* 117–152.

Boynton-Jarrett, R., Wright, R. J., Putnam, F. W., Hibert, E. L., Michels, K. B., Forman, M. R., & Rich-Edwards, J. (2012). Childhood abuse and age at menarche. *Journal of Adolescent Health,* n.p. doi: 10.1016/j.jadohealth.2012.06.006

Broen, A. N. (2005). Reasons for induced abortion and their relation to women's emotional distress: A prospective, two-year follow-up study. *General Hospital Psychiatry, 27,* 36–43.

Bumgarner, A. (2007). Right to choose?: Sex selection in the international context. *Duke Journal of Gender Law & Policy, 14,* 1289–1310.

Campbell, J. C. (2002). Health consequences of intimate partner violence. *The Lancet, 359,* 1331–1336. doi:10.1016/S0140-6736(02)08336-8

Campbell, J. C., Campbell, J., García-Moreno, C., & Sharps, P. (2004). Abuse during pregnancy in industrialized and developing countries. *Violence against women, 10,* 770–789.

Campbell, J. C., Glass, N., Sharps, P. W., Laughton, K., & T. Bloom (2007). Intimate partner homicide: Review and implications of research and policy. *Trauma, Violence, & Abuse, 8,* 246–269. doi: 10.1177/1524838007303505

Campbell, J. C., Webster, D., Koziol-McLain, J., Block, C., Campbell, D., Curry, M. A., . . . Laughon, K. (2003). Risk factors for femicide in abusive relationships: Results from a multisite case control study. *American Journal of Public Health, 93,* 1089–1097.

Center for Genetics and Society. (n.d.). Sex selection. Retrieved from http://www.geneticsandsociety.org/section.php?id=29

Centers for Disease Control and Prevention. (2013). Adverse Childhood Experiences (ACE) Study. Retrieved from http://www.cdc.gov/ace/findings.htm

Chamberlain, L. & Levenson, R. (2012). *Addressing intimate partner violence, reproductive and sexual coercion: A guide for obstetric, gynecologic and reproductive health care settings* (2nd ed.). San Francisco, CA: Futures Without Violence. Retrieved from http://www.acog.org/About_ACOG/ACOG_Departments/Violence_Against_Women/~/media/Departments/Violence%20Against%20Women/Reproguidelines.pdf

Chambliss, L. R. (2008). Intimate partner violence and its implication for pregnancy. *Clinical Obstetrics and Gynecology, 51,* 385–397.

Chan, K. L., Brownridge, D. A., Fong, D. Y. T., Tiwari, A., Leung, W. C., & Ho, P. C. (2012). Violence against pregnant women can increase the risk of child abuse: A longitudinal study. *Child Abuse & Neglect, 36,* 275–284. doi: 10.1016/j.chiabu.2011.12.003

Coker, A. L. (2007). Does physical intimate partner violence affect sexual health? A systematic review. *Trauma, Violence & Abuse, 8,* 149–177.

Coker, A. L., Sanderson, M., & Dong, B. (2004). Partner violence during pregnancy and risk of adverse pregnancy outcomes. *Paediatric and Perinatal Epidemiology, 18,* 260–269. DOI: 10.1111/j.1365-3016.2004.00569.x

Colen, S. (1995). "Like a mother to them": Stratified reproduction and West Indian childcare workers and employers in New York. In F. D. Ginsburg & R. Rapp (Eds.), *Conceiving the new world order: The global politics of reproduction* (pp. 78–102). Berkeley: University of California Press.

Cripe, S. M., Sanchez, S. E., Perales, M. T., Lam, N., Garcia, P., & Williams, M.A. (2008). Association of intimate partner physical and sexual violence with unintended pregnancy among pregnant women in Peru. *International Journal of Gynecology, and Obstetrics, 100,* 104–108.

D'Angelo, D. V., Gilbert, B. C., Rochat, R. W., Santelli, J. S., & Herold, J. M. (2004). Differences between mistimed and unwanted pregnancies among women who have live births. *Perspectives on Sexual and Reproductive Health, 2004, 36,* 192–197.

Danis, J. (1995). Sexism and "The Superfluous Female": Arguments for regulating pre-implantation sex selection. *Harvard Women's Law Journal, 18,* 219–264.

de Melo-Martin, I. (2013). Sex selection and the procreative liberty framework. *Kennedy Institute of Ethics Journal, 23,* 1–18.

Denmark, F.L, & Williams, D. (In Press). The Cycle of Violence. In J.A. Sigal & F.L. Denmark (Eds.) *Violence against Girls and Women: International Perspectives* (Vol 1, pp 21–38). Santa Barbara, CA: Praeger.

Devries, K. M., Kishor, S., Johnson, H., Stöckl, H., Bacchus, L., García-Moreno, C., & Watts, C. (2010). Intimate partner violence during pregnancy: Prevalence data from 19 countries. *Reproductive Health Matters, 18*(36), 1–13.

Dietz, P. M., Spitz, A. M., Anda, R. F., Williamson, D. F., McMahon, P. M., Santelli, J. S., . . . Kendrick JS. (1999). Unintended pregnancy among adult women exposed to abuse or household dysfunction during their childhood. *Journal of the American Medical Association, 282,* 1359–1364.

Dong, M., Anda, R. F., Dube, S. R., Giles, W. H., & Felitti, V. J. (2003). The relationship of exposure to childhood sexual abuse to other forms of abuse, neglect, and household dysfunction during childhood. *Child Abuse and Neglect, 27,* 625–630.

Ebenstein, A., & Sharygin, E. J. (2009). The Consequences of the "missing girls" of China. *World Bank Economic Review, 23,* 399–425.

Felitti, V. J., Anda, R. F., Nordenberg, D., Williamson, D. F., Spitz, A. M., Edwards, V., . . ., Marks, J. S. (1998). Relationship of childhood abuse and household dysfunction to many of the leading causes of death in adults: The Adverse Childhood Experiences (ACE) Study. *American Journal of Preventive Medicine, 14,* 245–258.

Foster, H., Hagan, J., & Brooks-Gunn, J. (2008). Growing up fast: Stress expo sure and subjective "weathering" in emerging adulthood. *Journal of Health and Social Behavior, 49,* 162–177. doi: 10.1177/002214650804900204

García-Moreno, C., & Watts, C. (2011). Violence against women: An urgent public health priority. *Bulletin of the World Health Organization, 89,* 2–3. doi:10.2471/BLT.10.085217

Garlough, C. (2008). The risks of acknowledgement: Performing the sex-selection identification and abortion debate. *Women's Studies in Communication, 31,* 368–394.

Garoma, S., Fantahum, M., & Worku, A. (2012). Maternal intimate partner violence victimization and under-five children mortality in western Ethiopia: A case–control study. *Journal of Tropical Pediatrics, 58,* 467–474. doi:10.1093/tropej/fms018

Gazmararian, J. A., Adams, M., Saltzman, L. E., Johnson C. H., Bruce, F. C., Marks, J. S., & Zahniser, S. C., for the PRAMS working group. (1995). The relationship between pregnancy intendedness and physical violence in mothers of newborns. *Obstetrics and Gynecology, 85,* 1031–1038.

Gee, R. E., Mitra, N., Wan, F., Chavkin, D. E., & Long, J. A. (2009). Power over parity: Intimate partner violence and issues of fertility control. *American Journal of Obstetrics and Gynecology, 201,* 148.e1–7.

Goodrum, S., Umberson, D., & Anderson, K. L. (2001). The batterer's view of the self and others in domestic violence. *Sociological Inquiry, 71,* 221–241.

Goodwin, M. A., Gazmararian, J. A., Johnson, C. H., Gilbert, B. C., Saltzman, L. E., & the PRAMS Working Group. (2000). Pregnancy intendedness and physical abuse around the time of pregnancy: Findings from the Pregnancy Risk Assessment Monitoring System, 1996–1997. *Maternal and Child Health Journal, 4,* 85–92.

Hesketh, T., & Xing, Z. W. (2006). Abnormal sex ratios in human populations: Causes and consequences. *Proceedings of the National Academy of Sciences of the United States of America, 103,* 13271–13275. doi:10.1073/pnas.0602203103

Human Rights Watch. (2011). *World report, 2011: Events of 2010.* New York, NY: Human Rights Watch.

Huth-Bocks, A. C., Levendosky, A. A., Theran, S. A., & Bogat, G. A. (2004). The impact of domestic violence on mothers' prenatal representations of their infants. *Infant Mental Health Journal, 25,* 79–98.

Kalfoglou, A. L., Scott, J., & Hudson, K. (2008). Attitudes about preconception sex selection: A focus group study with Americans. *Human Reproduction, 23,* 2731–2736.

Kishor, S., & Johnson, K. (2004). *Profiling domestic violence: A multi-country study.* Calverton, MD: ORC Macro.

Klasen, S., & Wink, C. (2003). "Missing women": Revisiting the debate. *Feminist Economics, 9,* 263–299

Lalor, K., & McElvaney, R. (2010). Child sexual abuse, links to later sexual exploitation/high-risk sexual behavior, and prevention/treatment programs, *Trauma, Violence, & Abuse, 11,* 159–177.

Lee, J., & Paik, M. (2006). Sex preferences and fertility in South Korea during the year of the horse. *Demography, 43,* 269–292.

Loo, K. K., Li, Y., Tan, Y., Luo, X., Presson, A., & Shih, W. (2010). Prenatal anxiety associated with male child preference among expectant mothers at 10–20 weeks of pregnancy in Xiangyun County, China. *International Journal of Gynaecology and Obstetrics, 111,* 229–232. doi:10.1016/j.ijgo.2010.07.010

Lopez, W. D., Konrath, S. H., & Seng, J. S. (2011). Abuse-related post-traumatic stress, coping, and tobacco use in pregnancy. *Journal of Obstetric, Gynecologic, & Neonatal Nursing 40,* 422–431. doi: 10.1111/j.1552-6909.2011.01261.x

Mahalingam, R., Haritatos, J., & Jackson, B. (2007). Essentialism and. the cultural psychology of gender in extreme son preference communities in India. *American Journal of Orthopsychiatry, 77,* 598–609. doi:10.1037/0002-9432.77.4.598

Mahalingam, R., & Wachman, M. (2012). Female feticide and infanticide: Implications for reproductive justice. In J. C. Chrisler (Ed.), *Reproductive justice: A global concern* (pp. 251–268). Santa Barbara, CA: Praeger.

Martin, S. I., Kilgallen, B., Tsui, A. O., Maitra, K., Singh, K. K., Kupper, L. L. (1999). Sexual behaviors and reproductive health outcomes: Associations with wife abuse in India. *Journal of the American Medical Association, 282,* 1967–1972.

Miller, E., Decker, M. R., McCauley, H. L., Tancredi, D. J., Levenson, R. R., Waldman, J., . . . & Silverman, J.G. (2010). Pregnancy coercion, intimate partner violence and unintended pregnancy. *Contraception, 81,* 316–322.

Miller, E., & Silverman, J. C. (2010). Reproductive coercion and partner violence: Implications for clinical assessment of unintended pregnancy. *Expert Review of Obstetrics & Gynecology, 5,* 511–515. doi: 10.1586/eog.10.44

Missmer, S., & Jain, T. (2007). Preimplantation sex selection demand and preferences among infertility patients in Midwestern United States. *Journal of Assisted Reproduction and Genetics, 24,* 451–457. doi:10.1007/s10815-007-9157-2

Moore, A. M., Frohwirth, L., & Miller, E. (2010). Male reproductive control of women who have experienced intimate partner violence in the United States. *Social Science and Medicine, 70,* 1737–1744. doi: 10.1016/j.socscimed.2010.02.009

Noll, J. G., Trickett, P. K., Harris, W. W., & Putnam, F. W. (2009). The cumulative burden borne by offspring whose mothers were sexually abused as children. *Journal of Interpersonal Violence, 24,* 424–449. doi: 10.1177/0886260508317194

Norsworthy, K., McLaren, M. A., & Waterfield, L. D. (2012). In J. Chrisler (Ed.), *Reproductive justice: A global concern* (pp. 57–76). Santa Barbara, CA: Praeger.

Pallitto, C. C., Campbell, J. C., & O'Campo, P. (2005). Is intimate partner violence associated with unintended pregnancy? A review of the literature. *Trauma, Violence, and Abuse, 6,* 217–235.

Pallitto, C. C., García-Moreno, C., Jansen, H. A., Heise, L., Ellsberg, M., & Watts, C. (2013). Intimate partner violence, abortion, and unintended pregnancy: Results from the WHO Multi-country Study on Women's Health and Domestic Violence. *International Journal of Gynecology and Obstetrics, 120,* 3–9. http://dx.doi.org/10.1016/j.ijgo.2012.07.003.

Pallitto, C. C., & O'Campo, P. (2004). The relationship between intimate partner violence and unintended pregnancy: Analysis of a national sample from Colombia. *International Family Planning Perspectives, 30,* 165–173.

Ptacek, J. (1997). The tactics and strategies of men who batter: Testimony from women seeking extreme orders. In A. P. Cardarelli (Ed.), *Violence between intimate partners: Patterns, causes, and effects* (pp. 104–123). Needham Heights, MA: Allyn & Bacon.

Ramiro, L. S., Madrid, B. J., & Brown, D. W. (2010). Adverse childhood experiences (ACE) and health-risk behaviors among adults in a developing country setting. *Child Abuse & Neglect, 34,* 842–855

Rapp, R. (2011). Reproductive entanglements: Body, state, and culture in the dys/regulation of childbearing. *Social Research, 778,* 693–718.

Ravindran, T. K. S., & Balasubramanian, P. (2004). "Yes" to abortion but "no" to sexual rights: The paradoxical reality of married women in rural Tamil Nadu, India. *Reproductive Health Matters, 12,* 88–99.

Rosen, D., Seng, J. S., Tolman, R. M., & Mallinger, G. (2007). Intimate partner violence, depression, and posttraumatic stress disorder as additional predictors of low birth weight infants among low-income mothers. *Journal of Interpersonal Violence, 22,* 1305–1314. doi: 10.1177/0886260507304551

Rowbottom, S. (2007). *Giving girls today and tomorrow: Breaking the cycle of adolescent pregnancy.* New York, NY: United Nations Population Fund.

Russo, N. F. (1976). The motherhood mandate. *Journal of Social Issues, 32,* 143–154.

Russo, N. F. (2006). Violence against women: A global health issue. In Q. Jing, M. R. Rosenzweig, G. d'Ydewalle, H. Zhang, H. Chen, & K. Zhang (Eds.), *Progress in psychological science around the world: Vol. 2. Social and applied issues* (pp. 181–198). Proceedings of the 28th International Congress of Psychology, Bejing, 2004. New York, NY: Psychology Press.

Russo, N. F., & Denious, J. E. (2001). Violence in the lives of women having abortions: Implications for public policy and practice. *Professional Psychology: Research and Practice, 32,* 142–150.

Salihu, H. M. (2004). Intimate partner violence and birth outcomes: A systematic review. *International Journal of Fertility and Women's Medicine, 49,* 159–164.

Sarkar, N. N. (2008). The impact of intimate partner violence on women's reproductive health and pregnancy outcome. *Journal of Obstetrics and Gynaecology, 28,* 266–271.

Secretariat of the Pacific Community for Ministry of Internal and Social Affairs. (2010). *Kiribati Family Health and Support Study: A study on violence against women and children.* Noumea, New Caledonia: Secretariat of the Pacific Community.

Sen, A. (2003). Missing women—revisited. *British Medical Journal, 327,* 1297–1298. doi:10.1136/bmj.327.7427.1297

Seng, J. S., Sparbel, K. J. H., Low, K. L., & Killion, C. (2002). Abuse-related post-traumatic stress and desired maternity care practices: Women's perspectives. *Journal of Midwifery & Women's Health, 47,* 360–370.

Sharps, P. W., Laughon, K., & Giangrande, S. K. (2007). Intimate partner violence and the childbearing year: Maternal and infant health consequences. *Trauma Violence Abuse, 8,* 105–116.

Silverman, J. G., Gupta, J., Decker, M. R., Kapur, N., & Raj, A. (2007). Intimate partner violence and unwanted pregnancy, miscarriage, induced abortion, and stillbirth among a national sample of Bangladeshi women. *British Journal of Obstetrics and Gynecology, 114,* 1246–1252.

Singh, S., Wulf, D., Hussain, R., Bankole, A., & Sedgh, G. (2009). *Abortion worldwide: A decade of uneven progress.* New York, NY: Guttmacher Institute.

Steinberg, J., & Russo, N.F. (2008). Abortion and anxiety: What's the relationship? *Social Science & Medicine, 67,* 238–252.

Tandon, S. L., & Sharma, R. (2006). Female foeticide and infanticide in India: An analysis of crimes against girl children. *International Journal of Criminal Justice Sciences, 1*(1). Retrieved from http://www.sascv.org/ijcjs/Snehlata.html

Tanha, M., Beck, C. J. Figueredo, A. J., & Raghavan, C. (2010, December 16). Sex differences in intimate partner violence and the use of coercive control as a motivational factor for intimate partner violence. *Journal of Interpersonal Violence, 25,* 1836–1854. doi:10.1177/0886260509354501.

Ullman, S. E., & Filipas, H. H. (2001). Predictors of PTSD symptom severity and social reactions in sexual assault Victims. *Journal of Traumatic Stress, 14,* 393–413.

United Nations. (1995). The Beijing Declaration and the platform for action: Fourth World Conference on Women: Beijing, China: 4–15 September, 1995. New York, NY: United Nations. UN/DPI/1766/Wom

Wall, L. L. (1998). Dead mothers and injured wives: the social context of maternal morbidity and mortality among the Hausa of northern Nigeria. *Studies in Family Planning, 29,* 341–359.

Wertz, D. C., & Fletcher, J. C. (1993). Prenatal diagnosis and sex selection in 19 nations. *Social Science & Medicine, 37,* 1359–1366.

World Health Organization. (2002). *World report on violence and health.* Geneva, Switzerland: Author.

World Health Organization. (2005). *WHO multi-country study on women's health and domestic violence against women.* Retrieved from http://www.who.int/gender/violence/who_multicountry_study/en

World Health Organization. (2010). *Preventing intimate partner and sexual violence against women: Taking action and generating evidence.* Geneva, Switzerland. Retrieved from http://www.who.int/violence_injury_prevention/publications/violence/9789241564007_en.

World Health Organization. (2012). *Gender and genetics.* Retrieved from http://www.who.int/genomics/gender/en/index4.html

Zabin, L. S., Emerson, M. R., & Rowland, D. L. (2005). Childhood sexual abuse and early menarche: The direction of their relationship and its implications. *Journal of Adolescent Health, 36,* 393–400.

Zeanah, C. H., Danis, B., Hirshberg, L., Benoit, D., Miller, D., & Heller, S. S. (1999). Disorganized attachment associated with partner violence: A research note. *Infant Mental Health Journal, 20,* 77–86.

Chapter 5

Child Sexual Abuse Issues: Prevalence, Sequelae, Treatment, and Prevention with a Focus on Cultural and Global Perspectives

Meagan A. Pagitt, Stephen P. Shewmake, Paula K. Lundberg-Love, Adam D. Garland, and Jeanine M. Galusha

INTRODUCTION

Child sexual abuse (CSA) was once believed to be a rare event in our society that only occurred in isolated areas (Bolen, 2001). However, over the past 30 years an ever-increasing amount of research and attention has focused on assessing the prevalence of CSA (Stoltenorgh, Ijzendoorn, Euser, & Bakermans-Kranenburg, 2011). What once was dismissed by most people as a situation that occurs only among the poor and culturally compromised has been proven to be commonplace among all social classes within our society. One past challenge that has made it difficult for the public to believe in the reality of CSA is that, historically, any suggestion that a child was being abused was treated as a private family matter and figuratively swept under the carpet. Despite the absence of an official mechanism in the United States for filing reports of CSA until the creation of the Child Abuse and Prevention Act in 1974, researchers have found evidence to suggest that children have been the victims of abuse since the beginning of our written history (Bolen, 2001). In 1974, DeMause wrote:

> The history of childhood is a nightmare from which we have only begun to awaken. The further back in history one goes, the lower the level of child care, and the more likely children were to be killed, abandoned, beaten, terrorized, and sexually abused. (p. 1)

As we began to recognize the prevalence of CSA within our society, many researchers and clinicians began to discuss and publish their information. Consequently, much effort has been devoted to understanding how to prevent, recognize, and help victims therapeutically recover from sexual abuse. The purpose of this chapter is to evaluate the current research describing the prevalence of CSA throughout the world, the impact of CSA on its victims, how an individual's cultural heritage may influence her or his perspective on CSA, therapeutic interventions available for recovery, and national and global efforts to help prevent and hopefully eliminate such abuse.

DEFINING CHILD SEXUAL ABUSE

Childhood sexual abuse encompasses a wide range of sexual misconduct involving children. Cultural and governmental factors can influence the criteria that constitute CSA across various nations. Therefore, it can be a challenge to iterate a global definition of CSA (Manly, 2005). In the United States, the primary federal legislation that defines CSA is the Child Abuse Prevention and Treatment Act (CAPTA; United States, 2011). This legislation defines CSA as:

> The employment, use, persuasion, inducement, enticement, or coercion of any child to engage in, or assist any other person to engage in, any sexually explicit conduct or simulation of such conduct for the purpose of producing a visual depiction of such conduct; or the rape, and in cases of caretaker or inter-familial relationships, statutory rape, molestation, prostitution, or other form of sexual exploitation of children, or incest with children. (U.S. Department of Health and Human Services [USDHHS], 2011, p. 2)

Although this thorough definition is useful conceptually, a global perspective of CSA needs a definition that includes specific criteria in the operational definition of CSA that accounts for the variance in cultural standards. For instance, the minimum age provisions for sexual contact vary from country to country. In Italy, the legal age of consent is 14 years old, whereas in Turkey an individual must be at least 18 years old to engage in sexual intercourse (Graupner, 2004). In the United States the age of consent is determined by state law, rather than at the federal level.

There are two categories of sexual abuse, contact abuse and noncontact abuse (Faller, 1988). Contact sexual abuse involves any inappropriate touching of intimate body areas as well as oral, vaginal, or anal intercourse. Contact CSA does not have to involve direct sexual interaction between the perpetrator and the victim. Forcing children to engage in creating child pornography and child prostitution falls under the crime of sexual exploitation (Faller, 1988). Noncontact sexual abuse refers to acts that involve no physical interaction. Things such as inappropriate sexual discussion, indecent exposure/flashing, voyeurism, and exposure to pornography fall within this category.

Another important variable with respect to CSA and its consequences is the nature of the relationship between the victim and the perpetrator. Intrafamilial sexual abuse involves a perpetrator who is a member of the child's family (Faller, 1988). This includes parents, siblings, uncles, aunts, grandparents, and other legal or blood relatives. Extrafamilial sexual abuse is committed by perpetrators with no legal or blood relationship to the victim. Consequently, one must take into account all of these variables when seeking to understand the prevalence and consequences of CSA.

Incidence and Prevalence of CSA

The precise percentage of children who are victims of CSA is unknown. Fallon et al. (2010) have identified several key factors that limit researchers' abilities to gather accurate prevalence and incidence rates of CSA. Unreported cases of CSA, varying research methodologies, and the aforementioned difficulty of defining CSA are just a few of the challenges that complicate the process of the conduct of research. Therefore, it is not surprising that results vary significantly from study to study. However, despite this incongruity, all data suggest that CSA is a startlingly common problem affecting children and families in all circumstances of life.

Statistical information about CSA is generally obtained through two types of sources: studies that use data collected by governmental agencies and clinical or epidemiological studies that collect data obtained through retrospective studies with adult populations (Goldman & Padayachi, 2000). Most experts maintain that data from retrospective studies better capture the magnitude of the problem of CSA, even given the limitation of memory issues, when compared to the data obtained from governmental agencies (London, Bruck, Ceci, & Shuman, 2011) because data obtained from the latter require that the abuse be reported and much CSA is not reported.

In the United States, the USDHHS, in conjunction with state agencies such as Child Protective Services (CPS), collect and publish data on the incidence of CSA in the United States (USDHHS, 2011). Efforts are being made to devise a national reporting system for crimes committed against children; however, there is no such system currently in place (Fallon et al., 2010). According to the Fourth National Incidence Study of Child Abuse and Neglect (NIS-4) conducted under the direction of the DHHS, there were an estimated 135,300 cases of CSA in the United States since 2005 (Sedlak et al., 2010). However, as we will see, this number is most likely a dramatic underestimate of the true incidence of CSA.

The main problem derived from reliance on data gathered from official agencies is a function of the low rate of reporting of CSA (London et al., 2011). Studies examining the current literature regarding disclosure rates of sexual abuse victims found that between 60% and 90% of victims do not report their abuse (London et al., 2011; Macmillian, Jamieson, & Walsh, 2003). Furthermore, CPS investigates as little as 50% of the reports of child abuse in a given year (Sedlak & Broadhurst, 1996) and without investigation, there can be no official report. Hence, data that only focus on the investigated incidences of CSA or even the reported occurrences of CSA fail to capture the prevalence of CSA within our society.

One way in which researchers have attempted to determine the prevalence of CSA in our society is through retrospective studies (London et al., 2011). Retrospective studies use a variety of data-gathering techniques to survey a sample of the adult population to obtain prevalence rates of CSA. Two of the most common techniques include face-to-face interviews and questionnaires. Prevalence estimates in these studies can vary dramatically with face-to-face interviews typically yielding higher rates than questionnaire data (Lundberg-Love, 2006). The methodology chosen is just one of the variables that can influence the results of this kind of study. Other major sources of variability in self-report studies come from the operational definition of CSA used, the population being sampled, and the format of the questions employed (Pereda, Guilera, Forns, & Gómez-Benito, 2009).

In 1983, Russell published a landmark study of the prevalence of CSA. This retrospective study used face-to-face interviews to assess participants' histories of CSA. Of the 930 randomly sampled women who participated in this study, 16% reported at least one experience of intrafamilial sexual abuse before age 18, and an additional 31% reported at least one incidence of extrafamilial sexual abuse before turning 18. Altogether, 38% of the women sampled reported at least one instance of sexual abuse before age 18 (Russell, 1983). Furthermore, Russell (1983) believed that it was likely that some of the participants were reluctant to disclose their history of abuse or had repressed their memories of abuse, and that the true prevalence rate of CSA in the sample might have been even higher. Still, Russell (1983) described the obtained prevalence rate as "astonishingly high" (p. 144).

Results from subsequent studies have reflected the findings of Russell's 1983 study. In a retrospective study investigating the prevalence of CSA in a sample of 338 African American and European American women, Wyatt, Loeb, Solis, Carmona, and Romero (1999) discovered that 34% reported at least one incident of sexual abuse before age 18. In a similar study, Briere and Elliott (2003) reported a CSA prevalence rate of 32.3% within a sample of 471 female subjects. In addition, Bolen and Scannapieco (1999) conducted a meta-analysis of 22 CSA prevalence studies and, from extrapolation, estimated that the prevalence rate of CSA in the female population was between 30% and 40%. Studies examining gender differences in prevalence rates of CSA estimate that girls are anywhere from two to five times more likely to be victimized (Walker, Carey, Mohr, Stein, & Seedat, 2004). However, the actual magnitude of the gender difference is difficult to determine, as boys are less likely to report abuse (Finkelhor, 1990).

The effort to reduce the variability in the estimation of incidence and prevalence rates of CSA is ongoing. To ameliorate this situation, better national and international reporting systems are needed, and agencies at all levels of government need to enhance their communication in reporting and investigating outcries of CSA. Retrospective studies need more standardized methodology to improve the precision of these studies. These problems notwithstanding, both sources of information indicate that millions of people are victims of sexual victimization.

EFFECTS OF SEXUAL ABUSE IN CHILDHOOD

The immediate physical injuries of CSA can include bleeding, vaginal and anal abnormalities, bruises, scratches, a damaged hymen, sexually transmitted diseases, and pregnancy (Fischer & McDonald, 1998). During the past 30 years, a substantial body of research investigating the consequences of CSA has been reported (Fergusson, Boden, & Horwood 2008). The majority of this research indicates that exposure to CSA in childhood increases the risk of developing a variety of medical, psychological, behavioral, and sexual disorders (Maniglio, 2009).

The symptomatology observed in victims of CSA encompasses a broad spectrum of disorders that can vary considerably from child to child. Factors that are positively correlated with an increase in the severity of symptomatology include an earlier onset of abuse, a greater frequency of abuse, longer duration of abuse, the amount of force or penetration involved in the abuse, and the identity of the perpetrator being a biological father or the stepfather (Beitchman, Zucker, Hood, Dacosta, & Akman, 1991; Olafson, 2011). All forms of sexual abuse in childhood can lead to severe consequences for the victim (Kendall-Tackett, 2002).

In many instances, the initial symptoms of CSA correlate with those seen in posttraumatic stress disorder (PTSD). Up to 80% of CSA victims may experience some symptoms of PTSD including reexperiencing the event through nightmares or invasive thoughts, affective numbing, anxiety, sleep disturbances, poor concentration, and other cognitive and affective symptoms (Wolfe, Sas, & Wekerle, 1994). Victims of CSA may also exhibit feelings of helplessness, guilt, and low self-esteem, as well as some degree of social incompetence due to their struggles with poor self-esteem and self-concept (Briere & Elliot, 1994) Hence, it is not uncommon for these victimized children to display wide ranges of behaviors that can encompass a spectrum of emotions from hostility and anger to withdrawal and fear (Maniglio, 2009). Additionally, victims of CSA may demonstrate poorer academic performance and be diagnosed with more learning disorders than their nonvictimized peers (Paolucci, Genuis & Violato, 2001). Furthermore, children with an abuse history are more likely to be held back in school and rated as lower performing by their teachers compared with nonvictims (Beitchman et al., 1991).

One of the most consistently noted behavioral problems in children who have been victims of sexual abuse is an increase in sexualized behavior (Beitchman et al., 1991). This is associated with age-inappropriate behaviors such as sexualized play with dolls, excessive or public masturbation, age-inappropriate sexual knowledge, and seductive behavior (Kendall-Tackett, Williams, & Finkelhor, 1993). Clinically, observations of sexualized behavior may be the most useful characteristic in predicting a history of sexual abuse in child patients (Kendall-Tackett et al., 1993). However, not all victims of CSA display overtly sexualized behavior, and nonvictims can also display age-inappropriate sexualized behavior (Deblinger, McLeer, Atkins, Ralphe, & Foa, 1989; Kendall-Tackett et al., 1993). As the victim ages, this sexualized behavior can evolve into risky sexual practices. Some research has supported the association of a CSA history with increases in promiscuity, inconsistent birth control usage, and early engagement in sexual behavior (Noll, Trickett, & Putnam, 2003; Purcell, Malow, Dolezal, & Carballo-Diéguez, 2004). However, some victims develop avoidant sexual behavior (Wilson &Widom, 2008). Problems with sexual functioning are more likely to occur in samples of female adult survivors when compared with women devoid of an abuse history (Zwickl & Merriman, 2011). Decreased sexual arousal, orgasmic difficulties, and low sexual desire are among the most common sexual dysfunctions reported by adult survivors of CSA (Zwicki & Merriman, 2011).

Depression is commonly observed in both children and adult survivors who have been sexually abused (Briere & Elliot, 1994). A study of children who were in outpatient therapy showed that those with a history of sexual abuse were four times as likely to have been diagnosed with major depressive disorder than those without a history of sexual abuse (Lanktree, Briere, & Zaidi, 1991). Indeed, adult survivors of CSA may be four times as likely to develop major depressive disorder in their lifetimes compared with adults without a history of sexual abuse (Stein, Golding, Siegel, Burnam, & Sorenson, 1988). Felitti (1991) found that 83% of participants in his study with a history of CSA suffered from depression compared with 32% of a control group.

Research investigating the link between CSA and mental disorders, including depression, has been criticized on the grounds that the influence of genetic and family environment factors cannot be excluded when considering the development of these disorders (Andrews, Corry, Slade, Issakidis, & Swanston, 2002). In response to these criticisms, twin studies have been conducted that have provided researchers the ability to investigate the outcomes of CSA while controlling for the confounds of genetic and family environmental factors (Andrews et al., 2002; Dinwiddie et al., 2000; Kendler et al., 2000; Nelson et al., 2002). Andrews et al. (2002) conducted an analysis of previous research published on the comparative health risks of CSA. This analysis included three twin studies that showed a consistent relationship between CSA and depression, especially in cases in which women had experienced severe contact forms of CSA (Andrews et al., 2002). Andrews et al. (2002) also found evidence of relationships between CSA and an increase in the prevalence of other forms of pathology including PTSD, alcohol abuse or dependence, and suicide attempts. Additionally, survivors of CSA are up to five times more likely to be diagnosed with at least one anxiety disorder compared with their nonabused peers (Briere & Elliot, 1994).

The increased risk of suicidal ideation and suicidal attempts in victims of CSA has been extensively documented in the literature (Maniglio, 2009; Neumann, Houskamp, Pollick, & Briere, 1996; Rind, Tromovitch, & Bauserman, 1998). Victims of CSA may be more than 3 times more likely to attempt suicide than those without a history of abuse (Dube et al., 2001). In a study performed in Australia, a cohort of patients that had previously been admitted to a hospital following incidents of CSA were shown to have a completed suicide rate that was more than 10 times that of the Australian national rate (Andrews et al., 2004; Plunkett et al., 2001). In another clinical study, it was found that patients with a history of CSA admitted to a hospital following a suicide attempt were more likely than nonabused patients to show a history of repeated suicide attempts (Ystgaard, Hestetun, Loeb, & Mehlum, 2004). Given the tragic loss of life sustained and the emotional torment suicide and suicide attempts can inflict on survivors, this is an area of great clinical concern and research. A more precise understanding of the contribution CSA makes to the manifestation of suicidal behaviors in victims is needed, but it is apparent that a history of CSA does elevate one's risk for attempting or completing suicide.

Although increased sexualized behavior, PTSD, and depression have been consistently associated with a history of CSA, researchers have also focused on other problems thought to coincide with CSA. Some research has indicated that victims of CSA compared with nonvictims are at higher risk for eating disorders, drug abuse and addiction, dissociation, borderline personality disorder, obsessive-compulsive disorder, and other behavioral problems (Beitchman et al., 1991; Kendall-Tackett, 2002). Clearly, a wide array of debilitating psychological sequelae that require further scientific research can emanate from CSA.

However, the possible consequences of CSA are not solely confined to the category of mental health. Victims of CSA are also at a higher risk for medical maladies (Irish, Kobayashi, & Delahanty, 2010). Researchers have identified several health consequences that occur at higher rates in victims of CSA. These problems include gastrointestinal (GI) symptoms, gynecological symptoms, pain disorders, cardiopulmonary symptoms, and obesity (Irish et al., 2010).

Female patients at a primary health clinic who reported a history of CSA were nearly three times as likely as nonvictims to report GI issues (Lechner et al., 1993). Hulme (2000) found similar results in her study of women patients at an academic family practice. An increased risk of developing chronic pelvic pain is a common finding in research relating to the gynecological symptoms experienced by victims of CSA (Hulme, 2000; Irish et al., 2010). Finestone et al. (2000) found that 69% of female participants in their study who had experienced CSA reported a chronic pain condition lasting longer than three months. Furthermore, these women reported a greater number of painful body areas, more diffuse pain, and more diagnoses of fibromyalgia than those in the control groups (Finestone et al., 2000). Reports of cardiopulmonary symptoms such as chest pain, shortness of breath, irregular heartbeat, and ischemic heart disease also occur more frequently in populations of CSA victims compared with samples of nonvictims (Irish et al., 2010). Research using community samples has demonstrated that individuals with a history of CSA are also at increased risk for developing obesity (Irish et al., 2010). Felitti et al. (2001) reported that survivors of CSA were 1.6 times as likely to develop severe forms of obesity compared with individuals devoid of such a history.

The role of CSA in the development of long-term physical problems is not readily apparent. One theory proposes that severe traumatic stress at an early age (like that which can occur in instances of CSA) may disrupt the regulation of the neuroendocrine and sympathetic nervous systems (SNS). The disruption of these systems then disrupts the function of other bodily systems (Irish et al., 2010; Shonkoff, Boyce, & McEwen, 2009). Additionally, victims of CSA are also more likely to engage in behaviors that increase the risk of developing other physical health symptoms. Substance use, smoking, risky sex behaviors, and lack of regular exercise are behaviors reported by CSA victims that can contribute to the development of illness (Irish et al., 2010; Kendall-Tackett, 2002).

Furthermore, the increased rates of psychopathology observed in CSA victims can contribute to the manifestation of physical symptoms (Irish et al., 2010). Additional research is required to determine the interaction and duration of the psychological and medical consequences of CSA.

As victims age, they often continue to struggle with the sequelae of CSA. Tragically, revictimization is common in CSA victims. They are more likely to be victims of domestic and sexual violence across their life spans than those who were not abused in childhood (Kendall-Tackett, 2002; Maniglio, 2009; Roodman & Clum, 2001). Therefore, it is critically important that children receive early therapeutic intervention to help them recover from such abuse. Considering the diverse spectrum of negative outcomes, improvements in detection and treatment of CSA will depend on the concerted efforts of researchers and clinicians.

CULTURAL PERSPECTIVES ON CSA

The cultural environment in which CSA occurs influences how the crime is viewed by the victim, the authorities, the child's family, and members of society. Empirical studies show that cultural attitudes and values play a pivotal role in the disclosure of the crime, not only affecting the likelihood that the child will disclose the sexual abuse but whether an adult will discover it or if the family will report the abuse to the authorities (Fontes & Plummer, 2010). Several key cultural factors that impact CSA disclosure are shame and fear of ruining the family's reputation, honor and respect toward elders and patriarchs, taboos on speaking about sex, modesty, the value of virginity, culturally based gender expectations, the unequal status of females, obligatory violence against the abuser and even the victim, religious values, and lack of economic and sociocultural resources (Admon, 2009; Fontes & Plummer, 2010; Liao, Lee, Roberts-Lewis, Hong, & Jiao, 2011; Ouis, 2009; Silberg & Dallam, 2009; Smith, Bryant-Davis, Tillman, & Marks, 2010). Following is a brief explanation of how several of these cultural issues influence CSA disclosure.

In some countries, CSA is hidden, and many victims and their families do not reveal crimes because of the shame and stigma associated with it. A 2009, situation analysis of gender-based sexual violence against women in Lebanon, the Occupied Palestinian Territories, and Yemen brought to light the honor ideology of the Middle East and how it creates three interconnected sexually based struggles for young girls—sexual abuse, honor violence, and forced early marriages (Ouis, 2009). The study found that victims of childhood sexual abuse are disgraced and people remain silent about the act because of the shame associated with sexual relations outside of marriage. Girls do not disclose the crimes because their families might take violent action against them or even force them to marry the abuser to prevent them from reporting the crime to the authorities. The author also explained the growing epidemic of "tourist marriages" in which wealthy men from Arab countries marry girls from impoverished families, engage in sexual relations, abandon them without providing a record of the marriage, and leave them stigmatized and often forced into prostitution.

Similarly, the shame associated with child sexual abuse is at the forefront for Latin American children as well as Latino families living in the United States (Fontes, 2007). Often victims of CSA are reluctant to come forward because of the taboo and aberrant nature of the acts perpetrated against them. Sexual acts such as incest, forced masturbation, anal penetration, sex with animals, and bondage are considered sexually deviant. Therefore, society believes that these victims will turn out to be sexually promiscuous or homosexual. Another source of shame for female CSA victims is the actual or perceived loss of virginity before marriage, leaving these girls feeling stigmatized and ruined. Pervasive negative attitudes about sexual abuse and its effect on child victims lead to the public shaming of victims, blaming them for the crimes, and discrimination against them and their families.

In many countries, the shame associated with CSA also encompasses the victims' families because of the cultural value of collectivism. In collectivist cultures, as opposed to those that are considered individualist, the goals and interests of the group take priority over those of the individual (Liao et al., 2011). Because children are viewed as extensions of their households, not as separate individuals, the shame and discrimination associated with CSA extend to the entire family. All of these underlying sources of shame are interconnected and serve as cumulative barriers to the disclosure of CSA.

Honor and respect for elders and patriarchs form another cultural issue that affects one's perspective on the disclosure of CSA. Liao et al. (2011) systematically reviewed empirical studies regarding child maltreatment in China, which included sexual abuse and the difficulty in understanding risk and preventive factors of violence and abuse against children. The study explained that one must be aware of how cultural factors, such as *filial piety*, or respect for one's elders and parents, are of overriding importance and can be used to justify abuse. Other parts of the world have cultural beliefs of filial piety, such as the South Asian concept of *izzat* (honor/respect) and *respecto* (respect) in Latino communities (Comas-Díaz, 1995, as cited in Fontes & Plummer, 2010; Gilligan & Akhatar, 2006). The importance placed on honor and respect of authority and parental figures in these societies often prevents children and families from disclosing instances of sexual abuse, particularly when it is perpetrated by the very figures to whom the respect is due (Fontes & Plummer, 2010).

Cultures that highly value modesty consider the discussion of sexual abuse inappropriate and taboo (Fontes & Plummer, 2010). Gupta and Ailawadi (2005, p. 180) told the story of a young Indian girl who was accused of being "a dirty girl with a vivid imagination" when she attempted to disclose to her mother the sexual abuse she experienced at the hands of their neighbor. Victims living in these environments are discouraged from disclosing abuse, may not be believed or helped when they do come forward, and thus often suffer through CSA in silence (Fontes & Plummer, 2010).

Gender issues are fully intertwined with the aforementioned cultural factors as well as the overall phenomenon of CSA, and they make it difficult for both girls and boys to disclose abuse or seek refuge from their abusers (Fontes & Plummer, 2010). The shame associated with a young girl's loss of virginity is a significant issue facing girls in many areas of the world. This loss, or even the perceived loss, of virginity, damages her reputation, reduces her marriage prospects, and may subject her to honor violence from family members to restore the family's reputation. Some cultural environments value men more than women, discount girls' disclosures as untrue, blame the girls for arousing their abusers, or dismiss the crime as simply men doing what men do (Smith et al., 2010). Cultures with clearly defined gender battle sexual scripts, which view sexual interaction as a male–female struggle, demand that men be masculine and assertive and that women remain pure, keep their legs closed, and refrain from tempting men (Fontes & Plummer, 2010). These sexual scripts create a strong barrier to disclosure for boys because reporting sexual abuse subjects them to humiliation for not being masculine enough, not wanting to engage in sexual relations, and being homosexual.

Religious beliefs also color the view of CSA and create powerful barriers to disclosure. For example, both Catholicism and Christianity teach that God does not give one more than he or she can handle, and it is one's duty to overcome the adversity in his or her own life (Fontes & Plummer, 2010; Kennedy, 2000). Buddhism's teaching of karma may lead victims to believe that their abuse is a "retribution for a misdeed committed in a previous life" or they may not prosecute an offender in an effort to "end the cycle of negative karma in this lifetime rather than extend it into the next lifetime" (Fontes & Plummer, 2010, p. 503). Jewish instructions to honor one's parents and to not speak ill of others may hinder CSA disclosure (Silberg & Dallam, 2009). People may use the Quran to justify child marriages and CSA by citing Mohammad's marriage to his bride Alisha when she was just 6 years old (Admon, 2009). Ouis (2009) brought to light what distinguishes religious factors from all other cultural characteristics that affect CSA: Religious beliefs are afforded a significant amount of respect and consideration. Even international, legally binding documents like the United Nation's Convention on the Rights of the Child allow for certain religious exemptions.

Clearly there are many cultural considerations affecting the disclosure and perception of CSA that one must take into account when dealing with victims, their family members, and perpetrators. Fontes and

Plummer (2010) provided specific questions for forensic investigators to ask themselves before, during, and after the interview that center on culturally based issues that might pertain to a child's particular situation. Fontes (2007) shared several recommendations on how authorities and interviewers could be culturally sensitive during CSA investigations, therapeutic intervention, and treatment. The techniques, aimed at counteracting victims' lack of self-worth and social worth stemming from the abuse, include being sensitive to the private and taboo nature of the sexual abuse topics by posing questions in a way that communicates their value rather than shaming them further and designing shame-releasing rituals to help them achieve closure. Culturally sensitive recommendations for working with family and community members advocate teaching all affected parties to reassign the responsibility of the crime to the actual offender, discouraging the teasing of male victims, showing concerned family members ways they can actively and positively participate in the victim's recovery, and organizing community psychoeducational classes and crime watch groups. Ouis (2010) stressed the need for changes on an international scale that address the manner in which child CSA is currently being covered up or justified as acts in accordance with a country's customs, culture, and religious beliefs. Whether in a local, national, or global arena, it is crucial that community leaders, authorities involved in the forensic process, and people who provide therapeutic intervention for CSA victims be cognizant of how cultural factors impact the identification and treatment of CSA. They also need to develop a cultural competency that is integrated into their investigations, treatments, and prevention efforts (Fontes, 2007; Fontes & Plummer, 2010; Ouis, 2010).

TREATMENT OF CSA

The treatment of CSA encompasses many approaches that may be implemented in a variety of environments. Although some methods focus solely on the victim, other practices treat the entire family and even the perpetrator, such as in cases of incestuous child sexual abuse (Cohen et al., 2012; Mohl, 2010). Clinicians may conduct sessions one-on-one with the victim, together with the child and his or her parents, solely with the parents, or with groups of children. The contexts in which therapy occurs are as diverse as the treatment modalities. They include clinical settings, schools, home visits, and children's advocacy centers (Cohen, Deblinger, & Mannarino, 2004; Tavkar & Hansen, 2011; Reardon, 2009; Staudt & Williams-Hayes, 2011). The most common CSA treatment methods are trauma-focused cognitive behavioral therapy, family therapy, group therapy, and play therapy (Bonner, 2004; Cohen et al., 2004, 2012; Harvey & Taylor, 2010; Mohl, 2010).

Trauma-focused cognitive-behavioral therapy (TF-CBT) is considered an evidence-based practice in the treatment of child sexual abuse victims because its efficacy is supported by a wealth of empirical research. It also has been demonstrated to be safe and effective (Chaffin & Friedrich, 2004). TF-CBT is designed to "reduce negative emotional and behavioral responses following CSA and other traumatic events" (Cohen et al., 2004, p. 4). Based on well-established learning, cognitive, and behavioral theories, TF-CBT helps victims overcome the trauma created by CSA by correcting their distorted, unhelpful, and maladaptive perceptions and beliefs related to the abuse and by modifying their habitual responses to stimuli associated with the traumatic experience. The parental educational aspect of TF-CBT focuses on helping nonoffending parents handle the emotional distress brought on by CSA and teaching them ways to respond effectively to their children in order to promote better communication with their children about CSA issues (Cohen et al., 2012).

Family therapy, like other forms of CSA treatment, seeks to protect the abused child first and foremost, but it is also concerned with repairing broken familial relationships, reducing at home risk factors for abuse, improving parent-child interactions, and inducing positive behavioral change (Ralston & Sosnowski, 2004; Saunders & Meinig, 2004; Tavkar & Hansen, 2011; Urquiza, 2004). Family crisis intervention comes to the aid of child victims and their families during the critical periods directly following the abuse, giving them the prompt mental health and legal support they need (Tavkar & Hansen, 2011). Parent–child interaction therapy (PCIT) aims to improve negative and coercive parent–child relationships that are often the result of abuse as well as an ongoing risk for further child maltreatment. PCIT promotes positive parent–child interactions by teaching parents how to use praise and direction properly and helping children with disobedience and other behavioral problems (Urquiza, 2004). Family treatment intervention (FTI) "focuses on identifying risk factors and required behavioral change and uses input from the caregiver regarding what will be needed to make the required change" (Ralston & Sosnowski, 2004, p. 67). For example, in circumstances wherein drug use is a risk factor for CSA, FTI hones in on eliminating said drug use to achieve the ultimate goals of increasing child safety, eliminating risk factors, clarifying the responsibility for the child abuse, strengthening the family, and reunifying them, if possible (Ralston & Sosnowski, 2004). Family resolution therapy (FRT) endeavors to repair families in which sexual abuse has occurred by helping them construct "safe, functional, and stable family structures and processes that will continue well after professional intervention with the family is completed" (Saunders & Meinig, 2004, p. 69). Although family therapy focuses on the family as a whole, the safety of the child is still paramount, and some treatment programs do end in complete termination of child-parent contact (Saunders & Meinig, 2011).

Group and play types of therapy are other familiar CSA treatments. Dynamic play therapy, a subtype of group therapy, gives the child a chance to interact with other kids in his or her "natural medium for expression and is a vehicle for emotional processing and behavior change" (Bonner, 2004, p. 34). Group therapies allow therapists to encourage interaction between victims of child abuse in a controlled environment. These therapies strive to correct emotional and behavioral problems that result from the powerful negative emotions related to their abuse, teach children to observe their peers' feelings and needs, and help them develop insight into their own needs and behavior (Bonner, 2004).

The neatly divided groupings of CSA treatments presented in this chapter are oversimplifications necessary for explanatory purposes. In reality, CSA treatment methods are not mutually exclusive, and they overlap a great deal. For instance, TF-CBT can be done individually with the victims, with groups of children, or with the entire family in a variety of settings, such as mental health facilities, hospitals, and in the home (Cohen et al., 2012). Research has shown that no one specific treatment is most effective in all child sexual abuse cases. In fact, the best determinant of treatment efficacy is whether the treatment program is tailored to the victim's specific symptom profile (Harvey & Taylor, 2010).

Hetzel-Riggin, Brausch, and Montgomery (2008) measured the effectiveness of several types of treatment in mediating various client symptoms, such as psychological distress (issues such as depression or anxiety), the promotion of self-esteem and a healthy self-concept, correcting behavioral problems, and treating social functioning deficits. They found that psychological stress was best alleviated using cognitive-behavioral and other types of individual therapies. Group therapies and abuse-specific therapies demonstrated the best results in treating behavioral problems. Self-esteem and self-concept problems responded most notably to cognitive-behavioral therapy, and play therapy was most effectual at addressing social functioning problems (Hetzel-Riggin et al., 2010). In a meta-analysis of the effect of different types of treatment on different secondary symptoms, Harvey and Taylor (2010) found that CBT and family approaches were most successful at treating the posttraumatic stress disorder symptoms associated with CSA.

CSA PREVENTION EFFORTS

Whereas CSA treatment programs are reactive in the sense that they help children and their families only after the crime has occurred, CSA prevention efforts are put in place to stop the abuse before it happens. CSA prevention methods fall into two categories: victimization prevention and perpetration prevention (Amick, Hafner, Hudson, & Rice, 2010; Chaffin & Friedrich, 2004; Renk, Liljequist, Steinberg, Bosco, & Phares, 2002).

Victimization prevention is directed at teaching children to be self-aware, recognize potentially dangerous situations in which CSA might arise, protect themselves from this maltreatment, and disclose any sexual abuse to a trusted adult (Putnam, 2003). The effectiveness of these programs is measured by the child's retention of prevention-related knowledge and acquisition of behavioral skills. Factors that mediate these positive results are the level of child involvement in the program, program length, and session frequency (Davis & Gidycz, 2000; Harvey & Taylor, 2010). When a child is more physically active in the treatment and has the opportunity to participate in activities such as modeling and role-playing, this dynamic participation increases children's attention, gives them a chance to practice key interpersonal behavioral skills, and promotes an increase in knowledge and behavioral modification. Longer prevention programs, specifically those that are spread over four or more sessions, give children the chance to learn material in smaller increments, increasing their knowledge retention and creating larger effect sizes in the measure of behavioral skills (Davis & Gidycz, 2000). It has also been shown that weekly treatment sessions produced more favorable outcomes than more frequent sessions (Harvey & Taylor, 2010).

Although victimization prevention programs are widespread and have been found to improve child awareness of the threatening situations and teach them how to act proactively as well as reactively to CSA, many authors emphasize that it is inappropriate to place the responsibility of preventing child sexual abuse on the shoulders of children (Amick et al., 2010; Renk et al., 2002). Instead, they reason that prevention programs should target adults who are in the position to take actions against CSA, specifically those who daily interact with children such as parents, teachers, community leaders, authority figures, and potential offenders. Instead of relying on young victims and other children to fight the battle alone, perpetration prevention efforts are comprehensive, community-wide programs that charge adults with ending child sexual abuse.

In 2010, Stop It Now!, a large-scale, successful perpetration prevention movement, surveyed more than 5,000 American adults in an effort to identify their knowledge level and attitudes about CSA (Amick et al., 2010; Tabachnick & Dawson, 2000;). Fortunately they found that most men and women are well informed about CSA. However, the study highlighted an important disconnect between what adults claim they would do in circumstances of suspected abuse and the actions they actually have taken: "nearly all adults say they will intervene when they suspect abuse, but when confronted by the likely abuse fewer say they did something" (Amick et al., 2010, p. 14).

This glaring inconsistency led Stop It Now! to call all community-wide prevention programs to action to empower adults to overcome the obstacles that currently inhibit them from actually taking a stand against CSA. The study urges programs to spread the message that any form of sexual activity with a child is inherently wrong, and adults can and should speak out without fear of judgment or retribution. Stop It Now!, along with other perpetration prevention programs, advocate taking steps to break the cycle of child abuse, including appropriately treating past offenders or those with sexual behavior problems and increasing support for programs that treat CSA's root causes (Amick et al., 2010).

GLOBAL EFFORTS TO PROMOTE CSA AWARENESS AND PROTECT CHILDREN

In recent years, key international organizations have sought to bring nations together so that they may set aside their cultural differences and protect our world's children against sexual abuse and other forms of maltreatment. There are hundreds of human rights organizations dedicated to fighting for children's rights, but the major parties involved in the global battle against child sexual abuse are the United Nations, the United Nations Children's Fund, the World Health Organization, and the International Society for Prevention of Child Abuse and Neglect. Following is a summary of recent key developments in the global fight against child abuse (Butchart & Harvey, 2006; Ebanks, Hanchett, & Kapell, 2009; United Nations Children's Fund [UNICEF], 2012; United Nations [UN] General Assembly, 1989).

In 1989, the UN General Assembly drafted the Convention on the Rights of the Child (CRC), which carefully articulates the rights of children and implements legally binding standards that nations must abide by with the intended goal of protecting children so that they are able to reach their full potential. The Convention's 54 articles and two Optional Protocols thoroughly define the inherent human rights of all children, including their civil, cultural, economic, political, and social rights. State Parties who ratify the CRC are subsequently bound by international law and must periodically appear before the United Nations Committee on the Rights of the Child and present evidence of progress made in the implementation of the articles of the Convention (UN General Assembly, 1989).

CRC articles 19 and 34 specifically address the issue of child sexual abuse. Article 34 demands the following from all parties who have adopted the CRC:

> State Parties undertake to protect the child from all forms of sexual exploitation and sexual abuse. For these purposes, State Parties shall in particular take all appropriate national, bilateral and multilateral measures to prevent: (a) The inducement or coercion of a child to engage in any unlawful sexual activity; (b) The exploitative use of

> children in prostitution or other unlawful sexual practices; (c) The exploitative use of children in pornographic performances and materials. (UN General Assembly, 1989, p. 10)

A decade later in 2000, the UN adopted the Optional Protocol to the Convention on the Rights of the Child on the Sale of Children, Child Prostitution and Child Pornography, which existing State Parties to the Convention could choose to separately ratify. This Optional Protocol promotes international awareness of these issues, instructs nations to band together to fight against them, and delineates measures State Parties must take in an effort to prosecute offenders, protect victims, assist other nations, and prevent future sexually based crimes against children (UN General Assembly, 2000a). Since the CRC's adoption in 1989, 193 countries have ratified the CRC, and 154 nations have ratified the aforementioned Optional Protocol (United Nations Treaty Collection, 2012a, 2012b).

Other international declarations have reaffirmed international dedication to the respect and protection of children's rights. These include the Declaration of Human Duties and Responsibilities, which was adopted in 1998 by the United Nations Educational, Scientific, and Cultural Organization (UNESCO) to commemorate the 50th anniversary of the adoption of the Universal Declaration of Human Rights and the Millennium Declaration, which was adopted by the United Nations during the Millennium Summit in 2000 (Goldstone, 1998; United Nations, 2011; UN General Assembly, 2000b). Both of these documents reiterate nations' commitments to ratify and fully implement the CRC and its Optional Protocols, thereby taking action to protect children from sexual abuse and other forms of maltreatment (Goldstone, 1998; United Nations, 2011; UN General Assembly, 2000b).

In 2008, government leaders, legal professionals, representatives of nongovernmental institutions, business people, academics, community leaders, and children and adolescents from over 170 countries convened at the World Congress III Against the Sexual Exploitation of Children held in Rio de Janeiro Brazil. This congress culminated in the drafting of the Rio de Janeiro Declaration and Call for Action to Prevent and Stop Sexual Exploitation of Children and Adolescents (Ebanks et al., 2009).

UNICEF plays an instrumental role in protecting our world's children from sexual abuse. The UNICEF Child Protection Strategy, which seeks to bring about systemic changes in societal and national support of legislation, policies, and social conventions that protect children, is dedicated to upholding the CRC, the goals of the Millennium Declaration, and the Rio de Janeiro Declaration (UNICEF, 2008a, p. ii, 2008b, 2012). UNICEF's comprehensive approach to the phenomenon of CSA seeks to

> [p]revent and respond to sexual violence by engaging different government sectors—justice, social welfare, education and health—as

> well as legislators, civil society, community leaders, religious groups, the private sector, media, families and children themselves. UNICEF supports governments in strengthening child protection systems at national and local levels—including laws, policies, regulations and the provision of comprehensive services to child victims. UNICEF also works with communities and the general public to raise awareness about the problem and address attitudes, norms and practices that are harmful to children. (UNICEF, 2012, para. 4)

The World Health Organization (WHO), a United Nations agency that is responsible for promoting international public health, is a vital warrior in the worldwide battle against child sexual abuse. Two of WHO's recent publications affecting global treatment and prevention are its guidelines for medico-legal care for victims of sexual violence and an instruction manual entitled "Preventing Child Maltreatment: A Guide for Taking Action and Generating Evidence," which WHO published in conjunction with the International Society for Prevention of Child Abuse and Neglect (Butchart & Harvey, 2006; Wells & Taylor, 2003).

The medicolegal guidelines provide health care professionals and policy makers with the valuable skills and knowledge necessary to respond to victims of sexual violence and set forth instructions on how to implement health care standards and forensic services (Wells & Taylor, 2003). These guidelines instruct professionals on how to establish adequate health care facilities, medically examine sexual abuse victims, record and classify victim injuries, collect forensic evidence, provide treatment and follow-up care, and document for medical records and court testimony. WHO also recommends that leaders use these guidelines in the training of health care professionals and the planning of health programs and procedures.

The child abuse prevention guide is intended to assist countries in designing and delivering programs for the prevention of child maltreatment perpetrated by parents and caregivers (Butchart & Harvey, 2006). It outlines various scientific research and data collection methods, such as epidemiological and ecological models, that professionals should employ to measure the extent of the violence perpetrated against children; the interaction of various contributing factors at the community, societal, and individual levels; and the overall effectiveness of the prevention programs and victim services already in place. When authorities evaluate the outcomes of their existing programs, they are to use the data to design and implement an improved national plan of action that better detects and responds to violence against children, prevents future child maltreatment, promotes gender and social equality, and adequately provides victim care and support services.

Although a single coordinated, universal effort to eradicate CSA is still lacking, various international organizations, governments, leaders, and concerned citizens have made great progress in clearly defining and raising awareness of every child's inherent rights, encouraging countries to implement and enforce laws that protect these rights, providing them with resources to do so, and promoting international cooperation in the worldwide fight against child sexual abuse and other modes of child maltreatment.

CONCLUSIONS

The focus of this chapter has been to educate the reader in the definition, prevalence, treatment, and prevention of CSA while describing the global effect it has on our society. As we have discussed earlier in this chapter, CSA does not discriminate among nations—it is a problem that plagues civilizations worldwide. Although it may seem that there is still much to do to resolve the multiple issues associated with the consequences of CSA, it is important to note that many victims do receive the help they need to recover from such trauma.

More important, however, is the emerging evidence that our society is beginning to accept the fact that CSA is happening and is moving from denial to active awareness and prevention efforts. Individuals, communities, and nations throughout the world are banding together to educate parents and families on how to protect their children from the terror of CSA. In many ways these efforts are already successful in teaching children the skills needed to protect themselves from their would be abusers; however, the work of raising awareness and prevention must continue to move forward at a more rapid pace (Finkelhor, 2009). There is evidence to suggest that these educational programs will almost certainly help protect children from future abusive situations, but it is clear that they will also increase the number of reported cases of CSA. In many cases, these additional outcries may be seen in a negative light to the lay reader. However, we can be confident in knowing that these children and families will then have the opportunity to receive the help they need to begin the process of healing.

REFERENCES

Admon, Y. (2009, March 8). Rising criticism of child bride marriages in Saudi Arabia. *Inquiry and Analysis, 502.* Retrieved from http://www.memri.org/report/en/0/0/0/0/0/131/3216.htm

Amick, T., Hafner, J., Hudson, S., & Rice, D.D. (2010). What do U.S. adults think about child sexual abuse? Measures of knowledge and attitudes among six states. Stop It Now! Retrieved from http://www.stopitnow.org/rdd_survey_report

Andrews, G., Corry, J., Slade, T., Issakidis, C., & Swanston, H. (2002). *Comparative risk assessment—Child sexual abuse. Final report.* Sydney, Australia: WHO

Collaborating Centre on Evidence and Health Policy in Mental Health, St. Vincent's Hospital.

Beitchman, J. H., Zucker, K. J., Hood, J. E., DaCosta, G. A., & Akman, D. (1991). A review of the short-term effects of child sexual abuse. *Child Abuse & Neglect, 15,* 537–556. Retrieved from https://ezproxy.uttyler.edu/login?url=http://search.ebscohost.com/login.aspx?direct=true&db=sih&AN=24486217&site=eds-live&scope=site

Bolen, R. M., & Scannapieco, M. (1999). Prevalence of child sexual abuse: A corrective metanalysis. *Social Service Review, 73,* 281–313.

Bolen, R. M. (2001). *Child sexual abuse: Its scope and our and failure.* New York, NY: Springer

Bonner, B. (2004). Cognitive-behavioral and dynamic play therapy for children with sexual behavior problems and their caregivers. In B. E. Saunders, L. Berliner, & R. F. Hanson (Eds.), *Child physical and sexual abuse: Guidelines for treatment* (Revised Report: April 26, 2004; pp. 34–36). Charleston, SC: National Crime Victims Research and Treatment Center.

Briere, J. N., & Elliott, D. M. (1994). Immediate and long-term impacts of child sexual abuse. *The Future of Children, 4,* 54–69.

Briere, J. N., & Elliott, D. M. (2003). Prevalence and psychological sequelae of self-reported childhood physical and sexual abuse in a general population sample of men and women. *Child Abuse & Neglect, 27,* 1205. doi:10.1016/j.chiabu.2003.09.008

Butchart, A., & Harvey, A. (2006). *Preventing child maltreatment: A guide to taking action and generating evidence.* World Health Organization and International Society for Prevention of Child Abuse and Neglect. Retrieved from http://libdoc.who.int/publications/2006/9241594365_eng.pdf

Chaffin, M., & Friedrich, B. (2004). Evidence-based treatments in child abuse and neglect. *Children and Youth Services Review, 26,* 1097–1113.

Cohen, J. A., Deblinger, E., & Mannarino, A. (2004). Trauma-focused cognitive-behavioral therapy for sexually abused children. *Psychiatric Time, 21.*

Cohen, J., Deblinger, E, Mannarino, A., Wilson, C., Taylor, N., & Igelman, R. (2012). Trauma-focused cognitive behavioral therapy: Addressing the mental health of sexual abused children. Child Welfare Information Gateway. Retrieved from www.childwelfare.gov/pubs/trauma/trauma.pdf

Davis, K. M., & Gidycz, C. A. (2000). Child sexual abuse prevention programs: A meta-analysis. *Journal of Clinical Child Psychology, 29,* 257–265.

Deblinger, E., McLeer, S. V., Atkins, M. S., Ralphe, D., & Foa, E. (1989). Post-traumatic stress in sexually abused, physically abused, and nonabused children. *Child Abuse & Neglect, 13,* 403–408.

DeMause, L. (1975). Our forbears made childhood a nightmare. *Psychology Today, 8,* 85–88.

Dinwiddie, S., Heath, A. C., Dunne, M. P., Bucholz, K. K., Madden, P. A., Slutske, W. S., . . . Martin, N. G. (2000). Early sexual abuse and lifetime psychopathology: A co-twin-control study. *Psychological Medicine, 30,* 41–52.

Dube, S., Anda, R., Felitti, V., Chapman, D., Williamson, D., & Giles, W. (2001). Childhood abuse, household dysfunction, and the risk of attempted suicide throughout the life span: Findings from the Adverse Childhood Experiences Study. *Journal of the American Medical Association, 286,* 3089–3096.

Ebanks, K., Hanchett, R. H., & Kapell, A. (2009). Rio de Janeiro declaration: A snapshot summary for children and adolescents. Retrieved from the ECPAT International website: www.ecpat.net/worldcongressIII/PDF/Publications/Child-friendly/RioDeclarationENG.pdf

Faller, K. C. (1988). *Child sexual abuse: An interdisciplinary manual for diagnosis, case management, and treatment.* New York, NY: Columbia University Press.

Fallon, B., Trocmé, N., Fluke, J., MacLaurin, B., Tonmyr, L., & Yuan, Y. (2010). Methodological challenges in measuring child maltreatment. *Child Abuse & Neglect, 34,* 70–79. doi:10.1016/j.chiabu.2009.08.008

Felitti, V. J. (1991). Long-term medical consequences of incest, rape, and molestation. *Southern Medical Journal, 84,* 328–331.

Felitti, V. J., Anda, R. F., Nordenberg, D., Williamson, D. F., Spitz, A. M., Edwards, V., . . . & Marks, J. S. (2001). Relationship of childhood abuse and household dysfunction to many of the leading causes of death in adults. In K. Franey, R. Geffner, & R. Faconer (Eds.), *The cost of child maltreatment: Who pays? We all do* (pp. 53–69), San Diego, CA: Family Violence and Sexual Assault Institute.

Fergusson, D., Boden, J., & Horwood, L. (2008). Exposure to childhood sexual and physical abuse and adjustment in early adulthood. *Child Abuse & Neglect, 32,* 607–619.

Finestone, H. M., Stenn, P., Davies, F., Stalker, C., Fry, R., & Koumanis, J. (2000). Chronic pain and health care utilization in women with a history of childhood sexual abuse. *Child Abuse & Neglect, 24,* 547–556.

Finkelhor, D. (1990). Early and long-term effects of child sexual abuse: An update. *Professional Psychology: Research and Practice, 21,* 325–330. doi:10.1037/07358.21.5.325

Finkelhor, D. (2009). The prevention of childhood sexual abuse. *The Future of Children, 19,* 169–194.

Fischer, D. G., & McDonald, W. L. (1998). Characteristics of intrafamilial and extrafamilial child sexual abuse. *Child Abuse & Neglect, 22,* 915–929. doi:10.1016/S0145-2134(98)00063-5

Fontes, L. (2007). Sin vergüenza: Addressing shame with Latino victims of child sexual abuse and their families. *Journal of Child Sexual Abuse, 16,* 61–83.

Fontes, L., & Plummer, C. (2010). Cultural issues in disclosure of child sexual abuse. *Journal of Child Sexual Abuse, 19,* 491–518.

Gilligan, P., & Akhtar, S. (2006). Cultural barriers to the disclosure of child sexual abuse in Asian communities: Listening to what women say. *British Journal of Social Work, 36,* 1361–1377.

Goldman, J. D. G., & Padayachi, U. K. (2000). Some methodological problems in estimating incidence and prevalence in child sexual abuse research. *Journal of Sex Research, 37,* 305–314. doi:10.1080/00224490009552052

Goldstone, R. (1998). *Declaration of Human Duties and Responsibilities, Background Documents.* Fundación Valencia Tercer Milenio, Valencia (pp. 29 ff). Retrieved from http://globalization.icaap.org/content/v2.2/declare.html

Graupner, H. (2004). Sexual consent: The criminal law in Europe and outside of Europe. *Journal of Psychology and Human Sexuality, 16,* 111–164.

Gupta, A., & Ailawadi, A. (2005). Childhood and adolescent sexual abuse and incest: Experiences of women survivors in India. In S. J. Jejeebhoy, I. Shah,

& S. Thapa (Eds.), *Sex without consent: Young people in developing countries* (pp. 171–202). New York, NY: Zed Books.

Harvey, S. T., & Taylor, J. E. (2010). A meta-analysis of the effects of psychotherapy with sexual abused children and adolescents. *Clinical Psychology Review, 30,* 517–535

Hetzel-Riggin, M. D., Brausch, A. M., & Montgomery, B. S. (2007). A meta-analytic investigation of therapy modality outcomes for sexually abused children and adolescents: An exploratory study. *Child Abuse & Neglect, 31,* 125–141

Hulme, P. A. (2000). Symptomatology and health care utilization of women primary care patients who experienced childhood sexual abuse. *Child Abuse & Neglect, 24,* 1471–1484.

Irish, L., Kobayashi, I., & Delahanty, D. (2010). Long-term physical health consequences of childhood sexual abuse: A meta-analytic review. *Journal of Pediatric Psychology, 35,* 450–461.

Kendall-Tackett, K. (2002). The health effects of childhood abuse: Four pathways by which abuse can influence health. *Child Abuse & Neglect, 26,* 715–729. doi:10.1016/S0145-2134(02)00343-5

Kendall-Tackett, K. A., Williams, L. M., & Finkelhor, D. (1993). Impact of sexual abuse on children: A review and synthesis of recent empirical studies. *Psychological Bulletin, 113,* 164–180. doi:10.1037/0033-2909.113.1.164

Kendler, K. S., Bulik, C. M., Silberg, J., Hettema, J. M., Myers, J., & Prescott, C. A. (2000) Childhood sexual abuse and adult psychiatric and substance use disorders in women: An epidemiological and cotwin control analysis. *Archives of General Psychiatry,* 57: 953–959.

Kennedy, M. (2000). Christianity and child sexual abuse: The survivor's voice leading to change. *Child Abuse Review, 9,* 121–141

Lanktree, C. B., Briere, J., & Zaidi, L. Y. (1991). Incidence and impacts of sexual abuse in a child outpatients sample: The role of direct inquiry. *Child Abuse& Neglect, 15,* 447–453.

Lechner, M., Vogel, M., Garcia-Shelton, L., Leichter, J., & Steibel, K. (1993). Self-reported medical problems of adult female survivors of childhood sexual abuse. *The Journal of Family Practice, 36,* 633–638.

Liao, M., Lee, A. S., Roberts-Lewis, A. C., Hong, J. S., & Jiao, K. (2011). Child maltreatment in China: An ecological review of the literature. *Children and Youth Services Review, 33,* 1709–1719.

London, K., Bruck, M., Ceci, S. J., & Shuman, D. W. (2005). Disclosure of child sexual abuse: What does the research tell us about the ways that children tell? *Psychology, Public Policy, and Law, 11,* 194–226. doi:10.1037/1076-8971.11.1.194

Lundberg-Love, P. K. (2006). Adult survivors of child sexual and emotional abuse. In P. K. Lundberg-Love & S. L. Marmion (Eds.), *Intimate violence against women: When spouses, partners, or lovers attack.* Westport, CN: Praeger.

MacMillan, H. L., Jamieson, E., & Walsh, C. A. (2003). Reported contact with child protection services among those reporting child physical and sexual abuse: Results from a community survey. *Child Abuse & Neglect, 27,* 1397–1408. doi:10.1016/j.chiabu.2003.06.003

Maniglio, R. (2009). The impact of child sexual abuse on health: A systematic review of reviews. *Clinical Psychology Review, 29,* 647–657. doi:10.1016/j.cpr.2009.08.003

Manly, J. (2005). Advances in research definitions of child maltreatment. *Child Abuse & Neglect, 29,* 425–439. doi:10.1016/j.chiabu.2005.04.00

Mohl, A. (2010). Sexual abuse of the child: A treatment model for the incestuous family. *The Journal of Psychohistory, 38,* 168–181.

Nelson, E. C., Heath, A. C, Madden, P. A., Cooper, M. L, Dinwiddie, S. H., Bucholz, K. K, . . . Glowinski, A. (2002). Association between self reported childhood sexual abuse and adverse psychosocial outcomes: results from a twin study. *Archive of General Psychiatry, 59,* 139–145.

Neumann, D. A., Houskamp, B. M., Pollock, V. E., & Briere, J. (1996). The long-term sequelae of childhood sexual abuse in women: A meta-analytic review. *Child Maltreatment, 1,* 6–16. doi:10.1177/1077559596001001002

Noll, J. G., Trickett, P. K., & Putnam, F. W. (2003). A prospective investigation of the impact of childhood sexual abuse on the development of sexuality. *Journal of Consulting and Clinical Psychology, 71,* 575–586. doi:10.1037/0022-006X.71.3.575

Olafson, E. (2011). Child sexual abuse: Demography, impact, and interventions. *Journal of Child & Adolescent Trauma, 4,* 8–21. doi:10.1080/19361521.2011.545811

Ouis, P. (2009). Honourable traditions? Honour violence, early marriage and sexual abuse of teenage girls in lebanon. *International Journal of Children's Rights, 17,* –474.

Paolucci, E.O., Genuis, M. L., & Violato, C. (2001). A meta-analysis of the published research on the effects of child sexual abuse. *Journal of Psychology: Interdisciplinary and Applied, 135,* 17–36. doi:10.1080/00223980109603677

Pereda, N., Guilera, G., Forns, M., & Gómez-Benito, J. (2009). The prevalence of child sexual abuse in community and student samples: A meta-analysis. *Clinical Psychology Review, 29,* 328–338. doi:10.1016/j.cpr.2009.02.007

Plunkett, A., O'Toole, B. I., Swanston, H., Oates, R. K., Shrimpton, S., & Parkinson, P. (2001). Suicide risk following child sexual abuse. *Ambulatory Pediatrics, 1,* 262–266.

Purcell, D. W., Malow, R. M., Dolezal, C., & Carballo-Diéguez, A. (2004). Sexual abuse of boys: Short- and long-term associations and implications for HIV prevention. In L. J. Koenig, L. S. Doll, A. O'Leary, W. Pequegnat, L. J. Koenig, L. S. Doll, . . . W. Pequegnat (Eds.), *From child sexual abuse to adult sexual risk: Trauma, revictimization, and intervention* (pp. 93–114). Washington, DC: American Psychological Association. doi:10.1037/10785-005

Putnam, F. W. (2003). Research Update Review: Ten-year research update review: Child sexual abuse. *Journal of the American Academy of Child & Adolescent Psychiatry, 42,* 269–278. doi:10.1097/00004583-200303000-00006

Ralston, M. E., & Sosnowski, P. B. (2004). Family focused, child centered treatment interventions in child maltreatment. In B. E. Saunders, L. Berliner, & R. F. Hanson (Eds.), *Child Physical and Sexual Abuse: Guidelines for Treatment (Revised Report: April 26, 2004)* (pp. 66–68). Charleston, SC: National Crime Victims Research and Treatment Center.

Reardon, C. (2009). Child advocates reduce trauma of abuse. *Social Work Today,* 6–9.

Renk, K., Liljequist, L., Steinberg, A., Bosco, G., & Phares, V. (2002). Prevention of child abuse: Are we doing enough? *Trauma, Violence, & Abuse, 3,* 68–84.

Rind, B., Tromovitch, P., & Bauserman, R. (1998). A meta-analytic examination of assumed properties of child sexual abuse using college samples. *Psychological Bulletin, 124,* 22–53.

Roodman, A. A., & Clum, G. A. (2001). Revictimization rates and method variance. A meta-analysis. *Clinical Psychology Review, 21,* 183–204. doi:10.1016/S0272-7358(99)00045-8

Russell, D. E. H. (1983). The incidence and prevalence of intrafamilial and extrafamilial sexual abuse of female children. *Child Abuse & Neglect, 7,* 133–146. Retrieved from https://ezproxy.uttyler.edu/login?url=http://search.ebscohost.com/login.aspx?direct=true&db=sih&AN=26051938&site=eds-live&scope=site

Saunders, B. E., & Meinig, M. B. (2004). Family resolution therapy (FRT). In B. E. Saunders, L. Berliner, & R. F. Hanson (Eds.), *Child Physical and Sexual Abuse: Guidelines for Treatment (Revised Report: April 26, 2004)* (pp. 69–70). Charleston, SC: National Crime Victims Research and Treatment Center

Sedlak, A., & Broadhurst, D. D. (1996). *Third national incidence study of child abuse and neglect: Final report.* Washington, DC: U.S. Department of Health and Human Services, Administration for Children and Families, Administration on Children, Youth and Families, National Center on Child Abuse and Neglect.

Sedlak, A.J., Mettenburg, J., Basena, M., Peta, I., McPherson, K., Greene, A., et al. (2010). *Fourth national incidence study of child abuse and neglect (NIS-4).* Washington, DC: U.S. Department of Health and Human Services.

Shonkoff, J. P., Boyce, W. T., & McEwen, B. S. (2009). Neuroscience, molecular biology, and the childhood roots of health disparities. Building a new framework for health promotion and disease prevention. *Journal of the American Medical Association, 301,* 2252–2259.

Silberg, J. L., & Dallam, S. (2009). Out of the Jewish closet: Facing the hidden secrets of child sex abuse—And the damage done to victims. In A. Neustein (Ed.), *Tempest in the temple: Jewish communities and child sex scandals* (pp. 77–104). Waltham, MA: Brandeis University Press.

Smith, K., Bryant-Davis, T., Tillman, S., & Marks, A. (2010). Stifled Voices: Barriers to help-seeking behavior for South African childhood sexual assault survivors. *Journal of Child Sexual Abuse, 19,* 255–274.

Staudt, M., & Williams-Hayes, M. (2011). A state survey of child advocacy center therapists' attitudes toward treatment manuals and evidence-based practice. *Journal of Child Sexual Abuse, 20,* 1–13.

Stein, J. A., Golding, J. M., Siegel, J. M., Burnam, M., & Sorenson, S. B. (1988). Long-term psychological sequelae of child sexual abuse: The Los Angeles Epidemiologic Catchment Area study. In G. Wyatt, G. Powell, G. Wyatt, & G. Powell (Eds.), *Lasting effects of child sexual abuse* (pp. 135–154). Thousand Oaks, CA: Sage.

Stoltenborgh, M., van Ijzendoorn, M. H., Euser, E. M., & Bakermans-Kranenburg, M. (2011). A global perspective on child sexual abuse: Meta-analysis of prevalence around the world. *Child Maltreatment, 16,* 79–101. doi:10.1177/1077559511403920

Tabachnick, J., & Dawson, E. (2000). Stop It Now! Vermont: A four year program evaluation, 1995–1999. *Offender Programs Report, 1,* 1–39. Retrieved from www.stopitnow.org/node/2054.

Tavkar, P., & Hansen, D. (2011). Interventions for families victimized by child sexual abuse: Clinical issues and approaches for child advocacy center-based services. *Aggression and Violent Behavior, 16,* 188–199

United Nations. (2011). *Millennium Development Goals Report 2011.* Retrieved from http://www.unhcr.org/refworld/docid/4e42118b2.html

United Nations Children's Fund. (2008a). *UNICEF child protection meta-evaluation: Final 15 may 2008.* New York, NY: Sheeran Consulting.

United Nations Children's Fund. (2008b). *Child protection strategy reference document.* Retrieved from http://www.unrol.org/doc.aspx?d=2622

United Nations Children's Fund. (2012). *Child protection from violence, exploitation and abuse: Sexual violence against children.* Retrieved from http://www.unicef .org/protection/57929_58006.html

United Nations General Assembly. (1989). Convention on the Rights of the Child. United Nations, Treaty Series, vol. 1577, p. 3; A/RES/44/25.

United Nations General Assembly. (2000a). Optional Protocol to the Convention on the Rights of the Child on the Sale of Children, Child Prostitution and Child Pornography. United Nations, Treaty Series, vol. 2171, p. 227; A/RES/54/263.

United Nations General Assembly. (2000b). United Nations Millennium Declaration. United Nations, Treaty Series, A/RES/55/2. Retrieved from http://www.un.org/millennium/declaration/ares552e.htm

United Nations Treaty Collection. (2012a). Multilateral treaties deposited with the secretary-general: Convention on the Rights of the Child. Retrieved from http://treaties.un.org/pages/ViewDetails.aspx?src=TREATY&mtdsg_no=IV-11&chapter=4&lang=en

United Nations Treaty Collection. (2012b). Multilateral treaties deposited with the secretary-general: Optional protocol to the convention on the rights of the child on the sale of children, child prostitution and child pornography. Retrieved from http://treaties.un.org/Pages/ViewDetails.aspx?src= TREATY&mtdsg_no=IV-11-c&chapter=4&lang=en

Urquiza, A. (2004). Parent–child interaction therapy (PCIT). In B. E. Saunders, L. Berliner, & R. F. Hanson (Eds.), *Child physical and sexual abuse: Guidelines for treatment* (Revised Report: April 26, 2004; pp. 81–83). Charleston, SC: National Crime Victims Research and Treatment Center.

U.S. Department of Health and Human Services, Administration for Children and Families. Administration on Children, Youth and Families, Children's Bureau. (2011). Definitions of child abuse and neglect. Retrieved from the Child Welfare Information Gateway: www.childwelfare.gov/systemwide/laws_policies/statutes/define.cfm

Walker, J. L., Carey, P. D., Mohr, N. N., Stein, D. J., & Seedat, S. (2004). Gender differences in the prevalence of childhood sexual abuse and in the development of pediatric PTSD. *Archives of Women's Mental Health, 7,* 111–121. doi:10.1007/s00737-003-0039-z

Wells, D., & Taylor, W. (2003). *Guidelines for medico-legal care for victims of sexual violence.* Geneva, Switzerland: World Health Organization. Retrieved from http://www.who.int/violence_injury_prevention/publications/violence/med_leg_guidelines/en/

Wilson, H. W., & Widom, C. (2008). An examination of risky sexual behavior and HIV in victims of child abuse and neglect: A 30-year follow-up. *Health Psychology, 27,* 149–158. doi:10.1037/0278-6133.27.2.149

Wolfe, D., Sas, L., & Wekerle, C. (1994). Factors associated with the development of posttraumatic stress disorder among child victims of sexual abuse. *Child Abuse & Neglect, 18,* 37–50

Wyatt, G. E., Loeb, T., Solis, B., Carmona, J., & Romero, G. (1999). The prevalence and circumstances of child sexual abuse: changes across a decade. *Child Abuse & Neglect, 23,* 45–60.

Ystgaard, M., Hestetuna, I., Loeb, M., & Mehiuma, L. (2004). Is there a specific relationship between childhood sexual and physical abuse and repeated suicidal behavior? *Child Abuse & Neglect, 28,* 863–875.doi:10.1016/j.chiabu.2004.01.009

Zwickl, S., & Merriman, G. (2011). The association between childhood sexual abuse and adult female sexual difficulties. *Sexual and Relationship Therapy, 26,* 16–32. doi:10.1080/14681994.2010.530251

Chapter 6

The Physical Abuse of Girls: Issues, Challenges, and Opportunities

Benjamin Freer, Ginny Sprang, and Sue-Huei Chen

The phenomenon of physical abuse against girls represents a convergence of biological and social factors, community norms and values, and economic and political priorities. Many countries have enacted laws to prevent, criminalize, and punish those who perpetrate violence against children; however, these efforts may be thwarted by variability in how physical abuse is defined and gender biases that may confound straightforward interpretations of intentional harm as abusive. These definitional and conceptual problems may produce inconsistent reporting resulting in variable and unreliable prevalence estimates.

No discussion of child abuse is complete without considering the effect such experiences can have on a child's development. Attainment of developmental milestones assumes exposure to a range of acceptable environments and experiences that nurture and support typical maturation (Gottesman, 1963). However, when the environment fails to meet adequate standards or is harmful, typical development can be impeded. In this way, child physical abuse (CPA) represents an assault on the health and well-being of the child (Cicchetti & Toth, 1995).

This chapter explores the definitions, prevalence, and effects of CPA perpetrated against girls. Current standards in assessment and treatment are offered, as well as perspectives on how gender may affect the identification of abuse and interfere with access to and use of appropriate treatment. Finally, the chapter concludes with recommendations to improve policy making and research in the subfield of physical abuse of girls.

DEFINITIONAL ISSUES

It is important to remember that definitions of what constitutes physical abuse are mediated by social and cultural norms. Azar (2005) reminded us that the physical treatment of girls must be considered in context of gender expectations and social pressures. Indeed, the literature is replete with examples of the social and cultural influences on how researchers, policy makers, and practitioners define physical abuse. Garbarino and Gillam (1980) stated that "physically abusive behaviors are those that include specific acts judged by a mixture of community values and professional expertise to be inappropriate and damaging" (p. 7). This definition, however, is technically imprecise and can lead to confusion regarding what specific outcomes might be considered physically abusive. For example, does physical abuse require demonstrable harm, or does endangerment (putting a child in harm's way) meet the definitional threshold? Furthermore, questions have been raised about what actions might be considered physically abusive (threatening and intimidation, failure to supervise, exposure to extreme violence). In some cultures or population subgroups, corporal punishment is an acceptable form of discipline, although its use raises concerns about the distinctions between this act and physical abuse. The Committee on the Rights of the Child defines corporal punishment as "any punishment in which physical force is used and intended to cause some degree of discomfort, however light" (Pinhero, 2006, p. 52). Humiliation, as a form of emotional abuse, is considered a component of corporal punishment (United Nations Children's Fund Innocenti Research Centre, 2009). The Child Welfare League of America (1998) has developed a set of standards for service for abused and neglected children and their families that provides for a definition of physical abuse that is widely used in the literature: "Physical acts by parents or caregivers that cause, or could have caused, physical injury to the child" (p. 3). Further clarifying the definition of what distinguishes physical abuse from acts of endangerment, the CWLA defines emotional maltreatment as "parental or other caregiver acts or omissions, such as rejecting, terrorizing, berating, ignoring, or isolating a child, that cause or are likely to cause the child serious impairment of his or her physical, social, mental, or emotional capacities" (p. 3).

The definitions of physical abuse detailed to this point reflect an emphasis of research on studies conducted in the North American and European countries. However, recent reports document an increase in child abuse rates in Asian countries, and in China specifically (Chou, Su, Wu, & Chen, 2011). Do these rates reflect an increase in the occurrence of child abuse or more accurate reporting? To answer this question, it is necessary to understand the impact of globalization on cultural standards. The world in general, and China and Taiwan specifically, is rapidly moving toward Westernization or globalization. As a result, traditional Chinese and Taiwanese ways of parenting (which includes physical battering), once accepted as appropriate, are now being reconsidered by many Asians as abusive. Thus, definitions of acceptable behavior in some parts of the world are evolving, and there is some difficulty reaching global consensus on what constitutes "abuse."

There is general agreement across cultures that no child at any age is psychologically prepared to experience and cope with sexual stimulation and intrusion. Therefore, there is more likely to be concurrence around definitions of child sexual abuse across cultures. Conversely, physical abuse requires a more culturally nuanced definition.

Debates regarding the definition of child abuse center on differing beliefs about the nature of the parent–child relationship and proper ways to discipline in various countries and cultures. For example, Collier and colleagues (1999) found that older Palau individuals were more likely to use guilt induction and physical punishment in their parenting practices than their younger counterparts. Conversely, Chan, Chun, and Chung (2008) found that in their sample of Asian adults, 34.2% did not consider battering to be CPA, and 62.8% did not consider slapping to be abusive behavior. Additional studies with Asian populations revealed that the outcome of discipline, not the caregiver intention, seemed to be important when making child abuse determinations; minor injuries inflicted by parents with "good intentions" were labeled as excessive child discipline (but not abusive), whereas those acts that produced severe injuries were labeled as abusive (Kwok & Tam, 2005). In some Eastern or African cultures, there may be confusion about evolving child protection standards in a particular community due to a conflict between cultural and family beliefs and emerging standards of care influenced by ongoing globalization. The problem is further complicated by a culture of silence, in which children may feel they dare not to tell or seek help because of a cultural emphasis on family privacy (e.g., "Don't wash your dirty laundry in public").

Acknowledging the definitional discrepancies across cultures and countries, this chapter uses the definition provided by the Child Abuse and Prevention Treatment Act (2010) that defines child abuse as "any recent act or failure to act on the part of a parent or caretaker, which results in death, serious physical or emotional harm, sexual abuse or exploitation, or an act or failure to act which presents an imminent risk of serious harm" (p. 6). Specifically, CPA refers to the injury of a child on purpose, including beating, biting, kicking, striking, or any action that leads to physical injury of the child.

Although there may be legal or statutory reasons to focus on acts or behaviors that constitute physical abuse, some may argue that child outcomes should be considered as well. Additionally, Sameroff and Chandler (1975) suggested that definitions of physical abuse consider the clustering or culmination of poor parenting practices over time, instead of focusing on singular events or acts. These contextual factors may provide for a more nuanced understanding of physical abuse and may have utility in crafting assessment, treatment, and policy responses to this type of child maltreatment.

GLOBAL PREVALENCE RATES OF CPA

Uwimana is a twelve-year-old girl from Rwanda who was the victim of physical abuse, and a witness to physical abuse of her mother and sexual abuse of her older sisters perpetrated by soldiers who broke into their home. Following the reported incident, the family went into hiding to avoid similar attacks and emigrated from Rwanda to live in the United States. Upon arrival to the United States, Uwimana and her siblings had difficulty socially integrating with their peers and teachers, due in part to language difficulties, social withdrawal, overly aggressive acts, and a lack of trust in others. This led to the referral of Uwimana and her siblings, by the school administration, to a clinical setting for assessment and treatment. During the initial session of assessment, Uwimana's father spoke for the family and would not allow the children to speak. When Uwimana's father left the room, Uwimana was hesitant to speak but stated that her father believed that their involvement in therapy brought shame on the family. In addition, Uwimana's father stressed the importance of silence regarding their earlier experience with the soldiers in Rwanda. After several sessions, Uwimana began to disclose, when her father was not present, about symptoms of dysregulation, such as nightmares and re-experiencing the soldiers' attack. In addition, Uwimana explained the steps she and her siblings took to protect their family from future attacks, such as barricading doors and boarding up windows. Despite progress made during individual sessions with Uwimana, the family remained isolated and unable to receive full beneficial support due to fears that there was something wrong with the family based on their experience.

The National Child Abuse and Neglect Data System recently reported that an estimated 896,000 children were victims of child abuse and neglect in the United States. Additionally, a large study in the United States found that 15% of children experienced physical abuse (Briere, Kaltman, & Green, 2008). However, the lifetime rate is higher in other regions of the world. A survey completed by 11- to 17-year-old children in the Kurdistan Province of Iran revealed that 38.5% of children surveyed reported experiencing mild to severe physical abuse in the family (Stephenson et al., 2006). Compared with these large epidemiologic studies, the majority of research on the prevalence of child abuse in Chinese societies has relied largely on small-scale studies, making accurate estimates of abuse difficult. Because it seems especially difficult to distinguish corporal punishment from physical maltreatment under Chinese culture (Tang, 2006), statistics for physical child abuse are difficult to determine. For example, with a Taiwanese sample of fourth to eighth graders at schools in a mixed type city near the capital of Taiwan, Chou and colleagues (2011) found a 34% overall lifetime prevalence of CPA, with Taiwanese boys presented at a significantly higher CPA prevalence than girls, 38.1% versus 29.8%, a difference similar to Western samples. However, a separate study revealed 54.6% of boys and 32.6% of girls had been hit or kicked on the head or body, and 39.0% and 28.5% had been beaten with an object (Chen, Dunne, & Han, 2006). In general, however, the rate of CPA among Asian countries is higher than in most European and North American countries. Among East and South Asian populations, the prevalence was between 40.3% and 65.0% (e.g., Back et al., 2003; Maker, Shah, & Agha, 2005; Segal, 1995; Yamamoto et al., 1999), whereas the lifetime prevalence of CPA ranged from 3.6% to 15.8% in Europe and the United States (e.g., Briere et al., 2008; Elklit, 2002; Hetzel & McCanne, 2005; Schaaf & McCanne, 1998). However, many agree that a lack of awareness of the problem, a paucity of well-designed prevalence studies, and intentional silence by the family, as seen in the case of Uwimana, contribute to an underreporting of the phenomenon worldwide (Runyan, Wattam, Ikeda, Hassan, & Ramiro, 2002).

EFFECTS OF CPA

Recent research estimates that 22% of children exposed to traumatic events will meet *Diagnostic and Statistical Manual of Mental Disorders* (4th ed.) diagnosis of posttraumatic stress disorder (PTSD), and an additional 32% display symptoms consistent with subthreshold PTSD (Silva et al., 2000). An estimated 3% to 15% of all girls and 1% to 6% of all boys receive a diagnosis of PTSD during childhood (National Center for PTSD, 2007). Over the life span, girls are twice as likely to be diagnosed with PTSD compared with boys (Tolin & Foa, 2006). Interest in the effect of trauma on children has increased because of the known deleterious effects of PTSD on the child's developing brain. The brain dramatically changes through pruning and the shaping of neural networks between the ages of 6 months and 3 years in myelination of the corpus callosum, subcortical gray matter, and limbic system structures (De Bellis et al., 1999), and changes in the prefrontal cortex (which has been linked to executive functioning) have been documented in adolescence (Anderson, 2002).

Effects on Behavior

Children who develop traumatic stress conditions exhibit a variety of behaviors that can lead to negative life outcomes. Adolescents with PTSD have higher rates of delinquency, violence, truancy, substance abuse, depression, anxiety, sleep disorders, suicidal behavior, and teenage pregnancy (Felitti et al., 1998). In addition, children demonstrate impaired social skills, social problem solving, and planning (Perry, 1993) and increased social withdrawal, aggression (Rogosch & Cicchetti, 1994), and perception of others as acting in hostile ways (Weiss, Dodge, Bates, & Pettit, 1992). In the case of Uwimana, she demonstrated impaired social functioning, social withdrawal, sleep trouble, and fear that others would attack or cause harm to her or her family. Although a variety of cognitive impairments may account for these behavioral deficits, it has been posited that a key factor may be deficits in executive function (Beers & De Bellis, 2002).

Neurobiological and Neurofunctional

Multiple interconnected neurobiological systems are affected by stressors associated with trauma exposure (De Bellis & Putnam, 1994). Individuals who have experienced a traumatic event may have elevated levels of glucocorticoids that produce a neurotoxic effect associated with synaptic destruction that have been connected to learning and concentration impairments (Edwards, Harkins, Wright, & Menn, 1990). In addition, individuals with postabuse traumatic distress have documented increases in norepinephrine in the hypothalamus, amygdala, and prefrontal cortex possibly reflecting heightened arousal and prolonged physiological dysregulation (De Bellis & Putnam, 1994).

In addition to these neurobiological findings, recent advancements in technology have allowed for the examination of internal brain structure and function in adults and children exposed to abuse to better understand the effect of exposure to traumatic events. This research is driven by the theory that the experience of traumatic events may alter the biological stress system that results in permanent atypical brain sequela (De Bellis et al., 1999). Research supporting this theory notes smaller frontal cortex volume and prefrontal cortex in children with traumatic stress disorders than normal controls (Carrion et al., 2001; Karl et al., 2006; Richert, Carrion,

Karchemskiy, & Reiss, 2006), and deficits in the anterior cingulate cortex (ACC) in adults (Stein, Hanna, Koverola, Torchia, & McClarty, 1997) and children (De Bellis, Keshavan, Spencer, & Hall, 2000). This deficit in the ACC may play a role in deficits of executive function because the ACC is believed to be a central location in the brain for information processing. Now that the postabuse reactions have been addressed, it is important to discuss the clinical challenges associated with assessing and treating girls who have been physically abused.

CLINICAL CHALLENGES

In 2005, Gerison Lansdown wrote, "Global solutions that define strategies for addressing need without also addressing the context in which those needs arise are not necessarily helpful" (p. 19). Indeed, gender-based roles and discriminatory societal and family practices fuel physical abuse against girls. Therefore, assessment and treatment must consider the role these structural and cultural factors have in the maintenance of family violence as well as individual responses to physical abuse.

Assessing Socially Influenced Family Dynamics

Vulnerable families are those that embrace corporal punishment and harmful family interaction patterns. Dynamic interactions in these family units perpetuate the notion that girls are inferior to boys through practices such as providing unequal access to education, limited career choices, and, more subtly, the prescription of subservient female roles and behaviors. Family and cultural ideals of femininity and masculinity that are dependent on the dominance of males and the subjugation of females can lead to the devaluing of human worth of girls, creating a condition of unequal power and regard in the family and the community. Clinicians should look for evidence that girls are being subjected to these practices but should also be aware of psychological manipulation by family members who want to gain their silence and forgiveness following abusive events. These attempts by the perpetrator to seek redemption, favor, or silence from their female victims by giving gifts, sharing secrets, or threatening retaliation are designed to keep the child in a subordinate position, and maintain the secrecy and power differential in the family and/or social group. Additionally, any report of male-on-female violence in the family is of concern, because gender-role conditioning and socialization occur as a result of observed and learned interactional norms and experiences. This finding is supported by studies that document that female victims and witnesses can develop anxious, avoidant, and inhibited behaviors, score lower on measures of social competence, and have poorer academic performance (Kitzmann, Gaylord, Holt, & Kenny, 2003; Wolfe, Crooks, Lee,

McIntyre-Smith, & Jaffe, 2003). Additionally, girls may overidentify with female victims in the family (who are viewed as helpless) and incorporate this way of relating to males in future intimate partner relationships (Edelson, 2006). Perry (1996) proffered the idea of a "vortex of violence" (p. 4) in which violent family behavior flows down a differential from most powerful to the weakest family member. Perry wrote:

> A typical flow of rage will start with a man frustrated and humiliated outside of the home. He will absorb this humiliation, modify some of it, and pass some on. At home, he will direct his anger and rage at his spouse—she will absorb, modify, and pass on. The overwhelmed and assaulted mother (usually when the father leaves) will pass the humiliation and violence on to the demanding children. The older children will absorb, modify, and pass it on to younger or weaker children. (1996, p. 4)

The most vulnerable children in the family may transmit this aggression toward family pets or other children at school. Cruelty to pets or other vulnerable children is a clue that the child may be at the eye of the vortex of violence in the family.

Certain parental behaviors and event-specific details may be warning signs that physical abuse is occurring in the home. Common characteristics of abusive caregivers are those who delay seeking treatment for a child's injuries, especially those that involve significant pain or discomfort; refuse to be interviewed by police or child protective service workers; blame others for the assault; or give ambiguous or conflicting statements to third parties (Peterson, Durfee, & Coulter, 2003). The nature and pattern of injuries is also an important warning, as are reports of other physical injuries in the family (including siblings and nonoffending parents), marks of abuse that resemble objects, bruises on the buttocks of infants, and radiograph images that document repeated fractures at various stages of healing. Parents who are actively abusing substances, have a criminal history, and who have a narrative representation of their female child as "unwanted" have been documented as at high risk for being physically abusive (Peterson et al., 2003).

Tools for Assessing Family Dynamics That May Lead to the Physical Abuse of Girls

Given the protective nature of secure parent-child relationships for young children, observational methods of understanding the strengths and deficiencies of caregiver–child interactions are highly recommended. The Crowell relationship assessment procedure for children 0 to 5 years of age and their caregivers (Crowell & Feldman, 1988) provides a method of observing and coding caregiver-child interactions in a clinical setting and determining the attachment qualities of a particular relationship. This is especially important in families in which family violence of any kind is suspected. Lyons-Ruth and Jacobvitz (1999) have documented that mothers who were victims of intimate partner violence may have disrupted attachment relationships with their children and can display negative, nonprotective, or harsh caregiving behaviors. Therefore, a parent's perception of his or her child can be influenced by trauma exposure and is crucial in understanding parenting behavior.

The Working Model of the Child Interview (WMCI; Zeanah, Benoit, Hirshberg, Barton, & Regan, 1994) is a semistructured interview designed to evaluate a caregivers' internal representations of their relationship with a particular child, and specifically provides a systematic assessment of a parent's perception of his or her child and the relationship with the child. The WMCI has a coding algorithm that allows for classification of representational features so that caregiver narratives can be classified into one of three groups that parallel the organized attachment categories seen in the Strange Situation (Ainsworth, Blehar, Waters, & Wall, 1978).

Assessing the propensity toward violence against children can be facilitated through the use of psychometric measures of attitudes or behaviors correlated with physical abuse, instruments that tap into the respondent's willingness and intentions to intervene and protect vulnerable children, and individual reports of gender role expectations and stereotyping. Community and climate measures have also been used to determine the presence of rude, aggressive, or violent behavior or attitudes in social groups, as well as measures that ascertain the presence of positive support and respect for female family members. Table 6.1 provides an abbreviated list of instruments that can be used to assess family and social attitudes and behavior that may increase the risk for physical abuse against girls.

Assessing a Child's Response to Physical Abuse

Any assessment of girls who have suffered physical abuse should include an evaluation of interactions among individual, dyadic, family, and systemic phenomena, as well as the investigation of adaptive and maladaptive responses to maltreatment. A child's response to physical abuse cannot be understood accurately without consideration of the relational and developmental status of the individual and the purpose and function of symptoms and functioning in the family. Therefore, a comprehensive assessment should include four domains of information: a trauma history, current and past symptom profiles, the context of abuse experiences (i.e., antecedents, consequences, cultural norms, the child's interpretation of the event), and a consideration of developmental status and functioning

Table 6.1 *Instruments to Assess Family and Social Attitudes and Behavior That May Increase the Risk for Physical Abuse against Girls*

Domain	Measure	Description	Citation
Attitudes toward gender roles and relations	Modern Sexism Scale	Thirteen items measuring overt, covert and subtle sexism	Swim & Cohen (1997)
	Attitudes toward Women Scale	A 55-item measure to assess opinions about the rights and roles of women	Spence & Hahn (1997)
Family violence	Conflict Tactics Scale	A 78-item scale designed to measure the use of reasoning, verbal aggression, and violence within family conflict	Straus, Hamby, & Warren (2003)
Propensity toward violence	Propensity for Abusiveness Scale	A 29-item self-report perpetrator profile for intimate abusiveness	Clift, Thomas, & Dutton (2005)
	Aggression Questionnaire	A revision of the Buss-Durkee Hostility Inventory; 29-item measure assessing hostility and aggression	Buss & Perry (1992)
	Child Abuse Potential Inventory	A 160-item screening tool designed for identifying individuals who share characteristics with known physical abusers	Milner (1989)
Community and Climate Measures	Measuring Violence-Related Attitudes, Behaviors and Influences among Youth	A compendium of ass-essment tools aimed at measuring school climate toward interpersonal violence	Dahlberg, Toal, Swahn & Behrens (2005)
	Peer Group Climate	U.S study constructed a measure of peer group climate or culture using individual-level measures of aggressive behaviors toward women and positive scales to measure support and respect of women	Rosen, Kaminski, Parmley, Knudson, & Fancher (2003)

before and after physical abuse. A structured or semistructured interview with the child and relevant caregivers should be guided by a trauma-informed approach to assessment that asks the meta-question, "What has happened to you?" instead of "What is wrong with you?" Trauma-informed approaches to assessment and treatment prioritize establishing and maintaining psychological and physical safety for the child, creating a clinical relationship that is hallmarked by trustworthiness, choice, and collaboration; restoration of a child's sense of control through healthy empowerment; and cultural competency in practice so that services are delivered in a manner that is accepted and utilized by the child and family (Harris & Fallot, 2001). The National Child Traumatic Stress Network has created a comprehensive intake schedule that includes background and contextual information about the child, family, relationships, and environment, indicators of problem severity, a developmental history, service utilization assessment, and a developmentally anchored trauma-detail form. This interview schedule provides the structure for a trauma-informed assessment of child functioning in the recommended four domains (see www.nctsn.org).

Any clinical intake should be complemented with a battery of child-focused trauma measures that tap into symptom and functioning problems associated with a continuum of traumatic stress reactions. This allows for an assessment of how symptom profiles and functional assessments converge or diverge across methods of data collection and considers variations or discrepancies between a girl's verbal descriptions of harm versus a caregiver's perceptions of what is relevant or injurious. There are a number of standardized assessments that are brief, age sensitive, and include underreporting scales (a common problem for young children). These are listed in Table 6.2 as an easy reference, but not an exhaustive list of measures currently available (for a more comprehensive list visit http://www.ptsd.va.gov/professional/pages/assessments/child-trauma-ptsd.asp).

Treating Physically Abused Girls and Their Families

Susie is a five-year-old child who was the victim of extreme physical abuse perpetrated by her biological father who was caring for her while her mother was at work. During the reported incident, she was held under water and choked as punishment for jumping on the bed. Susie's mother returned home to find her daughter bruised and struggling to breathe, and called 911 for assistance. Susie's father was removed from the family home by police, and a child protection case was opened. During the dispositional hearing, Susie's father described Susie as a hard to control child and asked for the court's assistance in securing mental health treatment for his daughter. Subsequently, the court mandated weekly family therapy services for all family members, as well as parenting classes for the father. During the initial session of treatment, Susie's father was loud, angry, and banged his fist on the table when describing his frustrations managing Susie's behavior. Susie's response to participation in treatment (the only

(*continued*)

time she had contact with her father) was to regress developmentally, and withdraw. She became enuretic and encopretic and began sucking her thumb. Her affect was restricted, she rarely talked, and lost interest in kindergarten and her friends. As a result, a treatment plan was drafted that identified Susie's internalization of distress as the primary family problem, and all attention became focused on "fixing Susie." However, over the course of the next three months in therapy, Susie became unable to sleep due to nightmares, she was increasingly dysregulated physiologically, and experienced significant dissociative symptoms. The therapist discussed the possibility of an inpatient admission for five-year-old Susie.

Just as the majority of trauma exposure in girls is interpersonally and relationally inflicted, a child's recovery from traumatic stress and related conditions is best organized around her fundamental developmental need to connect to others. Therefore, inclusion of a nonoffending, primary caregiver in treatment is crucial to create a relational context for sharing and support that will aid in the child's healthy adaptation and healing. For example, the family silence surrounding Uwimana's experience hindered treatment. It is important to note however, that a child cannot be expected to recover from traumatic stress while being retriggered through contact with the perpetrator and in the midst of ongoing exposure to violence or threats of violence. Psychological and physical safety must be a primary treatment goal, established and reinforced within a context of healthy, protective interpersonal relationships. In Susie's case, the therapist followed the court's order of family therapy, even though forced interaction between Susie and her father only served to retraumatize Susie and create an atmosphere of danger and insecurity. Susie's developmental regression and behavioral distress was a clear marker of traumatic stress, which was being misunderstood and conceptualized as a behavioral disturbance.

Similarly, gender-based theories of psychopathology suggest that psychological distress is environmentally influenced and culturally determined. Therefore, the therapeutic environment must be reconstructed to minimize gender bias and gender-role stereotypes, promote gender equality through the nomenclature of the therapeutic process, and avoid assigning blame to an individual when the source of the abuse is attributable to situational or cultural factors (Prochaska, DiClemente, & Norcross, 2003). The ideal therapeutic relationship between a clinician and a physically abused girl is one of empathy, mutual respect, and equality. The drafting of a treatment plan that identified a family therapy goal of "fixing Susie" only served to pathologize and invalidate her experience as a victim of abuse and sent a strong message that the critical incident was not the physical abuse but rather Susie's behavior before and after the abuse.

Table 6.2 *Brief, Age-Sensitive Standardized Assessments That Include Under-reporting Scales*

Measure	Description	Citation
Child PTSD Reaction Index (CPTS-RI)	Interview for children aged 6–17, includes 20 items about a single incident	Nader (1996)
Child PTSD Symptom Scale (CPSS)	Self-report measure for children 8–18, includes 26 items about multiple traumas; corresponds to DSM-IV criteria	Foa, Johnson, Feeny, & Treadwell (2001)
Clinician-Administered PTSD Scale for Children & Adolescents (CAPS-CA)	Interview for children aged 7–18, includes 33 items about multiple traumas; corresponds to DSM-IV criteria	Nader, Kriegler, Blake, Pynoos, Newman, & Weathers (1996)
Trauma Symptom Checklist for Children (TSCC)	Interview for children aged 6–17 that includes 54 items that allow for reporting on multiple traumas	Briere (1996)
Trauma Symptom Checklist for Young Children (TSCYC)	Caregiver report for children 3–12; includes 54 items that allow for reporting on multiple traumas	Briere (2005)
UCLA PTSD Index for DSM-IV	Self-report for children aged 7–12; includes 48 items and allows reporting on multiple traumas; corresponds to DSM-IV criteria	Steinberg, Brymer, Decker, & Pynoos (2004)
Parent Report of Child's Reaction to Stress	Caregiver report of children (age not specified), includes 79 items that allow for reporting about multiple traumas	Fletcher (1996)
Traumatic Events Screening Inventory (TESI)	Interview for children aged 4 and older that includes 18 items, allows for reporting about multiple traumas, and corresponds to DSM-IV criteria	Ribbe (1996)

Note: DSM-IV = *Diagnostic and Statistical Manual of Mental Disorders* (4th ed.); UCLA = University of California at Los Angeles.

There are a number of trauma-informed evidence-based practices that have emerged as treatment options for physically abused girls that are structured to prevent these types of assessment and treatment errors. Trauma-focused cognitive behavioral therapy (TF-CBT) (Cohen & Mannarino, 1996) provides a trauma-informed framework for understanding a child's response to and recovery from physical abuse. It is a manualized, components-based model of psychotherapy that addresses the unique needs of children (aged 3–18) with posttraumatic stress, depression, behavior problems, and other difficulties related to exposure to traumatic life experiences. Essential elements of TF-CBT are safety skills training and the psychoeducation of parents and children about the impact of trauma exposure. TF-CBT is the most investigated child-focused intervention (Cohen, Deblinger, Mannarino, & Steer, 2004; Cohen & Mannarino 1997; Deblinger, Steer, & Lippmann, 1999; Stauffer & Deblinger, 1996), and as designed, it is consistent with the gender- and culture-sensitive practices outlined earlier. Additionally, Alternative for Families—A Cognitive Behavioral Therapy (AF-CBT; Kolko & Swenson, 2002) represents an approach to working with physically abused children (aged 5–15), like Susie, and their offending caregivers. It incorporates behavior therapy and CBT procedures that address child and caregiver thoughts and behaviors associated with abusive experiences and specifically targets attitudes in the larger familial culture that promote and sustain physical force and aggression. Several studies have established efficacy of AF-CBT compared with routine community service models (Chalk & King, 1998; Kolko, 2002). For very young children (aged 0–5), Child-Parent Psychotherapy (CPP) incorporates tenets of developmental, attachment, trauma, social learning, psychodynamic, and cognitive behavioral theories to address exposure to violence in children and their caregivers. It has been culturally adapted to be used with diverse population subgroups and has been found to be efficacious in preventing a girl's exposure to violence and addressing subsequent traumatic stress and behavioral disturbance (Lieberman, Van Horn, & Ghosh-Ippen, 2006; Toth, Maughan, Manly, Spagnola, & Cicchetti, 2002). In Susie's case, all of these interventions would include Susie and her biological mother, as long as safety could be ensured and maintained. Susie's father would be excluded from participation in these interventions until he successfully completed treatment for his anger control issues and accepted responsibility for the abuse. Once these issues were addressed, the therapist, in collaboration with Susie and her mother, would decide when, and if, his inclusion in the therapeutic process or ongoing visitation should be resumed.

There are widely accepted, and empirically supported essential elements that can be identified in most trauma-informed, evidence-based practices. These treatment components constitute the standard of practice in the treatment of CPA and should be implemented considering the girl's stage of development, with an eye toward strengthening the bond between the child and a nonoffending caregiver. These common elements include establishing physical and psychological safety, psychoeducation about the impact of trauma, addressing maladaptive cognitions, affect regulation, trauma integration, and addressing problems associated with collaboration and interface with child-serving systems of care.

McMaster's model of family functioning (Epstein, Baldwin, & Bishop, 1983) can be instructive in developing treatment approaches for physically abusive and nonoffending parents. The approach assumes that family functioning and organization influence parent behavior, and transactional processes within a family shape the interaction patterns of its members. This model identifies six primary intervention goals that include problem solving, behavioral control, affective attunement and responsiveness, affective involvement, communication, and adequate distribution of familial roles and responsibilities (Epstein et al., 1983). These tasks can be completed through a variety of interventions that target a parent's skill deficits in each domain, while respecting the reciprocal process of interactions that can maintain or work to extinguish abusive behavior. Saunders, Berliner, and Hanson (2004) published *Child Physical and Sexual Abuse: Guidelines for Treatment,* which provide a compendium of family, parent-child and parent-focused interventions that target increasing child safety, reducing risk, and clarifying responsibility in CPA situations. Although not gender-specific, these guidelines provide a roadmap for practitioners to evaluate the effectiveness, goodness of fit, and overall quality of mental health treatments and represent a database of information describing available treatments for physically abusive caregivers.

Barriers to Effective Assessment and Intervention

Gender bias can interfere with the development and execution of clinical interventions and services designed to protect children. Farmer and Owen's (1998) ethnographic case study of child welfare and families noted that casework tended to focus on addressing maternal capacities and risk reduction, even when the identified perpetrator of physical abuse was the father. Noting an inclination toward identifying the mother as the primary caretaker and an aversion to working with belligerent or hostile men as a potential practice biases, these findings serve as a reminder that gender-based stereotypes and attitudes may exist within a professional milieu. It is the responsibility of all child-serving professionals to avoid the recapitulation of gender bias that may be occurring in these physically abusive families by guarding against discriminatory practices in the way services are delivered to these girls and their families.

Almost 20% of all youth have mental health problems that significantly impair their academic, familial, and community functioning (New Freedom Commission on Mental Health, 2003). Children living in poverty, those from diverse racial or ethnic groups, and those with language barriers are disproportionately affected (Garland et al., 2005; Howell, 2004; Kataoka, Zhang, & Wells, 2002). Kataoka and colleagues (2002) reported that approximately 80% of the children in the United States who are assessed as in need of mental health services do not get the mental health care they need. Unfortunately, access to child focused, evidence-based assessment and treatment services for traumatic stress conditions is inadequate in most parts of the world. Implementation challenges such as lack of availability of qualified providers, gender stereotypes in service systems, inadequate mental health service financing, problems transporting evidence-based protocols from one population and culture to another, and inadequate sustainability plans have slowed the translation of science to real world practice (McKay et al., 2004; Schoenwald et al., 2008). The next section of this chapter identifies the research implications of these clinical challenges with access to and delivery of quality, nonbiased services and provides suggestions as to how the research field can provide necessary information that will address the needs of physically abused girls.

Research Challenges

As discussed throughout this chapter, there is a lack of conceptual and empirical clarity regarding the best way to conceptualize, document, and treat girls who have been physically abused. Thus, researchers must increase efforts to ascertain a more accurate understanding of physical abuse throughout the world and clearly articulate the policy and practice implications of their work.

Because physical abuse cannot be reasonably predicted and ethical concerns about withholding intervention in the wake of an allegation prevail, the use of a typical experimental designs are often prohibited. Additionally, problems such as the difficulty in measuring the frequency and severity of the physical abuse for each child, distinguishing co-occurring problems (e.g., physical abuse and sexual abuse; physical abuse and childhood depression), and creating matched control groups abound. Although it is unlikely these issues can be fully addressed within the context of studies with human subjects, it is essential that researchers augment the understanding of physical abuse through the use of animal studies. Although animal models cannot replicate the human experience due to differences in the behaviors, cognitive function, brain anatomy, and genetics, these investigations provide enough similarities that allow for great advancements in the field's understanding of how humans may be affected by physical abuse.

Finally, as evident in some parts of the current chapter, the literature examining gender differences of children who have been physically abused, compared with those who have been sexually abused, is relatively scarce. This indicates a real need for researchers to examine female physical abuse as a unique phenomenon and to develop sampling frames that allow for cross-group comparisons.

RECOMMENDATIONS

The good news is that a number of strategies can be used to address the clinical and research challenges associated with the physical abuse of girls. These strategies address measurement problems, the need to address perpetration, and integrated models of service delivery.

Need for Gender and Culturally Specific Measures

As discussed in the section on clinical challenges, the field has a multitude of validated assessment and treatment programs when working with a child who has been physically abused; however, the large majority of these programs were established and are currently used in North America and Europe. Researchers have long held that assessment tools that were created and normalized with Western populations cannot be applied to individuals outside that majority who differ by language or cultural and societal norms and expectations (Padilla, 2001). It is important for researchers to understand that a simple translation of the text is rarely an adequate solution. Such translation of the assessment tool or treatment program will likely not communicate the same psychological constructs due to the possibility that the construct does not exist or is expressed in a different manner (van de Vijver & Poortinga, 1982). Thus, research attempting to adapt current assessment and treatment to other cultures must first determine whether translation is an adequate solution and then must either gather normative data with the translated tool or attempt to create a measure that is culturally specific and relevant. Furthermore, gender-specific differences exist in how questions are framed and interpreted, and tools that are normed on homogeneous gender groups may perpetuate stereotypes and fail to detect group differences.

Treating Perpetrators of Female CPA

Within the current literature on the physical abuse of children, one of the least examined areas is how to best intervene for the perpetrators of physical abuse (Schellenbach, 2006). As discussed earlier, various cultural and societal values are risk factors for the likelihood of an individual becoming a perpetrator of physical abuse (e.g., anger problems, low self-esteem, lack of social support), and a growing field is establishing the most effective methods of intervention with these perpetrators. Research has investigated the use of cognitive-behavior intervention strategies, social support groups, and multidimensional treatments to improve the parent–child relationship and minimize the likelihood of future physical abuse of the child. To this point, the research on these treatments is extremely limited and many studies lack experimental rigor, such as the inclusion of control groups or appropriate sample size. Finally, although the majority of these programs currently address parents, caregivers, and other adults who have physically abused a child, the development of such programs for parents at risk to physically abuse their child would likely benefit as well as a preventative measure (see Schellenbach, 2006, for more in-depth review).

Coordination and Integration of Services

The current system response to suspected CPA can involve myriad agencies and individuals, such as police, legal prosecutors, mental health workers, medical staff, and victim advocates, who are charged with the task of determining whether abuse has taken place and the appropriate plan of action. These various individuals often work independently from each other with no contact or collaboration regarding the specific case (i.e., the child). This lack of coordination can lead to fragmented care and poor interagency communication and can impede effective policy development (Pence, 1999). One possible solution to such problems is the establishment of *coordinated community services* that aim to unite the various individuals working on a case of child abuse (or any interpersonal crime) to reflect an understanding of the multiple contexts in which a victim and perpetrator receive services (Campbell & Ahrens, 1998). Although this solution seems reasonable, there is currently debate as to whether coordinated community services can be effectively implemented because of concerns regarding staff burden, conflicting interests and priorities across systems, and a need for improved communication pathways. Even so, recent research regarding service delivery models for rape victims reveals that a coordinated services approach can have a positive impact on client-level outcomes (Martin, 2005).

CONCLUSION

How a society treats its children is a reflection of cultural and community values regarding gender roles and responsibility, parental authority, and structures created by child protection policies and practices. Approaches to addressing this problem must respect these values, norms, and practices yet clearly specify the parameters that distinguish discipline from abuse and the most appropriate ways to protect girls in diverse families. A global approach to trauma-informed care involves the essential elements of trauma-focused screening and assessment, gender- and culture-specific perspectives, evidence-informed care, individual- and family-focused interventions, and coordinated service delivery. If these goals are met, regardless of the culture, country, or system, the psychosocial care of physically abused girls will be transformed.

REFERENCES

Ainsworth, M., Blehar, M., Waters, E., & Wall, S. (1978). *Patterns of Attachment.* Hillsdale, NJ: Erlbaum.

Anderson, V. (2002). Executive function in children: Introduction. *Child Neuropsychology, 8,* 69–70.

Azar, S. (2005). Child maltreatment and childhood injury research: A cognitive behavioral approach. *Journal of Pediatric Psychology, 30,* 598–614.

Back, S. E., Jackson, J. L., Fitzgerald, M., Shaffer, A., Salstrom, S., & Osman, M. M. (2003). Child sexual and physical abuse among college students in Singapore and the United States. *Child Abuse & Neglect, 27,* 1259–1275.

Beers, S. R., & De Bellis, M.D. (2002). Neuropyschological function in children with maltreatment-related posttraumatic stress disorder. *The American Journal of Psychiatry, 27,* 204–207.

Briere, J. (1996). *Trauma Symptom Checklist for Children: Professional manual.* Florida: Psychological Assessment Resources Inc.

Briere, J. (2005). *Trauma Symptom Checklist for Young Children: Professional manual.* Lutz, FL: Psychological Assessment Resources.

Briere, J., Kaltman, S., & Green, B. L. (2008). Accumulated childhood trauma and symptom complexity. *Journal of Traumatic Stress, 21,* 223–226.

Buss, A. H., & Perry, M. (1992). The aggression questionnaire. *Journal of Personality and Social Psychology, 63,* 452–459.

Campbell, R., & Ahrens, C. E. (1998). Innovative community services for rape victims: An application of multiple case study methodology. *American Journal of Community Psychology, 26,* 537–571.

Carrion, V. G., Weems, C. F., Eliez, S., Patwardhan, A., Brown, W., Ray, R. D., & Reiss, A. L. (2001). Attenuation of frontal asymmetry in pediatric posttraumatic stress disorder. *Biological Psychiatry, 50,* 943–951.

Chalk, R., & King, P. A. (Eds.). (1998). *Violence in families: Assessing prevention and treatment programs.* Washington, DC: National Academy Press.

Chan, Y., Chun, P. R., & Chung, K. (2008). Public perception and reporting of different kinds of family abuse in Hong Kong. *Journal of Family Violence, 23,* 253–263.

Chen, J., Dunne, M. P., & Han, P. (2006). Prevention of child sexual abuse in China: Knowledge, attitudes, and communication practices of parents of elementary school children. *Child Abuse & Neglect, 31,* 747–755.

Child Abuse and Prevention Treatment Act. (2010). Retrieved from the Administration for Children & Families website: http://www.acf.hhs.gov/programs/cb/laws_policies/cblaws/capta/capta2010.pdf

Child Welfare League of America. (1998). *CWLA Standards of Excellence for Services for Abused or Neglected Children and Their Families.* Washington, DC: Author.

Chou, C. S., Su, Y., Wu, H., & Chen, S. (2011). Child physical abuse and the related PTSD in Taiwan: The role of Chinese cultural background and victims' subjective reaction. *Child Abuse & Neglect, 35,* 58–68.

Cicchetti, D., & Toth, S. L. (1995). A developmental psychopathology perspective on child abuse and neglect. *Journal of the American Academy of Child and Adolescent Psychiatry, 34,* 541–565.

Clift, R. J. W., Thomas, L. A., & Dutton, D. G. (2005). Two-year reliability of the Propensity for Abusiveness Scale. *Journal of Family Violence, 20,* 231–234.

Cohen, J. A., Deblinger, E., Mannarino, A. P., & Steer, R. (2004). A multisite, randomized controlled trial for children with sexual abuse-related PTSD symptoms. *Journal of the American Academy of Child & Adolescent Psychiatry, 43,* 393–402.

Cohen, J. A., & Mannarino, A. P. (1996). A treatment outcome study for sexually abused preschool children: Initial findings. *Journal of the American Academy of Child and Adolescent Psychiatry, 35,* 42–50.

Cohen, J. A., & Mannarino, A. P. (1997). A treatment study of sexually abused preschool children: Outcome during one-year follow-up. *Journal of the American Academy of Child and Adolescent Psychiatry, 36,* 1228–1235.

Collier, A. F., McClure, F. H., Collier, J., Otto, C., & Polloi, A. (1999). Culture-specific views of child maltreatment and parenting styles in a Pacific-island community. *Child Abuse & Neglect, 23,* 229–244.

Crowell, J. A., & Feldman, S. S. (1988). Mothers' internal models of relationships and children's behavioral and developmental status: A study of mother–child interaction. *Child Development, 59,* 1273–1285.

Dahlberg, L. L., Toal, S. B., Swahn, M. H., & Behrens, C. B. (2005). *Measuring violence-related attitudes, behaviors, and influences among youths: A compendium of assessment tools* (2nd ed.). Atlanta, GA: Centers for Disease Control and Prevention, National Center for Injury Prevention and Control.

De Bellis, M. D., Keshavan, M. S., Clark, D. B., Casey, B. J., Giedd, J. N., Boring, A. M., . . . Ryan, N. D. (1999). AE Bennett Research Award: Developmental traumatology, part II: brain development. *Biological Psychiatry, 45,* 1271–1284.

De Bellis, M. D., Keshavan, M. S., Spencer, S., & Hall, J. (2000). N-acetylaspartate concentration in the anterior cingulated of maltreated children and adolescents with PTSD. *American Journal of Psychiatry, 157,* 1175–1177.

De Bellis, M. D., & Putnam, F. W. (1994). The psychobiology of childhood maltreatment. *Child and Adolescent Psychiatric Clinics of North America, 3,* 663–677.

Deblinger, E., Steer, R. A., & Lippmann, J. (1999). Two-year follow-up study of cognitive behavioral therapy for sexually abused children suffering post-traumatic stress symptoms. *Child Abuse and Neglect, 23,* 1371–1378.

Edleson, J. L. (2006). Emerging responses to children exposed to domestic violence. Retrieved from http://www.vawnet.org

Edwards, E., Harkins, K., Wright, G., & Menn., F. (1990). Effects of bilateral adrenalectomy on the induction of learned helplessness. *Behavioral Neuropsychopharmacology, 3,* 109–114.

Elklit, A. (2002). Victimization and PTSD in a Danish National Youth Probability Sample. *Journal of the American Academy of Child and Adolescent Psychiatry, 41,* 174–181.

Epstein, N., Baldwin, L, & Bishop, D. (1983). The McMaster Family Functioning Assessment Devise. *Journal of Marriage and Family Therapy, 9,* 171–180.

Farmer, E., & Owen, M. (1998). Gender and the child protection process. *British Journal of Social Work, 28,* 545–564.

Felitti, V. J., Anda, R. F., Nordenberg, D., Williamson, D. F., Spitz, A. M., Edwards, V., . . . Marks, J. S. (1998). Relationship of childhood abuse and household dysfunction to many of the leading causes of death in adults. The Adverse Childhood Experiences (ACE) study. *American Journal of Preventive Medicine, 14,* 245–258.

Fletcher, K. (1996). Psychometric review of the Parent Report of Child's Reaction to Stress. In B. H. Stamm (Ed.), *Measurement of stress, trauma, and adaptation* (pp. 225–227). Lutherville, MD: Sidran Press.

Foa, E. B., Johnson, K. M., Feeny, N. C., & Treadwell, K. R. H. (2001). The Child PTSD Symptom Scale: A preliminary examination of its psychometric properties. *Journal of Clinical Child Psychology, 30,* 376–384.

Garbarino, J., & Gilliam, G. (1980). *Understanding abusive families.* Lexington, MA: Lexington Books.

Garland, A. F., Lau, A. S., Yeh, M., McCabe, K. M., Hough, R. L., & Landsverk, J. A. (2005). Racial and ethnic differences in utilization of mental health services among high-risk youths. *American Journal of Psychiatry, 162,* 1336–1343.

Gottesman, I. I. (1963). Genetic aspects of intelligent behavior. In N. R. Ellis (Ed.), *Handbook of mental deficiency: Psychological theory and research* (pp. 253–296). New York, NY: McGraw-Hill.

Harris, M., & Fallot, R. D. (Eds.). (2001). *Using trauma theory to design service systems: New directions for mental health services.* New York, NY: Jossey-Bass

Hetzel, M. D., & McCanne, T. R. (2005). The roles of peritraumatic dissociation, child physical abuse, and child sexual abuse in the development of posttraumatic stress disorder and adult victimization. *Child Abuse & Neglect, 29,* 915–930.

Howell, E. (2004). *Access to children's mental health services under Medicaid and SCHIP.* Washington, DC: Urban Institute.

Karl, A., Schaefer, M., Malta, L.S., Dorfel, D., Rohleder, N., & Werner, A. (2006). A meta-analysis of structural brain abnormalities in PTSD. *Neuroscience & Biobehavioral Reviews, 30,* 1004–1031.

Kataoka, S., Zhang, L., & Wells, K. (2002). Unmet need for mental health care among U.S. children: Variation by ethnicity and insurance status. *American Journal of Psychiatry, 159,* 1548–1555.

Kitzmann, K., Gaylord, N., Holt, A., & Kenny, E. (2003). Child witnesses to domestic violence: A meta-analytic review. *Journal of Consulting and Clinical Psychology, 71,* 339–352.

Kolko, D. J. (2002). Child physical abuse. In J. E. B. Myers, L. Berliner, J. Briere, C. T. Hendrix, C. Jenny, & T. Reid (Eds.), *APSAC handbook of child maltreatment* (2nd ed., pp. 21–54). Thousand Oaks, CA: Sage.

Kolko, D. J., & Swenson, C. C. (2002). *Assessing and treating physically abused children and their families: A cognitive behavioral approach.* Thousand Oaks, CA: Sage.

Kwok, S., & Tam, D. M. (2005). Child abuse in Chinese families in Canada. Implications of child protection practice. *International Social Work, 48,* 341–348.

Lansdown, G. (2005). *Innocenti Insight: The evolving capacities of the child.* Florence, Italy: UNICEF Innocenti Research Centre.

Lieberman, A. F., Van Horn, P., & Ghosh Ippen, C. (2006). Child–parent psychotherapy: 6-month follow-up of a randomized control trial. *Journal of the American Academy of Child and Adolescent Psychiatry, 45,* 913–918.

Lyons-Ruth, K., & Jacobvitz, D. (1999). Attachment disorganization: Unresolved loss, relational violence, and lapses in behavioral and attentional strategies. In J. Cassidy & P. R. Shaver (Eds.), *Handbook of attachment* (pp. 520–554). New York, NY: Guilford Press.

Maker, A. H., Shah, P. V., & Agha, Z. (2005). Child physical abuse: Prevalence, characteristics, predictors, and beliefs about parent-child violence in South Asia, Middle Eastern, East Asian, and Latina women in the United States. *Journal of Interpersonal Violence, 20,* 1406–1428.

Martin, P. Y. (2005). *Rape work: Victims, gender and emotions in organization and community context.* New York, NY: Taylor & Francis Group.

McKay, M. M., Hibbert, R., Hoagwood, K., Rodriguez, J., Murray, L., Legerski, J., & Fernandez, D. (2004). Integrating evidence-based engagement interventions into "real world" child mental health settings. *Brief Treatment and Crisis Intervention, 4,* 177–186.

Milner, J. S. (1989). Additional cross-validation of the Child Abuse Potential Inventory. *Psychological Assessment: A Journal of Consulting and Clinical Psychology, 1,* 219–223.

Nader, K. (1996). Psychometric review of Childhood PTS Reaction Index (CPTS-RI). In B. H. Stamm (Ed.), *Measurement of stress, trauma, and adaptation* (pp. 83–86). Lutherville, MD: Sidran Press.

Nader, K., Kriegler, J. A., Blake, D. D., Pynoos, R. S., Newman, E., & Weathers, F. W. (1996). *Clinician Administered PTSD Scale, Child and Adolescent Version.* White River Junction, VT: National Center for PTSD.

National Center for PTSD. (2007). PTSD in children and teens. Retrieved from http://www.ptsd.va.gov/public/pages/ptsd-children-adolescents.asp

New Freedom Commission on Mental Health. (2003). Achieving the promise: Transforming mental health care in America. Final report (DHHS Pub. No. SMA-03-3832). Rockville, MD: U.S. Department of Health and Human Services, Substance Abuse and Mental Health Services Administration. Retrieved from http://www.mentalhealthcommission.gov/reports/report.htm

Padilla, A. M. (2001). Issues in culturally appropriate assessment. In L. A. Suzuki, J. G. Ponterroto, & P. J. Meller (Eds.), *Handbook of multicultural assessment: Clinical, psychological, and educational applications* (pp. 5–27). San Francisco, CA: Jossey-Bass.

Pence, A. R. (1999). "It takes a village . . .," and new roads to get there. In D. P. Keating & C. Hertzman (Eds.), *Developmental health and the wealth of nations: Social, biological, and educational dynamics* (pp. 322–336). New York, NY: Guilford Press.

Perry, B.D. (1993). Neurodevelopmental and the neurophysiology of trauma: Conceptual considerations for clinical work with maltreated children. *The Advisor, 6,* 1–18.

Perry, B. D. (1996). Neurodevelopmental adaptations to violence: How children survive the intergenerational vortex of violence. In *Violence and Childhood Trauma: Understanding and Responding to the Effects of Violence on Young Children.* Cleveland, OH: Gund Foundation.

Peterson, M. S., Durfee, M., & Coulter, K. (Eds.). (2003). *Child abuse and neglect: Guidelines for identification, assessment, and case management.* Volcano, CA: Volcano Press.

Pinhero, P. S. (2006). *World report on violence against children. United Nations Secretary General's Study on Violence against Children.* Geneva, Switzerland: World Health Organization.

Prochaska, J. O., DiClemente, C. C., & Norcross, J. C. (2003). In search of how people change: Applications to addictive behaviors. In P. Salovey, A. J. Rothman (Eds.), *Social psychology of health* (pp. 63–77). New York, NY: Psychology Press.

Ribbe, D. (1996). Psychometric review of Traumatic Event Screening Instrument for Children (TESI-C). In B. H. Stamm (Ed.), *Measurement of stress, trauma, and adaptation* (pp. 386–387). Lutherville, MD: Sidran Press.

Richert, K. A., Carrion, V. G., Karchemskiy, A., & Reiss, A. L. (2006). Regional differences of the prefrontal cortex in pediatric PTSD: An MRI study. *Depression and Anxiety, 23,* 17–25.

Rogosch, F. A., & Cicchetti, D. (1994). Illustrating the interface of family and peer relations through the study of child maltreatment. *Social Development, 3,* 291–308.

Runyan, D., Wattam, C., Ikeda, R., Hassan, F., & Ramiro, L. (2002). Child abuse and neglect by parents and other caregivers. In E. G. Krug, J. A. Mercy, L. L. Dahlberg, & A. B. Zwi (Eds.), *World report on violence and health* (pp. 59–86). Geneva, Switzerland: World Health Organization.

Sameroff, A., & Chandler, M. (1975). Transactional models in early social relations. *Human Development, 18,* 65–79.

Saunders, B. E., Berliner, L., & Hanson, R. F. (Eds.). (2004). *Child physical and sexual abuse: Guidelines for treatment* (rev. report, April 26, 2004). Charleston, SC: National Crime Victims Research and Treatment Center.

Schaaf, K. K., & McCanne, T. R. (1998). Relationship of childhood sexual, physical, and combined sexual and physical abuse to adult victimization and posttraumatic stress disorder. *Child Abuse & Neglect, 22,* 1119–1133.

Schellenbach, C. J. (2006). Child maltreatment: A critical review of research on treatment for physically abusive parents. In P. K. Trickett & C. J. Schellenbach (Eds.), *Violence against children in the family and the community* (pp. 251–268). Washington, DC: American Psychological Association.

Schoenwald, S. K., Chapman, J. E., Kelleher, K., Hoagwood, K. E., Landsverk, J., Stevens, J., . . . Rolls-Reutz, J. (2008). A survey of the infrastructure for children's mental health services: Implications for the implementation of empirically supported treatments (ESTs). *Administration and Policy in Mental Health and Mental Health Services Research, 35,* 84–97.

Segal, U. A. (1995). Child abuse by the middle class? A study of professionals in India. *Child Abuse & Neglect, 19,* 217–231.

Silva, R.R., Alpert, M., Munoz, D., Singh, S., Matzner, F., & Dummit, S. (2000). Stress and vulnerability to posttraumatic stress disorder in children and adolescents. *American Journal of Psychiatry, 157,* 1229–1235.

Spence, J. T., & Hahn, E. D. (1997). The Attitudes Toward Women Scale and attitude change in college students. *Psychology of Women Quarterly, 21,* 17–34.

Stauffer, L. B., & Deblinger, E. (1996). Cognitive behavioral groups for nonoffending mothers and their young sexually abused children: A preliminary treatment outcome study. *Child Maltreatment, 1,* 65–76.

Stein, M. B., Hanna, C., Koverola, C., Torchia, M., & McClarty, B. (1997). Structural brain changes in PTSD: Does trauma alter neuroanatomy. *Annals New York Academy of Sciences, 3,* 76–82.

Steinberg, A., Brymer, M., Decker, K., & Pynoos, R. S. (2004). The UCLA PTSD Reaction Index. *Current Psychiatry Reports, 6,* 96–100.

Stephenson, R., Sheikhattari, P., Assassi, N., Eftekhar, H., Zamani, Q., Maleki, B., & Kiabayan, H. (2006). Child maltreatment among school children in the Kurdistan province, Iran. *Child Abuse & Neglect, 30,* 231–245.

Straus, M. A., Hamby, S. L., & Warren, W. L. (2003). *The Conflict Tactics Scales handbook.* Los Angeles, CA: Western Psychological Services.

Swim, J. K., & Cohen, L. L. (1997). Overt, covert, and subtle sexism: A comparison between the Attitudes Toward Women and Modern Sexism scales. *Psychology of Women Quarterly, 21,* 103–118.

Tang, C. (2006). Corporal punishment and physical maltreatment against children: A community study on Chinese parents in Hong Kong. *Child Abuse & Neglect, 30,* 893–907.

Tolin, D. F., & Foa, E. B. (2006). Sex differences in trauma and posttraumatic stress disorder: A quantitative review of 25 years of research. *Psychological Bulletin, 132,* 959–992.

Toth S. L., Maughan A., Manly J. T., Spagnola M., & Cicchetti D. (2002). The relative efficacy of two interventions in altering maltreated preschool children's representational models: Implications for attachment theory. *Developmental Psychopathology, 14,* 877–908.

United Nations Children's Fund Innocenti Research Centre. (2009). A study on violence against girls: Report on the International Girl Child Conference, The Hague, Netherlands.

van de Vijver, F. J. R., & Poortinga, Y. H. (1982). Cross-cultural generalization and universality. *Journal of Cross-Cultural Psychology, 13,* 387–408.

Weiss, B., Dodge, K. A., Bates, J. E., & Pettit, G. S. (1992). Some consequences of early harsh discipline: Child aggression and maladaptive social information processing style. *Child Development, 63,* 1321–1335.

Wolfe, D. A., Crooks, C. V., Lee, V., McIntyre-Smith, A., & Jaffe, P. G. (2003). The effects of children's exposure to domestic violence: A meta-analysis and critique. *Clinical Child and Family Psychology Review, 6,* 171–187.

Yamamoto, M., Iwata, N., Tomoda, A., Tanaka, S., Fujimaki, K., & Kitamura, T. (1999). Child emotional and physical maltreatment and adolescent psychopathology: A community study in Japan. *Journal of Community Psychology, 27,* 377–391.

Zeanah, C. H., Benoit, D., Hirshberg, L., Barton, M. L., & Regan, C. (1994). Mothers' representations of their infants are concordant with infant attachment classifications. *Developmental Issues in Psychiatry and Psychology, 1,* 9–18.

Chapter 7

Female Genital Mutilation

Roswith Roth

KEY FACTS

Female genital mutilation (FGM), as defined by the World Health Organization (WHO) and the United Nations (UN) agencies, comprises all procedures that involve partial or total removal of the external female genitalia or other injury to the female genital organs for nonmedical reasons. The practice is also known as female genital cutting (FGC), female genital mutilation/cutting (FGM/C), and female circumcision.

The procedure has no health benefits for girls and women, and procedures can cause severe bleeding, problems urinating, and subsequent childbirth complications and newborn deaths. An estimated 100 to 140 million girls and women worldwide are currently living with the consequences of FGM; it is mostly carried out on young girls sometime between infancy and age 15 years. In Africa, an estimated 92 million girls aged 10 years and older have undergone FGM. The practice is internationally recognized as a violation of the human rights of girls and women (WHO, 2012; UN, 2011; United Nations Population Fund [UNFPA], 2011; United Nations Children's Fund [UNICEF], 2005).

CLASSIFICATION

WHO groups FGM into four types (WHO, 1995; WHO/UNICEF/UNFPA, 1997):

1. Excision of the prepuce (the fold of skin surrounding the clitoris), with or without excision of part or the entire clitoris (*clitoridectomy*).
2. Excision of the clitoris with partial or total excision of the labia minora (the smaller inner folds of the vulva) with or without excision of the labia majora (*excision*).
3. Narrowing of the vaginal orifice with creation of a covering seal by cutting and appositioning the labia minora and/or the labia majora, with or without excision of the clitoris (*infibulation*).
4. *Unclassified,* which includes pricking, piercing, or incising of the clitoris and/or labia; stretching of the clitoris and/or labia; cauterization by burning of the clitoris and surrounding tissue; scraping of tissue surrounding the opening of the vagina (*angurya* cuts) or cutting of the vagina (*gishiri* cuts); introduction of corrosive substances or herbs into the vagina to cause bleeding or to tighten or narrow the vagina; and any other procedure that can be included in the definition of female genital mutilation.

The procedure is generally carried out on girls between the ages of 4 and 14; it is also done to infants, women who are about to be married and, sometimes, to women who are pregnant with their first child or who have just given birth. It is often performed by traditional practitioners, including midwives and barbers, without anesthesia, using scissors, razor blades, or broken glass (UNICEF, 2005).

TERMINOLOGY

FGM or FGC was called female circumcision until the early 1980s. The term FGM was adopted at the Third Conference on the Inter-African Committee on Traditional Practices Affecting the Health of Women and Children in Addis Ababa, Ethiopia. In 1991, WHO recommended use of the term to the United Nations (WHO, 2008b). The word *mutilation* differentiates the procedure of FGM from male circumcision and stresses its severity. Other terms in use are female genital cutting, female genital surgery, and genital modification. Some organizations think that the term *cutting* is better received than mutilation. Thus, both FGM and FGC are used, and some groups, such as UNFPA and United States Agency for International Development (USAID), use the combined term FGM/C.

Several countries refer to Type I FGM as *sunna circumcision.* Type III FGM (infibulation) is also known as *pharaonic circumcision* or *Sudanese circumcision*. Local terms in various countries are often words synonymous with purification. The term FGM is not applied to medical or elective procedures such as labiaplasty and vaginoplasty or procedures in sex reassignment surgery (WHO, 2008b).

IMMEDIATE AND LATE COMPLICATIONS

The effects of genital mutilation can lead to death. At the time the mutilation is carried out, pain, shock, hemorrhage (often from rupture of the blood vessels of the clitoris), and damage to the organs surrounding the clitoris and labia resulting from the lack of surgical expertise of the person performing the procedure and the aggressive resistance of the patient when anesthesia is not used can occur. Afterward, urine may be retained, caused by swelling and inflammation and serious infections including tetanus and septicemia, due to the use of using unsterilized or poorly disinfected equipment develop. Use of the same instrument on several girls without sterilization can cause the spread of HIV (Dejene, Kebede, Alemu, Gundenffa, & Hassen, 2009; WHO, n.d.-c).

More commonly, the chronic infections, intermittent bleeding, abscesses, and small benign tumors of the nerve that can result from clitoridectomy and excision cause discomfort and extreme pain. Chronic infections of the bladder and vagina in Type III FGM (urine and menstrual blood can only leave the body drop by drop) lead to dysmenorrhea, or extremely painful menstruation; buildup and fluid retention inside the abdomen often cause infections and inflammation in the urinary and reproductive tracts and pelvic infections that can lead to infertility. Additional infibulation can have even more serious long-term effects: stones in the bladder and urethra, kidney damage, excessive scar tissue, keloids (raised, irregularly shaped, and progressively enlarging scars) at the site of the operation and formation of cysts on the stitch line.

First sexual intercourse can only take place after gradual and painful dilation of the opening left after mutilation. In some cases, cutting is necessary before intercourse. In one study carried out in Sudan, 15% of women interviewed reported that cutting was necessary before penetration could be achieved. In most cases, not only must the woman be reopened for each childbirth, but also on her wedding night, when the excisor may have to be called in to open her so she can consummate the marriage. Some new wives are seriously damaged by unskillful cutting carried out by their husbands. A possible additional problem resulting from all types of female genital mutilation is that lasting damage to the genital area can increase the risk of HIV transmission during intercourse (Dejene et al., 2009).

During childbirth, existing scar tissue on excised women may tear. Infibulated women, whose genitals have been tightly closed, have to be cut to allow the baby to emerge. Reinfibulation must be performed each time a child is born. When infibulation (Type III) is performed, the opening left in the genital area is too small for the head of a baby to pass through. Failure to reopen this area can lead to death or brain damage of the baby, and death of the mother. The excisor must reopen the mother and re-stitch her again after the birth. In most ethnic groups, the woman is restitched as before, leaving the same tiny opening. In other ethnic groups the opening is left slightly larger to reduce painful intercourse. The constant cutting and restitching of a woman's genitals with each birth can result in tough scar tissue in the genital area (Amnesty International, 1997; WHO, 2000, 2008a, 2012; WHO Study Group on Female Genital Mutilation and Obstetric Outcome, 2006).

The psychological effects of FGM are more difficult to investigate scientifically than the physical ones. A small number of clinical cases of psychological illness related to genital mutilation have been reported. Despite the lack of scientific evidence, personal accounts of mutilation reveal feelings of anxiety, terror, humiliation, and betrayal, all of which would be likely to have long-term negative effects. Personal reports from women who experienced FGM underline these assumptions (Wairi, 1998; Ali, 1997). Some experts suggest that the shock and trauma of the operation may contribute to the behavior described as "calmer" and "docile," considered positive in societies that practice female genital mutilation.

Some of the psychological impacts of FGM appear to be Pavlovian in nature and affect women who have undergone any form of FGM. The attendant painful rituals are so traumatizing that women can only associate their genitals with pain and possible death from childbirth. These associations appear with a much higher possibility in circumcised than in uncircumcised women, with the idea of sexual intercourse as a pleasurable activity is inconceivable for most of them (United Nations Development Program [UNDP/UNFPA/WHO/World Bank Special Programme of Research, Development and Research Training in Human Reproduction, 2011a; WHO/UNFPA, 2010; UNDP/UNFPA/WHO/World Bank, 2010).

Festivities, presents, and special attention at the time of mutilation may mitigate some of the trauma experienced, but the most important psychological effect on a woman who has survived is the feeling that she is acceptable to her society, having upheld the traditions of her culture and made herself eligible for marriage, often the only role available to her. It is possible that a woman who did not undergo genital mutilation could suffer psychological problems as a result of rejection by the society (WHO, 1999). Where the FGM-practicing community is in a minority, women are thought to be particularly vulnerable to psychological problems, caught as they are between the social norms of their own community and those of the majority culture (UNDP/UNFPA/WHO/World Bank, 2011b).

Prevalence in Various Countries Following the WHO Classification

FGM/C occurs throughout the world. WHO estimates that between 100 million and 140 million girls and women alive today have experienced some form of the practice (WHO, 2012). It is further estimated that up to 3 million girls in sub-Saharan Africa, Egypt, and Sudan are at risk of genital mutilation annually. Global prevalence rates display significant regional and geographic variations. In northeastern Africa, prevalence varies from 97% in Egypt to 80% in Ethiopia. In western Africa, 99% of women in Guinea, 71% in Mauritania, 17% in Benin, and 5% in Niger have undergone FGM/C. Where data are available for southeastern Africa, the prevalences are 32% in Kenya, for example, and 18% in the United Republic of Tanzania. FGM is also found among ethnic groups in Oman, United Arab Emirates, and Yemen as well as in parts of India, Indonesia, and Malaysia (UNICEF, 2005; Program for Appropriate Technology in Health [PATH], n.d.; Yoder & Khan, 2008; see also Wikipedia: Female genital mutilation).

CULTURAL ASPECTS

FGM is a cultural practice that started in Africa approximately 2,000 years ago. It is primarily a cultural not a religious practice, although some religions do include FGM as part of their practices. FGM is so well ingrained that it defines membership in these cultures (or being a member of these cultures). To eliminate the practice, one must eliminate the cultural belief that a girl will not become a woman without the procedure.

Religion, Ethnicity, and Culture

Although religion can help explain FGM distribution in many countries, the relationship is not consistent. In six of the African countries where data on religion are available (i.e., Benin, Côte d'Ivoire, Ethiopia, Ghana, Kenya, and Senegal), Muslim population groups are more likely to practice FGM/C than Christian groups. In five countries, there seems to be no significant differences, whereas in Niger, Nigeria, and the United Republic of Tanzania the prevalence is greater among Christian groups.

Looking at religion independently, it is not possible to establish a general association with FGM status. The most marked differences can be observed in Benin, Côte d'Ivoire, Ghana, and Senegal. In Côte d'Ivoire, for example, 79% of Muslim women have undergone FGM, compared with 16% of Christian women (Yoder & Mahy, 2001; Yoder, Abderrahim, & Zhuzhuni, 2004). Even among immigrants from Africa surveyed in Austria, where 35% had their daughters subjected to FGM, more than one-third were Christians (Afrikanische Frauenorganisation in Wien, 2000).

This trend is reinforced in the analysis of FGM status of daughters. In four countries, Muslim women are more likely to have circumcised daughters than women of other religious affiliations. In Ethiopia, Kenya, Niger, and the United Republic of Tanzania, prevalence of FGM/C is higher among daughters of Christian women than among daughters of Muslim women. This could be attributed, however, to other factors such as ethnicity and the overall distribution of the various religious groups within these countries. FGM is a doctrine in neither Islam nor Christianity, and the majority of interviewed individuals believe strongly in FGM regardless of their religion. This is further affirmation of the practice as a tradition based on cultural values rather than on religious ones.

Among all socioeconomic variables, ethnicity appears to have the most determining influence over FGM distribution within a country. Many researchers have noted that FGC prevalence varies with ethnicity or that FGC serves as an ethnic marker. In discussing the role of ethnicity, Ellen Gruenbaum (2001, p. 102) writes: "Female circumcision practices are deeply entwined with ethnic identity wherever they are found. Understanding this should provide an important insight into the tenacity of the practice and people's resistance to change efforts, and it can help to explain why the practice may even spread in certain situations" (Yoder & Mahy, 2001; Yoder et al., 2004).

FGM is found extensively in Africa and is also indigenous to other parts of the world. The age and time at which FGM is practiced differs from community to community and can be carried out from as early as a few days after birth to immediately after the birth of a woman's first child. One of the notable trends in global FGM today is the progressive lowering of the age at which girls undergo the practice.

According to Amnesty International (1997), in certain societies women who have not had the procedure are regarded as too unclean to handle food and water, and there is a belief that a woman's genitals might continue to grow without FGM, until they dangle between her legs. Some groups see the clitoris as dangerous, capable of killing a man if his penis touches it or a baby if the head comes into contact with it during birth (Amnesty International, 1997; Momoh, 2005).

Not so long ago in western cultures as well, irrational beliefs resulted in cruel procedures. In the nineteenth century, gynecologists in England and the United States would remove the clitoris to "cure" insanity, masturbation, and nymphomania (Momoh, 2005). The first reported clitoridectomy in the west was carried out in 1822 by a surgeon in Berlin on a teenage girl regarded as an "imbecile" who was masturbating (Elchalal et al., 1997). Isaac Baker Brown (1812–1873); an English gynecologist who was president of the Medical Society of London in 1865, believed that the "unnatural irritation" of the clitoris caused epilepsy, hysteria, and mania and would remove it "whenever he had the opportunity of doing so" (Kent, 1999). Also an

Austrian psychiatrist reported cases of "pathological sexuality" of women having orgasms and advised clitoridectomies (Krafft-Ebing, 1886/1912). As late as the 1960s, American obstetricians performed clitoridectomies to treat erotomania, lesbianism, hysteria, and clitoral enlargement (Cutner, 1985).

The practice of FGM is underpinned by a variety of beliefs promoting it for perceived health and hygiene benefits, religious, traditional, or gender-related reasons. It is often viewed as a rite of passage for a girl ensuring her status and marriageability within the community. Prevention of promiscuity and genital cleanliness were other reasons cited for FGM. On its role in ensuring cleanliness of the female external genitalia, it was reported in interviews and group discussions in Nigeria that certain whitish itching organisms known as "Eta" are hidden underneath the prepuce, and these make a woman or girl uncomfortable if not circumcised. Regardless of how often a woman washes this part, the itching would cease only when the clitoris and prepuce are removed (Adeneye, Oke, & Adeneye, 2009).

The decision to have the girl cut is usually made by her parents or other close family members. A choice to leave the girl uncut is often met with strong opposition from the community because FGM is a deeply entrenched tradition within social, economic. and political structures (Ending Female Genital Mutilation, 2009; UNDP/UNFPA/WHO/World Bank, 2010b). Among communities that practice FGM, the procedure is a highly valued ritual, the purpose of which is to mark the transition from childhood to womanhood. In these traditional societies, FGM represents part of the rites of passage or initiation ceremonies intended to impart the skills and information a woman will need to fulfill her duties as a wife and mother (Yoder et al., 2004).

The Role of Males and Females in FMG

All members of communities practicing FGM have a role in perpetuating it. Families of girls or women who undergo FGM support it because it makes their daughters marriageable; the operation ensures that their daughters will have ready suitors and a satisfactory bride price. In these communities, no eligible man would consider marrying a girl who had not undergone the procedure, so FGM makes a woman culturally and socially acceptable. It is in this important way that female genital mutilation is supported and encouraged by men.

Women in the community have a role too, because it is they who arrange for and perform the operation. Typically, the procedure is arranged by the mother or grandmother and, in Africa, is usually performed by a traditional birth attendant, a midwife, or a professional circumciser.

In communities practicing FGM there is literally no place for a woman who has not undergone the procedure. Such societies have sanctions, which are brought to bear on the woman and her family, ensuring that the woman's relatives enforce compliance. Other circumcised girls will no longer associate with her. She is called derogatory names and is often denied the status and access to positions and roles that "adult" women in that community can occupy. Ultimately, an uncircumcised woman is considered to be a child (UNDP/UNFPA/WHO/World Bank, 2010b).

In traditional societies that offer women few options beyond being a wife and mother, there is great pressure to conform. Women who lack the education to seek other opportunities are doubly constrained in terms of the choices open to them. These women also typically come from communities that do not have alternatives to the traditional economy and modes of production, such as farming, fishing, or pastoralism.

Staying with the practice of FGM, even if individuals are aware of campaigns against the practice, is explained in the framework of functionalist theory (Cohen, 1968; Ritzer, 2000). Shared values are seen as key to the origin and maintenance of order and stability in the society. Societies are constrained by social facts—by ways of acting, thinking, and feeling—beyond the individual's control, and religion reinforces the collective consciousness and promotes social solidarity by defining certain social actions such as FGM as sacred.

ALTERNATIVE RITES TO FGM

Recently, an "alternative rites" strategy is being used by NGOs in FGM-practicing communities. This strategy is intended to retain the rites of passage or initiation that the girls would traditionally undergo, with the exception of FGM. The girls are still encouraged to learn what it means to be a woman in their respective communities but do not have to endure the agony of the cut. This procedure is being tested in several communities around the world and has registered some success. However, alternative rites have also faced serious opposition and even led to lowering of the age at which FGM is practiced in certain communities. The Massai of Kenya, for example, responded to aggressive anti-FGM campaigns by cutting girls as young as age 4, rather than teenage girls (African Medical Research and Education Foundation, 2011; Population Reference Bureau, 2008; UNFPA, 2011; WHO, 2000).

RESEARCH ON FMG

Research continues to be needed on aspects that will contribute to the elimination and prevention of FGM and better care for girls and women who have been subjected to the practice.

The risk of obstetric complications was estimated based on a 2006 WHO study of 28,393 women. The costs of each complication were estimated in purchasing power parity dollars (I$) for 2008 and discounted at

3%. The model also tracked life years lost owing to fatal obstetric hemorrhage. Multivariate sensitivity analysis was used to estimate the uncertainty around the findings.

Calculations entailed unit costs associated with caesarean delivery, maternal hemorrhage, extended maternal hospital stay, infant resuscitation, inpatient perinatal death, and episiotomy. Estimating the obstetric costs of female genital mutilation in six African countries, the study found that on average, a girl of 15 years who undergoes FGM Type III will lose nearly one-quarter of a year of life and impose on the medical system a cost of I$5.82 over her lifetime. The other types of FGM also reduce survival and lead to monetary losses over each woman's life span, but to a lesser extent.

The annual costs of FGM-related obstetric complications in the six African countries studied amounted to I$3.7 million and ranged from 0.1% to 1% of government spending on health for women aged 15 to 45 years. In the current population of 2.8 million 15-year-old women in the six African countries, a loss of 130,000 life years is expected owing to FGM's association with obstetric hemorrhage. This is equivalent to losing half a month from each life span. Because FGM violates a series of human rights, financial concerns are not the main motivation to work toward its abolition. However, because efforts to combat FGM have been traditionally underfunded, knowing that investment in the prevention of FGM also contributes to savings in the health system, including through a prevention of birth complications, should contribute to increased funding to support measures for the prevention of FGM. If the health system were to spend as much as I$5.82 per FGM Type III prevented or I$2.50 per FGM Type II prevented, the value of avoided obstetric complications would entirely offset the costs of prevention.

The abandonment of FGM would also benefit societies, families, and individuals through reduction of other costs not measured here, including the costs of treating other FGM-related complications (Adam et al., 2006; UNPD et al., 2011a; WHO Study Group, 2006).

Women who have undergone female genital mutilation rarely have access to the reconstructive surgery that is now available with positive outcomes (Foldès, Cuzin, & Andro, 2012). Defibulation (reconstructive surgery of the infibulated scar) to treat FGM was conducted in one study and the physical and sexual outcome and satisfaction of both wives and husbands were evaluated and found to be positive (Nour, Michels, & Bryant, 2006). In individual cases as well it has been shown that defibulation resolves symptoms and problems (Nour, 2006). In general, Western gynecologists are sometimes not very familiar with FGM and how to proceed during childbirth; clinical and cultural guidelines have been developed for doctors, midwives, nurses, and medical students to guide treatment (Nour, 2004; WHO, 2000, 2001a, 2001b, 2001c).

Prevalence and Attempts to End the Practice

According to WHO, FGM is practiced in 28 countries in western, eastern, and northeastern Africa; in parts of Asia and the Middle East; and within some immigrant communities in Europe and North America. Type I and Type II operations account for 85% of all FGM. Type III (infibulation) is common in Djibouti, Somalia, and Sudan and in parts of Egypt, Ethiopia, Kenya, Mali, Mauritania, Niger, Nigeria, and Senegal.

FGM is still predominantly performed by "traditional" female circumcisers (91% in Côte d'Ivoire, 95% in Eritrea, 88% in Mali). Typically, it is performed with sharp stones, broken glass, scissors, or unsterilized razor blades without anesthesia. Health providers (such as doctors, nurses, and midwives) are increasingly performing FGM. In Egypt, girls are three times more likely (54.8%) to have FGM done by health providers than did their mothers (17.3%). Although this trend might reduce the pain and/or the risk of infection, it will not prevent other complications (PATH, n.d.).

Global efforts to stop FGM are increasingly supported by various programs, human rights efforts, policy, and legislation (PATH, n.d.). The pace of efforts to eliminate the practice of FGM has picked up over the past 30 years, and although a decline has been evident, this has occurred at a slower rate than was hoped. Interventions have been poorly evaluated thus far to allow both international and national NGOs and governments to know where best to place their limited resources and prevent as many girls from undergoing the practice. The review conducted by PATH on behalf of the WHO looked at which anti-FGM interventions work and which do not (Donors Working Group on Female Genital Mutilation/Cutting, 2008; WHO, 1999, 2011a, 2011b). Interventions that worked included those that involved coordination between NGOs and governments. This has ensured that governments have begun their initial efforts in taking FGM as a serious health issue, evident with the introduction of anti-FGM laws although improvements in enforcement of these laws are required. Furthermore, at the community level, behavioral change interventions are proving to be successful, specifically that of communication for change projects and alternative passage rituals (coming-of-age ceremonies). Mass media through radio, music, storytelling, and poems has also encouraged the behavior change intervention approach. However, the assessment did show areas of weaknesses. Governments, although beginning to engage with anti-FGM programs, are not providing the financial and technical support required by the majority of agencies. Poor training for health care professionals in treating FGM means that many women and girls leave consultations without gaining all the information they need. Furthermore, certain community-level programs such as income for excisors and increased FGM awareness may be ineffective because they do not aim to change the cause of the practice—the "mental map." This mental map incorporates myths, beliefs, values, and codes of conduct that cause the whole community to view women's external genitalia as potentially dangerous and that, if not eliminated, has the power to negatively affect women who have not undergone FGM, their families, and their communities. Interventions were not developed using research-based evidence that could ensure the correct allocation of limited resources. Finally, and most important, the majority of anti-FGM interventions failed incorporate an evaluation program. This is crucial because interventions that work can be implemented by NGOs and governments worldwide, saving many women and girls from the practice (WHO, 1999, 2011a).

In more than 20 African countries, the Inter-African Committee on Traditional Practices (IAC) with the collaboration of local NGOs has launched an extensive educational campaign aimed at eliminating FGM. Women in Egypt and Sudan recommended education as the best means to end this practice. Various African NGOs are involved in research and eradication campaigns. These include the Comité National de Lutte contre la Pratique de l'Excision in Burkina Faso, the National Association of Nigerian Nurses and Midwives, the Maendeleo Ya Wanawake Organization in Kenya, the National Research Network in Senegal, the National Union of Eritrean Youth, and the Seventh Day Adventist Church in Kenya.

Technical assistance, advocacy, and funding are being provided by various national and international development agencies such as PATH, RAINBE (Research, Action, and Information Network for Bodily Integrity of Women), Equality Now, the Centre for Development and Population Activities (CEDPA), Population Council, Wallace Global Fund, and Women's International Network.

Education about the harmful effects of FGM and its illegality is provided to African immigrants in Australia, Canada, France, Holland, Norway, Sweden, the United Kingdom, and the United States. United Nations agencies (UNICEF/UNFPA/WHO, 1997, 2008b) issued a joint position paper and are increasing their efforts to eradicate FGM. WHO recently launched a 15-year strategy to accelerate these activities.

USAID recently reviewed its FGM programming and increased its support for FGM eradication programs by working with technical agencies such as PATH, RAINBE, International Center for Research on Women, CEDPA, the Focus Project, and the Population Council.

Attempts to End the Practice: Africa

The IAC is an NGO that seeks to change social values and raise consciousness toward eliminating FGM and other traditional practices that affect the health of women and children in Africa.

The "International Day of Zero Tolerance to Female Genital Mutilation" is a UN-sponsored awareness day that takes place February 6 each year. It is an effort to make the world aware of female genital mutilation and to promote its eradication. On February 6, 2003, Stella Obasanjo, the First Lady of Nigeria and spokesperson for the Campaign Against Female Genital Mutilation, made the official declaration on "Zero Tolerance to FGM" in Africa during a conference organized by the IAC. Then the UN Sub-Commission on Human Rights adopted this day as an international awareness day. (See the accompanying boxed text with the 2011 statement of UNFPA Executive Director Dr. Babatunde Osotimehin and UNICEF Executive Director Anthony Lake on International Day of Zero Tolerance to FGM/C.)

Statement by UNFPA Executive Director Dr. Babatunde Osotimehin and UNICEF Executive Director Anthony Lake on International Day of Zero Tolerance to FGM/C

NEW YORK, 6 February 2011 — All girls deserve to grow up free from harmful practices that endanger their health and well-being. But every year, three million women and girls in Africa alone face the prospect of female genital mutilation and cutting (FGM/C), a practice with serious immediate and long-term health effects and a clear violation of fundamental human rights. Worldwide, 100 to 140 million have already undergone the practice.

In Africa, communities are coming together to put an end to FGM/C. Through a joint program UNFPA and UNICEF are working to support their efforts. Governments, non-governmental organizations, religious leaders, and community groups are making real progress. Three years into the program, more than 6,000 communities in Ethiopia, Egypt, Kenya, Senegal, Burkina Faso, the Gambia, Guinea, and Somalia have already abandoned the practice. Social norms and cultural practices are changing, and communities are uniting to protect the rights of girls.

To mark the International Day of Zero Tolerance to Female Genital Mutilation/Cutting, we are renewing our own commitment to put an end to FGM/C. We call on the global community to join us in this critical effort. Together, we can abolish FGM/C in one generation and help millions of girls and women to live healthier, fuller lives.

Since the beginning of this century, a downward trend in the percent of women cut in some countries indicates that abandonment of FGM/C seems to be taking hold, although in others, there still is little or no apparent change.

Nonpracticing Countries: Policies, Legislation

In industrialized countries, genital mutilation occurs predominantly among immigrants from countries where mutilation is practiced. It has been reported in Austria, Australia, Canada, Denmark, France, Italy, the Netherlands, Sweden, the United Kingdom, and the United States. Girls or female infants living in industrialized countries are sometimes operated illegally by doctors from their own community who are resident there. More frequently, traditional practitioners are brought into the country or girls are sent abroad to be mutilated. No figures are available on how common the practice is among the populations of industrialized countries (Amnesty International, 1997). As Western governments became more aware of the practice, legislation was passed to make it a criminal offense, although enforcement may be a low priority.

Efforts in different countries are being made to support campaigns to end FGM. Amnesty International now has taken up the fight to do away with this practice that mutilates millions of girls each year. Today FGM is seen as a human rights issue and is recognized at an international level. FGM was in the universal framework for protection of human rights that was tabled in the 1958 United Nation agenda. It was during the UN Decade for Women (1975–1985) that a UN Working Group on Traditional Practices Affecting the Health of Women and Children was created. This group helped to develop the 1994 Plan of Action for the Elimination of Harmful Traditional Practices Affecting the Health of Women and Children. WHO, UNICEF, and UNFPA unveiled a plan in April 1997 that would bring about a major decline in FGM within 10 years and the complete eradication of the practice within three generations.

FGM IN EUROPE

As noted previously the practice of FGM is widespread in large parts of Africa, some countries in the Middle East, and in some parts of Asia and Latin America. The practice is also prevalent in the European Union (EU) among certain communities originally from places where FGM is practiced. The exact number of women and girls living with FGM in Europe is still unknown, although the European Parliament estimates that it is around 500,000 with another 180,000 women and girls at risk of being subjected to the practice each year.

The *Strategy for the European Union Institutions* (End FGM, 2009a) has been launched in the following six cities by local NGOs:

1. Lisbon, Portugal, February 8, 2010, by the Association of Family Planning
2. Vienna, Austria, February 17, 2010, by FGM-Hilfe (http://www.stopfgm.net)

3. Nicosia, Cyprus, February 24, 2010, by Mediterranean Institute of Gender Studies
4. Brussels, Belgium, March 4, 2010, by GAMS Belgium
5. London, United Kingdom, March 22, 2010, by FORWARD
6. A national-level launch held by AkiDwA and Amnesty International Ireland in Dublin, Ireland, February 4, 2010

This campaign contributes to an international mobilization that recognizes the need to join forces to end the practice of FGM. This international mobilization is illustrated by the adoption of the UN interagency statement (in 2008), the UNHCR guidance on FGM (in 2009), several calls by UN Special Procedures, and by treaty monitoring bodies. The creation of the Donors Working Group on Female Genital Mutilation/Cutting, of which the European Commission is a partner, contributes to it. This mobilization is also taking place at a national level within the EU with the development of National Action Plans on FGM in several Member States.

END FGM is led by Amnesty International Ireland, working in partnership with a number of organizations in EU Member States: FGM-HILFE in Austria, GAMS in Belgium, MIGS in Cyprus, Vantaan Nicehearts RY in Finland, GAMS in France, AkiDwA in Ireland, AIDOS in Italy, Moteru informacijos centras in Lithuania, FSAN in the Netherlands, APF in Portugal, Female Integrity in Sweden, and Forward in the United Kingdom. The action plans were developed as part of a Daphne project, financed by the European Commission, coordinated by Euronet-FGM and have been presented by NGOs to EU Member States and Norway in 2008–2009. New action plans were developed in eight countries: Austria, Denmark, Greece, Ireland, Portugal, UK, Germany, and Italy. Four countries already had plans (Belgium, France, Netherlands, Norway) but succeeded in raising the issue of FGM or providing new input to an existing plan (the Netherlands). At the final stage of the project (May 2009), Finland announced that it was going to develop a national action plan to prevent FGM. Sweden previously had an action plan, but it has expired and a follow-up has not yet been developed.

The campaign aims to put an end to FGM high on the EU agenda and to echo the voices of women and girls living with FGM and those at risk of it. The campaign advocates for the recognition of human rights and lobbies EU institutions to ensure that the EU adopts a comprehensive and coherent approach toward ending FGM (Ending Female Genital Mutilation. A Strategy for the European Union Institutions, 2009a, 2009b).

CONCLUSION

Action taken at international, regional, and national levels over the past decades to stop the practice of FGM has begun to bear fruit. Increasing numbers of women and men from groups that have condoned the practice in the past have begun to declare support for discontinuing it, and in several countries, the prevalence has decreased significantly. However, the reduction in prevalence is not as substantial as hoped for in many places, and in a few, no declines can be noted.

Several reviews and studies have helped improve our understanding of FGM and will allow us to address the emotional and physical needs of girls and women who have undergone this traditional practice or who are at risk for undergoing it. Such work will also support the development of community-oriented programs based on social theories that take society-building mechanisms into account and offer alternative rites and customs for the passage of girls into womanhood. Educational efforts considering the influence of FGM on women's and men's sexuality and health should be a priority, and economic aspects must also be taken into consideration.

REFERENCES

Adam, T., Bathija, H., Bishai, D., Bonnenfant, Y. T., Darwish, M., Huntington, D., & Johansen, E. (2010). Estimating the obstetric costs of female genital mutilation in six African countries. *Bulletin of the World Health Organization, 88,* 281–288. Retrieved from http://www.who.int/bulletin/volumes/88/4/09-064808.pdf

Adeneye, A. K., Oke, E. A., & Adeneye, A. A. (2009). Socio-economic factors associated with the practice of female genital mutilation in Oyo State, Nigeria. *Journal on Female Genital Mutilation and Other Harmful Traditional Practices, 2(1),* 2–13.

Afrikanische Frauenorganisation in Wien. (2000). Die Anwendung der Female Genital Mutilation (FGM) bei MigrantInnen in Österreich (The application of FGM in migrants). Retrieved from http://vgarchiv.orf.at

Amnesty International. (1997). *What is female genital mutilation?* Retrieved from http://www.amnesty.org/en/library/asset/ACT77/006/1997/en/3ed9f8e9-e984-11dd-8224-a709898295f2/act770061997en.html

African Medical Research and Education Foundation. (2011, August 17). AMREF's position on female genital mutiliation. Retrieved from http://amref.ichameleon.com/news/amref-position-statements/amref-position-on-female-genital-mutilation/

Bundesministerium für Gesundheit und Frauen. (2006). *Genitalverstümmelung in Österreich—eine Umfrage unter niedergelassenen Gynäkolog/inn/en und Kinderärzt/inn/en sowie unter Krankenanstalten.* Retrieved from http://www.unicef.at/fileadmin/medien/pdf/FGM_Studie_OE.pdf

Cohen, P. (1968). *Modern social theory.* London, England: Heinemann Books.

Cutner, W. (1985). Female genital mutilation. *Obstetrical & Gynecological Survey, 40,* 437–443.

Dejene, A., Kebede, A., Alemu, B., Gundenffa, A., & Hassen, F. (2009). Linking HIV/AIDS and harmful practices in Ethiopia. *Journal on Female Genital Mutilation and Other Harmful Traditional Practices, 2*(1), 14–26.

Donors Working Group on Female Genital Mutilation/Cutting. (2008). *Platform for Action towards the abandonment of female genital mutiliation/cutting (FGM/C).*

A matter of gender equality. Retrieved from http://www.fgm-cdonor.org/publications/dwg_platform_action.pdf

Elchalal, U., Ben-Ami, B., Gillis, R., & Brzezinski, A. (1997). Ritualistic female genital mutilation: Current status and future outlook. *Obstetrical & Gynecological Survey, 52,* 643–651.

End FGM. (2009a). *Ending female genital mutilation: A strategy for the European Union institutions.* Retrieved from http://www.endfgm.eu/content/assets/END_FGM_Final_Strategy.pdf

End FGM. (2009b). Executive summary. In *Ending female genital mutilation: A strategy for the European Union institutions.* Retrieved from http://www.endfgm.eu/content/assets/END_FGM_Final_Strategy_Summary.pdf

Foldès, P., Cuzin, B., & Andro, A. (2012). Reconstructive surgery after female genital mutilation: A prospective cohort study. *The Lancet, 380,* 134–141.

Gruenbaum, E. (2001). *The female circumcision controversy: An anthropological perspective.* Philadelphia: University of Pennsylvania Press.

Hirsi Ali, A. (2006). *Infidel.* New York, NY: Free Press.

Kent, S. K. (1999). *Gender and power in Britain, 1640–1990.* London, England: Routledge.

Krafft-Ebing, R. von (1886/1912). *Psychopathia Sexualis.* Berlin, Germany: Mathes & Seiz.

Momoh, C. (2005). *Female genital mutilation.* Abingdon, England: Radcliffe.

Nour, N. M. (2004). Female genital cutting: Clinical and cultural guidelines. *Obstetrics & Gynecology Survey, 59,* 272–279.

Nour, N. M. (2006). Urinary calculus associated with female genital cutting. *Obstetrics & Gynecology, 107,* 521–523.

Nour, N. M. (2008). Female genital cutting: A persisting practice. *Reviews in Obstetrics and Gynecology, 1,* 135–139.

Nour, N. M., Michels, K. B., & Bryant, A. E. (2006). Defibulation to treat female genital cutting: Effect on symptoms and sexual function. *Obstetrics & Gynecology, 108,* 55–60.

Population Reference Bureau. (2008). *Female genital mutilation/cutting: Data and trends.* Retrieved from http://www.prb.org/pdf08/fgm-wallchart.pdf

Program for Appropriate Technology in Health: Female Genital Mutilation—The Facts. (n.d.). Retrieved from http://www.path.org/files/FGM-The-Facts.htm

Ritzer, G. (2000). *Sociological theory* (4th ed.). Singapore: McGraw-Hill.

United Nations. (2011). *Top UN officials call for abolishing female genital mutilation.* Retrieved from http://www.un.org/apps/news/story.asp?Cr1=health&NewsID=37478&Cr=women

United Nations Children's Fund. (2005). *FCG—Female genital mutilation/cutting. A statistical exploration.* Retrieved from http://www.unicef.org/publications/files/FGM-C_final_10_October.pdf

United Nations Development Program/United Nations Population Fund/WHO/World Bank Special Programme of Research, Development and Research Training in Human Reproduction. (2010a). *Men's and women's perceptions of the relationship between female genital mutilation and women's sexuality in three communities in Egypt.* Retrieved from http://www.who.int/reproductivehealth/publications/fgm/rhr_hrp_10_17/en/index.html

United Nations Development Program/United Nations Population Fund/World Health Organization/World Bank Special Programme of Research, Development and Research Training in Human Reproduction. (2010b). *Dynamics of decision-making and change in the practice of female genital mutilation in the Gambia and Senegal.* Retrieved August 20, 2012, from http://www.who.int/reproductivehealth/publications/fgm/rhr_hrp_10_16/en/index.html

United Nations Development Program/United Nations Population Fund/World Health Organization/World Bank Special Programme of Research, Development and Research Training in Human Reproduction. (2011a). *Estimating the obstetric costs of female genital mutilation in six African countries. Research summary.* Retrieved from http://www.who.int/reproductivehealth/publications/fgm/rhr_11.17/en/index.html

United Nations Development Program/United Nations Population Fund/World Health Organization/World Bank Special Programme of Research, Development and Research Training in Human Reproduction. (2011b). Sociocultural motivations for female genital mutilation: Matrimonial strategies, family motivations and religious justifications among the Al Pulaar and the Soninké in the River Senegal Valley. Retrieved from http://www.who.int/reproductivehealth/publications/fgm/rhr_11_16/en/index.html

United Nations Population Fund. (2011). *Ending female genital mutilation/cutting.* Retrieved from http://www.unfpa.org/gender/practices3.html

Waris, D. (1998). *Desert flower.* New York, NY: William Morrow.

World Health Organization. (1995). *Classification of female genital mutilation (FGM).* Retrieved from http://www.who.int/reproductivehealth/topics/fgm/overview/en/index.html

World Health Organization. (1999). *Female genital mutilation: Programmes to date: what works and what doesn't. A review.* Retrieved from http://www.who.int/reproductivehealth/publications/fgm/wmh_99_5/en/index.html

World Health Organization. (2000). *Female genital mutilation: A handbook for frontline workers.* Retrieved from http://www.who.int/reproductivehealth/publications/fgm/fch_wmh_005/en/index.html

World Health Organization. (2001a). *Management of pregnancy, childbirth and the postpartum period in the presence of female genital mutilation.* Retrieved from http://www.who.int/reproductivehealth/publications/maternal_perinatal_health/RHR_01_13_/en/index.html

World Health Organization. (2001b). *Female genital mutilation: Integrating the prevention and the management of the health complications into the curricula of nursing and midwifery. Teacher's guide.* Retrieved from http://www.who.int/reproductivehealth/publications/fgm/RHR_01_16/en/index.html

World Health Organization. (2001c). *Female genital mutilation: Integrating the prevention and the management of the health complications into the curricula of nursing and midwifery. A student's guide.* Retrieved from http://www.who.int/reproductivehealth/publications/fgm/RHR_01_17/en/index.html

World Health Organization. (2008a). *Effects of female genital mutilation on childbirth in Africa.* Retrieved from http://www.who.int/reproductivehealth/publications/fgm/effect_of_fgm_on_childbirth_africa.pdf

World Health Organization. (2008b). *Eliminating female genital mutilation—An interagency statement—OHCHR, UNAIDS, UNDP, UNECA, UNESCO, UNFPA, UNHCR, UNICEF, UNIFEM.* Retrieved August 20, 2012, from http://www.who.int/reproductivehealth/publications/fgm/9789241596442/en/index.html

World Health Organization. (2010). *Global strategy to stop health-care providers from performing female genital mutilation UNFPA, UNHCR, UNICEF, UNIFEM, WHO, FIGO, ICN, MWIA, WCPA, WMA.* Retrieved from http://www.who.int/reproductivehealth/publications/fgm/rhr_10_9/en/index.html

World Health Organization. (2011a). *Female genital mutilation programmes to date: What works and what doesn't.* Retrieved from http://www.who.int/reproductivehealth/publications/fgm/rhr_11_36/en/index.html

World Health Organization. (2011b). *An update on WHO's work on female genital mutilation.* Retrieved from http://www.who.int/reproductivehealth/publications/fgm/rhr_11_18/en/index.html

World Health Organization. (2012). *Female genital mutilation. Fact Sheet No. 241.* Retrieved from http://www.who.int/mediacentre/factsheets/fs241/en/

World Health Organization. (n.d.-c). *Health complications of female genital mutilation.* Retrieved from http://www.who.int/reproductivehealth/topics/fgm/health_consequences_fgm/en/index.html

World Health Organization, Study Group on Female Genital Mutilation and Obstetric Outcome. (2006). Female genital mutilation and obstetric outcome: WHO collaborative prospective study in six African countries. *Lancet, 367,* 1835–1841. Retrieved from http://www.thelancet.com/journals/lancet/article/PIIS0140-6736(06)68805-3

World Health Organization, UNICEF, and UNFPA. (1997). *A joint WHO/UNICEF/UNFPA statement* (pp. 1–2). Geneva, Switzerland: World Health Organization.

World Health Organization/United Nations Population Fund. (2010). *Measuring sexual health: conceptual and practical considerations and related indicators.* Retrieved from http://www.who.int/reproductivehealth/publications/monitoring/who_rhr_10.12/en/index.html

Yoder, P. S., & Khan, S. (2008). Numbers of women circumcised in Africa: The production of a total. Calverton, MD: ORC Macro.

Yoder, P. S., & Mahy, M. (2001). *Female genital cutting in Guinea: Qualitative and quantitative research strategies* (DHS Analytical Studies No. 5). Calverton, MD: ORC Macro. Retrieved from http://pdf.usaid.gov/pdf_docs/PNACN178.pdf

Yoder, P. S., Abderrahim, N., & Zhuzhuni, A., (2004). *Female genital cutting in the demographic and health surveys: A critical and comparative analysis* (DHS Comparative Reports No. 7). Calverton, MD: ORC Macro. Retrieved from http://www.measuredhs.com/pubs/pdf/CR7/CR7.pdf

Chapter 8

Ending Child Trafficking as a Human Rights Priority: Applying the Spectrum of Prevention as a Conceptual Framework

Yvonne Rafferty

Human trafficking is regarded as a low-risk criminal enterprise and is one of the fastest growing and most lucrative criminal activities driven by its ability to generate immense profits with no real risk (Hill & Carey, 2010). It is the third most profitable criminal activity after illicit trade in drugs and arms, generating illicit profits estimated at U.S. $32 billion annually, with one-third generated in Asia (International Labour Organization [ILO], 2005). Trafficking for commercial sexual exploitation (CSE) is particularly lucrative and has been described as one of the most profitable illicit activities in the world (Kara, 2010). Unlike drugs or arms, children who are sold into sexual slavery can be sold over and over again, making huge profits for their traffickers, with the price the trafficker receives often portrayed as an agent's fee (End Child Prostitution and Trafficking International [ECPAT], 2008a; Hodge, 2008). This egregious crime has been described as one of the most pervasive and systematic human rights violations in the world today (Bump & Duncan, 2003; Inter-Parliamentary Union & United Nations Office of Drugs and Crime [IPU & UNODC], 2009).

Human trafficking is not a new phenomenon; it has existed for thousands of years (Laczko, 2005). The first known phase occurred during the latter half of the Middle Ages and the early Renaissance, when women and children from East Prussia, the Czech lands, Poland, Lithuania, Estonia, and Latvia were sold into the slave markets of Italy, southern France, and the Middle East. Later, after the Ottoman Empire conquered Constantinople, Western European countries turned to West Africa as a source of slaves (Laczko, 2005; Scarpa, 2006; Sychov, 2009). By the early 19th century, however, the European industrial revolution made trade in goods more profitable than the exploitation of colonies through slave labor (Sychov, 2009).

Although rape was also common during the 19th century, due to the belief that sexual intercourse could cure medical ailments, depression, and venereal disease (deMause, 1998), the first large-scale trafficking for CSE did not take place until the end of the 19th century when Chinese and Japanese women and girls were imported into Southeast Asia to provide sexual services to Chinese male migrant workers. Shortly thereafter, during the early 20th century, a new form of human trade emerged: known as "the white slave traffic," it consisted of the abduction of young girls and women for sexual and labor exploitation and was widespread around the world (Andrews, 2004; Doezema, 2000; Gozdziak & Collett, 2005; Scarpa, 2006; Sychov, 2009).

The next big wave of CSE coincided with the Vietnam War and the influx of American soldiers into Southeast Asia during the 1960s (Andrews, 2004; Kuo, 2000). The signing by the U.S. government of a "Rest and Recreation" agreement with Thailand in 1967 to promote the use of its country and its services to sustain the morale of the American soldiers tremendously influenced the development of an active sex industry in Southeast Asia and greatly contributed to the transformation of Thailand into the "Sexual Disneyland of the World" (Andrews, 2004; Kuo, 2000; Rho-Ng, 2000). Following the war, the development strategy of governments in Southeast Asia, who were left with the challenge of replacing the capital garnered from the brothels during the war, included the continued use of brothels and marketing strategies that contained the established stereotypes of Asian women and girls and the luring of wealthy foreign tourists (Kuo, 2000).

The rapid pace of urbanization and industrialization provided a significant population of relatively wealthy men eager to spend their money on the purchase of sexual services and as such, a surplus of brothels developed in commercial and residential neighborhoods (Schwartz, 2004). As the high demand from new clientele prospered during the middle of the 20th century, when large numbers of single young men with disposable incomes moved to Southeast Asia, children were increasingly being trafficked to meet the growing demand of clients in the sex industry. By 1987, 70% of foreign tourists to Thailand were single men (Andrews, 2004). Sex tour packages offering young, beautiful, and submissive girls at low rates became a foundation of the Thai, Cambodia, and Filipino tourism industries (Schwartz, 2004). During the 1990s, as a result of geopolitical changes (e.g., the end of the Cold War and the opening of borders in Europe and elsewhere), there was a sharp increase in the flow of undocumented migrants from the world's underdeveloped areas, some of whom fell into the clutches of human traffickers (Sychov, 2009).

The global enslavement of children today affects countless numbers of victims who are transported away from their homes across borders, or trafficked within their home countries, and treated as commodities to be bought, sold, and resold for criminal purposes, labor or sexual exploitation (Rafferty, in press). Sadly, efforts to combat this international shame are all too often inefficient and uncoordinated (UNODC, 2006). This chapter describes the scope of this modern-day slavery, including its trends, forms, and manifestations, as well as the challenges relating to the lack of reliable statistical data that captures its various dimensions. It also provides an overview of the United Nation's response, highlighting the international legal rights framework and the Recommended Principles and Guidelines on Human Rights and Human Trafficking. Finally, it introduces the Spectrum of Prevention as a viable theoretical framework to guide the development of research, policy, and practice.

KEY CONCEPTS AND SCOPE

Definition of Child Trafficking

The most widely endorsed definition of *trafficking in persons* is found in the Protocol to Prevent, Suppress, and Punish Trafficking in Persons, Especially Women and Children, Supplementing the UN Convention against Transnational Organized Crime (Article 3) (UN, 2000). Known as the Palermo Protocol or the Trafficking Protocol, it is the first international instrument to explicitly define human trafficking. It also aims to prevent and combat human trafficking, protect and assist victims, and promote cooperation among state parties. Notably, it has had the greatest impact on the wording of national laws that make it an offense to traffic human beings (Chase & Statham, 2005; IPU & UNODC, 2009; UNODC, 2006, 2008).

Trafficking in persons is defined in Article 3(a) as

> the recruitment, transportation, transfer, harbouring or receipt of persons, by means of the threat or use of force or other forms of coercion, of abduction, or fraud, of deception, of the abuse of power or of a position of vulnerability or of the giving or receiving of payments or benefits to achieve the consent of a person having control over another person, for the purpose of exploitation. Exploitation shall include, at a minimum, the exploitation or the prostitution of others

or other forms of sexual exploitation, forced labour or services, slavery or practices similar to slavery, servitude or the removal of organs.

The Palermo Protocol also distinguishes between trafficking in adults and children. Article 3(b) explains that "consent" is irrelevant where any of the means set forth in Article 3(a) have been used. It further stipulates (Article 3c) that because children cannot consent under international law, it is a case of trafficking if the victim is a child regardless of whether or not fraud and deception are used. The term *child* is defined by the Convention on the Rights of the Child (CRC), Article 1 (UN, 1989), as an individual under the age of 18.

Child Trafficking Versus Migration and Smuggling

Human trafficking and migration are distinct, yet related crimes differing in three areas: (a) the status of crime (illegal migration is a crime against the nation whereas human trafficking is a crime against an individual), (b) the method of crime (illegal migration is a voluntary act whereas human trafficking is an act of violence or deception whereby an individual becomes a victim of exploitation), and (c) the purpose of crime (an illegal migrant's desire to attain improved well-being whereas the purpose of human trafficking is sexual or labor exploitation of entrapped people; UNODC, 2010). In contrast to trafficking and migration, smuggling requires the crossing of borders and the illegal entry into a different nation; it does not involve an element of coercion because the participants are willing to be smuggled and no subsequent exploitation is intended (IPU & UNODC, 2009; Staiger, 2005).

Definition of Commercial Sexual Exploitation

The First World Congress against the Commercial Sexual Exploitation of Children, held in Stockholm in 1996, focused on the need to create awareness about and develop measures to combat the commercial sexual exploitation (CSE) of children (Andrews, 2004; World Congress, 1996). Participants reaffirmed their commitment to the CRC and pledged to commit themselves to a partnership against the CSE of children. A definition of the practice was also provided noting that the remuneration factor distinguishes the concept of CSE from sexual abuse in which commercial gain is apparently absent, although sexual exploitation is also abuse. The CSE of children includes pornography, juvenile prostitution, trafficking for sexual purposes, and international and national sex tourism.

Participants at the conference also unanimously adopted a Declaration and Agenda for Action, which recognized for the first time CSE as a human rights, labor, health, education, and law enforcement problem (Andrews,

2004; Mahler, 1997; World Congress, 1996). Progress made subsequent to the conference was later reviewed during the Second World Congress, held in Japan in 2001 (World Congress, 2001), and later, during the Third World Congress in Rio de Janeiro in 2008 (Dottridge, 2008; ECPAT, 2008b, 2009). During each review, the lessons learned and key challenges were reviewed, and participants committed themselves to the implementation of goals and targets of a Call for Action to prevent, prohibit and stop the sexual exploitation of children and adolescents, and to provide the necessary support to children who had fallen victim to it (ECPAT, 2008b).

Magnitude

Finding reliable statistics on the extent of human trafficking is virtually impossible; thus, the exact number of people who are trafficked annually worldwide is not known (Ezeilo, 2009; H. M. Smith, 2011). Available data are elusive, confusing, and unreliable in view of (a) the clandestine nature of trafficking; (b) the fact that it is a criminal activity and lawmakers and public officials find it difficult to acknowledge the magnitude of the problem; (c) uncoordinated data collection and statistics ridden with methodological problems making it hard to evaluate the validity and reliability of available data; and (d) the lack of precise, consistent, unambiguous, and standard operating definitions as to what constitutes the act of trafficking, trafficker, trafficked person, and child (Andrews, 2004; Arnold & Bertone, 2002; Gozdziak, 2008; Gozdziak & Collett, 2005; ILO, 2009a; IPU & UNODC, 2009; Laczko, 2002; Organization for Security and Cooperation in Europe (OSCE), 2010; UNODC, 2006).

Some definitions of child trafficking, for example, include all children and youth under the age of 18 who have been recruited to be exploited, whereas others include only those who have been moved from one place to another (Dottridge, 2008; Staiger, 2005). In the United States, for example, the Trafficking Victims Protection Act (TVPA) and its reauthorizations specifically define anyone under the age of 18 who is "induced to perform" a commercial sexual act as a victim of human trafficking and entitled to protection (U.S. Department of State, 2012). In addition, the phrases "commercial sexual exploitation of children" and "child sex trafficking" are used interchangeably. As noted by ECPAT (2012), "Neither force nor movement across countries, across state lines or even across the street are required for child trafficking under the definition of the TVPA" (p. 7). Finally, the data that are available are rarely disaggregated by gender and age. Despite these caveats and inconsistencies in reports, the most widely cited statistics are as follows.

- There are approximately 20.9 million victims of forced labor at any time, 25% of whom are below age 18 (5.5 million; ILO, 2012). In contrast with the earlier estimates, this number does not disaggregate victims of human trafficking. The ILO (2012) also reports that of the 20.9 million victims, (a) 14.2 million (68%) are victims of forced labor exploitation by individuals or enterprises in the private economy (e.g., construction, domestic work, manufacturing), with children under age 18 accounting for 27% of the total; 4.5 million (22%) are victims of forced sexual exploitation (98% are female), with children under age 18 accounting for 21% of the total; and 2.2 million (11%) are victims of state imposed forced labor (e.g., in prisons or in work imposed by the state military or by rebel armed forces), with children under age 18 accounting for 33% of the total.

- There are approximately 12.3 million adults and children in forced labor, bonded labor, and forced prostitution around the world (ILO, 2005, 2008a, 2009a).
- Out of 12.3 million forced labor victims worldwide, around 2.4 million were trafficked.
- There are approximately 2.4 million adults and children trafficked each year for forced labor and sexual exploitation (ILO, 2002, 2005, 2008a).
- There are approximately 1.2 million children trafficked globally each year for forced labor and sexual exploitation (ILO, 2002; 2008a; UNODC, 2009).
- Most victims were trafficked for sexual sexploitation. On the basis of a global assessment of human trafficking trends in 155 countries, the most prominent form of trafficking (accounting for 79% of the total) is for CSE (UNODC, 2009).
- The majority of trafficking victims identified are women and children who make up 88% of all victims (66% of victims are women, 13% girls, 9% boys, and 12% men; UNODC, 2009).

Regions

Human trafficking is a highly complex global phenomenon, with no region of the world free of the practice. It involves internal trafficking within the borders of a country as well as cross-border international trafficking; countries may be designated as source, transit, or destination countries or any combination of these (ILO, 2009a; IPU & UNODC, 2009; UNODC, 2009). Human trafficking affects people from 127 countries who are being exploited in 137 countries (UNODC, 2008, 2009). On the basis of its most recent estimate of forced labor, the ILO (2012) reported that the largest number of forced laborers are located in Asia and the Pacific region (which includes South Asia), with 56% of the total (11.7 million), followed by Africa with 18% of the total (3.7 million), and Latin America with 9% of the total (1.8 million; ILO, 2012).

Victim Characteristics

- **Gender.** The most powerful predictor of being trafficked as a child is being female (Staiger, 2005). All over the world, girls are particularly vulnerable to being trafficked into the sex trade (ILO, 2005, 2009a).
- **Age.** Additional risk factors include age, with girls between the ages of 12 and 16 years at greatest risk, although children as young as 6 years have been identified as being for sale (Dottridge, 2002). In the United States, pimps have recruited girls as young as age 12 for prostitution (Lloyd, 2011; Shared Hope, 2008). A 2010 survey of 47 Cambodian men in male-frequented establishments such as beer gardens and snooker clubs found that many local men (aged 19–59) reported that they prefer younger girls (Chan, 2010). In addition, a recent study conducted in the United States, which involved 218 men between the ages of 18 and 67 (mean age 33 years) who responded to an advertisement on the Internet, found that although many of the men who exploit children were not seeking adolescent females per se, almost half were willing to pay for sex with a young female when they knew for sure that she was an adolescent (Schapiro Group, 2010). In addition, the demand for virgins, or "clean girls," and the belief (especially on the African continent) that younger girls are "safer" as sex objects because they reduce the risks associated with HIV/AIDS, has led to an increase in the number of younger girls (aged 13 or younger) among trafficked victims (Dottridge, 2002; Hoot, Tadesse, & Abdella, 2006; Ireland, 1993; Lalor, 2004; Orchard, 2007; Snell, 2003).
- **Ethnicity.** Ethnic minority status has also been identified as a risk factor for child trafficking and CSE. Identified groups include gypsy; the Gakauz Turkic-speaking minority in the Republic of Moldova; children from the Roma communities; Burma's ethnic minority people, including Shans, Akha, Lisu, Lahu, and others; the T'ai Lue (Dai in Mandarin) from China's Yunnan district; and those who are refugees or stateless (Beyrer & Stachowiak, 2003; Gjermeni et al., 2008; UNICEF, 2009a).
- **Disability status.** Young girls with disabilities have been recruited in Russia by marriage and adoption agencies and are subsequently marketed to individuals with sexual fetishes involving various disabilities (Hughes, 2004).
- **Risk factors within the family setting.** A number of risk factors within the family setting increase children's vulnerability and place

them at higher risk of being trafficked. The African tradition of "confiding children"—that is, sending them to stay with other families to have the opportunity to receive an education in exchange for domestic work, for example—has been associated with determining children's vulnerability to being trafficked (Dottridge, 2002; Gozdziak, 2008; OSCE, 2010; Scarpa 2006). A number of children who had been trafficked in the United States, for example, had been sent to live with family members from other countries and ended up being trafficked (Gozdziak, 2008). Additional risk factors include inadequate family protection, such as impoverished and dysfunctional families, experience of violence or abuse, substance abuse, neglect, family breakdown, domestic violence, parents dying of HIV/AIDS, and interpersonal problems (Aghatise, 2004; Beyrer, 2001; Dottridge, 2006; Flowers, 2001; Gjermeni et al., 2008; Staiger, 2005; UNODC, 2009). Furthermore, children who have run away from home, in some cases fleeing abuse or neglect by their own parents, and are living on the streets, as well as those who are in "out-of-home" placements, including youth shelters, group homes, and foster care facilities, are at greater risk for becoming victims of trafficking (Boak, Karklina, & Kurova, 2003; Coy, 2009; Gjermeni et al., 2008; Ireland, 1993; Snell, 2003). In Ethiopia, for example, it is estimated that 28% of children who are living on the streets are engaged in prostitution (Hoot et al., 2006).

- **Migration.** Children who have migrated and are cut off from family and community have also been identified as being at an increased risk for trafficking (ILO, 2004; Lay & Papadopoulos, 2009; Zimmerman & Borland, 2009). Migration is attractive and promising to children, especially in rural areas, when they finish school at age 12 or 14 and confront scarce employment, extreme poverty, and a lack of any social protection and social security schemes (OSCE, 2010; UNICE, 2009a). In other cases, minors who have been trafficked had initially migrated from their homes to escape traumatic and abusive experiences within the family context or within relationships with boyfriends or fled their countries of origin because of persecution, armed conflict, and other violent threats or natural disasters (Laczko, 2005).

Facilitators

A range of individuals and groups contribute to the trafficking of children and include community members, private sectors, and organized criminal networks, with some cases involving family members and relatives (Farr, 2005). In some regions, traffickers recruit their prey through bogus or semilegitimate employment agencies, through fake advertisements in local newspapers, or through mail-order bride catalogues

(UNODC, 2006). Most children, however, are recruited by "family friends" or other casual acquaintances in the community, although some parents have knowingly sold their children to traffickers or brothel owners. Although most trafficking is done by men, some reports in Southeast Asia show a growing tendency for women who have returned from oversees to act as suppliers of children to those who will exploit them (Yunnan Province Women's Federation, 2002).

Those who facilitate the trafficking of children also include the men from industrialized and developing countries who add to the coffers of corrupt officials through their purchase, exploitation, and abuse of children (Malarek, 2009). Each year, foreign travelers from predominantly western countries visit developing nations where they purchase sexual services. The practice of "sex tourism" is now so widely acknowledged that the Oxford Dictionary added the phrase to its publication in 1998 (Andrews, 2004). A review of 160 foreigners arrested in Asia for sexual abuse of children between 1992 and 1994 showed that 25% came from the United States, followed by Germany (18%), Australia (14%), the United Kingdom (12%), and France (6%) (Arnvig, 1993). More recently, data on 240 foreigners who sexually abused children in Asian countries indicate that 25% came from the United States, followed by Germany (16%), the United Kingdom (13%), Australia (12%), and France and Japan (7% each) (Andrews 2004). Finally, the largest portion of foreign sex offenders against children in Thailand between 1995 and 2006 (31%) were identified as being Australian (The Protection Project, 2007).

Local demand for commercial sex with children, however, accounts for the majority of demand, a fact that is often overlooked. For example, 43 of 44 adults in Cambodia who entered the sex industry when they were minors indicated that their usual clients were Cambodian men, not foreigners (Chan, 2010). Additionally, the Coalition Against Trafficking in Women reports that 4.6 million Thai men regularly, and 500,000 foreign tourists annually, use prostituted women and girls; they also report that 90% of Southeast Asian men have visited a prostituted woman or girl at least once and that 60% are regulars (Hughes, Sporcic, Mendelsohn, & Chirgwin, 1999). Finally, in a study by Chan (2010), 13 of the 19 girls who reported that their first sexual intercourse was with a client reported that their virginity was sold to a Cambodian client.

Studies also indicate that social and cultural norms and area of residence plays a role. For example, 7% of men in Great Britain reported that they had purchased sex in contrast with 39% of the men in Spain and 73% of the men in Thailand, although caution is warranted due to the use of different research methodologies (Hughes, 2004; Yen, 2008). Chan (2010) found that the major reasons cited for purchasing sex included cheap and easily available sexual services, a form of male-bonding and male socializing, sexual needs, the nature of social relationships in

Cambodia (not favoring sex before marriage for women and strongly valuing a woman's virginity), and the role of peer pressure in pressuring men to prove their masculinity by visiting brothels.

A number of studies also describe the motivations, characteristics, and behaviors of the heterogeneous population of those who purchase sex. Abusers of both boys and girls through CSE are, for the most part, heterosexual men (Montgomery-Devlin, 2008). Only a small percentage is considered to be "pedophiles" from a clinical point of view (Andrews, 2004; Barnitz, 2001). In addition to male gender, studies have also identified the typical sex buyer as being about 30 years old, married, and employed full-time with no previous criminal record, although they come from all age groups and occupational backgrounds (Andrews, 2004; Barnitz, 2001; Staiger, 2005; Yen, 2008). More recently, Farley, MacLeod, Anderson, and Golding (2011) found that men who purchased sex more frequently were more likely to report having committed sexual aggression against women who were not being prostituted and to report a greater degree of acceptance of myths about prostitution.

In contrast with the heterogeneous population of sex buyers, data on those who pimp children and youth (those who make money through the sale of another for CSE) indicates that a substantial number meet clinical criteria to be classified as psychopaths, displaying the behaviors required on the Hare Psychopathy Checklist-Revised (i.e. cunning/manipulative, lack of remorse or guilt; Hare, 2003). For example, of 22 prisoners who were doing time for sexual trafficking, more than one-third was diagnosed as being a psychopath (Spidel et al., 2006). This highlights the concern for victims–it is hard for the girls to "break free" considering their psychological and emotional attachment to the pimp and fear of violent retaliation (Reid, 2008; Spidel et al., 2006). In some cases, traffickers/pimps manipulate victims' reality and contribute to their loss of identity; the pimps give the children a new name and brand them with their own symbol or name, usually with tattoos; girls and young women are frequently tattooed with the initials or street names of pimps. Marks also include gang symbols and dollar signs or other symbols for the money the girls earn for the pimp (Hughes, 2009).

Processes: Factors Associated with Recruitment and Retention

Once children have been trafficked, a number of psychological tactics of power and control, similar to those seen in situations involving domestic violence, are used to manipulate victims and ensure dependence (Hodge & Lietz, 2007). Traffickers use a variety of coercive methods designed to destroy their hostages' physical and psychological defenses, create dependency, and limit chances for escape (Rafferty, 2007, 2008). The basis of their strategy is to understand the psychology of youth and to apply these principles to successfully create and exploit the vulnerabilities of their victims. The trafficker/pimp identifies the child's needs (i.e. physical, psychological) and aims to fill them to make the child dependent on the trafficker/pimp (e.g., fulfilling the need of a parent or a place to sleep). In some cases, pimps use psychological theory (e.g., Maslow's Hierarchy of Needs) to manipulate and control their victims (Maslow, 1943).

By identifying gaps caused by past sexual abuse or family dysfunction, for example, the traffickers can strategically provide safety, security, love, and belonging to establish a "trauma bond" keeping the youth vulnerable to the pimp as a provider. They also discredit the youth's families, the public, and law enforcement. These strategies are similar to those used by cult leaders, referred to as "brainwashing." Once control of the girls has been achieved, they are often exploited into the sex industry where they have no control over the type or number of clients they are required to serve or the acts they are compelled to perform (Raymond, 2004). The power and control strategies that are used include isolation, manipulation, coercion, threats and violence (emotional, physical, and sexual; L. A. Smith, Vardaman, & Snow, 2009).

Impact on Children

When children are trafficked away from their families, communities, and support networks and are consequently isolated in areas unknown to them, they are extremely vulnerable to exploitation. Those who have been trafficked across international borders are even more disempowered because they do not speak the local language and are less able to escape or seek assistance. Young victims are dependent on their traffickers for food, shelter, and other basic necessities, and the degree of experienced violence can range from coercive strategies, such as physical and verbal threats, to extreme physical abuse or torturelike violence (Zimmerman & Bortland, 2009). As a result of these harsh conditions, as well as the trauma involved, children who have been trafficked and/or commercially sexually exploited experience numerous adverse outcomes including physical health problems (e.g., broken bones, burns, sexually transmitted infections, HIV/AIDS, and complications from unwanted pregnancies and unsafe abortions) and mental health problems (e.g., hopelessness, despair, suicidal ideation and attempts, anxiety disorders, low self-esteem, depression, and posttraumatic stress syndrome/disorder; cf., Rafferty, in press).

COMBATING CHILD TRAFFICKING: THE UN RESPONSE

The International Legal Rights Framework: UN Instruments

There is a broad institutional base within the UN to combat human trafficking (Ezeilo, 2009, 2011; Scarpa, 2006; Sychov, 2009). First and foremost is the Universal Declaration of Human Rights, proclaimed by the UN General Assembly in 1948, which sets out basic rights and freedoms to which all human beings are entitled, recognized that all human beings deserve equal treatment and respect, and laid the foundation for international human rights law (UN, 1948). Together with the International Covenant on Civil and Political Rights and its two Optional Protocols, as well as the International Covenant on Economic, Social and Cultural Rights and its Optional Protocol, it forms the so-called International Bill of Rights. Human rights law legally guarantees human rights by protecting human beings against actions that interfere with their dignity and fundamental freedoms; it also obligates Member States of the UN to preserve and protect human rights without distinction as to race, color, sex, language, religion, political or other opinion, national or social origin, property, birth or other status (UNFPA & UNICEF, 2011). In addition, a number of other international agreed commitments designed to combat human trafficking (briefly discussed below) are legally binding for States that are party to them.

(a) The UN Trafficking Protocol. The most important treaty dealing with human trafficking is the UN Protocol to Prevent, Suppress and Punish Trafficking in Persons, Especially Women and Children, supplementing the UN Convention Against Transnational Organized Crime, which was adopted in Palermo in 2000 (UN, 2000). Together with the Protocol against the Smuggling of Migrants by Land, Sea and Air, it supplements the UN Convention against Transnational Organized Crime. The Trafficking Protocol contains measures designed to prevent human trafficking, to protect victims, including by defending their internationally recognized human rights, and to prosecute and punish traffickers. It stresses that States Parties should consider adopting prevention policies, cooperating through the exchange of information, providing training for their officials, strengthening border controls, issuing travel or identity documents that cannot be easily falsified and verifying upon request by another State Party the validity of travel or identity documents suspected of being used in the trafficking of persons. It also provides for States Parties to criminalize trafficking in human beings and to punish the attempt to commit, take part in, or organize offences related to trafficking. Finally, it requires States Parties to protect the identity and privacy of trafficking victims, and to guarantee them physical, psychological, and social assistance, as well as the opportunity to find a job and to attend professional courses. It further emphasizes that, in granting assistance to and protection of trafficking victims, special attention should be paid to children, in particular insofar as this concerns housing, education, and care.

(b) The UN Convention on the Rights of the Child. The UN Convention on the Rights of the Child (CRC) is an international convention establishing the civil, political, economic, social, and cultural rights of children

(UN, 1989). Because trafficking is a serious violation of child rights (ILO, 2009a), the CRC is the main human rights treaty for the protection of children's rights, including all forms of abuse, violence, neglect, and exploitation and is the main reference as regards to the situation of children who have been trafficked. Articles 32, 35, 36, and 39, for example, indicate that child trafficking violates the human rights guaranteed to children under the CRC (UN, 1989). In addition, the CRC imposes obligations on governments to protect against CSE. Article 34, for example, requires States Parties to "protect the child from all forms of sexual exploitation and sexual abuse . . . unlawful sexual activity . . . prostitution or other unlawful sexual practices . . . pornographic performances and materials."

(c) Optional Protocol to the CRC on the Sale of Children, Child Prostitution and Child Pornography. An Optional Protocol to the CRC on the Sale of Children, Child Prostitution and Child Pornography, adopted in 2002, expands upon the CRC and outlines measures that States Parties need to take to protect children from trafficking, prostitution, and pornography (Cedrangolo, 2009; Scarpa, 2006). Article 3, for example, prohibits abuse associated with trafficking and calls on participating countries to criminalize certain offenses, including the domestic or transnational sale of minors committed by an individual or by an organized group for the purposes of sexual exploitation, removal or organs, forced labor, or illegal adoption. States must also take appropriate measures to protect the rights and interests of child victims. Articles 8, 9, and 10 provide for victims' assistance, prevention policies and international cooperation and coordination among states, international organizations, and NGOs. Finally, it requires States to "take all feasible measures" to ensure all appropriate assistance to children who are victims of offences mentioned in the Protocol, "including their full reintegration and their full physical and psychological recovery."

(d) ILO Convention Number 182 on the Worst Forms of Child Labour. ILO Convention No. 182 concerning the Prohibition and Immediate Action for the Elimination of the Worst Forms of Child Labour, which came into force in November 2000, requires States to prohibit the involvement of any child under age 18 in any of the worst forms of child labor (Dottridge, 2008; Scarpa, 2006). It targets such practices as the use of children in slavery, forced labor, trafficking, debt bondage, serfdom, prostitution, pornography, forced or compulsory recruitment for armed conflict, illicit activities, and various forms of hazardous work (defined as work that is likely to harm the health, safety, or morals of children). In determining the hazardous nature of work, nations are required to give special attention to activities that expose children to sexual, psychological, or physical abuse. It also considers "the sale and trafficking of children" and "the use, procuring, or offering of a child for prostitution, for the production of pornography, or for pornographic performances" as forms of slavery or practices similar to slavery to be eliminated as a matter of urgency.

(e) Convention on the Elimination of All Forms of Discrimination Against Women (CEDAW). The Convention on the Elimination of All Forms of Discrimination Against Women (UN, 1979), adopted in 1979, was the first international treaty to address trafficking from a human rights perspective (Scarpa, 2006; UNODC, 2009). It recognized that both CSE and trafficking in girls and women are forms of gender inequality and calls upon States Parties to "take appropriate measures to suppress all forms of traffic in women and exploitation of prostitution of women" (Article 6).

The adherence of Member States to other international and regional instruments relevant to the issue of trafficking in women and girls further strengthen the key international instruments discussed above. They include, for example, the Council of Europe Convention against Trafficking in Human Beings and the Convention on Preventing and Combating Trafficking in Women and Children for Prostitution adopted by the States members of the South Asian Association of Regional Cooperation. In addition, a number of other international conventions contain provisions that address human trafficking, including the 1949 Convention for the Suppression of the Traffic in Persons and of the Exploitation of the Prostitution of Others and the 1993 Hague Convention on Protection of Children and Co-operation in respect to Intercountry Adoption (cf. IPU & UNODC, 2009).

The International Human Rights Framework

Noting that human trafficking is an attack on the dignity and integrity of the individuals involved and constitutes a violation of human rights, the UN High Commission for Human Rights adopted an international "soft law" instrument in May 2002 to promote and facilitate an appropriate human rights–based perspective into national, regional, and international antitrafficking interventions, policies, and laws (Pillay, 2009). The "Recommended Principles and Guidelines on Human Rights and Human Trafficking," with 17 principles and 11 guidelines, are designed to provide practical, rights-based policy guidance on both the prevention of trafficking and the protection of victims; it also highlights the need for law enforcement, protection, empowerment, and participation of affected and at-risk children, their families, and communities (Ezeilo, 2009; Pillay, 2009; Scarpa, 2006; UNICEF, 2008)

The international human rights-based approach is a "person-centered" framework that places children at the center of all efforts to combat trafficking and recognizes their right to a remedy and prioritized prevention, assistance to victims, and an appropriate response for perpetrators. The best interests of the child must be a primary consideration in all actions concerning trafficked children, whether undertaken by public or private social welfare institutions, courts of law, administrative authorities, or legislative bodies. Thus, in addition to providing a strong national legal framework, an effective rights-based approach to child trafficking helps us to understand that the human rights embedded in treaties must be translated into services on the ground (Pillay, 2009).

INNOVATIVE STRATEGIES TO COMBAT CHILD TRAFFICKING AS A HUMAN RIGHTS PRIORITY

Conceptual Models

Child trafficking and CSE are preventable (Rafferty, in press). However, although a number of innovative strategies have been identified, they are often listed in the literature without a viable theoretical framework to guide the development of research, practice, and social policy. The Ecological Model (Bronfenbrenner, 1979) and the Spectrum of Prevention (Cohen & Swift, 1999), both of which have been endorsed and applied in a variety of disciplines including public health and community psychology, are presented here as viable options to guide the development of research, policy, and practice in these areas. Both models go beyond working at the level of the individual and emphasize efforts to change community, organizational, and social norms (Lee, Guy, Perry, Sniffen, & Mixsom, 2007).

(a) The ecological model emphasizes the relationship between people and their environment, rather than examining the characteristics of either in isolation. According to Bronfenbrenner (1979): "The ecology of human development involves the scientific study of the progressive, mutual accommodation between an active, growing human being and the changing properties of the immediate settings in which the developing person lives, as this process is affected by relations between these settings, and by the larger contexts in which the settings are embedded" (p. 21). It aims to identify potential prevention strategies on four levels: (1) individual (e.g., gender), (2) relationships (e.g., influence of parents, significant others), (3) community (e.g., social and cultural norms, traditional practices), and (4) societal (e.g., broad social forces such as gender inequalities and public policies; Heise, 1998). When applied to child trafficking and CSE, Bronfenbrenner's ecological framework might focus on (a) micro-level factors, including demographic characteristics of potential victims (e.g., gender, age, ethnicity, disability status) and other childhood experiences (e.g., risk factors within the family setting, out of home placement, migration); (b) exo-level factors, including the presence of sporting events, armed conflict, disasters; and (c) broader contextual factors at the macro-level including: (i) poverty and economic inequality; (ii) the lack of access to education, decent work, and an adequate standard of living; and (iii) gender-based discrimination that fuels inequality and the demand for CSE (e.g., cultural beliefs and practices; unequal access to education).

(b) The Spectrum of Prevention is a comprehensive strategy that delineates a systems approach to prevention practice. Activities are focused not only on individuals but also on their environments, such as through organizational practice and policy change (Davis, Parks, & Cohen, 2006). Spectrum strategies have been applied in communities to a variety of issues, including traffic safety, nutrition, physical activity, and violence prevention (Davis et al., 2006). The following section introduces the Spectrum of Prevention as a viable theoretical framework to guide the development of research, policy, and practice involving child trafficking and CSE.

The Spectrum of Prevention comprises six interrelated action levels of increasing scope and is designed to support developing comprehensive efforts on multiple levels: (1) strengthen individual knowledge and skills; (2) promote community education; (3) educate providers; (4) foster coalitions and networks; (5) change organizational practices; and (6) influence policy and legislation (Davis et al., 2006). Activities at each of these six levels have the potential to support each other and effectively combat child trafficking and CSE. For example, efforts to influence policy (Level 6) will have a better chance of being enacted when public awareness and support are garnered through education (Levels 1 and 2) and a variety of partners in different sectors are working to effect the desired change (Levels 3–5). The following section applies the model to the prevention of child trafficking and CSE. The literature reviewed included academic publication as well as governmental and nongovernmental reports.

THE SPECTRUM OF PREVENTION

Level 1: Strengthen Individual Knowledge and Skills

One crucial step to prevent trafficking and CSE is to increase the capacity of potential victims by providing them with essential personal resources to enhance their competencies within high-risk settings. This section focuses on two major strategies to reduce children's vulnerabilities to human trafficking.

1. Promote Empowerment Through Expanding Access to Education and Training

Communities that are known as "sending areas" typically suffer from inadequate educational opportunities as they push children into exploitative situations. Therefore, expanding access to education and training in high-risk communities is vital (Gjermeni et al., 2008; ILO, 2009b; UNICEF, 2009b). To address this identified need, a number of prevention strategies have focused on providing children with education and training to empower them when they confront the "real world," including the inducements that often precede trafficking.

In southern Albania, the prevention work of the Terre des Hommes Foundation and its partner Ndihmë për Fëmijët, known as Help the Children, focused on keeping ethnic minority children at school until the end of compulsory education (Dottridge, 2006). Specific strategies included the provision of material assistance in the home, educating members of the child's household with information about family involvement in the schools, providing remedial assistance to children who were failing, and persuading school directors to reintegrate children who had dropped out of school. In China, more than 40,000 middle school girls were trained on child protection issues, which were integrated into the education curricula. The training was designed to enhance girls' self-protection skills and to teach them how to look for jobs safely. Through participatory training involving simple practical stories and role-plays, girls were introduced to likely situations they could meet while job hunting and were taught how to deal with them. It also alerted girls to local or common trafficking schemes and offered them guidance on safely entering the labor market and responding to suspicious situations (Dottridge, 2008; UNICEF, 2009a). Finally, some innovative programs have incorporated education sessions and skills-building workshops to help change gender norms, improve communication in relationships, and empower girls and women in other ways (Kim et al., 2009; Mansson & Farnsveden 2012).

2. Enhance Competence Through Life Skills Development

The acquisition of life skills has been identified as being a vital tool to prevent trafficking (Dottridge, 2008; World Health Organization [WHO], 2009a). In one notable example, the Child Rights Information Centre (CRIC) initiated "Life Skills Education for the Prevention of Trafficking and Unemployment" in residential schools in the Republic of Moldova (Guzun, 2004). Children who had been placed in such facilities due to poverty, abandonment, abuse, or disability were targeted by ministries of education in some areas (e.g., throughout southeastern Europe) because previous research had identified them as being 10 times more vulnerable to human trafficking. Baseline surveys identified low levels of self-appreciation (15%), poor communication skills (67%), inadequate decision-making skills (70% of the girls and 62% of the boys), and inadequate conflict resolution skills (70% of the girls, 50% of the boys). On the basis of these findings, the program was modified based on student input (e.g., they requested a shift in emphasis from the dangers that children might face after leaving school to immediate issues such as acquiring skills in communication, teamwork, decision making, and conflict resolution).

A "Guide for Graduates" was developed for students in the final year of compulsory education (ages 15 and 16) that contained information on trafficking, advice on how to get a job, and contact details for officials responsible for child protection. Recognizing the importance of child participation (Blanchet-Cohen, 2009), students were involved in the development of the curriculum as well as peer-to-peer educators. One of the main findings from the evaluation of the intervention was that life skills education is an efficient method for preparing children and youth for independent life after graduation, and for the prevention of social risks and trafficking.

Level 2: Promote Community Education

Identifying specific segments of the general public and targeting them for awareness-raising, advocacy campaigns, outreach activities to raise knowledge of trafficking, and other prevention measures are essential components of any successful antitrafficking strategy; they can also be highly effective (OSCE, 2010). Community education aims to reach the population at large, or smaller groups of people in a particular setting; increase awareness; change attitudes; foster public support for healthier behavior, norms, and policy change; improve safety; prevent sexual violence; develop effective trafficking prevention strategies; and provide a context in which other strategies can succeed, such as public policy changes (Davis et al., 2006; Jernigan & Wright, 1996). Raising awareness of equality issues is also vital if communities are to learn to view girls as equal human beings instead of as a burden (ILO, 2009b). The following section highlights the importance of raising awareness for various groups.

1. Children Who Are Planning to Migrate

Because children who opted to leave home are often subsequently trafficked, migration has been identified as a key risk factor for human trafficking and other forms of exploitation. It is therefore important to increase the protection of these vulnerable children to enable them to better protect themselves (Flamm, 2010; Van de Glind, 2010). In one notable example, the Project for the Prevention of Adolescent Trafficking in Latvia (PPAT-Latvia), targeted youth between the ages of 14 and 25 and focused on providing education about the realities of migration. The ultimate goal was to empower potential migrants to make informed decisions "whether migrating for work is the best choice and, if so, how and when to go" (Boak et al., 2003). Program components included an outreach and education program, public service announcements during popular youth television programs, and career workshops.

Another project, the "Be Smart Be Safe Campaign," was designed to raise awareness among children and youth in Lao PDR based on research that had found young people were trafficked through brokers who specifically approached them in their villages, offering them attractive job opportunities in Thailand, where they were subsequently exploited (Chamberlain et al., 2004). This campaign used seven types of mediums to teach young people how to migrate safely and how to avoid being trafficked, including posters, leaflets, an emergency contact card, billboards displayed throughout the country, a radio drama, a karaoke CD, and a film titled "Lessons of Life."

The "Travel Smart, Work Smart Campaign" in the Greater Mekong Subregion of Southeast Asia, was designed to ensure safe migration to minimize the risks of migrants and their families from falling into the hands of traffickers (ILO, 2007a, 2009b). On the basis of multicountry research, guidelines were developed on decent migration recruitment practices and a training program on applying the guidelines. Midlevel government officials and workers' and employers' representatives were trained on ways to improve existing migrant recruitment systems. Materials included an easy-to-read informational booklet, which provided valuable guidelines on human rights, advice on staying safe, and helpful hotlines with information on where to go for help in Thailand.

2. Family and Community Members

Parents and other adults, who are sometimes involved in decisions that may place their children into the hands of a relative, friend, or intermediary to earn money elsewhere, should be empowered by providing them with information and knowledge and by pointing out the abuse their child may be subjected to if their child leaves home (Ezeilo, 2009; UNODC, 2008). Consequently, UN agencies have engaged in a number of awareness-raising and advocacy campaigns: the UN Interregional Crime and Justice Research Institute targeted political and religious leaders, public institutions, and the general public in various Member States including Costa Rica, Italy, Nigeria, and Ukraine; the UN Development Fund for Women has used alternative media and theatre for skill-building, research, awareness-raising, and advocacy; and the International Organization for Migration (IOM) has been actively involved in educating communities in both source and destination countries (Ban, 2008a). Nongovernmental organizations have also implemented a number of awareness raising campaigns using a variety of media strategies (Rafferty, under review).

3. Workers Who Are Likely to Come into Contact with Victims

Some examples have focused on community members who are likely to come into contact with potential victims of human trafficking while they are at work. For example, the Philippines Ports Authority personnel, the crew of shipping companies, port police, coast guard, and port workers were targeted for monthly awareness seminars based on evidence that traffickers use sea routes in the Philippines across the archipelago of more than 7,000 islands (Dottridge, 2008). Other innovative practices have involved community watch teams that report on activities in their areas, or informants (e.g., food vendors) at transport hubs such as bus and train stations, because places of transit are particularly dangerous for young migrants (Flamm, 2010).

4. Those Who Might Exploit Children Who Have Been Trafficked (Buyers/Facilitators)

There have also been attempts to target potential consumers, including those who might donate money to beggars who have been trafficked, and the men and boys who purchase sex from children who are being exploited, including those involved in armed conflict, as well as those attending high-risk events such as sporting events (Dottridge, 2006).

Some notable programs work with male peer groups as partners against gender-based violence, address attitudes and stereotypes associated with violence, and aim to engage men and boys in violence prevention programs (Eriksson, 2009; Instituto Promundo, 2012; WHO, 2009b; Yen, 2008). Eriksson (2009), for example, described how training and community mobilization have influenced men in Kenya to challenge unequal power relations between men and women. According to one program participant, "I discovered that cultural norms were designed by men to suit them and could be changed" (p. 22). Other key strategies include well-trained facilitators, community ownership of interventions, the concurrent use of a variety of methods and activities, adequate and sustained funding, and the support of high-level political decision makers (WHO, 2009c).

A study conducted in Latin America that focused on the male image and increasing awareness and behavioral change among men, showed a high tolerance of sexual exploitation of children among men of all educational levels, ages, social classes, and places of residences. Training and awareness-raising activities included participants from trade unions, law enforcement agencies, the military, public institutions, and NGOs. The results from this study were subsequently translated into a range of short briefing notes and targeted at a specific group, such as police officers, teachers, and migration officers highlighting the role that various stakeholders can play in the fight against the CSE of girls (ILO, 2007b).

Recognizing the need to focus on members of the armed forces and military recruits, some programs have targeted them for awareness-raising programs (Ban, 2008a). The UN Department of Peacekeeping Operations, for example, adopted a policy of zero tolerance for trafficking in 2003 and developed special training and awareness-raising materials for peacekeepers worldwide.

Some campaigns were organized in eastern Europe in areas with a strong military presence and were aimed at people visiting bars and at international peacekeepers. In the UN-Administered Province of Kosovo, for example, the IOM organized an information campaign about victims of trafficking, aimed principally at men from overseas who were working in the area. The campaign slogan was "You pay for her for a night: she pays with her life." In addition, the UN Interim Mission in Kosovo (UNMIK) developed a list of bars and premises where it was suspected that prostitution was occurring. These places were declared off-limits to individuals employed by UNMIK and to foreign military personnel. Although this strategy was aimed at curbing the demand for commercial sex in general, it is widely regarded as having led to a reduction in the numbers of women and girls trafficked into the area.

Finally, the implementation in a number of member states of programs for those who sexually exploit children (e.g., Johns' School) require men who are arrested for buying the services of women and children who have been prostituted to participate in an 8-hour seminar or face prosecution. Designed to educate and rehabilitate men who pay for sex from children and women who have been prostituted, programs typically consist of informational campaigns designed to promote behavior change and prevent further acts of violence (Andrews, 2004; Barnitz, 2001; Ban, 2008b; Yen, 2008). Topics include discussion of the harm of prostitution and trafficking and men's roles as catalysts for change. According to Barnitz (2001),

> Former victims educate offenders about how prostitution hurts women and children and how they place themselves and others at risk of deadly disease and violence by buying sex acts. Few offenders participating in the Johns' School have been rearrested for participation in prostitution. (p. 605)

Level 3: Educate Providers

It is essential that governmental and nongovernmental service providers receive appropriate education and training to ensure that they have adequate knowledge to ensure their own awareness and understanding of the issues. This section highlights some innovative strategies that have been designed to enhance knowledge among law enforcement personnel as well as teachers and other school-based personnel.

1. Provide Adequate Training to Law Enforcement Personnel to Foster Effective Coalitions and Networks for Demand

An effective response to combat demand will require States Parties to implement a number of strategies, including methods to ensure that relevant officials, such as police, border guards and immigration officials, are adequately trained in the identification of persons who have been trafficked, in confiscating assets connected to the crime, in understanding the rights of children, and in ensuring that remedial proceedings are not detrimental or prejudicial to the rights of persons who have been trafficked and their psychological and physical safety (Ezeilo, 2011).

In one notable example, UNODC launched "Affected for Life," an anti–human trafficking film primarily for use in the delivery of training to criminal justice actors, including prosecutors, judges, law enforcement officers, and other specialized audiences who have a key role to play in the fight against trafficking, but also to be shown more broadly as an awareness-raising tool for a wider audience. The film uses the testimonies of victims of human trafficking from all over the world and focuses on raising awareness of core concepts and issues regarding human trafficking (UNODC & Danish Doc Production, 2009).

Another notable example involves one of the key capacity building initiatives implemented by the UN Inter-Agency Project on Human Trafficking (UNIAP) over the past several years, the Regional Training Program (RTP), which was established as a core component of the Coordinated Mekong Ministerial Initiative against Trafficking (COMMIT). This antitrafficking collaboration mechanism, involving six governments within the Greater Mekong Subregion (Cambodia, China, Lao PDR, Myanmar, Thailand, Vietnam), was established in 2004 and receives broad support from a wide range of interagency partners, including UN agencies (e.g., IOM, ILO, UNICEF), NGOs (e.g., World Vision), donor organizations (e.g., the Asian Development Bank, and the Australian Government-funded Asia Regional Trafficking in Persons Project), intergovernmental organizations, and academic organizations. Project offices have been established in each of the GMS country capitals, with a regional headquarter in Bangkok, Thailand. The training program brings together government and law enforcement officials, members of judiciaries, NGOs, and victim support agencies three to four times a year for a weeklong training covering all aspects of the antitrafficking response (e.g., appropriate law enforcement responses, victim identification and support, and procedures for the identification, arrest, and detention of perpetrators).

2. Train Teachers and Other School Staff to Address Discriminatory and Sociocultural Attitudes Through School-Based Interventions

Breaking gender stereotypes requires educating teachers how the education system can be used to change discriminatory sociocultural attitudes that perpetuate women's subordinate status in society and promote a culture of human rights and gender equality (Ban, 2008b). A series of examples that have been implemented in a number of nations to address discriminatory attitudes include training teachers on gender equality, gender equality education, eliminating gender stereotypes from textbooks, and mainstreaming gender perspectives in teaching materials and strategies (Ban, 2008b). School-based interventions also aim to help students learn about different types of abuse, gender stereotypes, violence-related attitudes, and society's acceptance of violence against girls and women; they also attempt to address gender norms and attitudes early in life, before gender stereotypes become deeply ingrained (WHO, 2009a). Some programs include role-playing to help participants confront sexist attitudes and to actively prevent violence. Others aim to promote new ideas of masculinity based on nonviolence and respect for girls and women as well as how to confront peers who joke or boast about gender-based violence (WHO, 2009c). A number of countries have also promoted formal, nonformal and peer education as well as integrated relevant training into school curricula.

Level 4: Foster Coalitions and Networks

Coalitions, partnerships, and networks that bring together diverse sectors of society are vital for accomplishing a broad range of goals that reach beyond the capacity of any individual member of the group. By working together, partners can conserve resources, foster cooperation between diverse sectors, and enhance the impact of their efforts. The following section highlights four innovative strategies.

1. Promote Empowerment Through Economic and Social Cooperatives

One example worth noting is Apne Aap's self-help model (Apne Aap, 2011). Apne Aap mobilizes and mentors community-based groups of trafficked and vulnerable girls and women to empower each other by organizing them into small community-based economic and social cooperatives (self-help groups). Cooperatives are designed to empower women and girls in the red-light districts and slums through livelihood trainings, access to educational services, and legal protection to build their capacities to resist violence and all forms of exploitation. Apne Aap has registered 200 self-help groups of girls and women in slums and brothels in India; enrolled at least 1,000 children, especially daughters of women in prostitution into mainstream schools; provided recurring training to 2,000 adult females on enrolling and monitoring children in schools; and helped 3,000 girls and women open bank accounts and start savings. The groups have also advocated for a change in antitrafficking law, the punishment of buyers, and greater protection for women and girls. Finally, it publishes its own newspaper, *Red Light Dispatch,* which is written by girls and women in prostitution for their sisters who are survivors and victims.

2. Enhance Effectiveness Through Interagency Collaboration and Communication

One notable example involves the antitrafficking approaches and activities undertaken by a Swedish NGO, Kvinnoforum, that works with disadvantaged women and girls, in partnership with five NGOs in the Baltic Sea and Nordic Region following the substantial increase in human trafficking in Europe as a result of the fall of the Iron Curtain in 1989. The projects aim to combat trafficking through research, information, and networking to create awareness of the complexity of trafficking and the serious human rights violations that it involves (Wennerholm, 2002). Their first strategy was to survey NGOs, researchers, and governmental organizations and to conduct interviews with key informants. Informed by the findings, Kvinnoforum established a national and regional network around the Baltic Sea designed to counteract trafficking and support victims. A resource book was published which provided vital information for cross-border antitrafficking work. Collaboration was later expanded to include NGOs in Finland, Estonia, Latvia, Lithuania, Denmark, and Sweden. Training workshops were provided by NGOs involving civil society, police, and migration services.

Other noteworthy strategies to reinforce preventive and protection measures have focused on linking different agencies mandated to protect children from trafficking and providing a framework for a coordinated response through the establishment of National Referral Mechanisms (NRMs). This strategy helps to ensure adequate cooperation between agencies involved in anti-trafficking action at the national level and includes the establishment of either a National Committee or a National Coordinator for Combating Human Trafficking, or, as in the Republic of Moldova, a subgroup for combating child trafficking. So far, however, NRMs have not been particularly attentive to the issue of prevention and have been weak in coordinating prevention activities (Dottridge, 2006).

3. Foster Collaboration among Governmental Agencies and/or NGOs

There have been various examples of government agencies in areas of recruitment and areas of exploitation establishing direct contact and improving their impact as a result. The experience in southeastern Europe and other parts of the world, for example, suggests that efforts to prevent child trafficking have benefited enormously from coordination between the areas where children are recruited and those where the same children are exploited. Bilateral agreements/treaties that formalize cooperation between countries and bind them to provide legal assistance to one another are useful for intercountry cooperation (Andrews, 2004). The effectiveness of such agreements, however, is compromised if they fail to include clear protection standards for victims of trafficking. The 2006 signed agreement between Greece and Albania, for example, was the first such agreement to include standards for the protection of children, such as issuing residence permits to victims, referral of victims to competent officials, appointment of a temporary guardian, and individual case assessment in determining durable solutions (Gjermeni et al., 2008).

For several years the Stability Pact for South Eastern Europe Task Force on Trafficking in Human Beings worked systematically to encourage cooperation between nations. Another notable example was the relationship developed by the Terre des Hommes Foundation and Ndihmë për Fëmijët (NPF) in Albania and Association for Social Support of Youth in Greece. However, because there is also a large internal population movement, internal MOUs have been established between internal "sending" and "receiving" regions, and/or clearly defined responsibilities between government departments and/or NGOs. In Albania, for example, six NGOs set up a coalition in 2001 called së Bashku Kundër Trafikimit të Fëmijëve (BKTF), All Together against Child Trafficking. It had nine member NGOs by the end of 2003 that continue to work separately but have coordinated activities on several occasions, for example, responding in 2003 to a new government draft strategy on child trafficking.

4. Develop Effective Partnerships Through Interagency Collaboration and Communication

The UN Inter-Agency Project on Human Trafficking (UNIAP) was established in June 2000 to strengthen and coordinate the policy and operational responses to human trafficking within the Greater Mekong Subregion (GMS; discussed earlier). UNIAP's ability to liaise with both governments and NGOs is what makes it an exemplary model (ILO, 2008b). The overarching goal of UNIAP is to reduce the severity and harm associated with human trafficking in the GMS by identifying and filling gaps in program implementation, adding value to existing programs, and promoting a more coordinated response approach among regional and national actors. The project aims to achieve its goals through interlinking services such as coordination, technical assistance, capacity building, issue analysis, research, and advocacy, in addition to addressing new and emerging issues. Projects typically cover a range of initiatives to prevent and combat trafficking, including awareness-raising; training of law enforcement, judicial and other personnel; enhancing victim support and assistance; economically empowering women and girls; rehabilitating and reintegrating rescued victims; exchanging information and best practices; and conducting studies on the scope and nature of trafficking.

Level 5: Change Organizational Practices

The organizational practices of institutions, including law enforcement, schools, corporations, the media, social service agencies and health departments can have a substantial impact on well-being. The following section highlights several innovative strategies.

1. Social Responsibility for Corporations

Employers and businesses have a pivotal role to play in the fight against human trafficking. The revelation by the media of child labor in clothing and sportswear companies such as Nike, Gap, Primark, and others called attention to the use of children as young as seven or eight toiling for long hours and low wages to make products for global multinational firms (Crane & Kazmi, 2009).

In one noteworthy example, the UN developed in 2011 the "Guiding Principles on Business and Human Rights: Implementing the United Nations 'Protect, Respect and Remedy' Framework," which was developed by the Special Representative of the Secretary-General on the issue of human rights and transnational corporations and other business enterprises (Ruggie, 2011). The "Guiding Principles" recognizes States' obligations to respect, protect, and fulfill human rights and to ensure that business enterprises comply with all applicable laws to respect human rights. It further requires States to take appropriate steps to prevent, investigate, punish, and redress such abuse through effective policies, legislation, regulations, and adjudication.

A second notable example is the work of the UN Global Initiative to Fight Human Trafficking (UN-GIFT), which was launched in 2007 by UNODC, in partnership with a number of UN organizations and agencies involved with human trafficking at the UN (e.g., the ILO, UNICEF, the Office of the UN High Commissioner for Human Rights, the Organization for Security and Cooperation in Europe (OSED), the IOM, and the Vienna Forum to Fight Human Trafficking). The major goals of UN-GIFT are to increase global awareness of trafficking; to deepen understanding of the crisis by improving data collection, analysis, sharing of knowledge and joint research initiatives; and to provide technical assistance to countries through the development of practical tools and manuals that are made available on their website (UN-GIFT, 2010).

The UN-GIFT website (www.ungift.org) contains a database of good practices with regard to corporate social responsibility, including the International Cocoa Initiative, which aims to eliminate child and forced labor in the West African cocoa sector; Manpower Inc., which aims to prevent the forced recruitment of children by illegal armed groups by enacting training and employment opportunities for potential victims; Public

Private Partnerships, which bring together representatives of the private section, governments, and NGOs in India to collectively provide rehabilitation programs to survivors of trafficking as well as prevention activities for those who are vulnerable.

2. Codes of Conduct for the Tourism Industry

A number of regulatory mechanisms, such as codes of conduct are increasingly being drawn up and adopted by the business community to prevent and mitigate child sex trafficking, as well as encourage a responsible, child-wise tourism industry (Ban, 2008a; Dottridge, 2008). The Code of Conduct for the Protection of Children from Sexual Exploitation in Travel and Tourism, created by ECPAT-Sweden in 1998, has been signed by more than 1,000 travel industry members across the world, including tour operators, hotels, travel agents, and airlines, for example. It is the only internationally accepted tool that sets a standard of responsible business practices to effectively crack down on the sexual exploitation of children. It engages the tourism industry to commit to and implement standards along the entire supply chain and to engage travelers. Codes of conduct, and other value statements, provide potential customers with a clear indication of what the company stands for as well as promoting awareness about child trafficking. Members adopting the code agree to establish an ethical policy regarding CSE, to train the personnel (e.g., Accor trained 13,000 employees in 34 countries), to include a clause in contracts with suppliers, stating a common repudiation of CSE, and to provide information to "key persons" at the destination (e.g., Accor displayed ECPAT campaign materials in its hotels to raise awareness amongst guests).

Level 6: Influence Policy and Legislation

Because institutional and legal policies and legislation can affect large numbers of people, influencing policy often presents a vital opportunity for substantial improvement in outcomes. The following section highlights three major policy changes that must be developed, implemented, and enforced to effectively end child trafficking as a human rights violation.

1. Implement a Human Rights-Based Approach to Prosecution of Traffickers and Their Associates

The most effective way to alleviate factors that make child trafficking and CSE possible is to combat the demand from employers, consumers and sex buyers, and other intermediaries involved in the process. As noted earlier, international law, particularly human rights law, requires States to criminalize trafficking and related offenses. Unfortunately, traffickers and their accomplices are seldom investigated, prosecuted, convicted, and punished (Gallagher & Karlebach, 2011; U.S. Department of State, 2012). Key elements and standards of a rights-based approach to prosecution of trafficking cases include criminalization of trafficking, no criminalization of trafficked persons, protection and support for victim-witnesses, due diligence in investigations and prosecutions, rights of suspects and the right to a fair trial, proportionality in sanctions, trafficking related corruption, asset recovery, and international cooperation in investigations and prosecutions (Gallagher & Karlebach, 2011). Toward this end, States parties must ratify applicable international obligations, enforce laws, and prosecute traffickers in a timely manner (Rafferty, in press). In some cases, laws and policies already exist that could protect children and youth, but an additional law, change in policy, better enforcement, or change in an organization's practice (Level 5) may be necessary to ensure its effectiveness (Davis et al., 2006).

2. Create Development and Employment Opportunities

Poverty and inequality of resources and opportunities within and between countries create vulnerability to child trafficking and CSE through a number of related risk factors (ILO, 2009a; Shifman, 2003; Sychov, 2009). Indeed, most victims of human trafficking come from families in poor communities lacking in economic and job opportunities (ECPAT, 2008a; Farr, 2005).

Recognizing the need for development strategies through which families can earn enough to survive, a number of states have implemented measures to reduce poverty through empowerment strategies that focus on education and training, employment opportunities, and local economic development (Gjermeni et al., 2008; ILO, 2009b; UNIFEM, 2011). New skills, for example, enable youth to find a job and to earn an income in their own country. However, it does not resolve a more fundamental problem: the shortage of jobs in high-risk settings. Recognizing the need to coordinate vocational training with job openings, one promising practice in China focused on cross-sectoral linkages and networking and matched employers' demand for certain skills in those rural areas with affordable skills training for girls in the same areas (ILO, 2007b). Social protection measures that target families in poverty can also play an important role (ILO, 2009b). Cash transfer programs, for example, are being effectively used to target and support vulnerable families, improving children's prospects for education and access to health care (Concern Worldwide and Oxfam GB, 2011; ILO, 2009b).

3. Challenge Discriminatory Social and Cultural Norms

The vulnerability of those living in poverty is further heightened through cultural traditions and social norms that perpetuate stereotypic attitudes and discrimination toward girls and women and fuels inequality and demand for CSE (ECPAT, 2008a; IPU & UNICEF, 2005; Mahler, 1997; Rafferty, 2013). In many parts of the world, for example, educating girls is viewed as a wasted investment, and consequently, girls are less likely than boys to be enrolled in school (UNICEF, 2006). In addition, even when they attend school, discriminatory attitudes prevail (Levine, Lloyd, Greene, & Grown, 2009). In addition to being marginalized from education, young girls remain particularly vulnerable to trafficking as a result of gender development processes that marginalize them from job opportunities (e.g., the existing gendered division of labor and associated attributes that relegate women to the unpaid care economy and men to the productive public sphere; UNDAW, 2002; UNICEF, 2008). Finally, a number of cultural beliefs related to gender discrimination further compromise the vulnerability of the girl child. For example, a youth-led study of children in the red light areas of Kolkata, India, highlighted the vulnerability of children and the need for greater action and meaningful policy change (Bhattacharya, 2010). In addition, the practice of prostitution of girls and young women who are part of the Devadasi (servant/slave of the god) in India is socially, economically, and culturally embedded in their history of former temple servants, artists, and prostitutes, and it remains a culturally and economically valued form of "work"; approximately 1,000 to 10,000 young girls are inducted into the system annually (Orchard, 2007).

A number of innovative interventions that challenge cultural and social norms have been widely used (WHO, 2009b), although few have been subject to any kind of scientific evaluation (WHO, 2009c). As a result, the evidence base for their effectiveness is weak, and additional rigorous evaluations of such interventions are required (Blanchet-Cohen, 2009; WHO, 2009b). Despite these limitations, the following section highlights UNICEF's Equity Approach as an innovative strategy to combat gender-based social and economic inequality experienced by females of all ages worldwide, including unequal access to food, education, and health care, which limits the capabilities and prospects of women and girls for development.

For UNICEF, equity means that all children have fair access to livelihoods, health, education, security, and resources, including participation in the political and cultural life of their community (UNICEF, 2010). Equity for children is defined as equal opportunity to realize their human rights, to survive, develop, and reach their full potential, without discrimination, bias, or favoritism. An equity-based approach to child protection emphasizes child protection systems (laws, policies, and service provision) as well as societal factors, including social norms, and seeks to understand how the two intersect. The equity-based approach in UNICEF's programs and policies seeks to understand and address the root causes of inequity so that all children, particularly those who suffer the worst deprivations in society, have equal access to education, health care, sanitation, clean water, protection, and other services and resources that are vital for their survival, growth, and development. It is consistent with the CRC, which guarantees the fundamental rights of every child regardless of gender, race, religious beliefs, income, physical attributes, geographic location, or other status. A focus on equity addresses discrimination through attention to diversity and differences in background, culture, race, and ethnicity.

In summary, addressing gender discrimination faced by girls is crucial to their development and to the realization of their rights (UNFPA & UNICEF, 2011). Comprehensive measures to secure gender equality and protect human rights, in accordance with the international human rights framework, are also vital for the effective prevention and elimination of all forms of violence against girls and women (UN, 2008). In addition, since the trafficking of girls for CSE is rooted in gender politics, gender-based discrimination, and patriarchal structures that condone the commercialization of girls and women, there must be a strong commitment to changing prevailing attitudes and social norms. Social norms and cultural traditions manifest in our attitudes, beliefs, and standards, and are powerful influences in shaping behavior (Davis et al., 2006). Within the context of sexual violence, they include norms about women (limited roles for and objectification and oppression of women), power (value placed on claiming and maintaining power over someone else), violence (tolerance of aggression and attribution of blame to victims), masculinity (traditional constructs of manhood, including domination, control and risk taking), and privacy (notions of individual and family privacy that fosters secrecy and silence; Davis et al., 2006).

Discussion and Conclusions

In 2000, Kofi Annan, then secretary general of the United Nations, called on Member States to take decisive action to halt human trafficking: "The trafficking of persons, particularly women and children, for forced and exploitative labour, including for sexual exploitation, is one of the most egregious violations of human rights which the United Nations now confronts" (Annan, 2000). Eight years later, on the International Day for the Abolition of Slavery, Ban Ki-moon, subsequent secretary general of the UN, called for innovative strategies to "deal with this old curse" (Ban, 2008a).

International and domestic child trafficking violates human rights in a number of ways, including the right to liberty, the right to dignity and security of person, the right not to be held in slavery or involuntary servitude, the right to be free from cruel and inhumane treatment, various economic and social rights, and specific rights of the child. It is a complex issue that has been linked with pervasive poverty and inequality of resources and opportunities within and between countries, gender-based discrimination, and the unrelenting demand for cheap labor and sex with children (Dottridge, 2006; Kang, 2008). Although the Universal Declaration of Human Rights was adopted by the General Assembly 60 years ago as a common standard of dignity and rights that all human beings are entitled to, it was recently described as an "empty hope" for the millions every year in every corner of the world who become victims of human trafficking (Kang, 2008, p. 2).

To truly make a difference, governments must first and foremost acknowledge that child trafficking is a persistent and widespread human rights violation and that the factors that fuel it must be alleviated. By incorporating human rights principles into national strategies and fulfilling their human rights obligations, governments are more likely to be successful in combating child trafficking, as well as meeting the Millennium Development Goals (to reduce poverty, hunger, and disease and promote gender equality, education, environmental sustainability and global partnerships) and in realizing the UN Charter's vision of a more equal and just world. Interventions to address child trafficking and CSE must, however, also include effective prevention programs and a stronger commitment to ensure a protective environment for children.

This chapter has identified the Spectrum of Prevention as a viable theoretical framework to guide the development of policy, practice and research on child trafficking and CSE. This multisectorial approach is designed to tackle various levels concurrently. As noted earlier, improving the legal and institutional framework for the protection of children is crucial to preventing child trafficking effectively. In her address to the United Nations General Assembly Special Thematic Debate on Human Rights (June 3, 2008), for example, Ms. Kyung-wha Kang, Deputy High Commissioner for Human Rights, reminded attendees that "Traffickers are able to operate with impunity in the face of weak or ineffective law enforcement, which is compounded, in some cases, by official corruption and complicity" (p. 2).

Thus, specific strategies should focus on the development and implementation of specific legislation on human trafficking, the criminalization of the offense of trafficking, and the adherence to human rights in all legislative responses. Efforts to combat demand will be enhanced if they are combined with other actions. For example, law enforcement and prosecution agencies must work together effectively, both locally and across borders, to fight criminal organizations involved in human trafficking. In addition, facilitators, such as advertising agencies on the Internet advertising sex for sale and mail-order bride agencies, as well as all others who profit from exploiting children for commercial gain should be prosecuted vigorously when found to be facilitators of commercial sexual services. Finally, improving the legal and institutional framework for the protection of children will be substantially enhanced if combined with appropriate training programs and other activities designed to raise awareness of this heinous crime.

An effective response to child trafficking will also require addressing the complete range of vulnerabilities that render children susceptible to exploitation, abuse, and neglect, as well as ensuring that all forms of protection to which they are entitled be made available to them by government agencies, including social services, the police, and child protection teams. Effective action includes identifying gaps in existing systems that are supposed to protect children against abuse, whether these are government-run systems (e.g., police, immigration services or local government child protection committees) or community-based (e.g., NGOs and intergovernmental organizations). In addition to the vital need to protect children at risk of trafficking, it is also crucial to target potential victims and potential offenders to change their awareness and to encourage their participation in genuine structural change.

Because child trafficking also has a negative impact on sustainable development, strategies must aim to promote systemic improvements in granting girls equal access to education, health care, and control over economic resources and to advance youth employment for children of working age—particularly in rural areas (Van de Glind, 2010). Furthermore, government must focus on ensuring safe migration, rather than stopping it. Countries with higher rates of emigration have a responsibility to ensure that good advice and support is available for young people thinking of emigrating for work. Finally, businesses must also be involved. Their corporate social responsibility policies should be designed to ensure that children who have been trafficked do not work for them and to ensure effective remediation if child labor is detected. In addition, they can provide training on child labor and child trafficking within their businesses and with business partners, and support national efforts to prevent child trafficking.

In conclusion, effective action to prevent and combat child trafficking and CSE will require a comprehensive, multifaceted, international approach. This includes a focus on prevention and the prosecution of traffickers, the provision of information about victim support services and advocacy for the implementation of legislation and resolutions to eliminate trafficking and to prosecute traffickers, and the use of media strategies to increase awareness. Their future is in our hands.

REFERENCES

Aghatise, E. (2004). Trafficking for prostitution in Italy. *Violence Against Women, 10,* 1126–1155.

Andrews, S. (2004). U. S. domestic prosecution of the American international sex tourist: Efforts to protect children from sexual exploitation. *The Journal of Criminal Law & Criminology, 94,* 415–454.

Annan, K. (2000). *Address at the opening of the signing conference for the United Nations Convention Against Transnational Organized Crime,* Palermo, Italy.Retrieved from www.unodc.org/unodc/en/about-unodc/speeches/speech_2000-12-12_1.html

Apne Aap Women Worldwide: A Grassroots Movement to End Sex Trafficking. (2011). *Apne Aap Women Worldwide Commits at the Clinton Global Initiative.* Retrieved from http://apneaap.org/news/latest-news/apne-aap-women-worldwide-commits-clinton-global-initiatve

Arnold, C., & Bertone, A.M. (2002). Addressing the sex trade in Thailand: Some lessons learned from NGOs. Part I. *Gender Issues, 20,* 26–52.

Arnvig, E. (1993). Child prostitution in Cambodia: Did the UN look away? *International Children's Rights Monitor, 3,* 4–6.

Ban, K. (2008a, August 4). *Trafficking in women and girls: Report of the Secretary General to the 63rd Session of the General Assembly* [A/63/215]. Retrieved from www.un.org/womenwatch/daw/documents/ga63.htm

Ban, K. (2008b, August 4). *Intensification of efforts to eliminate all forms of violence against women: Report of the Secretary General to the 63rd Session of the General Assembly* [A/63/214]. Retrieved from http://daccess-dds-ny.un.org/doc/UNDOC/GEN/N08/449/55/PDF/N0844955.pdf?OpenElement

Barnitz, L. (2001). Effectively responding to the commercial sexual exploitation of children: A comprehensive approach to prevention, protection, and reintegration services. *Child Welfare, 80,* 597–610.

Beyrer, C. (2001). Shan women and girls and the sex industry in Southeast Asia: Political causes and human rights implications. *Social Science & Medicine, 53,* 543–550.

Beyrer, C., & Stachowiak, J. (2003). Health consequences of trafficking of women and girls in Southeast Asia. *Brown Journal of World Affairs, 10,* 105–117.

Bhattacharya, I. (2010). *Vulnerability of children living in the red light areas of Kolkota, India.* Kolkata, India: Sanlaap. Retrieved from www.ecpat.net/ei/Publications/CYP/YPP_Research_indial.pdf

Blanchet-Cohen, N. (2009). *Children, agency and violence: In and beyond the United Nations study on violence against children* (Innocenti Working Paper No. IDP –10). Florence, Italy: UNICEF, Innocenti Research Center. Retrieved from www.unicef-irc.org/publications/pdf/iwp_2009_10.pdf

Boak, A., Karklina, V., & Kurova, T. (2003). Preventing youth trafficking: Lessons learned from the project for the prevention of adolescent trafficking. In A. Boak, A. Boldosser, & O. Biu (Eds.), *Smooth flight: A guide to preventing youth trafficking* (pp. 40–49). New York: International Organization for Adolescents (IOFA).

Brofenbrenner, U. (1979). *The ecology of human development.* Cambridge, MA: Harvard University Press.

Bump, M. M., & Duncan, J. (2003). Conference on identifying and serving child victims of trafficking. *International Migration, 41,* 201–208.

Cedrangolo, U. (2009). *The optional protocol to the Convention on the Rights of the Child on the sale of children, child prostitution and child pornography and the jurisprudence of the Committee on the Rights of the Child* (Innocenti Working Paper No. 2003–03). Florence, Italy: UNICEF, Innocenti Research Centre. Retrieved from www.unicef-irc.org/publications/pdf/iwp_2009_03.pdf

Chamberlain, J., Phomsombath, P., Vangmua, V., Oudone, P., Vixaysak, T., & Chittanavanh, K. (2004). *Broken promises shattered dreams: A profile of child trafficking in the Lao PDR.* UNICEF & Ministry of Labour and Social Welfare, Lao, PDR. Retrieved from www.unicef.org/media/files/BrokenPromisesFULLREPORT.pdf

Chan, I. (2010). *Addressing local demand for commercial sex with children in Cambodia: A recommended strategy for ECPAT—Cambodia.* Retrieved from www.ecpatcambodia.org/documents/Research_on_Local_Demand_for_Commercial_Sex.pdf

Chase, E., & Statham, J. (2005). Commercial and sexual exploitation of children and young people in the United Kingdom: A review. *Child Abuse Review, 14,* 4–25. doi: 10.1002/car.881

Cohen, L., & Swift, S. (1999). The spectrum of prevention: Developing a comprehensive approach to injury prevention. *Injury Prevention, 5,* 203–207.

Concern Worldwide and Oxfam GB. (2011). *Walking the talk: Cash transfers and gender dynamics.* Retrieved from www.oxfam.org.uk/resources/policy/gender/downloads/rr-walking-the-talk-cash-transfers-gender-120511-en.pdf

Coy, M. (2009). "Moved around like bags of rubbish nobody wants": How multiple placement moves can make young women vulnerable to sexual exploitation. *Child Abuse Review, 18,* 254–266.

Crane, A., & Kazmi, B. A. (2009). Business and children: Mapping impacts, managing responsibility. *Journal of Business Ethics, 91,* 567–586. doi: 10.1007/s10551-009-0132-y

Davis, R., Parks, L. F., & Cohen, L. (2006). *Sexual violence and the spectrum of prevention: Towards a community solution.* Enola, PA: National Sexual Violence Resource Center. Retrieved from www.preventioninstitute.org/component/jlibrary/article/id-97/127.html

deMause, L. (1998). The history of child abuse. *Journal of Psychohistory, 25,* 216–236.

Doezema, J. (2000). Loose women or lost women? The re-emergence of the myth of "white slavery" in contemporary discourses of "trafficking in women." *Gender Issues, 18,* 23–50.

Dottridge, M. (2002). Trafficking in children in West and Central Africa. *Gender & Development, 10,* 38–42.

Dottridge, M. (2006). *Action to prevent child trafficking in South Eastern Europe. A preliminary assessment.* Geneva, Switzerland: UNICEF & Terre des Hommes. Retrieved from www.unicef.org/ceecis/Assessment_report_June_06.pdf

Dottridge, M. (2008). *Child trafficking for sexual purposes: A contribution of ECPAT International to the World Congress III against sexual exploitation of children and adolescents.* Rio de Janeiro, Brazil: ECPAT International. Retrieved from www.ecpat.net/WorldCongressIII/PDF/Publications/Trafficking/Thematic_Paper_Trafficking_ENG.pdf

End Child Prostitution and Trafficking International. (2008a). *Question and answer about the commercial sexual exploitation of children.* Bangkok, Thailand: Author. Retrieved from www.ecpat.net/ei/Publications/About_CSEC/FAQ_ENG_2008.pdf

End Child Prostitution and Trafficking International. (2008b). *The Rio de Janeiro declaration and call for action to prevent and stop sexual exploitation of children and adolescents.* World Congress against Sexual Exploitation of Children and Adolescents, Rio de Janeiro, Brazil. Retrieved from www.ecpat.net/WorldCongressIII/PDF/Outcome/WCIII_Outcome_Document_Final.pdf

End Child Prostitution and Trafficking International. (2009). *Report of the World Congress III against sexual exploitation of children & adolescents.* Bangkok, Thailand: Author. Retrieved from www.ecpat.net/WorldCongressIII/PDF/Publications/ECPATWCIIIReport_FINAL.pdf

End Child Prostitution and Trafficking International. (2012). NGO response to the periodic report of the United States of America to the UN Committee on the Rights of the Child concerning the optional protocol to the Convention on the Rights of the Child on the Sale of children, Child Prostitution and Child Pornography. Retrieved from http://ecpatusa.org/wp-content/uploads/2012/04/Alt-Report-USA-2012-Final-with-submitting-orgs -2-19-2012.pdf

Eriksson, A. (Ed.) (2009). *Defying the odds: Lessons learnt from men for gender equality now.* Nairobi, Kenya: Men for Gender Equality Now, African Women's Development and Communication Network (FEMNET), & United Nations Development Fund for Women (UNIFEM). Retrieved from www.peacewomen.org/assets/file/Resources/NGO/hr_mengenderequalitynow_eriksson_2009.pdf

Ezeilo, J. N. (2009, February 20). *Promotion and protection of all human rights, civil, political, economic, social and cultural rights, including the right to development.* Report submitted to the Human Rights Council by the Special Rapporteur on trafficking in persons, especially women and children. UN Doc. A/HRC/10/16. Retrieved from www2.ohchr.org/english/issues/trafficking/docs/HRC-10-16.pdf

Ezeilo, J. N. (2011, April 13). *Promotion and protection of all human rights, civil, political, economic, social and cultural rights, including the right to development.* Report of the Special Rapporteur on trafficking in persons, especially women and children submitted to the Human Rights Council by the Special Rapporteur on trafficking in persons, especially women and children. UN Doc. A/HRC/17/35. Retrieved from http://daccess-dds-ny.un.org/doc/UNDOC/GEN/G11/127/97/PDF/G1112797.pdf?OpenElement

Farley, M., MacLeod, J., Anderson, L., & Golding, J. M. (2011). Attitudes and social characteristics of men who buy sex in Scotland. *Psychological Trauma: Theory, Research, Practice, and Policy, 3,* 369–383. doi: 10.1037/a0022645

Farr, K. (2005). *Sex trafficking: The global market in women and children.* New York, NY: Worth.

Flamm, S. (2010). The linkage between migration and child labor: An international perspective. *Stanford Journal of International Relations, 12,* 15–25.

Flowers, R. B. (2001). The sex trade industry's worldwide exploitation of children. *Annals of the American Academy of Political and Social Science, 575,* 147–157.

Gallagher, A. T., & Karlebach, N. (2011). *Prosecution of trafficking in persons cases: Integrating a human rights-based approach in the administration of criminal justice.* Geneva, Switzerland: United Nations. Retrieved from http://works.bepress.com/cgi/viewcontent.cgi?article=1019&context=anne_gallagher

Gjermeni, E., Van Hook, M., Gjipali, S., Xhillari, L., Lungu, F. & Hazizi, A. (2008). Trafficking of children in Albania: Patterns of recruitment and reintegration. *Child Abuse & Neglect, 32,* 941–948.

Gozdziak, E. (2008). On challenges, dilemmas, and opportunities in studying trafficked children. *Anthropological Quarterly, 81,* 903–923.

Gozdziak, E. M., & Collett, E. A. (2005). Research on human trafficking in North America: A review of literature. *International Migration, 43*(1/2), 99–128.

Guzun, I. (Ed). (2004). *Life skills education for prevention of trafficking in human beings, evaluation report.* Chisinau, Moldova: Child Rights Information Center Moldova. Retrieved from www.crin.org/docs/resources/treaties/crc.40/GDD_2005_Moldova_Life_skills_in_institutions.pdf

Hare, R. D. (2003). *Manual for the Hare psychopathy checklist-revised* (2nd ed.). Toronto, ON: Multi-Health Systems.

Heise, L. (1998). Violence against women: An integrated, ecological framework. *Violence Against Women, 4,* 262–290.

Hill, A., & Carey, R. (2010). The trade in human lives. *Americas Quarterly, 4,* 84–89.

Hodge, D. R. (2008). Sexual trafficking in the United States: A domestic problem with transnational dimensions. *Social Work, 53,* 143–152.

Hodge, D. R., & Lietz, C. A. (2007). The international sexual trafficking of women and children: A review of the literature. *Affilia: Journal of Women and Social Work, 22,* 163–174.

Hoot, J., Tadesse, S., & Abdella, R. (2006). Voices seldom heard: Child prostitutes in Ethiopia. *Journal of Children & Poverty, 12,* 129–139.

Hughes, D. M. (2004). *Best practices to address the demand side of sex trafficking.* Retrieved from www.uri.edu/artsci/wms/hughes/demand_sex_trafficking.pdf

Hughes, D. M. (2009, August 10). *Tattoos of girls under pimp control and pimp rules for the control of victims.* Retrieved from http://citizensagainsttrafficking.com/uploads/Tattoos_and_Control_of_Victims.pdf

Hughes, D. M., Sporcic, L. J., Mendelsohn, N. Z., & Chirgwin, V. (1999). *The factbook on global sexual exploitation.* Coalition Against Trafficking in Women. Retrieved from www.catwinternational.org/factbook/Asia_Pacific.php

Instituto Promundo. (2012). *Engaging men to prevent gender-based violence. A multi-country intervention and impact evaluation study. Report for the UN Trust Fund.* Washington, DC: Promundo. Retrieved from http://www.promundo.org.br/wp-content/uploads/2012/04/UNT_Eng_10-1.pdf

International Labour Organization. (2002). *Every child counts: New global estimates on child labour.* Geneva, Switzerland: Author. Retrieved from www.ilo.org/ipecinfo/product/download.do?type=document&id=742

International Labour Organization. (2004). Strangers in a foreign land–Migration's hidden risk: Increased child trafficking. *World of Work, 50,* 17–18. Retrieved from www.ilo.org/global/publications/magazines-and-journals/world-of-work-magazine/articles/WCMS_081346/lang--en/index.htm

International Labour Organization. (2005). *A global alliance against forced labour: Global report under follow-up to the ILO declaration on fundamental principles and rights at work.* Geneva, Switzerland: Author. Retrieved from http://www.ilo.org/global/publications/books/WCMS_081882/lang--en/index.htm

International Labour Organization. (2007a). *Travel smart—work smart: A "smart" guide for migrant workers in Thailand.* Retrieved from www.ilo.org/public/english/region/asro/bangkok/child/trafficking/downloads/english-ts-ws.pdf

International Labour Organization. (2007b). *Guidelines on the design of direct action strategies to combat commercial sexual exploitation of children.* Geneva, Switzerland: Author. Retrieved from http://www.ilo.org/ipecinfo/product/viewProduct.do?productId=8270

International Labour Organization. (2008a). *ILO action against trafficking in human beings.* Geneva, Switzerland: Author. Retrieved from http://www.ilo.org/wcmsp5/groups/public/---ed_norm/---declaration/documents/publication/wcms_090356.pdf

International Labour Organization. (2008b). *Meeting the Challenge: Proven practices for human trafficking prevention in the Greater Mekong Sub-region*. International Labour Office, International Programme on the Elimination of Child Labour (IPEC). Geneva, Switzerland. Retrieved from http://www.ilo.org/public/english/region/asro/bangkok/child/trafficking/downloads/building-knowledge/meetingthechallenge.pdf

International Labour Organization. (2009a). *Training manual to fight trafficking in children for labour, sexual, and other forms of exploitation: Textbook 1: Understanding child trafficking*. Geneva, Switzerland: International Labour Office, International Programme on the Elimination of Child Labour (IPEC). Retrieved from http://www.ilo.org/ipecinfo/product/viewProduct.do?productId=10771

International Labour Organization. (2009b). *Training manual to fight trafficking in children for labour, sexual, and other forms of exploitation: Textbook 2: Action against child trafficking at policy and outreach levels*. International Labour Office, International Programme on the Elimination of Child Labour (IPEC). Geneva, Switzerland: Author. Retrieved from http://www.ilo.org/ipecinfo/product/viewProduct.do?productId=10772

International Labour Organization. (2012). ILO Global Estimate of Forced Labour 2012: Results and Methodology. Geneva, Switzerland: Author. Retrieved from www.ilo.org/sapfl/Informationresources/ILOPublications/WCMS_182004/lang--en/index.htm

Inter-Parliamentary Union and United Nations Children Fund. (2005). *Combating child trafficking: Handbook for parliamentarians, No. 9*. Retrieved from http://www.unicef.org/ceecis/IPU_combattingchildtrafficking_GB.pdf

IPU & UNODC: Inter-Parliamentary Union & the United Nations Office of Drugs and Crime. (2009). *Combating trafficking in persons: A handbook for parliamentarians*. Vienna: Austria: Author. Retrieved from http://www.unodc.org/documents/human-trafficking/UN_Handbook_engl_core_low.pdf

Ireland, K. (1993). Sexual exploitation of children and international travel and tourism. *Child Abuse Review, 2*, 263–270.

Jernigan, D. H., & Wright, P. A. (1996). Media advocacy: Lessons from community experiences. *J. Public Health Policy, 17*, 306–330.

Kang, K. (2008). Address of Ms. Kyung-wha Kang, Depute High Commissioner for Human Rights to the United Nations General Assembly Thematic Debate on Human Rights. Retrieved from http://www.un.org/ga/president/62/ThematicDebates/humantrafficking/unhcr.pdf

Kara, S. (2010). *Sex trafficking: Inside the business of modern slavery*. New York, NY: Columbia University Press.

Kim, J., Ferrari, G., Abramsky, T., Watts, C., Hargreaves, J., Morison, L., . . . Pronyk, P. (2009). Assessing the incremental benefits of combining health and economic interventions: Experiences from the IMAGE Study in rural South Africa. *Bulletin of the World Health Organization, 87*, 824–832. doi:10.2471/BLT.08.056580

Kuo, M. (2000). Asia's dirty secret. *Harvard International Review, 22*, 42–45.

Laczko, F. (2002, November). *Human trafficking: The need for better data*. Washington, DC: Migration Policy Institute. Retrieved from the Migration Information Source Website http://www.migrationinformation.org/Feature/display.cfm?ID=66

Laczko, F. (Ed.) (2005). Data and research on human trafficking: A global survey. Offprint of the *Special Issue of International Migration, 43*(1/2), 1–342.

Lalor, K. (2004). Child sexual abuse in Tanzania and Kenya. *Child Abuse & Neglect, 28,* 833–844. doi:10.1016/j.chiabu.2003.11.022

Lay, M., & Papadopoulos, I. (2009). Sexual maltreatment of unaccompanied asylum seeking minors from the Horn of Africa: A mixed method study focusing on vulnerability and prevention. *Child Abuse & Neglect, 33,* 728–738.

Lee, D. S., Guy, L., Perry, B., Sniffen, C. K., & Mixson, S. A. (2007). Sexual violence prevention. *The Prevention Researcher, 14,* 15–20.

Levine, R., Lloyd, C. B., Greene, M., & Grown, C. (2009). *Girls count: A global investment and action agenda.* Washington, DC: The Center for Global Development. Retrieved from http://www.coalitionforadolescentgirls.org/sites/default/files/Girls_Count_2009.pdf

Lloyd, R. (2011). *Girls like us: Fighting for a world where girls are not for sale, an activist finds her calling and heals herself.* New York, NY: HarperCollins.

Mahler, K. (1997). Global concerns for children's rights: The World Congress against sexual exploitation. *International Family Planning Perspectives, 23,* 79–84.

Malarek, V. (2009). *The Johns: Sex for sale and the men who buy it.* New York, NY: Arcade.

Mansson, A. N., & Farnsveden, U. (2012). *Gender and skills development: A Review.* (Background paper for the EFA global monitoring report, United National Girls' Education Initiative). Retrieved from http://www.ungei.org/resources/index_2943.html

Maslow, A. H. (1943). A theory of human motivation. *Psychological Review, 50,* 370–396.

Montgomery-Devlin, J. (2008). The sexual exploitation of children and young people in Northern Ireland: Overview from the Barnardo's Beyond the Shadow service. *Child Care in Practice, 14,* 381–400.

Orchard, T. R. (2007). Girl, woman, lover, mother: Towards a new understanding of child prostitution among young Devadasis in rural Karnataka, India. *Social Science & Medicine, 64,* 2379–2390.

Organization for Security and Cooperation in Europe. (2010). *Unprotected work, invisible exploitation: Trafficking for the purpose of domestic servitude.* Vienna, Austria: Author. Retrieved from www.childtrafficking.com/Docs/osce_10_unprotected_work_0411.pdf

Pillay, N. (2009, October 22). *Giving voice to the victims and survivors of human trafficking.* Conference—United Nations Office of the High Commission for Human Rights, New York, NY. Retrieved from http://www.unausa.org/page.aspx?pid=1674

The Protection Project. (2007). *International child sex tourism: Scope of the problem and comparative case studies.* Washington, DC: Johns Hopkins University. Retrieved from: www.protectionproject.org/wp-content/uploads/2010/09/JHU_Report.pdf

Rafferty, Y. (2007). Children for sale: Child trafficking in Southeast Asia. *Child Abuse Review, 16,* 401–422. doi: 10.1002/car.1009

Rafferty, Y. (2008). The impact of trafficking on children: Psychological and social policy perspectives. *Child Development Perspectives, 2,* 13–18.

Rafferty, Y. (in press). Child trafficking and commercial sexual exploitation: A review of promising prevention policies and programs. *American Journal of Orthopsychiatry.*

Rafferty, Y. (2013). International dimensions of discrimination and violence against girls: A human rights perspective. *Journal of International Women's Studies, 14,* 1–23.

Rafferty, Y. (2013). *The role of the media in protecting children from trafficking and commercial sexual exploitation.* Manuscript submitted for publication.

Raymond, J. G. (2004). Prostitution on demand. *Violence Against Women, 10,* 1156–1186.

Reid, J. (2008). *Rapid assessment of domestic minor sex trafficking in the Clearwater/Tampa Bay area.* Clearwater, FL: Shared Hope International. Retrieved from http://works.bepress.com/cgi/viewcontent.cgi?article=1001&context=joan_reid

Rho-Ng, E. (2000). The conscription of Asian sex slaves: Causes and effects of U.S. military sex colonialism in Thailand and the call to expand U.S. Asylum Law. *Asian Law Journal, 7,* 103–117.

Ruggie, J. (2011). *Report of the Special Representative of the Secretary-General on the issue of human rights and transnational corporations and other business enterprises, John Ruggie: Guiding Principles on Business and Human Rights: Implementing the United Nations "Protect, Respect and Remedy"* Framework. Retrieved from www.ohchr.org/Documents/Issues/Business/A-HRC-17-31_AEV.pdf

Scarpa, S. (2006). Child trafficking: International instruments to protect the most vulnerable victims. *Family Court Review, 44,* 429–437.

Schapiro Group. (2010). *Men who buy sex with adolescent girls: A scientific research study.* Atlanta, GA: Author. Retrieved from www.womensfundingnetwork.org/sites/wfnet.org/files/AFNAP/TheSchapiroGroupGeorgiaDemandStudy.pdf

Schwartz, A. (2004). Sex trafficking in Cambodia. *The Journal of Asian Law, 17,* 372–432. Retrieved from www.columbia.edu/cu/asiaweb/v17n2_371_Schwartz.html

Shared Hope International. (2008). *Demand: A comparative examination of sex tourism and trafficking in Jamaica, Japan, the Netherlands, and the United States.* Retrieved from http://www.sharedhope.org/Resources/DEMAND.aspx

Shifman, P. (2003). Trafficking and women's human rights in a globalized world: An interview by Pamela Shifman. *Gender and Development, 11,* 125–132.

Smith, H. M. (2011). Sex trafficking: Trends, challenges and the limitations of international law. *Human Rights Review, 12,* 271–286.

Smith, L. A., Vardaman, S.H., & Snow, M.A. (2009). *The national report on domestic minor sex trafficking: America's prostituted children.* Vancouver, WA: Shared Hope International. Retrieved from http://www.sharedhope.org/Portals/0/Documents/SHI_National_Report_on_DMST_2009.pdf

Snell, C. (2003). Commercial sexual exploitation of youth in South Africa. *Journal of Negro Education, 72,* 506–514.

Spidel, A., Greaves, C., Cooper, B. S., Hervé, H., Hare, R. D., & Yuille, J. C. (2006). The psychopath as pimp. *The Canadian Journal of Police and Security Services, 4,* 193–199.

Staiger, I. (2005). Trafficking in children for the purpose of sexual exploitation in the EU. *European Journal of Crime, Criminal Law and Criminal Justice, 13,* 603–624.

Sychov, A. (2009). *Human trafficking: A call for global action.* Stony Brook, NY: Globality Studies Journal. Retrieved from Stony Brook University, Institute for Global Studies website: http://globality.cc.stonybrook.edu/?p=114

United Nations. (1948). *The universal declaration of human rights.* Retrieved from www.un.org/en/documents/udhr/index.shtml

United Nations. (1979). *Convention on the elimination of all forms of discrimination against women.* Retrieved from www2.ohchr.org/english/law/cedaw.htm

United Nations. (1989). *Convention on the rights of the child.* Retrieved from www.unicef.org/crc

United Nations. (2000). *Protocol to prevent, suppress and punish trafficking in persons, especially women and children, supplementing the United Nations convention against transnational organized crime.* Retrieved from www.osce.org/odihr/19223

United Nations. (2008, August). *Intensification of efforts to eliminate all forms of violence against women: Report of the Secretary General* (A/63/214). Retrieved from http://daccess-dds-ny.un.org/doc/UNDOC/GEN/NO8/449/55/PDF/NO844955.pdf?OpenElement

United Nations Children Fund. (2006). *The state of the world's children 2007: Women and children—The double dividend of gender equality.* New York, NY: Author. Retrieved from http://www.unicef.org/publications/index_36587.html

United Nations Children Fund. (2008). *Child trafficking in Europe: A broad vision to put children first.* Florence, Italy: UNICEF Innocenti Research Center. Retrieved from http://www.unicef.at/fileadmin/medien/pdf/ct_in_europe_full.pdf

United Nations Children Fund. (2009a). *South Asia in action: Preventing and responding to child trafficking: Analysis of anti-trafficking initiatives in the region.* Florence, Italy: Innocenti Research Center. Retrieved from http://www.unicef-irc.org/publications/pdf/ii_ct_southasia_analysis.pdf

United Nations Children Fund. (2009b). *Reversing the trend: Child trafficking in East and South-East Asia.* Bangkok, Thailand: Author. Retrieved from www.unicef.gr/pdfs/Unicef_Trafficking_Report_Aug09.pdf

United Nations Children Fund. (2010). *Progress for children: Achieving the MDGs with equity* (No. 9). NY: Author. Retrieved from http://www.unicef.org/protection/Progress_for_Children-No.9_EN_081710.pdf

United Nations Development Fund for Women. (2011). *Investing in gender equality: Ending violence against women and girls.* Retrieved from http://www.endvawnow.org/uploads/browser/files/genderequality_vaw_leaflet_en_web.pdf

United Nations Division for the Advancement of Women & United Nations Office on Drugs and Crime. (2002, November). *Trafficking in women and girls.* Report of the Expert Group Meeting, Glen Cove, NY. Retrieved from http://www.un.org/womenwatch/daw/meetings/consult/CM-Dec03-CRP2.pdf

United Nations Global Initiative to Fight Human Trafficking. (2010). *Human trafficking and business: Good practices to prevent and combat human trafficking.* Retrieved from www.ilo.org/sapfl/Informationresources/NonILOpublications/WCMS_142722/lang--en/index.htm

United Nations Office of Drugs and Crime. (2006). *Trafficking in persons: Global Patterns.* Retrieved from http://www.unodc.org/documents/human-trafficking/HT-globalpatterns-en.pdf

United Nations Office of Drugs and Crime (2008). *Toolkit to combat trafficking in persons: Global programme against trafficking in human beings.* Vienna, Austria: Author. Retrieved from http://www.unodc.org/documents/human-trafficking/HT_Toolkit08_English.pdf

United Nations Office of Drugs and Crime. (2009). *Global report on trafficking in persons.* Retrieved from http://www.unodc.org/documents/human-trafficking/Global_Report_on_TIP.pdf

United Nations Office of Drugs and Crime & Danish Doc Production. (2009). *Affected for life: An anti-human trafficking training film.* Available from www.unodc.org/unodc/en/human-trafficking/2009/affected-for-life.html

United Nations Population Fund & United Nations Children Fund. (2011). *Women's and children's rights: Making the connection.* New York, NY: Author. Retrieved from http://www.unfpa.org/webdav/site/global/shared/documents/publications/2011/Women-Children_final.pdf

United States Department of State. (2012). *Trafficking in persons report 2012.* Retrieved from http://www.state.gov/g/tip/rls/tiprpt/2012/index.htm

Van de Glind, H. (2010). *Migration and child labour: Exploring child migrant vulnerabilities and those of children left behind* (working paper). Geneva, Switzerland: International Labour Office, International Programme on the Elimination of Child Labour (IPEC). Retrieved from http://www.ilo.org/ipecinfo/product/viewProduct.do?productId=14313

Wennerholm, C. J. (2002). Crossing borders and building bridges: The Baltic Region Networking Project. *Gender and Development, 10,* 10–19.

World Congress. (1996, August). *First World Congress against the commercial sexual exploitation of children.* Stockholm, Sweden. Retrieved from http://www.csecworldcongress.org/en/stockholm/index.htm

World Congress. (2001, December). *Second World Congress against commercial sexual exploitation of children.* Yokohama, Japan. Retrieved from http://www.csecworldcongress.org/en/yokohama/index.htm

World Health Organization. (2009a). *Violence prevention: The evidence: Preventing violence by developing life skills in children and adolescents.* Geneva, Switzerland: Author. Retrieved from http://whqlibdoc.who.int/publications/2009/9789241597838_eng.pdf

World Health Organization. (2009b). *Violence prevention: The evidence: Changing cultural and social norms that support violence.* Geneva, Switzerland: Author. Retrieved from http://whqlibdoc.who.int/publications/2009/9789241598330_eng.pdf

World Health Organization. (2009c). *Violence prevention: The evidence: Promoting gender equality to prevent violence against women.* Geneva, Switzerland: Author. Retrieved from http://whqlibdoc.who.int/publications/2009/9789241597883_eng.pdf

Yen, I. (2008). Of vice and men: A new approach to eradicating sex trafficking by reducing male demand through educational programs and abolitionist legislation. *Journal of Criminal Law & Criminology, 98,* 653–686.

Yunnan Province Women's Federation. (2002). *Yunnan Province, China–Situation of trafficking in children and women: A rapid assessment.* Bangkok, Thailand: ILO & IPEC. Retrieved from http://www.ilo.org/wcmsp5/groups/

public/---asia/---ro-bangkok/documents/publication/wcms_bk_pb_12_en.pdf

Zimmerman, C., & Borland, R. (Eds). (2009). *Caring for trafficked persons: Guidance for health providers.* Geneva, Switzerland: International Organization for Migration (IOM), London School for Hygiene and Tropical Medicine (LSHTM), and United Nations Global Initiative to Fight Trafficking in Persons (UN.GIFT). Retrieved from http://publications.iom.int/bookstore/free/CT_Handbook.pdf

Chapter 9

Cyberbullying among and against Girls, Female Adolescents, and Women: National and International Trends

June F. Chisholm

INTRODUCTION

Computers and other information communication technologies (ICTs; e.g., mobile phones such as Androids and iPhones; tablets such as the iPad, etc.) have created a global, interactive communication and social networking community via social networking sites that transcends personal, geographic, geopolitical, and socioeconomic boundaries (Blood, 2002). In 2005, there were more than 1 billion Internet users and 2 billion mobile phone users worldwide (Privetera & Campbell, 2009). Zizek (2004) argues that the social function of cyberspace in our society today is to bridge the gap between an individual's public symbolic identity and that identity's fantasmatic background. Ideas, fantasies, beliefs—all part of the inner world—are more readily and immediately projected into the public symbolic space. The technological phenomenon of the "screen," and the mechanics of its functioning, create a logic that has an impact on other spheres of psychological/social functioning of the user, especially for youth (Wallace, 1999).

ICTs continue to evolve, and unfortunately, cyberbullying persists into the second decade of the 21st century. Since the beginning of the new century, efforts to improve computer use by girls in schools and the ubiquitousness of cell phones has increased the number of females using ICTs (American Association of University Women, 2000; A. Smith & Williams, 2004). As female participation has increased in what had been considered a "male domain," gender differences in online behavior, including cyberbullying, have emerged.

Another area of increasing concern, stemming from a distinct but perhaps related social phenomenon as those associated with bullying and cyberbullying, has been the emergence of the "mean girl" phenomenon. In the late 1980s, much of the research on youth aggression and violence focused on physical violence (e.g., fighting, gang violence, school violence, shootings), primarily among male youth. In the late 1990s, the discourse shifted from physical violence primarily among boys to relational violence among girls, and from physical violence in real time to virtual violence in cyberspace. Researchers have referred to female bullying behavior as *relational aggression* (Mikel-Brown, 2003), social aggression (Underwood, 2003), or alternative aggression (Simmons, 2002) characterized by catty, vengeful, deceitful, manipulative, back-stabbing, or just plain mean-spirited behavior. Simmons (2002) referred to this as a *hidden culture of aggression* among girls. Ringrose (2006) wrote:

> This discourse of the new universal mean girl is distinctly postfeminist and works to re-establish the bounds of femininity disrupted by feminism. The dual dynamic of both fear and repudiation of feminism . . . is indicated by the enormous panic girls' aggression incites—because at the fault line of feminine repression is violent excess. We see the fear of the return of the repressed, the explosion of this meanness into something beyond repression. So while the mean girl's feminine lack re-affirms contemporary conditions of successful, adaptive but necessarily pathological femininity, the overtly aggressive girl is transgressive of both traditional norms of feminine passivity and the newer successful, mean girls. She is a deviant, whose qualities cannot easily be reconciled with the feminine. (p. 419)

Thus, this female phenomenon is seen as an outgrowth of and reaction to cultural expectations that distinguish between what are acceptable attitudes and behaviors for girls and boys based on gender, which impose structural–systemic inequitable distributions of power creating dominant (male)–subordinate (female) groups (Miller, 1976). These cultural beliefs about gender and how they manifest in social contexts are the basis for contemporary gender stereotypes about girls and female adolescents as being more communal in their relationships and males as being more instrumental and more agentic (Eagly, Wood, & Diekman, 2000; Ridgeway and Correll, 2004). Society, through parents, peers, social institutions, and the mass media encourage cooperation and emotional support among girls but competition, independence, and aggression among boys, albeit in ways, according to the relational perspective within psychology, that foster disconnections for both males and females (Jordan, Kaplan, Miller, Stiver, & Surrey, 1991; Miller, 1976; Robb, 2006).

Psychological perspectives on bullying and gender have traditionally emphasized explanations involving personal traits, or deficits in communication–interpersonal skills. Relational theory offers an alternative model for understanding violence in general and bullying in particular. From this perspective, the bully and the bullied are "in a relationship" characterized by disconnections (i.e., ways of engaging with the other that thwart emotional growth, healthy self-esteem, and reciprocal self-validation). The bully's stance conceals aspects of the self—his or her perceived vulnerabilities—that then inflate a pseudo-self-esteem. The inherent interactions associated with this stance paradoxically serve to protect the bully from experiencing the demands of a healthy, mutually satisfying relationship of sharing thoughts, feelings, hopes, and so on while enabling him or her to establish and maintain a disconnected–dysfunctional one. Relational theory refers to these disconnections as relational violations that cause "the relational paradox: trying to keep out of a relationship so that [one] can stay in it" (Robb, 2006, p. 304). These psychological perspectives offer insights into the motivations of some youth, both males and females, who cyberbully.

Youth and adults of both sexes who misuse or abuse ICTs continue to endanger the physical and psychological well-being of everyone; when a child, adolescent, or adult is targeted, the impact affects not just the bully and the bullied but ripples through their family, community, and institutions alike, undermining healthy functioning across domains from the micro (intrapersonal) to the macro (systemic) levels. Although there is no consensus on the estimates of the prevalence of cyberbullying nationally and internationally, a broader analysis, one that examines the complexities embedded in the impact of ICTs on culture and society, is much needed but difficult to research (Livingstone et al., 2011).

Patchin and Hinduja's (2010) findings are apropos; they found that both the cyberbully and those cyberbullied suffer from significantly lower levels of self-esteem, which compromises their academic and behavioral performance and adversely affects the climate of the school.

The social problems occurring in cyberspace are not limited to the United States. The scope of this phenomenon is international, involving many countries (Australia, Belgium, Brazil, Canada, Germany, Japan, New Zealand, Russia, Singapore, Scotland, the United Kingdom, and

Turkey, to name a few), affecting people all around the world from all walks of life (e.g., adults and children, men and women, rich and poor, privileged and disenfranchised). For example, Liau, Khoo, and Ang (2005) explored risky Internet behavior among adolescent Internet users in Singapore and found that those adolescents who were frequent users of the Internet (e.g., daily online activity) participated in chat rooms and online games, disclosed personal information online, and had face-to-face meetings with someone first encountered online. In Scotland and New Zealand, social problems have emerged with the increased use of cell phones, especially text messaging, to such an extent that some schools have banned mobile phones (A. Smith & Williams, 2004). Aricak et al (2008) found among Turkish secondary school students that more than a third of the 269 participants were exposed to cyberbullying; approximately one quarter were bullied through their cellphones. Livingstone et al. (2011) surveyed 25,000 children and their parents across 25 European countries and created a country classification based on children's online use and risk: (a) lower use, lower risk (e.g., Austria, Belgium, France, Germany, Greece, Italy, and Hungary), (b) lower use, some risk (e.g., Ireland, Portugal, Spain, Turkey), (3) higher use, some risk (e.g., Cyprus, Finland, the Netherlands, Poland, Slovenia, the UK), and (4) higher use, higher risk (e.g., Bulgaria, the Czech Republic, Denmark, Estonia, Lithuania, Norway, Romania, Sweden). The researchers noted: "A country's socioeconomic stratification, regulatory framework, technological infrastructure and educational system all shape children's online risks." They also pointed out that "at risk" does not necessarily mean "harmed by." These researchers found that the risk of being cyberbullied upset children the most when compared with the risks of exposure to sexual images, sexual messages, or meeting online contacts offline.

Within the past 15 years, a concerted effort by different agencies, organizations, and national and international groups has generated policies to promote cyberspace safety. The discussion in this chapter gives an overview of the definitions of cyberbullying and its impact on the psychological and physical well-being of children, adolescents, and young adults with an emphasis on gender distinctions, especially those discussed in feminist discourse on the meaning of the "mean girls" phenomenon; current research and future directions for research are discussed. It concludes with a review of policy recommendations and preventative strategies for promoting cyber safety to ensure the psychological well-being of children, adolescents, and young adults in our digital age.

Many youth today are more technologically sophisticated in their knowledge about how to use ICTs than are their parents, teachers, and other adults in their lives and use them regularly and frequently (Yan, 2006). This poses significant challenges for caregivers who are charged with guiding, supervising, and protecting youth, online as well as offline.

Indeed, a large-scale survey on adolescents and texting conducted by the Pew Internet and American Life Project (Pew Research Center, 2010) found that 75% of 12- to 17-year-olds own cell phones in the United States, and 72% of all adolescents (88% of cell phone users) use text messaging regularly; 75% of teenagers who use cell phones have service plans for unlimited text messaging, and 54% contact friends daily via text messaging (Lenhart, Madden, & MacGill, 2010; Underwood, Rosen, More, Ehrenreich, & Gentsch, 2012).

"Texting" is a common form of online social interaction among millennials (those who have come of age within the digital era; Pew Research Center, 2010). It consists of its own unique language, a text-based form of communication that helps to forge an identity of membership in a group and/or community. The following text message illustrates this: "lmao ur funny ill c u latr iight" translates into, " Laugh my ass off, you are funny I'll see you later, alright?" Users thus have a sense of belonging and are sensitive to signs of being included or excluded, valued, and criticized, for example. Research suggests that individuals who do not receive text messages when they expect to feel left out and dejected (Taylor & Harper, 2003).

Twitter, a popular free micro-blogging and social networking service that enables its users to send and read other users' updates known as *tweets*, illustrates another aspect of the psychological and social function of cyberspace. Tweeting has become so popular since it was created in 2006 that outages from traffic overloads have occurred. On August 6, 2009, Twitter suffered a denial-of-service attack, causing the website to be offline for several hours (Claburn, 2009). Advocates, youth and adults maintain that tweets allow busy people to keep in touch. Others, grappling with higher cell-phone bills and messages at odd hours from family, friends, and acquaintances telling them in 140 characters or less about mundane, trivial daily routines, are less positive about the phenomenon (Lavallee, 2007). Research examining the impact of Twitter on the psychological functioning of youth who use this technology is needed. The extent to which this technology is being used by cyberbullies needs to be explored. Researchers using macro-perspectives need to explore the ways in which this technology has become, in and of itself, the cyberbully, constantly bombarding or harassing our "collective" consciousness. Unlike oral communication or hardcopy written communication that over time becomes part of the past, all twitter messages, including "mean tweets" sent from March 2006 forward are being archived by the Library of Congress with the potential of haunting youthful "offenders" years into the future (Holladay, 2010).

Despite understanding the technical complexity of ICTs, research suggests that some youth do not fully comprehend the ramifications of some of the uses to which these technologies are applied, especially the complexities associated with social networking and communication (Yan, 2006). Concerns about the abuse and misuse of ICTs as well as the harmful effects on victims of some online activity have been discussed in the literature and researched in child and adolescent populations (Bruno, 2004; Cowie & Colliety, 2010; Wolak, Finklehor, Mitchell, & Ybarra, 2010). Little is known about cyberbullying and cyberstalking among college students or older adults aside from anecdotal accounts. College administrators and faculty are beginning to take note of the occurrence of cyberbullying and cyberstalking on campus; much more research with these populations is needed (Finn, 2004; Kraft & Wang, 2010).

CYBERBULLYING DEFINED

Cyberbullying is the intentional and repeated harm inflicted through the use of computers, cell phones, and other electronic devices (Kowalski & Limber, 2007; Patchin, Burges, & Hinduja, 2009, 2010). In some respects, it is similar to traditional bullying in terms of the characteristics outlined in the American Psychological Association (APA, 2004) document that include behaviors such as teasing, name-calling, social exclusion, and physical or sexual harassment directed toward individuals perceived to be "different" (e.g., members of "outgroups" such as sexual minorities, ethnic minorities, children and youth with disabilities).

Some research analyzing the differences between traditional bullying and cyberbullying suggest that cyberbullying is a variant of traditional bullying and associated more with children and adolescents (e.g., many victims know their online harasser; APA, 2004; Kowalski & Limber, 2007; Li, 2007; Snider, 2004). Others view cyberbullying as distinct from traditional bullying because of the unique psychological processes involved in cyberbullying and being cyberbullied (Beckerman & Nocero, 2003; Harris, Petrie, & Willoughby, 2002; Van der Wal, de Wit, & Hirasing, 2003; Willard, 2003; Ybarra & Mitchell, 2004a). Cyberstalking, defined similarly to cyberbullying, includes the ideas that these behaviors "would make a reasonable person afraid or concerned for their safety" and may involve criminal activity (Finn, 2004, p. 469). Cyberstalking is associated more with an older population (e.g., college students, adults).

More specifically, cyberbullying entails one or more of the following socially inappropriate online behaviors: harassing, humiliating, intimidating, sending derogatory insults or threats in messages, teasing, posting compromising and/or suggestive photos, using inappropriate language, and cheating. Harassment, for instance, consists of a range of activities including impersonating others online, posting defamatory or embarrassing personal information about others, physical and emotional abuse, stalking people online, and threatening violence (Menesini, Nocentini, & Calussi, 2011; Mitchell, Becker-Blease, & Finkelhor, 2005; P. K. Smith et al., 2008).

Examples of how cyberbullying differs from what is usually deemed to be bullying behavior include the following: (1) the rapid, extensive circulation and proliferation of threatening information or pictures to the targeted individual and simultaneously to a multitude of strangers online; (2) the practice of online "slamming" in which "bystanders" participate in the online harassment; (3) "flaming" (an antagonistic, "in-your-face" argumentative style of online communication used primarily, but not exclusively, by males); (4) cheating, forming roving gangs, and blocking entryways in games; and (5) shock trolling (usually offensive or superfluous posts or messages in an online community intentionally designed to anger, frustrate, and or humiliate someone to provoke a response; Annese & Jorgensen, 2012; Beran & Li, 2005; Espelage & Swearer, 2003; Fekkes, Pijpers, & Verloove-Vanhorick, 2005; Herring, 1994; Muir, 2005). (The latter is illustrated in the posting of offensive images and comments to the Staten Island, New York, family grieving the loss of their teenage daughter, Amanda Cummings, who committed suicide in January 2012 after having been cyberbullied.)

WHAT IS IT ABOUT ICTs THAT SEEMS TO PREDISPOSE SOME TO CYBERBULLY?

Anonymity and disinhibition are two characteristics that distinguish traditional bullying and other forms of harassment from cyberbullying–cyberstalking. Anonymity typically occurs with the creation of a screen name, an avatar, or both enabling the user to act out fantasies online without their real identity being disclosed. A normally withdrawn person can act out aggressions online that s/he would never express in public. I. Berson, Berson, and Ferron (2002) discussed the *culture of deception* and anonymity prevalent in online communication as serious concerns because they lead to disinhibition.

Online disinhibition refers to the loosening of psychological barriers that serve to block the release of innermost, private thoughts, feelings, and needs. In short, online social interactions can and often do change the way in which an individual generally self-discloses and self-creates. Parks and Floyd (1996) noted that youth tend not to think about the risks involved in disclosing personal information online. The effect of disinhibition may be benign or "toxic" contingent on whether the risk to explore aspects of one's self occurs in a safe online environment or on the "dark side" of the Internet in unsafe sites or in inappropriate ways. Millennials who spend a major segment of their day online in chat rooms, sending e-mails and instant messages (IMs), blogging, and playing online games (massively multiplayer online games—MMOGs) are vulnerable and at risk, albeit in different ways associated with their respective developmental and maturational processes and stage of development.

Suler's (2005) discussion of nine characteristics of cyberspace that may affect psychological functioning and predispose vulnerable individuals to act out online or be targeted for abuse supports Zizek's perspective. These characteristics include altered perception, equalized status, identity flexibility, media disruption, reduced sensation, social multiplicity, temporal flexibility, texting, and transcended space.

The following discussion of *identity flexibility, temporal flexibility,* and *texting,* elucidates the complexities of the interaction of these characteristics influencing the online behavior of millennials that, depending on one's perspective, promotes healthy online transactions with self and others or compromises it. Identity flexibility is a consequence of texting because of the lack of face-to-face cues and the sense of anonymity. Therefore, one has options with how they present themselves; that is, texting as a written form of communication, permits opportunities to experiment with self-expression (e.g., being younger or older, male or female, changing ethnicity, etc.) in a variety of cyberspace environments.

Cyberspace creates a unique temporal space and temporal flexibility in which the ongoing, interactive time together stretches out. During chats and IMs one has from several seconds to a minute or more to reply to the other person—a significantly longer delay than in face-to-face meetings. In e-mails, blogs, and newsgroups, one has hours, days, or even weeks to respond. This provides a convenient zone for reflection and/or for misunderstandings and festering negative emotions. Compared with face-to-face encounters, one has significantly more time to mull things over independent of nonverbal language cues from the other. The reduced social cues (RSC) model (Kiesler, Siegel, & McGuire, 1984) suggests that the lack of feedback about the affective component of communication could result in a deficiency in affective empathy and therefore contribute to the deregulated behavior of both boys and girls in cyberspace.

The consequences of cyberbullying can shift from the psychological to the physical, from cyberspace to a real physical location. For example, an 11-year-old Japanese girl fatally stabbed a classmate in the schoolyard after an intense online argument the night before (Nakamura, 2004). Nansel et al (2003) found that those students bullied outside of school online were more likely to carry a weapon to school. Slonje and Smith (2008) found that 25% of cyberbullies and their victims were identified as being from the same school. Hinduja and Patchin (2007, 2009) found that youth reporting problem offline behaviors (e.g., alcohol and drug use, cheating, truancy) were also cyberbullied.

Some cyberbullies, like their traditional counterparts, thrive on an audience of bystanders. The audience, witnessing the bullying as well as the behavior of the victim, makes the bully feel powerful. Unlike face-to-face bullying, because of the cyberbully's enhanced capacity to reach targets and bystanders with these technologies, the audience of bystanders to the cyberbully can range from a few to several hundred "friends" on MySpace or Facebook to several million on YouTube. Because the bully in cyberbullying bullies in cyberspace (i.e., is not physically and/or even temporally present) as is the case in traditional bullying, she or he has more ubiquitous and pernicious ways of reaching and hurting targets, anonymously, anytime, anywhere, and quickly. The technology allows for the effects of the bullying to spread quickly throughout the online community, greatly intensifying the pressure and experience of harm, humiliation, or exploitation for the victim as well as potential bystanders. Palfrey and Gasser (2008) stated,

> Though there is no fundamental change in what is occurring when the online world is the stage rather than the playground, there are differences in the way the impact is felt by the person attacked and by those who can observe its occurrence . . . a local dispute, carried out in online public spaces, can become an international news story. (p. 92)

The ultimate power cyberbullies have over their victims stems from the extent of their competence to use the technology and their ability to hide their identity online while engaged in this activity, not only escaping detection but also avoiding any responsibility and consequence for their actions (Patchin & Hinduja, 2006). Hence, the cyberbully can act anonymously with little to no fear of punishment, before a much larger audience, also anonymous and unimaginably huge, spanning continents, cultures, nationalities, as well as time.

GENDER DIFFERENCES IN CYBERBULLYING AND ONLINE BEHAVIOR

Research findings on gender differences in cyberbullying show some inconsistencies. Several studies in the United States and Sweden found that teenage girls are equally likely as boys to cyberbully or to be cyberbullied (Hinduja & Patchin, 2008; Slonje & Smith, 2008; Williams & Guerra, 2007; Ybarra & Mitchell, 2004a). A Canadian study observed no significant gender difference in victimization, although more boys were found to be perpetrators (Li, 2007). According to a Turkish study, boys are more involved in cyberbullying, both as perpetrators and as victims (Aricak et al., 2008). However, studies from the United Kingdom and the United States have concluded that girls are more likely to be victimized, and boys are more likely to perpetrate; furthermore, females are more likely bullied by females and males, whereas males are more likely bullied by males (APA, 2004; Chisholm, 2006; Dehue, Bolman, & Vollink, 2008; Kowalski & Limber, 2007; Li, 2007; Pellegrini & Long, 2002; Wright et al., 2009). There are studies that found no difference in the percentages of victims of cyberbullying by gender. However, clear qualitative differences across gender in the experience of being cyberbullied and in their emotional response to victimization have been noted (Burgess-Proctor, Patchin, & Hinduja, 2009; Chisholm, 2006; Dehue et al., 2008; Smith et al., 2008; Wang et al., 2009; Wright et al., 2009). Inexperienced, immature young men and women seeking companionship may tend to act inappropriately online.

Former undergraduate students in my course "Psychology of Women" gave me permission to use their online experiences that caused discomfort for them or others to illustrate what has been reported in the literature on gender differences with ICT misuse discussed earlier. Their comments follow.

Anecdote I

I went through all of middle school, and even all of high school, never once seeing or experiencing cyberbullying. I would watch Lifetime TV dramas depicting this apparent "epidemic" and think, "Wow, I must be really lucky!" Then, I went to college.

My first experience was relatively harmless. My college roommate chose to air her frustrations with me on her Internet blog. She was kind enough to leave my name out, referring to me as "roommate." At the end of a long letter expressing her frustration that I routinely annoyed her by staying up too late doing homework, she exclaimed, "I am not talking to you at all tomorrow, maybe then you will get the message." I was shocked and upset, because my roommate never said anything to me about how my habits bothered her. I would offer to move to the library at night, but she would always tell me to stay, that it was "fine." I wanted to talk to her about the issue but felt so embarrassed by it. I wrote her a letter, apologizing for keeping her up but also requesting that any future problems be brought to me in person so we could discuss it as two adults. She never acknowledged the letter, or the blog. She rarely talked to me at all for the remainder of the year. Fortunately, my experience with all roommates since then has been wonderful. And compared with some of the other roommate stories I have heard, mine seems pretty bearable.

My second experience dwarfs the first, but I guess it would have to because it involves an ex-boyfriend, and romance is nothing if not a catalyst for drama. Before I explain what happened, it needs to be mentioned that the man, and I use that term loosely, who did this was 22 years old. He was college educated and even employed with a major company earning a decent salary for someone his age. After we broke up, he, for some reason, chose to post a fake sex ad on Craigslist, in which he included my name, school, age, and cell phone number. Fortunately, after I contacted Craigslist, they pulled down the ad and gave me some basic information on the user who posted it (an Optimum Online customer from the Bronx). Apparently, impersonation is a recurring problem for them. I do not see what my ex-boyfriend got out of this prank, since he was nowhere near me on Easter

Sunday at 9 PM (this was the precise time that my phone started ringing off the hook with countless men looking to answer the ad). He did not get to read the disgusting text messages I received, nor did he listen to the disturbing voicemails that filled my inbox. The only thing he got was a message from me asking if he did it. I did not want to accuse him, but Craigslist would only release his IP address if I had a police warrant, which I could have easily received (I went to the local precinct with a printout of the ad and e-mails I exchanged with Craigslist and filed a report; I was told this was a case of aggravated assault). I explained to him that he was the only person I knew from the Bronx and that if he were not the perpetrator, I would have to follow through and press charges to determine exactly who did it. However, I certainly had no desire to have the police trace the IP address to my ex, since I feared such actions would ruin his life by leaving him with a misdemeanor on a once spotless record. He confessed, completely mortified and seemingly shocked that I took any steps at all to find out who did this to me.

Today, I can laugh about both these stories. Although that is not to say that I consider myself completely unscathed. I still find myself paranoid about my roommates, bombarding them with questions that go something like: "Do you mind if I . . ." "Are you sure?" Also, I simply don't trust Craigslist, at all. I hear people talk about the apartments and jobs they find there, and every time I look at the site, I automatically assume everything posted is illegitimate or based on some kind of sexual exchange. But if cyberbullying has done nothing other than make me annoyingly polite and leery of an already risky website, I have to say things could certainly be worse. (M. S., 2009)

This student's recollections convey several important points. She had reached late adolescence in this Digital Age without an incident of cyberbullying, but the experiences she had as a young adult were significant and caused her considerable pain and suffering at the time of the occurrences and afterward. Researchers need to look into the complex social interactions in "real" time among children, adolescents, and adults complicated by the differences in their use and/or abuse of ICTs. This student's roommate cyberbullied her by airing her grievances publicly on a blog instead of speaking with her privately, face-to-face. This student had to cope with someone close to her using the Internet to vent their frustration in a way that was hurtful, harassing, and characteristic of relational aggression discussed earlier and in the next section.

This student's second experience with an ex-boyfriend demonstrates, once again, differences in how peers use/abuse ICTs for communication and social networking and how that difference can negatively impact social interactions among them in "real" time and contribute to relational disconnections intra- and interpersonally. Moreover, inappropriate online activity seems to increase and/or may be exacerbated when negative emotions are triggered as in this case when a romantic relationship ended. The young man's behavior represents a particularly insidious type of cyberbullying that is extreme and criminal in nature. Her appropriate response to stop it, as well as her thoughtful and compassionate reaction/stance toward him (i.e., determining that he was responsible for the onslaught of interests in the bogus sex posting, confronting him and getting an admission, and then not pursuing criminal charges to avoid ruining his life) reflect a young woman who is considerate, intelligent, and mature by our societal standards. The young man's behavior, on the other hand, characterizes the harmful effects of anonymity and disinhibition experienced by some digital natives who then without insight or reflection engage in cyberbullying (or in this case) criminal behavior.

Subrahmanyam et al. (2006) found gender differences in identity presentation and sexual exploration in monitored and unmonitored online teen chat rooms. Specifically, youth who self-identified as younger and female were more likely to participate in a protected environment of monitored chat than were those youth who self-identified as older and male. The latter were more likely to participate in unmonitored chat rooms. Also, females were more likely to produce implicit sexual communication (e.g., "eminem is hot"), whereas males tended to produce more explicit sexual communication (e.g., "whats up horny guys IM me" (p. 399). Herring (1992) noted differences in online communication styles based on gender. Females use more supportive language, express appreciation more directly, and foster community building. Males use adversarial language (e.g., sarcasm) and self-promotion more than community building, as well as "flaming" (antagonistic, confrontational speech). Hence, the potential danger in cyberspace is in part due to the desires and needs of those who use Internet online services for social communication.

RELATIONAL AGGRESSION AMONG GIRLS AND FEMALE ADOLESCENTS

As mentioned earlier, the literature on gender differences in the expression of aggression finds that girls tend to engage in a passive, relational style of aggression that extends into their online behavior (e.g., spreading rumors, the threat of withdrawing affection, excluding someone from a social network or important social function; Crick, Casa, & Nelson, 2002; Nansel et al., 2001, 2003). Relational aggression can also include such behavior as ignoring someone, excluding someone, name-calling, making sarcastic verbal comments toward someone, using negative body language, and threatening to end a relationship if the girl does not get her way (Artz, 1998; Dellasega & Nixon, 2003; Mikel-Brown 2003; Remillar & Lamb 2005; Simmons, 2002).

This passive aggression is more covert and tends to be overlooked, its potential harm underestimated, by teachers, guidance counselors, and parents (Merten, 1997; Simmons, 2002). However, the impact on the targeted girls and adolescents is clearly shown in their poorer academic performance, lack of confidence, and low self-esteem, higher incidences of depression, loneliness, emotional distress, and alienation (Dellasega & Nixon, 2003).

Social aggression is specifically intended to damage self-esteem or social status (Underwood, 2003). These forms of aggression often co-occur, becoming a part of the "rites of passage" among girls that presumably will eventually be outgrown. In this regard, "meanness" is seen as a phase that girls are simply supposed to transcend (Merten, 1997). Thus, parents and teachers often dismiss this kind of behavior by calling it "normal" girl behavior. However, Remillar and Lamb (2005) found that girls are far more likely than boys to perceive this type of aggression as hurtful and damaging. With respect to online bullying, "mean girls" is one kind of bullying done in a group, for "fun" at the expense of the feelings of the target (STAR-W, 2005). Lauren Newby and Megan Meier were victims of this type of bullying.

Lauren Newby, a high school sophomore from Dallas, Texas, was victimized by nasty messages posted on a message board (e.g., "Lauren is a fat cow MOO BITCH"; "People don't like you because you are a suicidal cow who can't stop eating"); a bottle of acid was thrown at her front door and her car was vandalized (Benfer, 2001). Megan Meier, a teenager from Missouri, committed suicide after discovering that two former friends and their parents were involved in a hoax, creating an online profile of a fictional boy who became friends with her and suggested via messages a romantic interest in her (Pokin, 2007).

Some research reports that the number of girls and adolescent females engaged in physical aggression comparable to their male counterparts has increased in recent years (Prothrow-Stith & Spivak,2005). The use of ICTs to record their violent behavior compounds this phenomenon. In January 2007, in Long Island, New York, a videotape of a group of girls beating a middle school girl was posted on YouTube, stunning not only the local community but the nation as well (CBSNEWS.com, January 30, 2007). A search for "girls fighting" on Youtube will generate many such posted videos. Additional research is needed to determine the differences between females who engage in relational aggression from those who engage in physical aggression.

Ringrose (2006) suggested that the form aggression takes among females (e.g., physical or relational) as depicted in the media is coded and reflects presumed differences among girls based on class and ethnic backgrounds (e.g., relational aggression associated more with white/middle-class girls and physical violence associated more with those of lower socioeconomic status and ethnic minorities (e.g., African Americans, Asians, and Hispanics). She wrote:

> Girlhood remains carefully regulated . . . through class and race specific categories of femininity, which continue to produce normative

> and deviant girls, with vastly different effects for different girls. Where middle class parents can buy books and employ the new experts of girls' aggression to speak in their schools and communities as ways of managing girl pathology, the effects of this narrative of girlhood for those girls who lie outside the boundaries of middle class meanness are quite different. New criminal categories such as the antisocial behavior bans draw particular girls . . . who defy the feminine, into growing webs of penal regulation . . . it is those rendered simultaneously invisible and "other" by the discourse of the universal mean girl who are bearing some of its most serious consequences. (p. 420)

The impact of violence, regardless of the form it takes, perpetrated by these "mean girls" and female adolescents harms not only the victim and the perpetrator (s) but the online and offline social network of the victim–perpetrator as well as the community-at-large. Regarding relational aggression, Wiseman (2002) offers the following advice to parents of adolescent girls:

> Welcome to the wonderful world of your daughter's adolescence. A world in which she comes to school one day to find that her friends have suddenly decided that she no longer belongs. Or she's teased mercilessly for wearing the wrong outfit or having the wrong friend. Or branded with a reputation she can't shake. Or pressured into conforming so she won't be kicked out of the group. For better or worse, your daughter's friendships are the key to enduring adolescence—as well as the biggest threat to her well-being. (p. 1)

Several factors trigger the "cycle of mean" behaviors mentioned here, which include but are not limited to the following: conflict over boys, jealousy, the threat of the "pretty girl," a girl thinking that "she is all that" or that "she is the boss," competition, showing off, popularity, or anyone who is unable to adhere to the "good friendship" expectations. These triggers speak of the competition for power within their social circles. Social power refers to an individual's ability to obtain the highest socially valuable possessions, such as a "prized/high status" boyfriend, the "best" friends, designer clothing, popularity, and the ability to tell others what to do to feel good.

Feminist scholars suggest that the motivation underlying relational aggression among girls and adolescent females pertains to their misguided efforts to control and exert power over "lesser" others like themselves. By so doing, they are attempting to compensate for the internalization of the dominant group's (e.g., men in a patriarchal society) beliefs that those who are subordinates are substandard, defective, and inferior. The internalization of this negativity turns into self-hatred, defended against by projecting the hostility horizontally onto the devalued other who is like them. Consequently, infighting among members of a subordinate group occurs. For girls and adolescent females, the infighting takes the form of relational/social aggression. From Miller's (1976) perspective, females, as a result of their gender, are likely to be victimized by other females due to gender inequality—that is, lack of power relative to males.

The following student's anecdotal account highlights her experience of this phenomenon as well as illustrates what has been reported in the literature on middle school youth and gender differences with ICT misuse discussed earlier.

Anecdote II

My only experience with cyberbullying has been instances where I was the bully, which is not something that I am proud of at all. As a person who does not like confrontation or to be confrontational, it was easier for me to express anger or dislike behind the cover of an IM chat or MySpace messaging. As I have gotten older, I have learned that this is not the way to handle situations, and after a few instances where my "bully-having" spilled over into real life, I have stopped using IM as a vehicle for my frustration with people. There is one experience in particular where my harsh way with words proved more harmful to me than to the other person. Of course I knew that conversations can be copied and pasted and shared with other people but I did not think that it would be used against me. However, it was, and my friends took the other person's side, so not only was I unnecessarily mean-spirited, but I also lost a lot of friends because of it. This particular instance taught me how detrimental cyberbullying can be for all the parties involved. (M.G., 2009)

This student's experience reveals how her use of ICTs when she was younger (in middle school) served defensive/self-protective purposes that enabled her to create a "psychological space" in cyberspace where she could vent angry feelings and release her frustrations on those (mental representations of others) whom she perceived to be responsible for her emotional distress. Without the benefit of face-to-face encounters, the development of social skills that would facilitate her capacity to assert herself in more age-appropriate ways when she felt wronged was delayed. Thus, she became handicapped by the technology; she failed to appreciate that her "angry" talk went beyond the bounds of an active fantasy life. Her "angry" IMs were her attempts to compensate for hurts in "real" life by projecting them into the social arena of "virtual" life in cyberspace (e.g., her IMs). The technology shielded her from the much-needed "real" process of social interactions from which she would adaptively learn to adjust or modify verbal and nonverbal communication; instead, she developed a style of engagement with others in virtual reality that constituted harassment. Ironically, it was the technology and her lack of technological sophistication to conceal her "real" identity that led to her undoing. The targeted victim of her wrath shared with others the product of her bullying (e.g., copies of the offensive IMs) by circulating these copies among their mutual network of friends.

In addition to the "mean girls" cyberbully, other types of cyberbullies have been identified based on their motivation and what they do online (STAR-W, 2005). The "vengeful angel" views himself or herself as defending a friend who is being or has been bullied in school by shifting the bullying online. "Power-hungry" cyberbullies resemble more closely the playground bullies who use coercion and intimidation to assert their power and control over others; when this bully has technical knowledge and uses the Internet as a tool for bullying, the term "Revenge of the Nerds" is used. This type of cyberbully can damage someone's computer by intentionally sending virus-infected e-mails, for example. The "inadvertent cyberbully" is one whose online reactions stem from misunderstandings online or misconstruing the meaning of a text message.

I. Berson and Berson (2003) found that 92% of 10,800 girls aged 12 to 18 who participated in an online survey use a home computer as their primary access site. When online, 58% of the girls spend their time sending instant messages or e-mails to friends; 20% surf for new things on the Internet, and 16% spend most of their time in chartrooms. Only 1% indicated that the majority of time online was spent working on building a website, reading discussion boards, interacting at game sites, or engaging in homework and research.

PREVALENCE OF CYBERBULLYING

Determining the prevalence of cyberbullying is difficult, in part because reporting and comparisons across studies are compounded by differences in age-related findings (Kowalski & Limber, 2007; Li, 2007; Patchin, & Hinduja, 2010; Privetera & Campbell, 2009; Williams & Guerra, 2007). Some studies focused on a narrow range of youth, and others studied large age ranges (e.g., "middle school aged," "older adolescents") and grade level (Palfrey & Gasser, 2008). As a result, cyberbully victims vary from a low of 4% (Ybarra & Mitchell, 2004a) to a high of 72% (Juvonen & Gross, 2008). Ybarra et al. (2004), reported that 3% of their U.S. sample of youth aged 10 to 17 years was cyberbullied three or more times in the previous year. According to Li (2007), 9% of middle school students indicated that they had been cyberbullied three or more times. According to Palfrey, Sacco, Boyd, and DeBonis (2009), few students are cyberbullied daily or weekly. Beran & Li (2007), in a Canadian study, found that 34% of students in grades 7 to 9 were cyberbullied once or twice, 19% reported "a few times," 3% "many times," and 0.01% reported being cyberbullied on a daily basis.

Research has found an overlap in victimization and perpetration; between 3% to 12% of youth have been both online harassers and victims of online harassment (Beran & Li, 2007; Kowalski & Limber, 2007). Patchin et al. (2009) found that 27% of female adolescents retaliate for being bullied online by "cyberbullying back." Research suggests some overlap between online and offline bullying and victimization. Patchin and Hinduja (2006) found that 42% of victims of cyberbullying were also victims of offline bullying and that 52% of cyberbullies were also offline bullies. Many young people who have had a negative online experience that caused discomfort do not report the incident or seek help to cope with their reaction (Beran & Li, 2005; Mitchell et al., 2005).

Earlier findings indicated that 1 out of every 17 youth reported being threatened or harassed while using the Internet, and 19% of youth between the ages of 10 and 18 had been either the perpetrator or victim of cyberbullying (Hinduja & Patchin, 2010; Ybarra & Mitchell, 2004a). A survey of 1,500 students in the United States, Grades 4 to 8, found that 42% had been victims of online bullying, and 21% had received mean-spirited or menacing e-mails/IMs (ISAFE, 2003). In another survey of 1,500 children between the ages of 10 and 17, 25% reported being exposed to unwanted sexual material while online; approximately 19% of these young people were propositioned while online (Mitchell, Finkelhor, & Wolak, 2001, 2003).

More recent findings challenge whether cyberbullying is increasing. Lenhart (2007) found that 67% of teenagers expressed that bullying happens more offline than online; 42% of cyberbully victims were also school bullying victims (Hinduja & Patchin, 2009); 54% of seventh-grade students were victims of traditional bullying with less than half that number (25%) reporting cyberbully victimization (Li, 2007). Victimization rates were found to be generally lower in early adolescence (Hinduja & Patchin, 2008; Lenhart, 2007; Ybarra & Mitchell, 2004a) and higher in mid-adolesce (Hinduja & Patchin, 2008; Kowalski & Limber, 2007; Slonje & Smith, 2008). Some studies suggest that eighth and ninth graders or 15 years of age is the peak period for online harassment (Hinduja & Patchin, 2008; Hinduja & Patchin, 2009; Sbarbaro & Enyeart Smith, 2011; Williams & Guerra, 2007; Wolak, Finkelhor, Mitchell, & Ybarra, 2007). The Bureau of Justice Statistics shows a decline in offline bullying from seventh to twelfth grades (Devoe et al., 2005), whereas P. K. Smith et al. (2008) found that cyberbullying tends to peak later in eighth grade and declines only slightly. Other findings suggest that cyberbullying remains level through the end of high school and persists in college (Finn, 2004). Recent research has begun to examine cyberbullying in the workplace among adults (Privetera & Campbell, 2009).

Menesini et al. (2011) identify three general characteristics of cyberbullying that also challenge researchers in their efforts to better understand its prevalence and nature, as well as its severity in a given population:

> First, the complexity and accelerated evolution of new technologies often renders any classification soon obsolete. Second, specific characteristics such as the anonymity of the acts and the public/private nature of the attacks should be considered in the definition. Third, the different use of technological devices across cultures can affect not only the frequency of each behavior, but also their cultural meaning. (p. 268)

Questionnaires and surveys are the methods typically used to collect data on cyberbullying and results are affected by the following: (a) the inherent limitations of self-report measures, (b) the nature of self-selected populations, (c) the ways in which the questions are asked and the actual definition of the behaviors and media used, and (d) cultural variations in terminology and salience of the behavior (e.g., is "cyperpesting" synonymous with cyberbullying?; Livingstone et al., 2011).

PSYCHOLOGICAL VULNERABILITIES AND THE IMPACT OF CYBERSPACE

Children experience different vulnerabilities and protective systems as they grow and mature (Masten et al., 1995). Emotional self-regulatory skills, so vital for self-concept and personality development, have been reported to be vulnerable to biological and environmental insult, and they have also been demonstrated to be amenable to environmental support (Raver, 2004). Executive function skills, associated with cognition, involve goal-directed problem solving and planning abilities—the identification of a problem, strategizing, execution, and evaluation of a plan (Seguin & Zelazo, 2005). To effectively accomplish the necessary steps of problem solving, an individual must also incorporate inhibition and working memory skills (Zelazo, Muller, Frye, & Marcovitch, 2003); information processing and self-regulation are critical aspects of executive function.

Children's milestones in affect regulation, cognition, empathy, motivation, object representation, physical growth, self-representation, and self-reflectiveness occur first within their families with their mothers, fathers, and significant others who are responsible for creating an atmosphere of care, love, nurturance, safety, and security for healthy development. As the child continues to grow, the environmental support broadens to encompass schools and other institutions within the community that contribute to their educational, physical, and social development.

Youth in our American pluralistic society learn formally and informally about how differences among people, especially those pertaining to race/ethnicity, gender, religion, age, sexual orientation, socioeconomic class, and disability support the continued use of stereotypes and contribute to prejudice and discriminatory behavior (at the individual level) and policies and systematic practices (at the institutional level). Indeed, more lesbian, gay, transgendered, and bisexual youth are reported victims of cyberbullying than other "minority" groups (Cassidy, Jackson, & Brown, 2009).

Knowledge about the influence of ICTs on the development of emotional self-regulatory and executive function skills discussed earlier is scarce, as is empirical studies on how millennials wrestle with the expression of powerfully felt emotions (e.g., anger, fear, frustration, hatred, hurt, humiliation, prejudice) online. This is especially salient when considering the vast range of experiences in ordinary living that may elicit negative emotions in children, adolescents, and adults. The conviction of Dharun Ravi who spied on his gay roommate Tyler Clementi's sexual encounter is apropos. Using a webcam on his computer and gossiping about Tyler on Twitter was deemed a crime not a prank by a jury. His defense's argument that his actions reflected immaturity not criminality and that he should not be held accountable for the tragic outcome (Clementi committed suicide by jumping off the George Washington Bridge after learning that his sexual encounter with a man had become public) failed to impress the jury. Ravi's sophisticated technological knowledge and skills to implement this malicious invasion of Tyler's privacy negated dismissing the charges based on a "youthfulness" defense (Glaberson, 2012).

The needs and motivations of adolescents have been well researched and presented in the psychological literature. They are focused on establishing an identity, intimacy, and self-esteem; they want to belong within their own social groups while becoming more autonomous and separating from family. They are striving to develop and maintain a more mature way of managing and regulating emotions and preparing for a career or occupation. In other words, adolescents are learning who they are, what is important to them, what they value, and how to relate to others; they are making friends and maintaining friendships, discovering what their goals for the future are, and developing skills and competencies to become productive citizens, to name a few of their concerns.

Cyberspace offers many opportunities for adolescents to satisfy the need to experiment with their identity and learn about the world. Indeed, this generation of adolescents and young adults has been described in the literature as being "always on"—that is, continually connected to ICTs in this digital age. According to Gross (2004), communication is the most important use of the Internet for today's adolescents. Although teens continue to learn critical thinking skills, they are not automatically inclined to apply these skills in their face-to-face social interactions as they strive for healthy emotional adjustment. Nor are they inclined, or indeed cognitively and emotionally capable, of applying these skills in their online activities. Aboujaoude (2011) noted that "The new disequilibrium, brought about by virtual life, between the brake system that keeps us in check and the stubborn (Hobbesian) urges that lie underneath the surface, helps unleash an online self that can be quite foreign to the person sitting behind the computer" (p. 286). Adolescents' increasing independence from adult scrutiny and their inclination to solve their problems without parental or adult assistance complicate efforts to develop effective prevention–intervention programs to minimize online victimization.

The following anecdotal account written by another former undergraduate student in my Psychology of Women class illustrates the points raised here.

Anecdote III

As of May 2004, I graduated from ______High School, a small Catholic school in California. When I was in school, the Internet was merely a tool used for research for upcoming research papers, but in the 2004–2005 school year, this changed drastically. During my spring semester of college at Pace, I became aware of an Internet service called "MySpace." It is a free website in which members join and then create their own web pages. On their pages, people put pictures of themselves, schools they have attended, bulletins, and other voluntary information about themselves. The biggest attraction of MySpace is something called a "wall"; each personal page has one. A person's wall consists of comments about them made by fellow MySpace friends (friends can only become friends by request and acceptance).

By May of 2005, I had joined MySpace after a friend told me about all the people from her past that she was able to reconnect with. When I joined MySpace, I was also able to get in touch with people I had not seen in years, I was able to talk to them and see how they were doing, and I loved the experience. As I spent more time on the actual site, I became aware that there were people using the site in a negative manner. While I was surfing pages one day, I came upon many pages from the kids who were in the grade below me in high school. They were now seniors and seemed to be out of control. Most of the pages I came across chronicled tales of people's drug abuse and underage drinking, and many of the girls' pages were laden with personal tales of their own sexual exploits. I was shocked to see these things because in my mind, these kids were still the innocent juniors I once knew. When I thought I couldn't be any more shocked, I read a bulletin (a mass message sent to all of one's MySpace friends) calling a girl a slut and listing her actual phone number "for a good time."

I went home for the summer and decided to ask one of my friend's younger sisters who was still at my high school about the MySpace usage. She told me of even more occurrences like the one above. She even told me about students starting sexual rumors about a teacher. The rumors got back to the school of course and the teacher was constantly harassed. After this, the school was forced to step in. The first step the school took was to attempt to ban My Space usage. This was of course impossible because it violated freedom rights of student; so they did the next best thing: held many conferences about it and eventually banned MySpace from all school computers. Today the exact same things are going on because students can of course go online at home and do whatever they want. There are a small but powerful group of people who are using this website negatively, and it is impacting the reputation of the school and girls everywhere. (M.H., 2005)

This student's account of her experience illustrates several issues. She is an older adolescent who observes that her response and participation in cyberspace differs from younger adolescents. The difference reflects not only maturational processes of adolescence but also the time frame in which digital technology has become a significant influence in our society and in the social functioning of youth. Her initial response mirrors how an entire generation, before the explosion of this technology, used computers. It is therefore important to include cohort variables when conducting research in this area. Second, what motivated her to explore this Internet site has been discussed in the literature on gender in which needs for social affiliation and communication are important for females. Third, the nature of the abuse she witnessed online has been discussed in the literature on belongingness theory (Baumeister & Leary, 1995); research on ostracism has demonstrated that simply being ignored and excluded is enough to produce depressive symptoms and lower self-reported satisfaction levels of self-esteem (A. Smith & Williams, 2004; Williams, 2001; Ybarra, Leaf, & Diener-West, 2004). Lastly, this student's commentary on the harmful effect of the behavior of a minority of users on themselves and the rest of the community of users underscores the need for appropriate intervention by the collaborative efforts of Internet service providers, social network sites, academia, education, child safety and public policy advocacy organizations, the technology industry, and parents to curb "out-of-control" behavior and promote safe online environments (Aftab, 2000; Chisholm, 2006; Palfrey et al., 2009).

AT-RISK ONLINE BEHAVIORS

The apparent ability to communicate online without revealing one's "true" identity—that is, the perceived security of being protected behind the computer screen (e.g., pseudo-anonymity)—can predispose children, youth, and some adults to succumb to pressures (social or intrapersonal) and behave online in ways that they know are unsafe or inappropriate. In 2011, the highly publicized downfall of New York Assemblyman Anthony Weiner, whose cell phone activity reflected, at the very least, immaturity and a significant lapse in judgment illustrates this point. At-risk online behaviors include the following: giving out personal information online, agreeing to meet with someone in person met online, receiving and sending inappropriate photos, receiving and sending suggestive or threatening e-mail, participating in chat rooms where the content results in discomfort (I. Berson, Berson, & Ferron, 2002; Hashima & Finkelhor, 1999). Research suggests that troubled youth and youth who tend to have high rates of Internet use, use chat rooms, talk with strangers online, or use the Internet in households other than their own tend to be at risk for online victimization (Mitchell et al., 2001).

Another potential risk factor deals with the ease with which our young can access global information and make use of information obtained through digital technologies. On one hand, this access has the potential to expand their awareness and exposure to diverse cultural and social worldviews. However, material obtained online may be illegal, inappropriate, age-restricted, or simply inaccurate or intentionally specious. Exposure to and acting on misinformation or inappropriate material online may be harmful to the cognitive–emotional or physical well-being of youth.

Use of various digital technologies allows millennials, young and older, many possibilities for recreating themselves and experimenting with different roles or lifestyles in a wide range of virtual platforms (e.g., multiple identities). Because of the nature of the Internet, with the increased capacity to track and record online activity, information about these identities may paradoxically bind, restrict, or harm youth by keeping these identities "alive" for perpetuity, long after they have forgotten, outgrown, and discarded them (e.g., Library of Congress archiving all tweet messages).

PREVENTION

Erikson's 1968 concept of *psychosocial moratorium* is as important today as it was when he introduced it more than 50 years ago. Society sanctions culturally or institutionally appropriate activities designed to facilitate the maturational and psychosocial development of adolescents. According to Erikson's perspective, society recognizes that adolescence is a period in psychological development in which youth consolidate earlier experiences of self into a cohesive self-concept through experimentation with opportunities to experience a variety of adult roles without being held fully responsible for the consequences of their actions while trying out those roles. Society, therefore, is obligated to assist youth who, upon successful transition through this psychosocial moratorium, are prepared to fully participate as adults, becoming the emotionally healthy, productive citizens who contribute to and function well within their complex society.

Preventative strategies need to advance Erikson's notion of psychosocial moratorium to cyberspace. For, as the National Crime Prevention Council indicates, about half the adolescent population has been affected by cyberbullying (Goldsborough, 2010). What can be learned from efforts to comprehend the salience of the "mean girls" discourse in the media and psychological literature on gender differences in aggression especially as it pertains to cyberbullying? That is, what are the policies and procedures necessary to ensure the safety of all those who use ICTs, and how are they to be implemented?

The complexity of the problem involving different constituencies, each with their own perspective and concerns as well as conflicting values, are reflected in the literature, which emphasizes the commonalities as well as the substantive differences between conventional bullying and cyberbullying for millennials (Bhat, 2008; Couvillon & Ilieva, 2011; Hinduja & Patchin, 2009; I-Safe, 2003; Katzer, Fetchenhauer, & Belschak, 2009; Privetera & Campbell, 2009; Wright et al., 2009). Advances in technology have led to the apprehension of perpetrators more quickly after a crime has been committed than ever before. What are the ethical, moral, legal ramifications of monitoring cyberspace activity and intervening in "suspect" activity?

Cyberbullying prevention requires a holistic approach, one that is complex and involves the commitment of financial resources to fund a variety of interventions. These interventions need to be informed by knowledge in which coordinated efforts across communities and domains including education, health, justice, the Internet community, and the workplace combat the social forces and norms that give rise to this form of online behavior (Palfry & Gasser, 2008). For example, the Children's Online Privacy Act (COPA) enhances monitoring online activities of youngsters. It went into effect in the United States in 2000 and requires that website operators and Internet service providers obtain verifiable parental consent when personal information is collected online from children under the age of 13 (COPA, 2006).

Preventing cyberviolence, especially cyberbullying among children and adolescents, is difficult because so much of this activity takes place between minors who know one another or know of one another through involvement in online and offline social networks (Hinduja & Patchin, 2007, 2009; Slonje & Smith, 2008). The problem is further complicated by the ways in which bullying moves between online and offline contexts as well as shifts between victims and perpetrators (e.g., reciprocal harassment). Modifying online pseudo-anonymity by creating online identity authentication for all online users regardless of age or using filters show promise in reducing online harassment because people could presumably be held accountable for their online behavior because their identity would be known and their access to sites and information would be restricted. However, implementing technological mechanisms would undoubtedly carry many hurdles, including, but not limited to, freedom of speech issues and legal and privacy concerns.

Many youth are capable of circumventing these technologies by using proxies to circumvent filters or to reformat their computers to remove parental controls; devices with Wi-Fi capabilities and unsecured wireless networks can be accessed anywhere. To date, most filtering technologies focus on sexual context and inappropriate language. Some fail to restrict access to violent content, hate content, and self-harm content. They also fail to address the rise of youth-generated problematic content distributed virally.

Additional preventative activities or strategies include development of awareness programs for administrators, employees, employers, educators at all grade levels, parents, and youth; legislation designed to criminalize certain inappropriate online activity (e.g., the Electronic Antistalking Act of 1995); hotlines where people can report illegal content on Internet sites; age-appropriate supervision and monitoring of online activity; discussion with parent(s) or other trusted adults about online safety; instruction by teachers about cybersafety; and technological developments that help to limit the amount of unwanted/harmful content (Shariff & Hoff, 2007).

Several initiatives have launched projects to accomplish these objectives. In the United States, the Multi-State Working Group on Social Networking, comprising 50 state attorneys general, charged the Internet Safety Technical Task Force to determine the extent to which today's technologies could help to address these online safety risks, with a primary focus on social network sites in the United States. Their final report makes a series of recommendations for public policy advocacy to promote youth online safety with the input from technology experts (Palfrey et al., 2009).

ECPAT International (End Child Prostitution, Child Pornography and Trafficking of Children for Sexual Purposes; www.ecpat.net) is a network of organizations and individuals working around the world to protect children from all forms of sexual exploitation and violence. As part of the 2005 United Nations' study on violence against children, ECPAT generated a report that contained a section on cyberbullying to contribute to the international effort to protect youth from violence (Muir, 2005).

I-SAFE America is a nonprofit educational foundation established in 1998 to provide students with the awareness and knowledge they need to recognize and avoid dangerous, harmful online behavior. This objective is accomplished through two major activities: providing the I-SAFE school education curriculum to schools nationwide and community outreach, which includes events for the community-at-large and school-based assemblies for the student population at which Internet safety issues are discussed (I-SAFE America, 2003).

ISG (the Internet Safety Group) from New Zealand is an independent organization whose members include educators at all levels of the school system (e.g., elementary grades through college), government groups, representatives of law enforcement agencies, the judiciary, community groups, businesses, libraries, and individuals. In 2000, the Internet Safety Kit for schools, the NetSafe website, and their toll-free NETSAFE Hotline was launched (www.netsafe.org.nz). What is stressed in these programs and projects is that education (curricula) designed for specific groups (e.g., youth, parents, teachers, school administrators, law enforcement, legislators) is crucial to reducing and/or eliminating at-risk online behavior. For example, from the parents' perspective, especially those born before the rise of the Digital Age, this technology is a tool to be used for practical and/or business purposes. Their children, however, view this technology as their way of being connected in their social world. Empowering parents with knowledge about existing unsafe activities and teaching them skills to adequately monitor and supervise online activities are deemed important components of many intervention strategies. It is noteworthy, however, that parental supervision techniques have not been too effective in lowering adolescent risky online activity. This may be due in part to the attitudes of teens who do not disclose information about their online activities with their parents, and studies measuring parental monitoring are in fact assessing level of parental knowledge rather than parents' efforts in tracking and surveillance (Kerr & Statin, 2000; Liau et al., 2005).

For youth and adult users to become "netizens," the literature encourages "netiquette" and "nethics" (i.e., online manners encouraging acceptable conduct when engaged in an interchange with people in cyberspace; M. J. Berson, 2000; Cole et al., 2001; Willard, 2002). Clearly articulated rules assist youth in behaving courteously and respectfully to others, facilitating positive social interactions with others. The application of the rules enables young people to apply critical thinking skills to online activity, thereby promoting healthy, productive social discourse and participation (Kubey, 2002).

Although these rules of "netiquette" make sense to more mature users who will follow them, younger or more psychologically immature users may not readily adopt sound online strategies, such as not sharing one's password with anyone or refraining from sharing secrets, photos, or anything online that might be embarrassing, humiliating, or, with older millennials, threatening if someone or an entire online community have access to them. Their inexperience as well as their cognitive, emotional, and social immaturity gives rise to a kind of reasoning that makes them vulnerable to abuse and be abused online. Moreover, many types of bullying involving texts, including those involving impersonation, password stealing, and the distribution of embarrassing images and video may confuse and intimidate younger users who may not feel comfortable disclosing their discomfort with an adult whose knowledge of the technology as a social tool is limited.

A colleague and friend of mine who is a social worker for a public elementary school in a township in New Jersey shared with me her overwhelmingly positive interactions with students who participated in the school implementation of the Netsafe school kit in 2008. Many of the children expressed delight and relief that there were adults with whom they could communicate their online experiences knowing that these adults would "understand" and "help" them (R. Walker, personal communication, 2008).

The shift in research design from self-report/survey methods to current research on examining variables hypothesized to be related to cyberbullying shows promise in formulating interventions to prevent cyberbullying. Apropos of Walker's (2008, personal communication) experience, Ybarra and Mitchell (2004b) suggested that supportive adult caregivers such as parents and teachers could serve as mentors to model appropriate empathic responses and reduce cyberbullying. Ang and Goh (2010) proposed including empathy training and education in cyberbullying intervention programs with emphasis on cognitive components of empathy for boys and affective components of empathy for girls. Underwood et al.'s (2012) methodology enabled researchers to study the actual behavior and content of adolescents' daily, online communication and how they engage in different types of communication with their peers, parents, love interests, and strangers. Contrary to survey research results, they found no gender differences in the frequency of texting between girls and boys or the length of text messages based on examination of billing records among college women and men.

HOW TO REPORT CYBERVIOLENCE

Incidents of cyberviolence can be handled in a variety of ways including reporting the incident to a supportive adult, CyberTipline, the ISP (internet service provider), school official(s), and/or the local police. Enlisting the aid of an adult may facilitate taking appropriate action to stop the bullying. Unsolicited, obscene materials or threats can be reported online to CyberTipline at http://www.missingkids.com/cybertip/ or by calling 1-800-843-5678. One can also report the harassment to the offender's Internet service and request that the abuser's account be suspended or blocked (it is important to note that some bullies have further harassed a victim by reporting the victim as the bully and having the victim's account blocked). Many schools now include online bullying in their antiharassment policies and code of conduct. Involving the police may be in order if the bullying behavior threatens violence and violates other laws as was illustrated in Anecdote III. There is software programming now that helps document Cyberbullying by saving a screen shot of the computer when one clicks on the Cyberbully Alert icon. This program costs a nominal annual fee and can be used on up to three computers per home (www.cyberbullyalert.com). The following three websites also offer invaluable information about online and offline actions to reduce cyberbullying:

- kidshealth.org/kid/grow/school_stuff/bullies.html
- stopbullyingnow.hrsa.gov/kids
- www.education.com/topic/school-bullying-teasing

Establishing a national registry for reporting all cyberbullying incidents and outcomes of preventive interventions similar to what was established by the medical community to combat pediatric cancers may lead to a decrease in these incidents as occurred in the decrease in pediatric cancer deaths. The success of the cooperative pediatric clinical trials groups in the United States and elsewhere (e.g., Children's Oncology Group—COG) shows how effective these collaborations are, suggesting they could be used as models for similar initiatives for other health concerns (Jemal et al., 2006).

Cyberbullying reflects the "dis-ease" so prevalent in our digital world; it is an international public health problem affecting the well-being of children, adolescents, and adults. A cyberbullying reporting system could be used to (a) identify trends in the incidence and prevalence of cyberbullying, (b) evaluate initiatives/programs promoting those that are shown to be effective, and (c) provide information for program planning and development.

DIRECTIONS FOR FUTURE RESEARCH AND TRAINING

The discussion on cyberbullying reflects the emergence of a new field of inquiry on how ICTs can be a detrimental influence in the lives of millennials of all ages. Psychological theories and research in this area are proliferating; however the findings to date have been primarily based on self-report/survey measures. The focus has mainly been on identifying types of online activities, the frequency of use and the electronic technology involved. Mitchell et al. (2005) have suggested that

> the implementation of population-based studies about Internet use and problematic Internet experiences should help in the development of norms in this area, which, in turn, is an important component in the development of public policy, prevention, and intervention in this field. More research is also needed concerning the mental health impact of various problematic Internet experiences. Internet problems may be adding some unique dynamics to

> the field of mental health that require special understanding, new responses, and interventions in some cases. . . . For example, are persons with impulse control problems drawn to certain aspects of the Internet, such as pornography and gaming, which could further exacerbate their symptoms? Does Internet exposure exacerbate preexisting mental health difficulties? (p. 507)

Greenfield and Yan (2006), surveying the empirical literature on the impact of virtual reality on psychosocial functioning of children and adolescents, asked the following: "How should we think of the Internet from a developmental perspective? What are the uses to which the Internet is put and what do children and adolescents get from it?" (p. 392). They suggested that the Internet, when viewed as a "new object of cognition" (p. 393; i.e., the interplay of Internet involvement and cognitive/emotional development of children, adolescents, and adults), is unlike other media and electronic devices (e.g., television) because Internet users participate in and coconstruct the virtual social and physical world of this phenomenon. Future research may explore developmental trends of bullying across age groups and domains. For example, are the schoolyard bullies of 15 years ago the online bullies of today in the workplace?

Cyberbullying requires much more empirical study to further our understanding of this phenomenon. Results from existing studies need to be replicated and validated. Future research needs to develop additional measures to determine how to reduce the risk of being victimized, identifying and assisting those who have been subjected to cyberbullying, and determining how to prevent it. Underwood et al.'s (2012) research design makes a significant contribution in this regard because its methodology allows researchers to actually examine the cyberbullying behavior through one of the mediums in which it occurs (i.e., text messages). It is important for researchers, clinicians, and other professionals who work with youth to better understand the diversity among the victims of cyberbullying as well as the diversity among cyberbullies. Current research indicates that considering the age, gender, social class, access to ICTs, and individual preferences regarding online activities of children and adolescents is crucial to understanding the interplay of the online activity and the user's experience of being bullied and bullying. The trend for younger and younger children to have access to this technology as the technology continues to evolve requires that researchers, experts in these technologies, and other professionals collaborate in earnest to promote the safe use of ICTs and facilitate healthy development for children and adolescents.

Existing support services need to become sensitized to the needs of millennials who have suffered abuse and/or are abusing others in this venue to appropriately address their vulnerability and victimization. As discussed in the literature, many youth never report their experience of cyberbullying and cope with the negative feelings and experience on their own. Therefore, additional training for mental health and other professionals is necessary to enable them to recognize the signs of cyberbullying, which contribute to psychological distress and interpersonal difficulties and interfere with developmental tasks throughout the life span.

REFERENCES

Aftab, P. (2000). *The parent's guide to protecting your children in cyberspace.* New York, NY: McGraw-Hill.

American Association of University Women. (2000). *Tech savvy: Educating girls in the new computer age.* Washington, DC: American Association of University Women Educational Foundation Research.

American Psychological Association. (2004, July). *APA resolution on bullying among children and youth.* Retrieved from http://www.apa.org/about/policy/bullying.pdf

Ang, R., & Goh, D. H. (2010). Cyberbullying among adolescents: The role of affective and cognitive empathy and gender. *Child Psychiatry and Human* Development, *41,* 387–397.

Annese, J., & Jorgensen, J. (2012, January). Cyberbullies insult the memory of Amanda Cummings, tragic Staten Island teen hit by bus. *Staten Island Advance.* Retrieved from http://silive.com/news/index.ssf/2012/01/cyberbullies_insult_the_memory.html

Aricak, T., Siyahhan, S., Uzunhasanoglu, A., Saribeyoglu, S., Ciplak, S., Yilmaz, N., & Memmedov, C. (2008). Cyberbullying among Turkish adolescents. *CyberPsychology & Behavior, 11,* 253–261.

Artz, S. (1998). *Sex, power & the violent school girl.* New York, NY: Teacher's College Press.

Baumeister, R. F., & Leary, M. R. (1995). The need to belong: Desire for interpersonal attachments as a fundamental human motivation. *Psychological Bulletin, 117,* 497–529.

Beckerman, L., & Nocero, J. (2003). You've got hate mail. *Principal Leadership, 3,* 38–41.

Benfer, A. (2001, July). Cyber slammed. *Salon.com.* Retrieved from http://dir.salon.com/mwt/feature/2001/07/03/cyber_bullies/index.html?sid=1039555

Beran, T., & Li, Q. (2005). Cyber-harassment: A study of a new method for an old behavior, *Journal of Educational Computing Research, 32,* 265–277.

Beran, T., & Li, Q. (2007). The relationship between cyberbullying and school bullying. *Journal of Student Wellbeing, 1,* 15–33.

Berson, I. (2003). Grooming cybervictims: The psychosocial effects of online exploitation for youth. *Journal of School Violence. 2,* 5 –18.

Berson, I., & Berson, M. (2002). *Evolving a community initiative to protect children in cyberspace.* Tampa: The Louis de la Parte Florida Mental Health Institute, University of South Florida.

Berson, I., & Berson, M. (2003). Digital literacy for effective citizenship. *Social Education, 67,* 164–167.

Berson, I., Berson, M., & Ferron, J. (2002). Emerging risks of violence in the digital age: Lessons for educators from an online study of adolescent girls in the United States. *Meridian: A Middle School Computer Technologies Journal, 5.* Retrieved from http://www.ncsu.edu/meridian/sum2002/cyberviolence/index.html

Berson, M. J. (2000). Rethinking research and pedagogy in the social studies: The creation of caring connections through technology and advocacy. *Theory & Research in Social Education, 28,* 121–131.

Bhat, C. S. (2008). Cyberbullying: Overview and strategies for school counselors, guidance officers, and all school personnel. *Australian Journal of Guidance and Counseling, 18,* 53–66.

Blood, R. (2002). *The weblog handbook: Practical advice on creating and maintaining your blog.* Cambridge, MA: Perseus.

Bruno, L. (2004, October). Blogging ban provokes debate over cyberspace. *Daily Record,* 1–6.

Burgess-Proctor, A., Patchin, J., & Hinduja, S. (2009). Cyberbullying and online harassment: Reconceptualizing the victimization of adolescent girls. In V. Garcia & J. Clifford (Eds.), *Female crime victims: Reality reconsidered* (pp. 162–176). Upper Saddle River, NJ: Prentice Hall.

Cassidy, W., Jackson, M., & Brown, K. (2009). Sticks and stones can break my bones, but how can pixels hurt me? Students' experiences with cyberbullying. *School Psychology International, 30,* 383–402.

CBS News. (2007, January 30). Teen fight caught on tape [video webcast]. Retrieved from http://www.cbsnews.com/video/watch/?id=2368636n&tag=related;photovideo

Children Online Privacy Protection Act. (2006). Retrieved from http://www.ftc.gov/bcp/conline/pubs/buspubs/coppa.htm

Chisholm, J. F. (2006). Cyberspace violence against girls and adolescent females. In F. Denmark, H. Krauss, E. Halpern, & J. Sechzer (Eds.), *Violence and exploitation against women and girls* (Vol. 1087; pp. 74–89). Boston, MA: Annals of the New York Academy of Sciences.

Claburn, T. (2009, August). Twitter downed by denial of service attack. *InformationWeek.* Retrieved from http://www.informationweek.com/news/security/attacks/showArticle.jhtml?articleID=219100308

Cole, J. I., Suman, M., Schramm, P., Coget, J-F., Firth, D., Fortier, D., . . . Aquino, J-S. (2001). UCLA Internet report 2001: Surveying the digital future: Year two. Los Angeles, CA: UCLA Center for Communication Policy. Retrieved from http://www.digitalcenter.org/wp-content/uploads/2013/02/2001_digital_future_report_year2.pdf

Couvillon, M., & Ilieva, V. (2011). Recommended practices: A review of schoolwide preventative programs and strategies on cyberbullying. *Preventing School Failure, 55,* 96–101.

Cowie, H., & Colliety, P. (2010). Cyberbullying: Sanctions or sensitivity? *Pastoral Care in Education, 28,* 261–268

Crick, N. R., Casa, J. F., & Nelson, D. A. (2002). Toward a more comprehensive understanding of peer maltreatment: Studies of relationship victimization. *Current Directions in Psychological Science, 11,* 96–101.

Dehue, F., Bolman, C., & Vollink, T. (2008). Cyberbullying: Youngsters' experiences and parental perception. *CyberPsychology and Behavior, 11,* 217–223.

Dellasega, C., & Nixon, C. (2003). *Girl wars: 12 strategies that will end female bullying.* New York, NY: Simon & Schuster.

Devoe, J. F., Peter, K., Noonan, M., Snyder, T. D., & Baum, K. (2005, November). Indicators of school crime and safety. Retrieved from the National Crimina Justice Reference Center, U.S. Department of Justice web site: http://www.ncjrs.gov/App/publications/abstract.aspx?ID=210697

Eagly, A. H., Wood, W., & Diekman, A. B. (2000). Social role theory of sex differences and similarities: A current appraisal. In T. Eckes & H. M. Trautner (Eds.), *The developmental social psychology of gender* (pp. 123–174). Mahwah, NJ: Erlbaum.

Erikson, E. H. (1968). *Identity: Youth and crisis.* New York: Norton.

Espelage, D. L., & Swearer, S. M. (2003). Research on school bullying and victimization: What have we learned and where do we go from here? *School Psychology Review, 32,* 365–383.

Fekkes, M., Pijpers, F. I. M., & Verloove-Vanhorick, S. P. (2005). Bullying: Who does what, when and where? Involvement of children, teachers and parents in bullying behavior. *Health Education Research, 20,* 81–91.

Finn, J. (2004). A survey of online harassment at a university campus. *Journal of Interpersonal Violence, 19,* 468–483.

Glaberson, W. (2012, March 18). Verdict repudiates notion of youth as legal defense. *New York Times,* p. A20.

Goldsborough, R. (2010). Technology today: Resources available to fight growing cyberbullying trend. *Community College Week.* Retrieved from http://www.ccweek.com/news/templates/template.aspx?articleid=1990&zoneid=3

Greenfield, P. M., & Yan, Z. (2006). Children, adolescents and the Internet: A new field of inquiry in developmental psychology. *Developmental Psychology, 42,* 391–394

Gross, E. F. (2004). Adolescent Internet use: What we expect, what teens report. *Journal of Applied Developmental Psychology, 25,* 633–649.

Harris, S., Petrie, G., & Willoughby, W. (2002). Bullying among 9th graders: An exploratory study. *NASSP Bulletin, 86,* 1630.

Hashima, P., & Finkelhor, D. (1999). Violent victimization of youth versus adults in National Crime Victimization Survey. *Journal of Interpersonal Violence, 14,* 799–819.

Herring, S. (1992). Gender and participation in computer-mediated linguistic discourse. Washington, DC: Eric Clearinghouse on Languages and Linguistics. Document no. ED345552.

Hinduja, S., & Patchin, J. (2007). Offline consequences of online victimization: School violence and delinquency. *Journal of School Violence, 6,* 89–112.

Hinduja, S., & Patchin, J. (2008). Personal information of adolescents on the Internet: A quantitative content analysis of MySpace. *Journal of Adolescence, 31,* 125–146.

Hinduja, S., & Patchin, J. (2009). *Bullying beyond the schoolyard: Preventing and responding to cyberbullying.* Thousand Oaks, CA: Sage.

Hinduja, S., & Patchin, J. (2010). Bullying, cyberbullying and suicide. *Archives of Suicide Research, 14,* 206–221.

Holladay, J. (2010). Cyberbullying: The stakes have never been higher for students—or schools. *Teaching Tolerance, 38,* 42–46.

I-SAFE America. (2002). Evaluability assessment: I-SAFE America, Inc. Retrieved from http://www.ncjrs.gov/pdffiles1/nij/ISAFE.pdf

Jackson, L. A., von Eye, A., Biocca, F. A., Barbatsis, G., Zhao, Y., & Fitzgerald, H. E. (2006). Does home Internet use influence the academic performance of low-income children? *Developmental Psychology, 42,* 429–435.

Jemal, A., Siegel, R., Ward, E., Murray, T., Xu, J., Smigal, C., & Thun, M. J. (2006). Cancer statistics, *CA: A Cancer Journal for Clinicians, 56,* 106–130.

Jordan, J. V., Kaplan, A. G., Miller, J. B., Stiver, I. P., & Surrey, J. L. (1991). *Women's growth in connection: Writings from the Stone Center.* New York, NY: Guilford Press.

Juvonen, J., & Gross, E. F. (2008). Extending the school grounds? Bullying experiences in cyberspace. *Journal of School Health, 78,* 496–506.

Katzer, C., Fetchenhauer, D., & Belschak, F. (2009). Cyberbullying: Who are the victims? A comparison of victimization in Internet chatrooms and victimization in school. *Journal of Media Psychology, 21,* 25–36.

Kerr, M., & Statin, H. (2000). What parents know, how they know it, and several forms of adolescent adjustment: Further support for a reinterpretation of monitoring. *Developmental Psychology, 36,* 366–380.

Kiesler, S., Siegel, J., & McGuire. T. W. (1984). Social psychological aspects of computer mediated communications. *American Psychologist, 39,* 1123–1134.

Kowalski, R. M., & Limber, S. P. (2007). Electronic bullying among middle school students. *Journal of Adolescent Health, 41,* S22–S30.

Kraft, E. M., & Wang, J. (2010). An exploratory study of the cyberbullying and cyberstalking experiences and factors related to victimization of students at a public liberal arts college. *International Journal of Technoethics, 1,* 74–91.

Kubey, R. (2002). How media education promotes critical thinking, democracy, health, and aesthetic appreciation. In *Thinking critically about media: Schools and families in partnership* (pp. 1–6). Alexandria, VA: Cable in the Classroom.

Lavallee, A. (2007, March). Friends swap twitters, and frustration. *The Wall Street Journal.* Retrieved from http://online.wsj.com/public/article/SB117373145818634482-ZwdoPQ0PqPrcFMDHDZLz_P6osnI_20080315.html

Lenhart, A. (2007). Cyberbullying and online teens. *PewInternet.* Retrieved from http:www.pewinternet.org/Reports/2007/cyberbullying

Lenhart, A., Ling, R., Campbell, S., & Purcell, K. (2010, April). Teens and mobile phones. Retrived from the PewInternet website: http://pewinternet.org/Reports/2010/Teens-and-Mobile-Phones.aspx

Lenhart, A., Madden, M., & MacGill, A. (2007). Teens and social media. Retrieved from from the PewInternet website: http://www.pewinternet.org/Reports/2007/Teens-and-Social-Media.aspx

Li, Q. (2007). New bottle but old wine: A research of cyberbullying in schools. *Computers in Human Behavior, 23,* 1777–1791.

Liau, A. K., Khoo, A., & Ang, P. H. (2005). Factors influencing adolescents engagement in risky Internet behavior. *CyberPsychology & Behavior, 8,* 513–520.

Livingstone, S., Olafsson, K., & Staksrud, E. (2011). Social networking, age and privacy. *EU Kids Online: Short report.* London, England: London School of Economics and Political Science.

Livingston, S., Haddon, L., Gorzig, A., & Olafsson, K. (2011). EU Kids Online Final Report. Retrieved from www.eukidsonline.net.

Masten, A. S., Coatsworth, J. D., Neemann, J., Gest, S. D., Tellegen, A., & Garmezy, N. (1995). The structure and coherence of competence from childhood through adolescence. *Child Development, 66,* 1635–1659.

Menesini, E., Nocentini, A., & Calussi, P. (2011). The measurement of cyberbullying: Dimensional structure and relative item severity and discrimination. *CyberPsychology, Behavior and Social Networking, 14,* 267–274.

Merten, D. (1997). The meaning of meanness: Popularity, competition and conflict among junior high schools. *Sociology of Education, 70,* 175–191.

Mikel-Brown, L. (2003). *Girlfighting: Betrayal and rejection among girls.* New York, NY: New York University Press.

Miller, J. B. (1976). *Toward a new psychology of women.* Boston, MA: Beacon Press.

Mitchell, K. J., Becker-Blease, K. A., & Finkelhor, D. (2005). Inventory of problematic Internet experiences encountered in clinical practice. *Professional Psychology: Research and Practice, 36,* 498–509.

Mitchell, K., Finkelhor, D., & Wolak, J. (2001). Risk factors for and impact of online sexual solicitation of youth. *Journal of the American Medical Association, 285,* 3011–3014.

Mitchell, K., Finkelhor, D., & Wolak, J. (2003). The exposure of youth to unwanted sexual material on the Internet: A national survey of risk, impact, & prevention. *Youth & Society, 34,* 330–358.

Muir, D. (2005). Violence against children in cyberspace. *ECPAT International.* Retrieved from ECPAT_cyberspace_2005_ENG

Nakamura, A. (2004, June). Killing stokes fears over impact of net. *The Japan News.* Retrieved from http://202.221.217.59/print/news/nn06-2004/mn20040605a5 .htm

Nansel, T. R., Overpeck, M. D., Haynie, D. L., Ruan, J. W., & Scheidt, P. C. (2003). Relationships between bullying and violence among U.S. youth. *Archives of Pediatrics & Adolescent Medicine, 157,* 348–353.

Nansel, T. R., Overpeck, M., Pilla, R. S., Ruan, J. W., Simons-Morton, B., & Scheidt, P. (2001). Bullying behaviors among U.S. youth: Prevalence and association with psychosocial adjustment. *Journal of the American Medical Association, 16,* 2094–2100.

Palfrey, J., & Gasser, U. (2008). *Born digital: Understanding the first generation of digital natives.* New York, NY: Basic Books

Palfrey, J., Sacco, D., Boyd, D., & DeBonis, L. (2009). *Enhancing child safety & online technologies: Final report of the Internet safety technical task force to the multi-state working group on social networking of state attorneys general of the United States.* Cambridge, MA: Berkman Center for Internet & Society at Harvard University.

Parks, M. R., & Floyd, K. (1996). Making friends in cyberspace. *Journal of Computer-Mediated Communication, 46,* 80–97.

Patchin, J., Burgess-Proctor, A., & Hinduja, S. (2009). Cyberbullying and online harassment: Reconceptualizing the victimization of adolescent girls. In V. Garcia & J. Clifford (Eds.), *Female victims of crime: Reality reconsidered* (pp. 162–176). Upper Saddle River, NJ: Prentice Hall.

Patchin, J., & Hinduja, S. (2006). Bullies move beyond the schoolyard: A preliminary look at cyberbullying. *Youth Violence and Juvenile Justice, 4,* 148–169.

Patchin, J., & Hinduja, S. (2010). Cyberbullying and self-esteem. *Journal of School Health, 80,* 614–621.

Pellegrini, A., & Long, J. (2002). A longitudinal study of bullying, dominance, and victimization during the transition from primary school through secondary school. *British Journal of Developmental Psychology, 20,* 259–288.

PewResearchCenter. (2010). Millennials: A portrait of generation next: Confident. Connected. Open to change. Retrieved from http://pewresearch.org/millennials

Pokin, S. (2007). Pokin around: A real person, a real death. *St. Charles County Suburban Journal.* Retrieved from http://www.stltoday.com/suburban-journals/stcharles/news/stevepokin/pokin-around-a-real-person-a-real-death/article_511f32a2-ebd1-5568-8a1a-b2218cc60135.html

Privetera, C., & Campbell, M. A. (2009). Cyberbullying: The new face of workplace bullying? *CyberPsychology & Behavior, 12,* 395–400.

Prothrow-Stith, D., & Spivak, H. (2005). *Sugar & spice and no longer nice: How we can stop girls' violence.* San Francisco, CA: Jossey-Bass.

Raver, C. C. (2004). Placing emotional self-regulation in sociocultural and socioeconomic contexts. *Child Development, 75,* 346–353

Remillar, A. M., & Lamb, S. (2005). Adolescent girls' coping with relational aggression. *Sex Roles, 53,* 221–229.

Ridgeway, C., & Correll, S. (2004). Unpacking the gender system: A theoretical perspective on gender beliefs and social relations. *Gender & Society, 18,* 510–531.

Ringrose, J. (2006). A new universal mean girl: Examining the discursive construction and social regulation of a new feminine pathology. *Feminism & Psychology, 16,* 405–424. Retrieved from http://fap.sagepub.com/content/16/4/405

Robb, C. (2006). *This changes everything: The relational revolution in psychology.* New York, NY: Farrar, Straus & Giroux.

Sbarbaro, V., & Enyeart Smith, T. M. (2011). An exploratory study of bullying and cyberbullying behaviors among economically/educationally disadvantaged middle school students. *American Journal of Health Studies, 26,* 139–151.

Seguin, J. R., & Zelazo, P. (2005). Executive function in early physical aggression. In R. E. Tremblay, W. W. Hartup, & J. Archer (Eds.), *Developmental origins of aggression* (pp. 307–329). New York, NY: Guilford Press.

Shariff, S., & Hoff, D. (2007). Cyberbullying: Clarifying legal boundaries for school supervision in cyberspace. *International Journal of Cyber Criminology, 1,* 76–118.

Simmons, R. (2002). *Odd girl out: The hidden culture of aggression in girls.* New York, NY: Harcourt Brace.

Slonje, R., & Smith, P. K. (2008). Cyberbullying: Another main type of bullying? *Scandinavian Journal of Psychology, 49,* 147–154.

Smith, A., & Williams, K. (2004) R U there? Ostracism by cell phone text messages. *Group Dynamics: Theory, Research and Practice, 8,* 291–301.

Smith, P. K., Mahdavi, J., Carvalho, M., Fisher, S., Russelll, S., & Tippett, N. (2008). Cyberbullying: Its nature and impact in secondary school pupils. *Journal of Child Psychology and Psychiatry, 49,* 376–385.

Snider, M. (2004, May 24). Stalked by a cyberbully. *Macleans, 117,* 76. Retrieved from http://www.macleans.ca/article.jsp?content=20040524_81183_81183

STAR-W (Students Using Technology to Achieve Reading and Writing). (2005). Bullies to buddies: 4 types of cyberbullies. Retrieved from http://www.starw.org/b2b/4TypesofCyberbullies.htm

Subrahmanyam, K., Greenfield, P., & Smahel, D. (2006). Connecting developmental constructions to the Internet: Identity presentation and sexual exploration in online teen chat rooms. *Developmental Psychology, 42,* 395–406.

Suler, J. (2005). The psychology of cyberspace. Rider University. Retrieved from www.rider.edu/suler/psycyber.html

Taylor, A. S., & Harper, R. (2003). The gift of the gab: A design oriented sociology of young people's use of mobiles. *Journal of Computer Supported Cooperative Work (CSCW), 12,* 267–296.

Underwood, M. (2003). *Social aggression among girls.* New York, NY: Guilford Press.

Underwood, M., Rosen, L. H., More, D., Ehrenreich, S. E., & Gentsch, J. K. (2012). The BlackBerry project: Capturing the content of adolescents' test messaging. *Developmental Psychology, 48,* 295–302.

Van der Wal, M. F., de Wit, C. A. M., & Hirasing, R. A. (2003). Psychosocial health among young victims and offenders of direct and indirect bullying. *Pediatrics, 111,* 1312–1317.

Wallace, P. (1999). *The psychology of the Internet.* Cambridge, England: Cambridge University Press.

Wang, J., Ianotti, R., & Nansel, T. R. (2009). School bullying among US adolescents: Physical, verbal, relational and cyber. *Journal of Adolescent Health, 45,* 368–375.

Willard, N. (2002). *Computer ethics, etiquette & safety for the 21st century student.* Eugene, OR: International Society for Technology in Education.

Willard, N. (2003). Off-campus, harmful online student speech. *Journal of School Violence, 1,* 65–93.

Williams, K. A. (2001). *Ostracism: The power of silence.* New York, NY: Guilford Press.

Williams, K., & Guerra, N. G. (2007). Prevalence and predictors of Internet bullying. *Journal of Adolescent Health, 41* (Suppl. 6), S14–S21

Wiseman, R. (2002). *Queen bees and wannabes. Helping your daughter survive cliques, gossip, boyfriends and other realities of adolescence.* New York, NY: Crown.

Wocker, C. (2002, July). Bash a Christian: Rappists' hi-tech message of hate. *The Daily Telegraph,* p. 3.

Wolak, J., Finkelhor, D., Mitchell, K., & Ybarra, M. (2010). Online predators and their victims: Myths, realities and implications for prevention and treatment. *Psychology of Violence, 1* (Suppl.), 13–35.

Wolak, J., Kimberley, J. D., Mitchell, J., & Finkelhor, D. (2007). Does online harassment constitute bullying? An exploration of online harassment by known peers and online-only contacts. *Journal of Adolescent Health, 41,* S51–S58.

Wright, V. H., Burnham, J. J., Inman, C. T., & Ogorchock, H. N. (2009). Cyberbullying: Using virtual scenarios to educate and raise awareness. *Journal of Computing in Teacher Education, 26,* 35–42.

Yan, Z. (2006). What influences children's and adolescents' understanding of the complexity of the Internet? *Developmental Psychology, 42* (Suppl. 1), 418–428.

Ybarra, M., Leaf, P., & Diener-West, M. (2004). Sex differences in youth-reported depressive symptomatology and unwanted Internet sexual solicitation. *Journal of Medical Internet Research, 6,* e5. Retrieved from http://www.jmir.org/2004/1/e5

Ybarra, M., & Mitchell, K. (2004a). Online aggressor/targets, aggressors, and targets: A comparison of associated youth characteristics. *Journal of Child Psychology and Psychiatry, 45,* 1308–1316.

Ybarra, M., & Mitchell, K. (2004b). Youth engaging in online harassment: Associations with caregiver-child relationships, Internet use, and personal characteristics. *Journal of Adolescence, 27,* 319–336.

Zelazo, P. D., Muller, U., Frye, D., & Marcovitch, S. (2003). The development of executive function in early childhood. *Monographs of the Society for Research in Child Development, 68,* 11–27.

Zizek, S. (2004). What can psychoanalysis tell us about cyberspace? *Psychoanalytic Review, 91,* 801–830.

Chapter 10

A Global Examination of Teen Relationship Violence

Emilio C. Ulloa, Jamie Kissee, Donna Castaneda, and Audrey Hokoda

On April 24, 2012, UK news organizations reported that a violent and jealous boyfriend, fearful his aspiring model girlfriend was being unfaithful to him, strangled her in bed. The 20-year-old strangled his 17-year-old girlfriend (name withheld) after some time arguing over his suspicions that she was having an affair. The prosecutor in the case told the jury that the couple had a short, volatile relationship that had included threats of murder and incidents of actual violence toward the young woman in front of friends. The young man had become angry over a Facebook picture of her "flirting with lads in a car" in New Zealand. He did not like that the clothes she wore he considered too revealing and called her a whore on the night the prosecution say he strangled her.

On August 14, 2011, African news reports shared photos of a young college woman who had survived an attack of concentrated acid on her face and body at the hands of her boyfriend, also a student from the same college. They reported that the young woman was attacked on her way to her hostel after school had ended for the day. Bystanders reported that she had stopped in front of one of the male hostels known as Suleiman Hall to answer a call when her boyfriend came from behind and reportedly poured the acid on her. The investigative authorities discovered that the relationship between them started on campus but had gone bad when the young woman tried to end the relationship, which her parents did not approve of. After the attack, other women at the university demonstrated and went on record to say that this was not the first time something like this had happened on their campus.

INTRODUCTION

Over approximately the past 30 years, researchers have worked to define teen relationship violence (TRV), measure its prevalence, track its consequences, recognize its predictors, and understand its mechanisms. What we have concluded is that TRV is a complex phenomenon, prevalent across the youth life span and across cultures and geographies. This chapter aims to describe the theory and empirical literature related to TRV with attention to the global nature of the phenomenon. We cover its prevalence, consequences, predictors, and mechanisms. As well, we describe the documented prevention and intervention efforts associated specifically with TRV.

DEFINITION OF ADOLESCENT DATING VIOLENCE

Because dating violence among adolescents was first identified in North America and the majority of research on this phenomenon has taken place in the United States and Canada, the definition of dating violence among adolescents emerged from this geographic region (e.g., Bergman, 1992; Wekerle & Wolfe, 1999). Most generally, it has been defined as "any attempt to control or dominate another person physically, sexually, or psychologically, causing some level of harm" (Wekerle &Wolfe, 1999, p. 436), and it is characterized first by occurring in the adolescent years and, second, in relationships in which partners are unmarried and do not cohabitate together (for a discussion, see Rey Anacona, 2008). The Centers for Disease Control and Prevention (CDC, 2009) went on to specifically describe each subcategory of intimate partner violence indicating that physical abuse refers to instances where a partner is hit, pinched, shoved, or kicked with the intention to harm, disable, or even kill. Sexual abuse refers to instances when a partner is forced to engage in a sex act when she or he does not or cannot give consent, whether or not the act is completed. It also refers to noncontact sexual abuse, such as verbal sexual harassment. Psychological abuse, which includes emotional abuse, refers to threatening a partner or harming her or his sense of self-worth. It can include shaming, bullying, or embarrassing a partner on purpose; name-calling; and keeping the partner away from friends and family.

As the issue of intimate partner violence has become more salient internationally, particularly violence against women, the World Health Organization (WHO) has also put forth a definition of intimate partner violence that is similar to that of the CDC. It refers to physical, sexual, and emotional abuse, as well as a fourth category of abuse referred to as "deprivation and neglect" (Garcia-Moreno, Jansen, Ellsberg, Heise, & Watts, 2005, p. 13; Krug, Dahlberg, Mercy, Zwi, & Lozano, 2002). In the 2005 WHO multicountry study on women's health and domestic violence, researchers found that women readily recognized the behaviors that made up physical and sexual violence on the part of relationship partners, but because of cultural variation by country, social class, and ethnicity within a country, less agreement was found on what behaviors constituted emotional abuse (Garcia-Moreno et al., 2005).

Unlike the CDC, WHO does not explicitly refer to adolescent dating violence as a separate category of intimate partner violence. The growing body of international research on adolescent relationship violence indicates that, despite varying geographic and cultural contexts, it is often defined in similar ways. That is, the focus includes physical, sexual, and psychological or emotional abuse between nonmarried couples (Chan, Straus, Brownridge, Tiwari, & Leung, 2008; Pradubmook-Sherer, 2011; Rivera-Rivera, Allen-Leigh, Rodríguez-Ortega, Chávez-Ayala, & Lazcano-Ponce, 2007; Sherer & Sherer, 2008).

Although development of a universal definition of adolescent dating violence is considered a priority (e.g., Bandyopadhyay, Deokar, & Omar, 2010) because it aids in attempts to understand adolescent dating relationship violence at the international level, some researchers and theorists point to the importance of continuing to include a contextual interpretive framework to better incorporate cultural construals of intimate partner violence behaviors and responses that may fall outside these standard definitions (Mason et al., 2008). This may be particularly important in the case of adolescent dating violence because it is still in the early stages of being recognized and researched in many countries. Adolescence itself, and thus adolescent dating relationships, may be viewed and understood differently based on religious, economic, historical, community, and cultural contexts, as well as degree of Westernization within and across particular countries, and this may increase the chance that more varied definitions exist of what constitutes violence within these relationships. For instance, research on adolescent dating violence in Spain has found that, although the Conflict in Dating Relationships Inventory, a frequently used measure of dating violence in adolescents, has similar reliability and validity across its subscales, the subscale on threatening behavior was not valid in the Spanish context (Fernández-Fuertes, Fuertes, & Pulido, 2006). Another study found that Iraqi immigrant youth identified a larger number of behaviors as constituting violence than African American youth, particularly behaviors that referred to emotional or verbal abuse (Black et al., 2009). Alternatively, as in a study with Thai adolescent girls, physical and emotional abuse may be viewed as dating violence, whereas forms of sexual violence and coercion may not readily be included in understandings of dating violence (Thongpriwan & McElmurry, 2009). Likewise, even if adolescent dating violence is defined similarly across geographic and cultural contexts, it is important to remember that interpretations of findings within any given country are embedded within the social, cultural, political, and historical changes specific to that particular nation or society. Some examples of changes that influence interpretations of adolescent dating violence data are the ongoing Arab–Israeli conflict (Sherer & Sherer, 2008) and its effect on attitudes toward violence in general; the collapse of socialism in Poland and resulting social and cultural changes in gender dynamics (Doroszewicz & Forbes, 2008); and coexisting traditional and nontraditional cultural values and norms surrounding adolescent dating in Thai society (Pradubmook-Sherer, 2011).

Eastern versus Western Definitions

Researchers have some trouble reaching a common definition of teen relationship violence. For example, there are differences of opinion on whether the definition needs to include intent to harm or whether sexual, physical, and verbal emotional abuse should all be included. But these differences among social scientists seem less consequential than the differences among youth in their own definitions of abusive or violent relationship behavior. The literature suggests that there may be different perceptions of TRV in different countries and cultures.

In Japan, dating violence is commonly referred to as forms of harassment (Ohnisihi et al., 2011). This can include such behaviors as controlling the activities and behavior on one's partner, checking cell phone records without permission, taking money out of their girlfriend or boyfriend's purse or wallet, and forcing unprotected sexual intercourse. However, the most commonly documented form of harassment is verbal harassment. Although harassment within dating relationships is common, with about 50% of adolescents reporting the perpetration of harassing behavior, few boys and girls recognize these activities as actual forms of harassment. This suggests that there is a disconnect between harassment and recognizing or acknowledging these behaviors as abusive.

In many Southeast Asian countries, spirituality plays an important role in how violence is defined, the reason for why violence occurs, and as a means for young girls to cope with abuse. For example, in Cambodia and Thailand, many women believe that they are reborn to experience abuse due to bad karma from a past life (Norsworthy, 2003). Alternatively, younger girls tend to find hope in their beliefs in karma, that they must endure abuse now to enjoy a better life in the future, which serves as a mechanism for coping (Thongpriwan & McElmurry, 2009). Additionally in China, one's *linghun,* or soul, is of utmost importance, and hindering or damaging one's *linghun* in any way can be considered a form of violence in a relationship (Wang & Ho 2007). However, in general, dating violence in China has not been well defined because of the lack of research and the varying dimensions of violence that can be included. Therefore, more attention to this area is needed to establish a comprehensive definition of dating violence and how it may look different across countries.

The definition of dating violence, specifically sexual abuse, is oftentimes unclear due to differing gender roles and expectations. Specifically, in the United Kingdom, male adolescents commonly initiate sexual advances toward a dating partner that cues girls to respond to advances with either a "yes" or a "no" (Hird, 2000). Although this seems straightforward, the answer of "no" is often misunderstood, which creates a negotiation between girls and boys. Girls have reported that they believe the verbal act of saying "no" is a sufficient means of expressing "no," and the sexual advance should be terminated. However, boys have reported that verbally expressing "no" is not enough, and to mean "no," girls should express it in various ways (e.g., verbally and physically pushing their hand away). In addition, there is social pressure on male adolescents to express their sexuality in relationships because it represents a compliment of one's prowess. In contrast, there is social pressure on female adolescents to defend their sexual reputations. As a result misunderstandings during the negotiation process coupled with differing gender expectations can lead to girls' compromising their own sexuality and blurs the line of what is considered sexual abuse (Hird, 2000).

In Africa, there appears to be more contextual consideration of abuse compared with Western societies. For example, in the context of high poverty and limited resources, the concept of detoothing among young African women, which involves the receiving of gifts or money in exchange for sex (Luke, 2003), is not often described as abusive. Cultural backdrops such as these have a profound effect on dating behaviors in Africa, such that young girls date much older men, and partners are sought out for their ability to provide necessities, in contrast to the types of attributes that Western young women seek out in partners. Research has suggested that the nature of the power imbalances between genders that this cultural backdrop creates is responsible for an environment where girls tend to give themselves sexually as a means to survive (Luke, 2003). Consequentially, many adolescents—even girls—report that they think rape is justified in cases of detoothing (Luke, 2003). Similarly, in South Africa, the male-dominated society is illustrated in that many adolescents believe physical violence is acceptable and furthermore is a demonstration of love in a relationship (Swart, Seedat, Stevens, & Ricardo, 2002).

Dating violence is highly influenced by the values upheld in patriarchal societies because of common socially accepted male-dominated behaviors. For example, Thailand has a predominant patriarchal society in which sexual power and sexual experience are important elements in defining one's masculinity (Pradubmook-Sherer, 2009). As a result, major incongruencies exist for sexual expectations between men and women. More specifically, a double standard exists for premarital sexual intercourse. Women are condemned for engaging in premarital sex, whereas men are encouraged by society to be sexually active. Additionally, women are often forced by their partners to consent to unwanted sex to prove their loyalty and affection. The acceptance of these forced actions by men encourages a society in which dating violence can easily occur. This similar pattern can be seen in Israeli–Arab societies in which the values and customs are well defined and reflect a patriarchal, nonegalitarian society (Haj-Yahia, 2000, 2003; Herzog, 2004). Violence is commonly viewed as an accepted form of problem solving, and abuse towards women is widely accepted by both men and women (Haj-Yahia, 2000, 2003). These defined gender roles that uphold men's superiority over women encourage an environment where dating violence can be accepted (Sherer, 2010). Furthermore, because these social norms in patriarchal societies are prominent in everyday life, many female adolescents find it difficult to seek help concerning their violent relationship experiences, which only perpetuates the cycle (Thongpriwan & McElmurry, 2009).

PREVALENCE OF TEEN RELATIONSHIP VIOLENCE

Available international-level research indicates that intimate partner violence among adolescents is common but that rates vary widely across studies and countries. Much of this information comes from studies that have been done as part of the International Dating Violence Study, a consortium of researchers from 32 nations investigating perpetration and being a victim of dating violence among university students in each country (see Straus, 2011) and utilizes the Revised Conflict Tactics Scale (Straus, Hamby, Money-McCoy, & Sugarman, 1996). Although data from this large research effort is important, it focuses on the upper age level of adolescence and fewer studies are available that examine the phenomenon of adolescent dating violence cross-culturally for individuals at early or midadolescence. This is the case despite evidence that dating violence is increasing among those at younger ages in many countries (Bandyopadhyay et al., 2010). Nonetheless, one of the studies to emerge from this research effort was done by Chan and colleagues (2008) and they found in their 21-country study (22 study sites) of dating violence prevalence among university students that the overall median rate of reported physical assault perpetration in dating relationships across countries was 30% (Germany) and ranged from a low of 17%

(Sweden) to a high of 44% (Mexico). The median rate of report of being a victim of physical assault was 26% (Hong Kong) and ranged from a low of 14% (Israel) to a high 39% (Mexico). The median rate of reported sexual coercion perpetration across the 21 countries was 20% (Switzerland) and rates ranged from a low of 8% (the Netherlands) to a high of 34% (Brazil). The median rate of reports of being a victim of sexual coercion was 24% (Singapore) and ranged from a low of 9% (the Netherlands) to a high of 46% (Greece). Another study conducted as part of the International Dating Violence Study found that college students across 32 nations showed an overall rate of reported female physical attacks on a dating partner of 31.6% and an overall rate of reported male physical attacks on a dating partner of 24.4% (Straus, 2008). The range in these rates of physical attacks on a dating partner, however, was considerable, from 95.5% and 71.4% for men and women, respectively, in Iran, to 10% and 15.8% among men in Singapore and women in Malta, respectively.

Studies of adolescent dating violence that focus on younger adolescents at middle and secondary school levels show varied rates as well. For example, rates of reported physical violence perpetration by girls in adolescent dating relationships are 20.99% in Mexico and 30.2% in Spain, whereas for boys the reported rates of physical violence perpetration are 19.54% in Mexico and 16.1% in Spain (Fernández-Fuertes & Fuertes, 2010; Rivera-Rivera et al., 2007). In South Africa and Tanzania, researchers also found varying rates of physical violence perpetration by adolescent girls at 8.6% to 17% and for boys at 11.1% to 21.8%; rates of physical violence victimization were 13.2% to 37.8% for girls and 10.2% to 35.8% for boys (Wubs et al., 2009). Another study that focused on South African adolescents found even higher rates of perpetration of physical violence, with a reported rate of 35% for boys and 44% for girls; reported rates of being a victim of physical violence in a dating relationship were 38% for boys and 42% for girls (Swart et al., 2002). A study of youth that had been referred to a youth mental health organization in Australia found that 11.3% of girls and 15.6% of boys reported being a victim of physical violence from a dating partner (Brown et al., 2009).

As in studies in the United States (for a review, Ulloa, Castañeda, & Hokoda, 2010; Ulloa, Watts, Ulibarri, Castañeda, & Hokoda, 2012), international research indicates that emotional, or verbal, abuse tends to show the highest prevalence rates among adolescents, both for perpetration and victimization, followed by physical abuse, where rates for perpetration and victimization tend to be more variable across studies, with sexual violence sometimes showing rates similar to or sometimes lower than physical abuse (e.g., Chan et al., 2008; Doroszewicz & Forbes, 2008; Fernández Fuertes & Fuertes, 2010; for a discussion on prevalence of sexual coercion in Spain see Fuertes Martín, Ramos Vergeles, & Fernández Fuertes, 2007; Sherer & Sherer, 2008; Swart et al., 2002; Wubs et al., 2009).

A large amount of research in the United States (Cano, Avery-Leaf, Cascardi, & O'Leary, 1998; O'Leary & Smith Slep, 2003; Ozer, Tschann, Pasch, & Flores, 2004; Silverman, Raj, Mucci, & Hathaway, 2001), and a growing amount of research at the international level (Fernández Fuertes & Fuertes, 2010; Rivera-Rivera et al., 2007; Swart et al., 2002), indicates that the three categories of adolescent dating violence in relationships—that is, physical, sexual, and psychological violence—can be described separately, but they are related to each other and often co-occur in dating relationships among adolescents. Likewise, international research shows that among adolescents, being a perpetrator of intimate partner violence is associated with being a victim of intimate partner violence (Fernández-Fuertes & Fuertes, 2010; Fernández-Fuertes, Fuertes, & Pulido, 2006; Swart et al., 2002).

In addition to evidence that adolescent dating violence is common across different types of countries and societies, the pattern of gender symmetry is also striking. Gender symmetry refers to similar rates of dating violence perpetration and victimization across adolescent girls and boys. Gender symmetry is a frequent finding in studies of adolescent dating violence with female and male adolescents (and young adults)—in fact, in a 32-nation study of dating violence in college students by Straus (2008) results showed that bidirectional physical assault—that both partners were violent—was the most common dating violence pattern, followed by assault on the female only, and lastly assault on the male only. These results are mirrored in a number of single-country studies with both college students and adolescents at the middle or secondary school age that show a higher prevalence of physical dating violence perpetration for girls than boys (Doroszewicz & Forbes, 2008; Rivera-Rivera et al., 2007; Swart et al., 2002). Despite the findings of gender symmetry, and even higher rates of dating violence perpetration by adolescent girls compared with boys in certain studies, some researchers continue to emphasize how complex social and cultural pressures, sexual double standards, gendered perceptions of blame and responsibility surrounding dating violence, as well as gendered power relations in adolescent heterosexual relationships may make girls more vulnerable than boys to dating violence (Chung, 2007; Thongpriwan & McElmurry, 2009).

In summary, despite the still limited research on adolescent dating violence at the international level, variability in measures used, and that studies do not necessarily measure all categories of dating violence or both victimization and perpetration, the picture that emerges with regard to the global prevalence of adolescent dating violence is one of variability across countries, types of violence, and across gender. Clearly, violence is often present in the dating relationships of adolescents and the growing global research emphasis on this issue points to the concern surrounding it and the need for a better understanding of its prevalence in differing parts of the world.

INTERNATIONAL PATTERNS AND PERSPECTIVES

TRV is an international phenomenon; however, until recently much of what we know is based on U.S. and Canadian samples. Although the research on TRV from countries other than the United States is less plentiful, what does exist provides an interesting picture of the patterns of similarities and differences in TRV internationally. In this section, we aim to synthesize these patterns of similarities and differences.

Patterns of Risk Factors

It is clear from the literature that some assumptions about patterns of risk factors for TRV simply do not hold true in all societies. One of the most apparent is the finding that neglectful, authoritarian childhood experiences are consistently predictive of TRV in adolescence. In fact, according to Strauss and Savage (2005), in a study of TRV across 17 countries, the more neglectful behaviors one experienced as a child, the more likely they were to physically assault a dating partner. Interestingly in Russia, perpetration rates of TRV are higher among females than among males (Lysova & Hines, 2008). This may be attributed to the fact that many men fear the consequence of being kicked out of school and forced to enroll in the army where life can be much more difficult. However, in a recent study of parental supervision in Thailand, researchers discovered a contradictory finding. Namely, in Thailand, the higher the parental supervision, the greater the risk for an adolescent to engage in an abusive relationship (Pradubmook-Sherer, 2009).

Patterns of Consequences

There are a multitude of dangerous consequences that can result from TRV. These consequences fall into two major categories including both direct and indirect effects to individuals involved. A major direct effect of dating violence is the physical and sexual harm suffered by the victim. Indirect effects include long-term effects of physical, sexual, and emotional well-being, in addition to social implications. There is evidence to suggest that these patterns of consequences hold across different cultures that have far-reaching effects on individuals and societies.

The major direct effect of TRV is the immediate physical and sexual harm that is inflicted upon an individual. The severity of this consequence is reflected in the rate of physical and sexual harm reported across countries, especially for girls. Chan and colleagues (2008) investigated dating violence in a sample of youth across 17 countries. They found that across all countries, the rate of perpetrating physical violence that resulted in injury and sexual coercion was higher for males than for females. Rates for perpetrating physical assault with less severe consequences were split in which 12 sites had higher rates among perpetration from women and 17 sites had higher rates for perpetration from men. High perpetration rates resulting in physical and sexual harm suggest that dating violence is prevalent and dangerous to one's personal safety across countries.

Consequences of dating violence can indirectly affect many areas of an adolescent's physical, sexual and emotional life that may not manifest until months or years have passed. For example, dating violence among adolescent girls in Africa is associated with unsafe sexual behaviors, increased risk of human immunodeficiency virus (HIV) infection, and other sexually transmitted infections (STIs) in Africa and Japan (Ohnishi et al., 2011; Jewkes et al., 2006; Luke, 2003). Unplanned pregnancy is commonly associated with dating violence and has been documented in Australia, Japan, and Canada (Chung, 2007; Ismail, Berman, & Ward-Griffin, 2007; Ohnishi et al., 2011). Maladaptive outcomes associated with sexual abuse victimization specifically include suicidal thoughts, self-harm (e.g., cutting behaviors), maladaptive dieting, early dating, substance use, and a heightened risk for lower safety at school, in a sample of Canadian youth (Chiodo, Wolfe, Crooks, Hughes, & Jaffe, 2009). In addition, physical dating violence has been found to be associated with older age and substance dependence, in a sample of Australian youth, which suggests that dating violence may contribute to the development of externalizing behaviors rather than internalizing behaviors (Brown et al., 2009). These effects of dating violence reach across physical, sexual, educational, and social domains, highlighting the widespread effects that TRV can have over time.

Mental health issues are often associated outcomes of dating violence that also affect individuals. Muñoz-Rivas, Graña, O'Leary, and González (2007) noted that psychological violence can cause great harm to a victim's mental health. In one study of Canadian adolescents, for example, many girls expressed difficulty in discussing the violence that had occurred in their relationships because people often did not take them seriously (Ismail, Berman, & Ward-Griffin, 2007). A similar phenomenon was documented in an Australian sample, in which girls reported that it is often difficult for them to speak up and seek help because many internalize the view that they are responsible for the violence that has occurred to them, in addition to being inadequate for not leaving their partner (Chung, 2007). The internalization of these thoughts can lead to great mental suffering (Ismail et al., 2007). For example, poor psychosocial functioning and a number of comorbid Axis I diagnoses have been identified in a sample of Australian youth involved in an abusive relationship both at the time of diagnosis and a 6-month follow-up (Brown et al., 2009). There is evidence to suggest that mental health issues can be sustained long after the abuse has occurred. Specifically, in Canada, ninth-grade students who were victims of sexual abuse reported they experienced emotional distress 2.5 years after the abuse had taken place (Chiodo et al., 2009). In addition, sustained fear of the perpetrator can also cause great emotional distress long after the relationship has ended, which has been documented in an Australian sample (Chung, 2007). These mental health issues can cause lasting and destructive damage.

In addition to mental health consequences, other outcomes of dating violence have been identified as important risk factors for future risky behavior, especially for girls. For example, Chiodo and colleagues (2009) noted that the immediate impact and long-term outcomes associated with sexual harassment victimization are often stronger and more negative for girls than boys in a sample of Canadian youth. For example, sexual harassment victimization in Grade 9 was associated with a higher risk for other forms of relationship violence, such as physical peer violence and sexual harassment victimization in Grade 11 (Chiodo et al., 2009). In addition, sexual harassment victimization in Grade 9 significantly predicted substance abuse and violent delinquency two and a half years later. Girls in particular grew more distressed over time and also acted out in a highly aggressive manner (Chiodo et al., 2009). Furthermore, in a sample of youth in South Africa, girls were particularly reluctant to terminate even unsatisfactory relationships because doing so increases the risk that they would experience additional physical violence and other compounded negative outcomes (Jewkes, Vundule, Maforah, & Jordaan, 2001).

The long-term effects of dating violence become especially important when considering the cycle of violence. Violence experienced during adolescent years can set the foundation for future relationship habits. When children experience abuse or witness other violent behaviors in the home, they increase their risk for dysfunctional and abusive relationships in adulthood. For girls in particular, it may be that these experiences shape a maladaptive expectation that abusive, demeaning, or controlling behavior is a normal part of relationships (Chiodo et al., 2009). Brownridge (2006) provided some evidence for this in a study of female university students from Canada, finding that witnessing interparental conflict had the largest impact on predicting the victimization of both physical assault and sexual coercion in dating relationships. This effect was stronger for experiencing sexual coercion than it was for experiencing physical assault. These results suggest that the cycle of violence can be intergenerational (Brownridge, 2006).

THEORIES OF TRV

In this section we aim to describe the most widely adopted different theoretical approaches to the phenomenon of TRV. Although the different theories each describe and attempt to explain the same phenomenon, they do so from different perspectives, with different foci, and consequently by emphasizing different factors. Their combined utility on the whole is high, because, when taken together, it provides a comprehensive set of lenses through which to think about TRV and helps researchers and practitioners alike to "see the bigger picture."

Feminist Theory

The feminist theory as applied to TRV, views violence against young women as one form of a more general global phenomenon of male attempts to control women. The theory was not developed with female adolescents in mind specifically, but nonetheless it has implications for teen female dating violence. The theory postulates that male violence toward women is rooted in patriarchal social structures and in the cultural roles of men and women, such that it is used to maintain subordinate social control and political status (Harway & O'Neil, 1999). Feminist theory focuses on the institutions and culture of different societies to explain male violence against women (Harway & O'Neil, 1999). It is used to explain heterosexual intimate partner violence perpetrated by men; however, it does not explain intimate partner violence in homosexual relationships or when females are the perpetrators.

Feminist theory focuses on patriarchal values that are learned and reinforced in most societies through gender role socialization, which establishes a belief in male entitlement, privilege and domination. Patriarchal values are transferred to young males through intergenerational transmissions or through a society's institutions, such as the legal system, mass media, and the educational system (Harway & O'Neil, 1999). When a society's institutions are male dominated, their practices and policies reinforce and allow patriarchal values to be legitimized and to flourish (Yodanis, 2004).

According to the feminist perspective, it is precisely the maladaptive patriarchal values adopted by both young men and women that foster expectations of inequitable power relationships. As such, the use of control, perhaps through threats of violence or actual violence become easy and accepted options used to maintain control and exert power over the perceived relatively powerless romantic partner (Yodanis, 2004). Feminist theory posits that the threat of violence can be as effective as actual physical violence (Harway & O'Neil, 1999).

Social Learning Theory

A popular approach to understanding any behavior, but aggressive behavior in particular, is by recalling Albert Bandura's (1971) social learning theory. According to Bandura, individuals learn behaviors by internalizing the behaviors modeled by their social network. When the individual reproduces the behavior on their own, these behaviors are then reinforced depending on whether they receive some direct or indirect positive feedback. When applied to TRV, social learning theory suggests that individuals learn maladaptive or aggressive conflict resolution tactics by internalizing behaviors witnessed at home (in their family of origin) or in their communities and then use similar conflict resolution tactics in their own intimate relationships. Put simply, teens who witness parental intimate partner violence or who experienced abuse as a child are more likely to experience violence in their own dating relationships. The literature on association between family of origin violence and TRV is inconsistent, however, which suggests there are multiple pathways from family of origin violence to later perpetration or victimization of dating violence. More recent consideration of gender socialization to Bandura's original theory has helped distinguish between some of the pathways from family of origin violence to later experiences of intimate partner violence. Gwartney-Gibbs, Stockard, and Bohmer (1987) suggested that because boys and girls are socialized differently, these early effects of socialized gender differences may lead to different pathways from family of origin violence to intimate partner violence among girls and boys. O'Keefe (1997), for example, found that low socioeconomic status, exposure to community and school violence, and acceptance of violence were the risk factors that predicted perpetration of dating violence in boys who also witnessed high levels of parent to parent violence. For girls, exposure to community and school violence and experiencing child abuse predicted perpetration of dating violence in females who had witnessed high levels of parent-to-parent violence. Sims, Dodd, and Tejeda (2008) found that severe family of origin abuse predicted later perpetration of dating violence better in males than in females.

Attachment Theory

When searching for explanations of aggression, many researchers focus on early life experiences. In fact, Bowlby's (1973) attachment theory in infants and young children has been drawn from and expanded to explain aggression, including intimate partner violence among adolescents and adults. According to Bowlby (1973) early life experiences can result in different attachment styles, three of which are often used to explain the relationship between young children and their caretakers. They include secure attachment, avoidant attachment, and anxious-ambivalent attachment. These attachment styles were distinguished by the behaviors the young children showed during separation from their caregiver (Bowlby, 1973). Bowlby posited that these attachment styles become internal working models that shape how an individual interacts with others. Attachment theory implies that adult attachment styles are extensions of our attachment style to our caregivers and therefore are characterized by certain beliefs and behaviors in our intimate relationships (e.g., Collins, Cooper, Albino, & Allard, 2002). As one might imagine, the interaction style an individual adopts toward significant others may have implications for their own teen romantic relationships. The adoption of attachment theory to explain relationships (in the form of adult attachment theory) proposes that TRV may be an extreme reaction to the perception that an intimate partner is unavailable or lacks commitment to the relationship (Mayseless, 1991).

Secure attachment in adulthood is characterized by trust in an intimate partner and the belief that one is loved and cared for by their partner. Those who enjoy secure attachments also have high expectations for their relationships, are comfortable with intimacy (Collins et al., 2002), and are less likely to use aggressive or violent conflict resolution tactics with intimate partners. Avoidant attachment in adulthood is characterized by an emphasis on self-reliance and an unwillingness to depend on others. Those who tend toward an avoidant attachment style view intimate partners as unreliable and are uncomfortable with intimacy (Collins et al., 2002; Mayseless, 1991). Adults with avoidant attachment may use passive-aggressive conflict resolution tactics such as disrespect, indifference, hostility, and contempt to distance themselves from an intimate partner. In contrast, individuals with an anxious-ambivalent attachment style in adulthood are characterized by an exaggerated need for closeness and intimacy. They may be unsure of the trustworthiness of their partner, may worry excessively about rejection (Collins et al., 2002), and these beliefs may lead to more aggressive responses to perceived threats to their relationship (Mayseless, 1991). Attachment theorists suggest that intimate partner violence is more likely to occur when one or both partners have an insecure attachment style (avoidant or anxious-ambivalent). Those who express insecure attachment styles are characterized by uncertainty about the availability and responsiveness of their intimate partner when a threat to the relationship is perceived. Paired with poor conflict resolution tactics, this uncertainty may lead to violence as a tool to keep the partner in the relationship or to distance themselves from an intimate partner (Mayseless, 1991).

Socioecological Model

Bronfenbrenner's ecological theory states that the healthy development of an individual is dependent on the interconnections between several levels of a person's social world. Using this framework to think about TRV means that one must recognize that aggressive behavior is complex and multiply determined. Ecological theory (sometimes referred to as socioecological theory) recognizes the influence from different "layers" of environment. These levels can include individual, family, and community factors (Bronfenbrenner, 1979). The interaction between factors in the model, such as personality, immediate family, school–peer environment, and the larger community environment determines social and behavioral outcomes. Banyard, Cross, and Modecki (2006) described the interconnections of these micro and macro levels as "a series of concentric circles of influence, which include intrapersonal, family, peer, community, and wider societal influences on behavior and development" (p. 1315). Dutton (1985) described Bronfenbrenner's theory as a nested ecological theory to highlight the importance of the interplay between a person's micro and macro influences on their development. Although many correlates of TRV have been individually identified, (e.g., low anger control, acceptance of violence, authoritarian parenting, low parental monitoring, parental conflict, peer norms, peers' involvement in delinquency, exposure to community violence, alienation in school) it is the interplay between these factors that, according to ecological theory, may create an environment conducive to the use of violence in dating relationships. The socioecological model lends itself well to research that explores different correlates, predictors, risk, and protective factors simultaneously. Statistical methods that model complex relationships (i.e., structural equation models) are ideal for exploring the phenomenon of dating violence among adolescents from this perspective. The ecological approach, more than others, provides the conceptual framework that encourages researchers to explore how, in particular, these layers can interact with one another. In other words, researchers should be wont to examine, not only different levels of influence on TRV, but also should attempt to identify the mechanisms that underlie their interactions as well.

PREVENTION AND INTERVENTION PROGRAMS

The research presented in the foregoing sections demonstrates the prevalence and seriousness of teen relationship violence in many countries across the world. As violence against women in teen and adult relationships is viewed as an international human rights and social justice issue (e.g., Amnesty International, 2004; Glass, Rollins, & Bloom, 2009), countries have established a variety of prevention and intervention programs that are influenced by culture, religion, and educational and political systems. As research guided by socioecological theory (e.g., Banyard, Cross, & Modecki, 2006; Dutton, 1985) identifies risk and protective factors associated with intimate partner violence across individual, peer, family, and community levels, more work is needed to apply this research to the development of effective prevention and intervention programs.

Existing primary prevention programs addressing teen relationship violence described in publications have mostly been implemented in Canada or the United States, and they generally involve psychoeducational lessons focused on individual factors associated with violence (Whitaker et al., 2006). For example, school-based programs have been implemented that focus on increasing knowledge about dating violence (e.g., Jaycox et al., 2006; Macgowan, 1997), and challenging attitudes and norms that demonstrate acceptance of violence beliefs and gender stereotyping (e.g., Avery-Leaf, Cascardi, O'Leary, & Cano, 1997; Jaycox et al., 2006; Macgowan, 1997). Similarly, prevention programs for sexual assault have traditionally focused on educating participants about prevalence rates and risk factors, as well as addressing gender role stereotypes and rape myths associated with perpetration of sexual violence (Kress et al., 2006). School-based prevention programs that focus on increasing high school students' knowledge about prevalence and consequences of dating violence and addressing gender and cultural norms are also offered in Mexico (e.g., Pick, Leenen, Givaudan, & Prado, 2010). Similarly, in Australia, "When Love Hurts," a web-based project (www.dvirc.org.au/whenlove), and the Domestic and Dating Violence Peer Education Program (Women's Council for Domestic and Family Violence Services, 2007) offered to secondary school students and teachers, were developed to raise awareness of dating and domestic violence, increase knowledge of available resources, and change attitudes that condone violence.

In addition to addressing individual-level risk factors, programs are increasingly strength-based and have focused on building protective factors for dating violence. For example, in addition to increasing knowledge and addressing social norms for violence, prevention programs are focused on building communication, anger management, and social problem-solving skills (e.g., Avery-Leaf et al., 1997; Foshee & Langwick, 2004; Schwartz, Magee, Griffin, & Dupuis, 2004; Wolfe et al., 1996). These skills negatively relate to perpetration of dating violence in adolescents from Mexico and the United States (e.g., Antônio & Hokoda, 2009; Clarey, Hokoda, & Ulloa, 2010; Feldman & Gowen, 1998; Kinsfogel & Grych, 2004; Wolf & Foshee, 2003). Research on adult couples involved in domestic violence suggests that interventions that teach anger management skills that deescalate conflicts may be effective for reciprocal and bidirectional violence (e.g., Holtzworth-Munroe, Meehan, Herron, Rehman, & Stuart, 2003; Holtzworth-Munroe & Stuart, 1994; O'Leary & Smith Slep, 2006) that is common in dating couples (Gray & Foshee, 1997). In addition to primary prevention programs, there are also secondary prevention efforts in Canada that have targeted maltreated youth at risk for teen relationship violence (Wolfe et al., 1996). Similar to the school-based programs described earlier, the Youth Relationships Project aims to increase knowledge about dating violence, increase awareness of gender stereotypes, and increase positive communication and problem-solving skills.

There are challenges to implementing these programs in other countries because of the large variance in social-political and educational systems, as well as, in people's definitions and perceptions of violence against women. For example, Garcia-Moreno et al. (2005) suggested that in particular, emotional violence and issues of power and control within a couple differ within cultures. Research examining the social norms held about the acceptability of physical violence by South African adolescents (Swart et al., 2002) and beliefs about sexual and abusive behaviors among men and women in Thailand and Israeli–Arab societies (e.g., Haj-Yahia, 2000, 2003; Pradubmook-Sherer, 2009) further demonstrate the challenges one would face implementing and adapting programs for different countries due to differences in definitions and beliefs about gender roles and abuse. Hamby, Nix, De Puy, and Monnier (2012) described the adaptation and challenges in implementing the Safe Dates prevention program originally developed for schools in the United States (Foshee & Langwick, 2004) for youth in Switzerland. Differences in defining *dating*, *violence*, and *domestic violence* were identified and need to be considered when adapting and implementing these programs in different countries (Hamby et al., 2012). Furthermore, the timing for implementing effective primary prevention programs (Catalano & Hawkin, 1996; Foshee & McNaughton-Reyes, 2009; Nation et al., 2003) are likely to differ across countries as dating is relevant to adolescents at different ages and the onset of experiences with different types of violence may differ as well.

In addition to identifying individual factors that should be targeted in school-based prevention programs, researchers have proposed ways to effectively educate and influence students. For example, studies indicate that the most effective university prevention programs for dating violence and sexual assault are interactive (Kress et al., 2006; Schwartz et al., 2006). However, psychoeducational lessons implemented as part of Safe Dates in the United States are less familiar to the youth in Switzerland (Hamby et al., 2012), and thus, research that determines effective ways to teach youth in different settings and countries is needed. Some programs have used interactive theater as a way to enhance school-based prevention programs (e.g., Foshee & Langwick, 2004; Fredland, 2010). In addition, in Germany, Sweden, and Belgium, a video game called CAVA (Changing Attitudes to Dating Violence in Adolescents) has been developed that encourages positive conflict resolution and problem solving by involving participants in simulated role-play scenarios (http://www.cavaproject.eu/content/project).

Researchers recommend that prevention programs address risk and protective factors for multiple problems across multiple social settings

(Foshee & Reyes, 2009; Nation, 2003). Because sexual and dating violence is linked to substance abuse, risky sexual behaviors, and teen pregnancy (Howard & Wang, 2005), prevention programs should be targeting these multiple problems together. Because various forms of interpersonal violence, including domestic and dating violence, child maltreatment, and gang violence, often co-occur and share risk and protective factors, it is recommended that programs address these multiple types of violence together (Kazdin, 2011). Other researchers recommend that interventions for dating violence also focus on mental health correlates and consequences of violence. For example, several authors (e.g., Chan et al., 2008; Chiodo et al., 2009: Chung, 2007) have suggested that depression, suicidal ideation, and self-harm be a focus of violence prevention programs.

Research is increasingly identifying risk and protective factors for intimate partner and sexual violence from broader ecological levels of influence, such as the family, peer, and community. Family risk and protective factors for dating violence include childhood exposure to family violence, punitive parenting, low parental monitoring, and sibling victimization (e.g., East, Chien, Adams, Hokoda, & Maier, 2010; Ehrensaft et al., 2003; Jouriles, Mueller, Rosenfield, McDonald, & Dodson, 2012; Simonelli, Mullis, Elliott, & Pierce, 2002; Straus & Savage, 2005). Despite the growing body of studies identifying family risk and protective factors associated with dating violence, this research has generally not been incorporated into prevention and educational programs for dating violence. However, interventions are targeting some of the individual cognitive and affective factors (e.g., trauma, hostility, emotional regulation, or anger control) that mediate the relationship between exposure to family violence and teen relationship violence (e.g., Boivin, Lavoie, Hébert, & Gagné, 2012; Jouriles et al., 2012; Jouriles, McDonald, Mueller, & Grych, 2012). In addition, programs targeting children exposed to domestic violence that address trauma, depressive symptoms, and positive conflict resolution skills (e.g., Graham-Bermann, 2011) serve as secondary prevention programs for teen relationship violence.Furthermore, a study examining a family-based prevention program, Families for Safe Dates, revealed promising results in increasing parent/caregiver self-efficacy for talking about dating violence and their knowledge about dating violence, and decreasing acceptance of violence beliefs (Foshee et al., 2011).

Research has also determined several risk factors associated with peers that relate to teen relationship violence. Having peers who have experienced dating violence, have acceptance of violence beliefs, and engage in delinquent acts increases risk of dating violence (Arriaga & Foshee, 2004; Capaldi, Dishion, Stoolmiller, & Yoerger, 2001; Foshee et al., 2004; Vézina, Hébert, Poulin, Lavoie, Vitaro, & Tremblay, 2011). Vézina et al. (2011) found that risky lifestyle mediates the relationship between deviant peer affiliation and dating violence victimization in adolescent girls in Canada and suggests that prevention programs for dating violence target deviant peer groups as well as risky lifestyle (i.e., risky sexual practices, substance use, antisocial and delinquent behaviors).

As research increasingly identifies risk and protective factors for intimate partner and sexual violence from these broader ecological levels of influence, interventions are being developed that expand beyond addressing individual attitudes and skills (e.g., Banyard, 2011; Casey & Lindhorst, 2009; Foshee et al., 2012). Recent strengths-based programs in Canada have focused on promoting healthy relationships and building youth leadership skills in peer mentors who help lead discussion circles and serve as role models (Crooks, Chiodo, Thomas, & Hughes, 2010). Positive psychology and youth development programs like these build community partnerships, are guided by social justice concepts, and encourage youth leadership and civic engagement (Prilleltensky, 2001). Broadening programs and building social support from peers, families, schools, and the community may help lessen the negative outcomes associated with teen relationship violence (e.g., Banyard & Cross, 2008; Holt & Espelage, 2005). For example, the perception that one is supported by one's parents and by one's neighbors is related to lowered suicidal thoughts for females victimized by sexual abuse, and perceived neighborhood support moderates the associations between victimization by physical abuse and substance use and school attachment (Banyard & Cross, 2008). The Cognitive Behavioral Intervention for Trauma in Schools is an example of a program that builds support within schools and school districts and is making macro-level changes to implement and sustain a school-based intervention (Nadeem, Jaycox, Kataoka, Langley, & Stein, 2011). Researchers and school professionals developing and implementing school-based programs for teen relationship violence can expand in scope by similarly following a community partnered research framework; addressing trauma by involving school staff, parents, and mental health professionals; and building long-term macro-level support (e.g., infrastructure changes in policy, financial and staff support) for their programs. Another program, "Bringing in the Bystander," broadens the scope of interventions addressing individual factors and focuses on building peer and community responses to sexual violence (Banyard, Moynihan, & Plante, 2007; McMahon, Postmus, & Koenick, 2011). McMahon and Banyard (2012) described a framework for strategies bystanders can do to proactively prevent possible sexual assault, as well as, reactive strategies for responding and helping victims of sexual violence. Bystander interventions have been offered to sororities, as well as fraternities and college athletic teams (e.g., Foubert & Perry, 2007; Miller et al., 2012; Moynihan, Banyard, Arnold, Eckstein, & Stapleton, 2011), and the research has implications for campus-wide policy changes that provide better coordinated community prevention and intervention programs for relationship violence (Moynihan et al., 2011). As researchers further identify individual and situational factors that support positive bystander and community responses (e.g., Casey & Ohler, 2012; McMahon, 2010) and cultural differences and influences on bystander behaviors (e.g., Knafo, Schwartz, & Levine (2009), this knowledge can inform the adaptation and implementation of bystander programs in various countries.

REFERENCES

Amnesty International. (2004). *It's in our hands: Stop violence against women.* New York, NY: Author.

Antônio, T., & Hokoda, A. (2009). Gender variations in dating violence and positive conflict resolution among Mexican adolescents. *Violence and Victims, 24,* 533–545. doi:10.1891/0886-6708.24.4.533

Arriaga, X. B., & Foshee, V. A. (2004). Adolescent dating violence: Do adolescents follow in their friends', or their parents' footsteps? *Journal of Interpersonal Violence, 19,* 162–184. doi:10.1177/0886260503260247

Avery-Leaf, S., Cascardi, M. M., O'Leary, K. D., & Cano, A. A. (1997). Efficacy of a dating violence prevention program on attitudes justifying aggression. *Journal of Adolescent Health, 21,* –17. doi:10.1016/S1054-139X(96)00309-6

Bandura, A. (1971). *Social learning theory.* New York, NY: General Learning Press.

Bandyopadhyay, A., Deokar, A., & Omar, H. A. (2010). Adolescent dating violence: A comprehensive review. *International Journal of Child and Adolescent Health, 3,* 305–320.

Banyard, V. L. (2011). Who will help prevent sexual violence: Creating an ecological model of bystander intervention. *Psychology of Violence, 1,* 216–229. doi:10.1037/a0023739

Banyard, V. L., & Cross, C. (2008). Consequences of teen dating violence: Understanding intervening variables in ecological context. *Violence Against Women, 14,* 998–1013. doi:10.1177/1077801208322058

Banyard, V. L., Cross, C. & Modecki, K. L. (2006). Interpersonal violence in adolescence: Ecological correlates of self-reported perpetration. *Journal of Interpersonal Violence, 21,* 1314–1332.

Banyard, V. L., Moynihan, M. M., & Plante, E. G. (2007). Sexual violence prevention through bystander education: An experimental evaluation. *Journal of Community Psychology, 35,* 463–481. doi:10.1002/jcop.20159

Bergman, L. (1992). Dating violence among high school students. *Social Work, 37,* 21–27.

Black, B. M., Peterson, B. L., Weisz, A. N., Kernsmith, P. D., Lewandowski, L. A., & Hedge, K. K. (2009). Definitions of violence: African-American and Iraqi refugee adolescents' perceptions. *International Journal of Adolescence and Youth, 14,* 313–331.

Boivin, S., Lavoie, F., Hébert, M., & Gagné, M. (2012). Past victimizations and dating violence perpetration in adolescence: The mediating role of emotional distress and hostility. *Journal of Interpersonal Violence, 27,* 662–684. doi:10.1177/0886260511423245

Bowlby, J. (1973). *Separation: Anxiety and anger*. London, England: Hogarth.

Bronfenbrenner, U. (1979). *The ecology of human development experiments by nature and design*. Cambridge, MA: Harvard University Press.

Brown, A., Cosgrave, E., Killackey, E., Purcell, P., Buckby, J. & Yung, A. R. (2009). The longitudinal association of adolescent dating violence with psychiatric disorders and functioning. *Journal of Interpersonal Violence, 24*, 1964–1979.

Brownridge, D. A. (2006). Intergenerational transmission and dating violence victimization: Evidence from a sample of female university students in Manitoba. *Canadian Journal of Community Mental Health, 25*, 75–93.

Cano, A., Avery-Leaf, S., Cascardi, M., & O'Leary, K. D. (1998). Dating violence in two high schools: Discriminating variables. *The Journal of Primary Prevention, 18*, 431–446.

Capaldi, D. M., Dishion, T. J., Stoolmiller, M., & Yoerger, K. (2001). Aggression toward female partners by at-risk young men: The contribution of male adolescent friendships. *Developmental Psychology, 37*, 61–73.

Casey, E. A., & Lindhorst, T. P. (2009). Toward a multi-level, ecological approach to the primary prevention of sexual assault: Prevention in peer and community contexts. *Trauma, Violence, and Abuse, 10*, 91–114. doi:10.1177/1524838009334129

Casey, E. A., & Ohler, K. (2012). Being a positive bystander: Male antiviolence allies' experiences of "stepping up." *Journal of Interpersonal Violence, 27*, 62–83.

Catalano, R. F., & Hawkins, J. (1996). The social development model: A theory of antisocial-behavior. In J. Hawkins (Ed.), *Delinquency and crime: Current theories* (pp. 149–197). New York, NY: Cambridge University Press.

Centers for Disease Control and Prevention. (2009). *Understanding teen dating violence: Fact sheet.* Retrieved from http://www.cdc.gov/violenceprevention/pdf/TeenDatingViolence2009-a.pdf

Chan, K. L., Straus, M. A., Brownridge, D. A., Tiwari, A., & Leung, W. C. (2008). Prevalence of dating partner violence and suicidal ideation among male and female university students worldwide. *Journal of Midwifery and Women's Health, 53*, 529–537.

Chiodo, D., Wolfe, D. A., Crooks, C., Hughes, R., & Jaffe, P. (2009). Impact of sexual harassment victimization by peers on subsequent adolescent victimization and adjustment: A longitudinal study. *Journal of Adolescent Health, 45*, 246–252. doi:10.1016/j.jadohealth.2009.01.006

Chung, D. (2007). Making meaning of relationships: Young women's experiences and understandings of dating Violence. *Violence Against Women 13*, 1274–1295.

Clarey, A., Hokoda, A., & Ulloa, E. C. (2010). Anger control and acceptance of violence as mediators in the relationship between exposure to interparental conflict and dating violence perpetration in Mexican adolescents. *Journal of Family Violence, 25*, 619–625. doi:10.1007/s10896-010-9315-7

Collins, N. L., Cooper, M. L., Albino, A., & Allard, L. (2002). Psychosocial vulnerability from adolescence to adulthood: A prospective study of attachment style differences in relationship functioning and partner choice. *Journal of Personality, 70*, 965–1008.

Crooks, C. V., Chiodo, D., Thomas, D., & Hughes, R. (2010). Strengths-based programming for First Nations youth in schools: Building engagement through healthy relationships and leadership skills. *International Journal of Mental Health And Addiction, 8,* 160–173. doi:10.1007/s11469-009-9242-0

Doroszewicz, K., & Forbes, G. B. (2008). Experiences with dating aggression and sexual coercion among Polish college students. *Journal of Interpersonal Violence, 23,* 58–73.

Dutton, D. G. (1985). An ecologically nested theory of male violence toward intimates. *International Journal of Women's Studies, 8,* 404–413.

East, P. L., Chien, N. C., Adams, J. A., Hokoda, A., & Maier, A. (2010). Links between sisters' sexual and dating victimization: The roles of neighborhood crime and parental controls. *Journal of Family Psychology, 24,* 698–708. doi:10.1037/a0021751

Ehrensaft, M. K., Cohen, P., Brown, J., Smailes, E., Chen, H., & Johnson, J. G. (2003). Intergenerational transmission of partner violence: A 20-year prospective study. *Journal of Consulting and Clinical Psychology, 71,* 741–753. doi:10.1037/0022-006X.71.4.741

Feldman, S. S., & Gowen, L. K. (1998). Conflict negotiation tactics in romantic relationships in high school students. *Journal of Youth and Adolescence, 27,* 691–717. doi:10.1023/A:1022857731497

Fernández Fuertes, A. A., & Fuertes, A. (2010). Physical and psychological aggression in dating relationships of Spanish adolescents: Motives and consequences. *Child Abuse and Neglect, 34,* 183–191.

Fernández Fuertes, A. A., Fuertes, A., & Pulido, R. F. (2006). Evaluación de la violencia en las relaciones de pareja de los adolescents: Validación del Conflict in Adolescent Dating Relationships Inventory (CADRI)—versión española. *International Journal of Clinical and Health Psychology, 6,* 339–358.

Foshee, V. A., Benefield, T. S., Ennett, S. T., Bauman, K. E., & Suchindran, C. (2004). Longitudinal predictors of serious physical and sexual dating violence victimization during adolescence. *An International Journal Devoted to Practice and Theory, 39,* 1007–1016.

Foshee, V. A., & Langwick, S. (2004). *Safe dates: An adolescent dating abuse prevention curriculum.* Center City, MN: Hazelden.

Foshee, V. A., & Reyes, H. (2009). Primary prevention of adolescent dating abuse perpetration: When to begin, whom to target, and how to do it. In D. J. Whitaker, J. R. Lutzker, D. J. Whitaker, & J. R. Lutzker (Eds.), Preventing partner violence: Research and evidence-based intervention strategies (pp. 141–168). Washington, DC: American Psychological Association. doi:10.1037/11873-007

Foshee, V. A., Reyes, H. L., Ennett, S. T., Cance, J. D., Bauman, K. E., & Bowling, J. M. (2012). Assessing the effects of families for safe dates, a family-based teen dating abuse prevention program. *Journal of Adolescent Health, 51,* 349–356. doi: 10.1016/j.jadohealth.2011.12.029

Foubert, J. D., & Perry, B. C. (2007). Creating lasting attitude and behavior change in fraternity members and male student athletes: The qualitative impact of an empathy-based rape prevention program. *Violence Against Women, 13,* 70–86. doi:10.1177/1077801206295125

Fredland, N. M. (2010). Nurturing healthy relationships through a community-based interactive theater program. *Journal of Community Health Nursing, 27,* 107–118.

Fuertes Martín, A., Ramos Vergeles, M., & Fernández Fuertes, A. A. (2007). La coerción sexual en las relaciones de los y las adolescentes y jóvenes: Naturaleza del problema y estrategias de intervención. *Apuntes de Psicología Colegio Oficial de Psicología, 25,* 341–356.

García-Moreno, C., Jansen, H. A. F. M., Ellsberg, M., Heise, L., & Watts, C. (2005). *WHO multi-country study on women's health and domestic violence against women: Initial results on prevalence, health outcomes and women's responses.* Geneva, Switzerland: WHO Press.

Glass, N., Rollins, C., & Bloom, T. (2009). Expanding our vision: Using a human rights framework to strengthen our service response to female victims of male intimate partner violence. In D. J. Whitaker, & J. R. Lutzker (Eds.), *Preventing partner violence: Research and evidence-based intervention strategies* (pp. 193–217). Washington, DC: American Psychological Association. doi:10.1037/11873-009

Graham-Bermann, S. A. (2011). Evidence-based practices for school-age children exposed to intimate partner violence and evaluation of the Kids' Club program. In S. A. Graham-Bermann, & A. A. Levendosky (Eds.), *How intimate partner violence affects children: Developmental research, case studies, and evidence-based intervention* (pp. 179–205). Washington, DC: American Psychological Association. doi:10.1037/12322-009

Gray, H. M., & Foshee, V. (1997). Adolescent dating violence: differences between one-sided and mutually violent profiles. *Journal of Interpersonal Violence, 12,* 126–141.

Gwartney-Gibbs, P.A., Stockard, J., & Bohmer, S. (1987). Learning courtship aggression: The influence of parents, peers, and personal experiences. *Family Relations, 36,* 276–282.

Haj-Yahia, M. M. (2000). Wife abuse and battering in the sociocultural context of Arab society. *Family Process, 39,* 237–255.

Haj-Yahia, M. M. (2003). Beliefs about wife beating among Arab men from Israel: The influence of their patriarchal ideology. *Journal of Family Violence, 18,* 193–206.

Haj-Yahia, M. M. (2003). Beliefs of Jordanian women about wife-beating. *Psychology of Women Quarterly, 26,* 282–291.

Hamby, S., Nix, K., De Puy, J., & Monnier, S. (2012). Adapting dating violence prevention to Francophone Switzerland: A story of intra-western cultural differences. *Violence and Victims, 27,* 33–42. doi:10.1891/0886-6708.27.1.33

Harway, M., & O'Neil, J. M. (Eds.). (1999). *What causes men's violence against women.* Thousand Oaks, CA: Sage

Herzog, S. (2004). Differential perceptions of the seriousness of male violence against female intimate partners among Jews and Arabs in Israel. *Journal of Interpersonal Violence, 19,* 891–900.

Hird, M. J. (2000). An empirical study of adolescent dating aggression in the U.K.. *Journal of Adolescence, 23,* 69–78.

Holt, M. K., & Espelage, D. L. (2005). Social support as a moderator between dating violence victimization and depression/anxiety among African American and Caucasian adolescents. *School Psychology Review, 34,* 309–328.

Holtzworth-Munroe, A., Meehan, J. C., Herron, K. Rehman, U., & Stuart, G. L. (2003). Do subtypes of martially violent men continue to differ over time? *Journal of Consulting and Clinical Psychology, 71,* 728–740.

Holtzworth-Munroe, A., & Stuart, G. L. (1994). The relationship standards and assumptions of violent versus nonviolent husbands. *Cognitive Therapy and Research, 18,* 87–103.

Howard, D. E., & Wang, M. (2005). Psychosocial correlates of U.S. adolescents who report a history of forced sexual intercourse. *Journal of Adolescent Health, 36,* 372–379. doi:10.1016/j.jadohealth.2004.07.007

Ismail, F., Berman, H., & Ward-Griffin, C. (2007). Dating violence and the health of young women: A feminist narrative study. *Health Care for Women International, 28,* 453–477.

Jaycox, L. H., McCaffrey, D., Eiseman, B., Aronoff, J., Shelley, G. A., Collins, R. L., & Marshall, G. N. (2006). Impact of a school-based dating violence prevention program among Latino teens: Randomized controlled effectiveness trial. *Journal of Adolescent Health, 39,* 694–704. doi:10.1016/j.jadohealth.2006.05.002

Jewkes, R., Vundule, C., Maforah, F., & Jordaan, E. (2001). Relationship dynamics and teenage pregnancy in South Africa. *Social Science and Medicine, 52,* 733–744.

Jewkes, R., Dunkle, K., Nduna, M., Levin, J., Jama, N., Khuzwayo, N., . . . Duvvury, N. (2006). Factors associated with HIV sero-status in young rural South African women: Connections between intimate partner violence and HIV. *International Journal of Epidemiology, 35,* 1461–1468.

Jouriles, E. N., McDonald, R., Mueller, V., & Grych, J. H. (2012). Youth experiences of family violence and teen dating violence perpetration: Cognitive and emotional mediators. *Clinical Child and Family Psychology Review, 15,* 58–68. doi:10.1007/s10567-011-0102-7

Jouriles, E. N., Mueller, V., Rosenfield, D., McDonald, R., & Dodson, M. C. (2012). Teens' experiences of harsh parenting and exposure to severe intimate partner violence: Adding insult to injury in predicting teen dating violence. *Psychology of Violence, 2,* 125–138. doi: 10.1037/a0027264.

Kazdin, A. E. (2011). Conceptualizing the challenge of reducing interpersonal violence. *Psychology of Violence, 1,* 166–187. doi:10.1037/a0022990

Kinsfogel, K. M., & Grych, J. H. (2004). Interparental conflict and adolescent dating relationships: Integrating cognitive, emotional, and peer influences. *Journal of Family Psychology, 18,* 505–515. doi:10.1037/0893-3200.18.3.505.

Knafo, A., Schwartz, S. H., & Levine, R. V. (2009). Helping strangers is lower in embedded cultures. *Journal of Cross-Cultural Psychology, 40,* 875–879.

Kress, V. E., Shepherd, J., Anderson, R. I., Petuch, A. J., Nolan, J., & Thiemeke, D. (2006). Evaluation of the impact of a coeducational sexual assault prevention program on college students' rape myth attitudes. *Journal of College Counseling, 9,* 148–157.

Krug, E. G., Dahlberg, L. L., Mercy, J. A., Zwi, A. B., & Lozano, R. (2002). Intimate partner violence. In *World report on violence and health* (Chapter 4). Geneva, Switzerland: World Health Organization. http://www.who.int/violence_injury_prevention/violence/global_campaign/en/chap4.pdf

Luke, N. (2003). Age and economic asymmetries in the sexual relationships of adolescent girls in sub-Saharan Africa. *Studies in Family Planning, 34,* 67–86.

Lysova, A. V., & Hines, D. A. (2008). Binge drinking and violence against intimate partners in Russia. *Aggressive Behavior, 34,* 416–427.

Macgowan, M. J. (1997). An evaluation of a dating violence prevention program for middle school students. *Violence and Victims, 12,* 223–235.

Mason, R., Hyman, I., Berman, H., Guruge, S., Kanagaratnam, P., & Manuel, L. (2008). "Violence Is an International Language": Tamil Women's Perceptions of Intimate Partner Violence. *Violence Against Women, 14,* 1397–1412.

Mayseless, O. (1991). Adult attachment patterns and courtship violence. *Family Relations, 40,* 21–28.

McMahon, S. (2010). Rape myth beliefs and bystander attitudes among incoming college students. *Journal of American College Health, 59,* 3–11.

McMahon, S., & Banyard, V. L. (2012). When can I help? A conceptual framework for the prevention of sexual violence through bystander intervention. *Trauma, Violence, and Abuse, 13,* 3–14. doi:10.1177/1524838011426015

McMahon, S., Postmus, J. L., & Koenick, R. (2011). Conceptualizing the engaging bystander approach to sexual violence prevention on college campuses. *Journal of College Student Development, 52,* 115–130. doi:10.1353/csd.2011.0002

Miller, E., Tancredi, D. J., McCauley, H. L., Decker, M. R., Virata, M. D., Anderson, H. A., & . . . Silverman, J. G. (2012). "Coaching boys into men": A cluster-randomized controlled trial of a dating violence prevention program. *Journal of Adolescent Health, 51,* 431–438. doi:10.1016/j.jadohealth.2012.01.018

Moynihan, M. M., Banyard, V. L., Arnold, J. S., Eckstein, R. P., & Stapleton, J. G. (2011). Sisterhood may be powerful for reducing sexual and intimate partner violence: An evaluation of the Bringing in the Bystander in-person program with sorority members. *Violence Against Women, 17,* 703–719.

Muñoz-Rivas, M. J., Graña, J., O'Leary, K. D., & González, M. P. (2007). Aggression in adolescent dating relationships: Prevalence, justification, and health consequences. *Journal of Adolescent Health, 40,* 298–304.

Nadeem, E., Jaycox, L. H., Kataoka, S. H., Langley, A. K., & Stein, B. D. (2011). Going to scale: Experiences implementing a school-based trauma intervention. *School Psychology Review, 40,* 549–568.

Nation, T. (2003). Creating a culture of peaceful school communities. *International Journal for the Advancement of Counseling, 25,* 309–315. doi:10.1023/B:ADCO.0000005530.72520.40

Nation, M., Crusto, C., Wandersman, A., Kumpfer, K. L., Seybolt, D., Morrissey-Kane, E., & Davino, K. (2003). What works in prevention: Principles of effective prevention programs. *American Psychologist, 58,* 449–456.

Norsworthy, K. L. (2003). Understanding violence against women in Southeast Asia: A group approach in social justice work. *International Journal for the Advancement of Counseling, 25,* 145–156.

Ohnishi, M., Nakao, R., Shibayama, S., Matsuyama, Y., Oishi, K., & Miyahara, H. (2011). Knowledge, experience, and potential risks of dating violence among Japanese university students: A cross-sectional study. *BMC Public Health, 11,* 1–8.

O'Keefe, M. (1997). Predictors of dating violence among high school students. *Journal of Interpersonal Violence, 12,* 546–568.

O'Leary, K. D., & Smith Slep, A. M. (2003). A dyadic longitudinal model of adolescent dating aggression. *Journal of Clinical Child and Adolescent Psychology, 32,* 314–327.

O'Leary, K. D., & Smith Slep, A. M. (2006). Precipitants of partner aggression. *Journal of Family Psychology, 20,* 344–347.

Ozer, E. J., Tschann, J. M., Pasch, L.A., & Flores, E. (2004). Violence perpetration across peer and partner relationships: Co-occurrence and longitudinal patterns among adolescents. *Journal of Adolescent Health, 34,* 67–71.

Pick, S., Leenen, I., Givaudan, M., & Prado, A. (2010). Yo quiero, yo puedo . . . prevenir la violencia: Programa breve de sensibilización sobre violencia en el noviazgo. *Salud Mental, 33,* 153–160.

Pradubmook-Sherer, P. (2009). Prevalence and correlates of adolescent dating violence in Bangkok, Thailand. *Journal of Sociology and Social Welfare, 36,* 9–37.

Pradubmook-Sherer, P. (2011). Youth attitudes toward dating violence in Thailand. *International Journal of Offender Therapy and Comparative Criminology, 55,* 182–206.

Prilleltensky, I. (2001). Value-based praxis in community psychology: Moving toward social justice and social action. *American Journal of Community Psychology, 29,* 747–778. doi:10.1023/A:1010417201918

Rey Anacona, C. A. (2008). Prevalencia, factores de riesgo y problemáticas asociadas con la violencia en el noviazgo: Una revisión de la literatura/Prevalence, risk factors, and problems associated with dating violence: A literature review. *Avances en Psicología Latinoamericana/Bogotá (Colombia), 26,* 227–241.

Rivera-Rivera, L., Allen-Leigh, B., Rodríguez-Ortega, G., Chávez-Ayala, R., & Lazcano-Ponce, E. (2007). Prevalence and correlates of adolescent dating violence: Baseline study of a cohort of 7960 male and female Mexican public school students. *Preventive Medicine, 44,* 477–484.

Schwartz, J. R., Griffin, L. D., Russell, M. M., & Frontaura-Duck, S. (2006). Prevention of dating violence on college campuses: An innovative program. *Journal of College Counseling, 9,* 90–96.

Schwartz, J. P., Magee, M. M., Griffin, L. D., & Dupuis, C. W. (2004). Effects of a group preventive intervention on risk and protective factors related to dating violence. *Group Dynamics: Theory, Research, and Practice, 8,* 221–231. doi:10.1037/1089-2699.8.3.221

Sherer, M. (2010). Attitudes toward dating violence among Jewish and Arab youth in Israel. *Youth and Society, 42,* 132–150.

Sherer, P., & Sherer, M. (2008). Exploring reciprocity in dating violence among Jewish and Arab youths in Israel. *International Journal of Intercultural Relations, 32,* 17–33.

Silverman, J. G., Raj, A., Mucci, L. A., & Hathaway, J. E. (2001). Dating violence against adolescent girls and associated substance use, unhealthy weight control, sexual risk behavior, pregnancy, and suicidality. *JAMA, 286,* 572–579.

Simonelli, C. J., Mullis, T., Elliott, A. N., & Pierce, T. W. (2002). Abuse by siblings and subsequent experiences of violence within the dating relationship. *Journal of Interpersonal Violence, 17,* 103–121. doi:10.1177/0886260502017002001

Sims, E. N., Dodd, V. J. N., & Tejeda, M. J. (2008). The relationship between severity of violence in the home and dating violence. *Journal of Forensic Nursing, 4,* 166–173, doi:10.1111/j.1939.2008.00028.x

Straus, M. (2011, August 19). International Dating Violence Study, 2001–2006 (ICPSR29583-v1). Ann Arbor, MI: Inter-university Consortium for Political and Social Research. doi:10.3886/ICPSR29583.v1

Straus, M. A. (2008). Dominance and symmetry in partner violence by male and female university students in 32 nations. *Children and Youth Services Review, 30,* 252–275.

Straus, M. A., Hamby, S. L., Money-McCoy, S., & Sugarman, D. B. (1996). The Revised Conflict Tactics Scale (CTS2): Development and preliminary psychometric data. *Journal of Family Issues, 17,* 283–316.

Straus, M. A., & Savage, S. A. (2005). Neglectful behavior by parents in the life history of university students in 17 countries and its relation to violence against dating partners. *Child Maltreatment, 10,* 124–135.

Swart, L., Seedat, M., Stevens, G. & Ricardo, I. (2002). Violence in adolescents' romantic relationships: Findings from a survey amongst school-going youth in a South African community. *Journal of Adolescence, 25,* 385–395.

Thongpriwan, V., & McElmurry, B. J. (2009). Thai female adolescents' perceptions of dating violence. *Health Care for Women International, 30,* 871–891.

Ulloa, E., Castaneda, D., & Hokoda, A. (2010). Teen relationship violence. In M. Paludi & F. Denmark (Eds.), *Victims of sexual assault and abuse: Resources and responses for individuals and families.* Santa Barbara, CA: Praeger.

Ulloa, E., Watts, V., Ulibarri, M., Castañeda, D., & Hokoda, A. (2012). Intimate partner violence among adolescent girls. In P. K. Lundberg-Love, K. L. Nadal, & M. A. Paludi, (Eds.), *Women and mental disorders, Vol. 2.* Santa Barbara, CA: Praeger.

Vézina, J., Hébert, M., Poulin, F., Lavoie, F., Vitaro, F., & Tremblay, R. E. (2011). Risky lifestyle as a mediator of the relationship between deviant peer affiliation and dating violence victimization among adolescent girls. *Journal of Youth and Adolescence, 40,* 814–824. doi:10.1007/s10964-010-9602-x

Wang, X., & Ho, P. S. Y. (2007). Violence and desire in Beijing. A young Chinese woman's strategies of resistance in father-daughter incest and dating relationships. *Violence Against Women, 13,* 1319–1338.

Wekerle, C., & Wolfe, D. A. (1999). Dating violence in mid-adolescence: Theory, significance, and emerging prevention initiatives. *Clinical Psychology Review, 4,* 435–456.

Whitaker, D. J., Morrison, S., Lindquist, C., Hawkins, S. R., O'Neil, J. A., Nesius, A. M., & . . Reese, L. (2006). A critical review of interventions for the primary prevention of perpetration of partner violence. *Aggression and Violent Behavior, 11,* 151–166. doi:10.1016/j.avb.2005.07.007

Wolf, K. A., & Foshee, V. A. (2003). Family violence, anger expression styles, and adolescent dating violence. *Journal of Family Violence, 18,* 309–316. doi:10.1023/A:102623791440610.1023/A:10262379144062003-09468-001

Wolfe, D. A., Wekerle, C., Gough, R. Reitzel-Jaffe, D. Grasley, C., Pittman, A., & Stumpf, J. (1996) *Youth Relationships manual: A group approach with adolescents for the prevention of woman abuse and the promotion of healthy relationships.* Thousand Oaks, CA: Sage.

Women's Council for Domestic and Family Violence Services, Western Australia. (2007). Domestic and Dating Violence Peer Education Program: A pilot project. Perth, Australia: Author.

Wubs, A. G., Aarø, L. E., Flisher, A. J., Bastien, S., Onya, H. E., Kaaya, S., & Mathews, M. (2009). Dating violence among school students in Tanzania and South Africa: Prevalence and socio-demographic variations. *Scandinavian Journal of Public Health, 37,* 75–86.

Yodanis, C. L. (2004). Gender inequality, violence against women, and fear. *Journal of Interpersonal Violence, 19,* 655–675. Doi:10.1177/0886260504263868

Chapter 11

Males, Masculinity, and Physical and Sexual Violence against Females

Kathy McCloskey

Male perpetration of physical and sexual abuse against women and girls is undeniably a global phenomenon because male violence is inflicted on women and girls in virtually all cultures. Internationally, male physical and sexual violence against women and girls appears in a remarkable variety of forms, "from sordid to sanitized, from secretive to sacred, in bedrooms and battlegrounds, censured as well as supported by courts, clergy, and communities throughout the world" (Fontes & McCloskey, 2011, p. 151). Unfortunately, because this type of male violence is so familiar and commonplace, the everyday male actions of emotionally abusing, slapping, beating, and sexually assaulting women and girls around the world have become almost invisible as a daily part of the social background (Watts & Zimmerman, 2002). Thus, when I began to contemplate "Who are these violent perpetrators?" while gathering information for this contribution, I realized that the problem is so widespread and so much a part of the global social fabric that determining predator characteristics could best be answered with one word: *males.*

I truly considered stopping right there. The answer seems so self-evident, the amassed evidence so overwhelming, that at first I believed I had nothing more to add. Then I began to think about how the global and privileged invisibility of males and their masculinity is the source of the problem, and how this keeps all of us from effectively intervening to stop their violence against women and girls (as well as boys and other men). Perhaps I did have something to add; a focus on males might assist in removing the social veil and lead us to both local and global solutions.

Before proceeding, I would like to address three common responses to the simple and accurate statement that males and their masculinities are the problem. First, acknowledging "what is" (that the problem is a male one) in no way implies human males are genetically or biologically determined to be violent, and by implication that all males are predators. This essentialist argument has been raised and debunked by better minds than I (e.g., Gurven & Hill, 2009; Hill 2010), although the disturbing evolutionary-testosterone argument for male violence and rape is far from dead in the 21st century (Kaighobadi, Shackelford, & Goetz, 2009; Liddle, Shackelford, & Weekes-Shackelford, 2012; McKibbin, Shackelford, Goetz, & Starratt, 2008; Miner, Shackelford, Block, & Starratt, 2012). In any case, I want to be clear that biological determinism is not the issue.

Second, the common response that "females do it too" in no way invalidates the fact that the overwhelming majority of public and private violence is perpetrated by males. In fact, this latter argument implies there is something inherently *social* that supports such violence but does so differentially for males and females and in fact suppresses female violence:

> [R]esearch on the history of . . . women's crimes is a valuable resource . . . as a way to understand the relationship between women's violence and women's lives. Whenever a woman commits murder, particularly if she is accused of murdering a family member, people immediately ask, "How could she do that?" Given the enormous costs of being born female, that may well be the wrong question . . . the real question is why so few women resort to violence in the face of such horrendous victimization—even to save their lives . . . [this] provides evidence that women's crimes parallel their assigned role in the rest of society. (Chesney-Lind & Pasko, 2004, pp. 97–98)

In other words, there is something within our worldwide social organization that supports male violence and suppresses female violence (Chopra, 2003; Meneley, 2000; Posel, 2005; Sitaker, 2009). This "something" is known as *patriarchal hierarchy* in which males are elevated over females throughout all known social spheres across the globe, from family structure to religion to economics to politics (Adeleye & Chizwuzie, 2007; Agathangelou & Ling, 2004; Cossins, 2007; Dobash & Dobash, 1981;

Lorber, 2002). Patriarchal hierarchy is found in virtually all nations and cultures, with few exceptions, and not only creates the legitimacy of male violence overall but also sustains and maintains it as natural and normal (Admon, 2009; Ahmed-Ghosh, 2004; Das Gupta, 1987; Hsu, 2008; Jha et al., 2006; Kaur, 2008; Levesque, 2011; Pinheiro, 2006; Rosenthal, 2001; Santhya & Jejeebhoy, 2005; Sidahmed, 2001; Skjelsbaek & Smith, 2001; United Nations [UN], 2002, 2006a, 2006b; UN Children's Fund, 2007; Yoon, 2006; Zorza & Pines, 2007). Such normality contributes to its invisibility—it constitutes the very social order within which we're personally embedded and therefore cannot often be perceived. This social context has profound influences on the propensity for males to feel free to use physical and sexual violence against females of all ages (Adinkrah, 2004, 2008; Sanghavi, Bhalla, & Das, 2009; University of Melbourne, 2000; Ward & Marsh, 2006; Watts & Zimmerman, 2002; Yang, 2004). For example, Table 11.1 shows how gendered control of female sexuality in Westernized and non-Westernized cultures creates just one type of social context within which male violence is bolstered, supported, and maintained; one will hopefully notice when perusing Table 11.1 that males, through various definitions of masculinity, are relatively free from highly sexualized social requirements around dress and appearance, body alterations, responsibility for rape perpetration, restricted movement in social spheres, policing of male virginity, or responsibility for birth control and pregnancy; the reverse is certainly not the case for females.

Which leads me to the third common response: When the problem of male violence is pointed out, there is often a visceral and overwhelmingly negative backlash against the messenger (e.g., Crowley, 2009; DeKeseredy, 1999). We are then left with a *female problem* because the focus must be shifted to females to maintain the privileged social status of males—otherwise, something would have to change within our gendered social structures (Berns, 2001; Brush, 2002; Jewkes, 2005; Jewkes et al., 2005). This brings me full circle within this introductory section. By focusing on male perpetrators, I hope not only to lift the veil of invisibility but also to contribute in some small way to shifting from patriarchal hierarchy to more egalitarian social structures.

THE EXTENT OF MALE VIOLENCE AGAINST FEMALES

Measurement Issues

It should not be surprising that measuring the extent of male violence against women and children is usually accomplished by focusing on the victims (victim surveys, health care visits for injury treatment, and so on). This is because asking males in general how often or how severely they

Table 11.1 *Definitions of Female Sexuality That Provide Social/Cultural Support for Male Violence against Females*

	Westernized Countries (general trends)	Non-Westernized Countries (general trends)
Dress and appearance	Highly revealing and sexualized (clothing, shoes, media representations including pornography; American Psychological Association [APA], 2007)	Various desexualized clothing requirements to reduce bodily exposure (*burqa* requirements, facial veils, and so on; Hussain, 2001; Jewkes, 2005; Lorber, 2002)
Body alteration	Plastic surgery (face, breasts, genitals; American College of Obstetricians and Gynecologists, 2007; Fitzpatrick, 2008)	Genital mutilation (United Nations Population Fund, 2007)
Responsibility for men's sexual actions	Rape myths and blaming the victim (not believed, socially ostracized, beliefs that men cannot control their sexualized actions, nonenforcement of criminal rape laws, and so on) (Gavey, 2005)	Rape myths and blaming the victim (not believed, socially ostracized, beliefs that men cannot control their sexualized actions, forced marriage to rapist, forced to bear rapists' children, lack of criminal laws or nonenforcement, and so on; Cáceres, 2005; Jewkes, Penn-Kekanna, & Rose-Junius, 2005; Karkera, 2006; Wilkinson, Bearup, & Soprach, 2005)
Freedom of movement within public spaces	Fear of sexual assault by male strangers constrains female movement (isolated locations, after dark, and so on; Gavey, 2005; Hollander, 2000)	Controlled and limited female movements to ensure sexual purity (chaperones, male accompaniment, etc.; Borka, 2009; Jewkes, 2005)
Virginity	"Slut versus Madonna" definitions of female sexual behavior (APA, 2007; Gavey, 2005)	Enforced virginity until marriage and severe punishments for perceived adultery ("honor" assaults and murders) (Borka, 2009; UN 2006a, 2006b; Vahdati, 2009)
Birth control and pregnancy	Responsibility for birth control and pregnancy with concomitant limits on that control (including abortion services and prenatal care) (Guldi, 2008; Meyers & Woods, 1996)	Responsibility for birth control and pregnancy with concomitant limits on that control (including abortion services and prenatal care; Adeleye & Chiwuzie, 2007; Panchanadeswaran et al., 2009; Rojanapithayakorn, 2006)

have been violent or coercive with the females in their lives is often met with blank stares, and if they admit such behaviors at all, they either downplay their abusive actions ("I only pushed her") or legitimize them ("She deserved it") (Blacklock, 2001; Cossins, 2007; Fisher & Hall; 2011; McCloskey, Sitaker, Grigsby, & Malloy, 2004; Muchoki, 2011). Furthermore, many males simply do not define their own actions against females as problematic, let alone harmfully violent to others; this is because standard definitions of masculinity (e.g., male gender role stereotypes) require males to maintain power, control, and often ownership over others within the family and community (Abrahams, Jewkes, Hoffman, & Laubsher, 2004; Fisher & Hall; 2011; Hamner, Itzin, Quaid, & Wigglesworth, 2000; Rivet & Rees, 2004). Because of this, females are then asked about their victimization to determine the actual extent of the problem, and the focus is once again taken away from violent males and placed on victimized females.

However, some types of information are available about violent males that do not require asking female victims about their perpetrators. In countries where legislation has been passed to curb male violence against women and girls, official police or court statistics are often available about perpetrators (UN, 2006a, 2006b, 2010). In addition, we may also obtain information about those who kill women and girls when homicide statistics are gathered that include both victim and perpetrator demographics. There are also a handful of available references that provide the perspective of male perpetrators about their violence against women and children (e.g., Abrahams et al., 2004; Blacklock, 2001; Fisher & Hall; 2011). As seen in the later section on perpetrator characteristics, males overall do not tend to take responsibility for their violent behavior against females, do not recognize the harm caused as a result, and blame others for their own violent behavior.

Thus, much of the multicountry information about male violence comes from reports by female victims, either in direct survey form or from face-to-face contacts during public health surveillance efforts. It should also be noted that when information about male perpetrators is obtained without involving information gathered from victims, it almost always comes from within a single Western region that has officially criminalized the violence, created surveillance systems to track these crimes, or has a governmental funding stream that supports research on perpetrators.

Male Violence within Intimate Relationships

The World Health Organization (WHO; 2005) completed a survey of 15 sites across 10 countries: Bangladesh, Brazil, Ethiopia, Japan, Peru, Namibia, Samoa, Serbia and Montenegro, Thailand, and the United Republic of Tanzania. The WHO report found that women reported high rates of physical violence at the hands of intimate male partners, ranging from 13% in Japan to 61% in Peru, with most sites reporting between 23% and 49%. For severe physical violence, the range was 4% in Japan to 49% in Peru, with most being physically assaulted by male partners more than once.

Most women reported that male violence was part of an ongoing pattern of verbal, physical, and sexual abuse, and all three types were most likely used by male perpetrators. For ever-partnered women, the WHO (2005) found that the prevalence of physical or sexual violence by males, or both, ranged from 15% to 71%. As noted in the WHO report, "Only in the urban settings in Brazil and Thailand, and in Japan and Serbia and Montenegro was the overlap between physical and sexual abuse less than 30%" (p. 7). Clearly, the physical abuse of women and girls cannot be understood without also taking into consideration the sexualized context of male violence. Furthermore, the extent of verbally abusive acts and controlling behaviors by male partners were associated with the risk of both physical and sexual assault. In terms of the extent of male verbal abuse and controlling behaviors, the WHO (2005) report stated that "[a]cross all countries, between 20% and 75% of women had experienced one or more of these acts" (p. xiii).

This violent male pattern within intimate relationships has also been found in Western countries (e.g., McFarlane & Malecha, 2005), such as the United States and Canada. In the United States, a large population survey conducted by the Centers for Disease Control and Prevention (CDC; 2010) also found that among female victims of partner violence, over one third experienced multiple forms of physical and sexual violence coupled with controlling behaviors (i.e., stalking) at the hands of males; similar patterns were also found in Canada (Canadian Centre for Justice Statistics [CCJS], 2011). Thus, across sites and countries, a pattern seems to emerge: M*ale perpetrators in intimate relationships combine physically assaultive acts against females with sexual violence, verbal and emotional abuse, and controlling/monitoring behaviors across time.*

Male Perpetrated Femicide

Where statistics are gathered (usually within Western countries), the rates of femicide are decreasing, yet males still constitute the vast majority of murderers. Within the United States, the total number of homicide victims related to intimate partner violence has declined over time (Catalano, 2007), and females still make up 70% to 80% of victims (Catalano, 2007; U.S. Justice Department [USJD], 2005). In 2007, intimate partners committed 14% of all homicides in the United States, and males were still the overwhelming majority of these murderers (Catalano, 2007). After 3 decades of a similar decline for femicide rates in Canada, the rates have stabilized since 2006; even so, males still constitute the overwhelming majority of murderers within intimate relationships (CCJS, 2011).

Problems with determining accurate rates of femicides committed in non-Western countries have been noted by many international organizations; this is because information about femicide must often be obtained from records provided by medical examiners, the courts, or the police, and in many areas this information is incomplete or simply not recorded (UN, 2006a; WHO, 2005, 2010). Nevertheless, available data suggest that femicide, whether or not it occurs within the context of an ongoing intimate relationship, overwhelmingly involves male perpetration (including sexual assault; Adinkrah, 2004, 2007); this is exemplified by the recent increase in such murders reported in Guatemala and Mexico (UN, 2006a):

> Official sources agree that more than 320 women have been murdered in Ciudad Juarez [Mexico], one third of whom were brutally raped . . . in Guatemala according to National Civil Police statistics, 1,467 women were murdered between 2001 and the beginning of 2004 . . . other sources claim the figure is higher, with 2,070 women murdered, mostly aged 14 to 35 . . . [male] impunity for these crimes is seen as a key factor in these occurrences. (p. 41)

Male Perpetrated Sexual Assault and Harassment

In terms of sexualized violence outside adult intimate partnerships, women in the WHO (2005) study reported that sexual assaults occurred at young ages (as early as age 8, well before marrying age) at the hands of males within their extended family or communities (including teachers). Indeed, regardless of location, females across the lifespan are at high risk for sexual assault by males. For example, McCloskey and Raphael (2005) found that males made up more than 90% of all sexual predators in the United States and that males assaulted child victims 25% of the time, adolescent victims 40% of the time, and adult victims 35% of the time, all overwhelmingly female. Multinationally, the UN (2006a) noted that women in Peru, Samoa, and the United Republic of Tanzania reported lifetime sexual assault at the hands of nonintimate males at rates of between 10% and 15%; women in Canada reported rates of about 11.5%, women in New Zealand and Australia reported between 10% and 20%, and results from Switzerland indicate women reported rates of about 22%.

In terms of sexual assault specifically during childhood years, up to 1 in 5 women report being sexually abused as young girls (WHO, 2005). Although males also sexually abuse boys within and outside the home, girls are still far more likely to be victimized in most cultures where data are available. Globally, extremely high numbers of girls are sexually abused by males both within their families (incest, forced sexual initiation, child brides, etc.) and outside the home (religious institutions, schools, camps, residential facilities, the workplace, on sports teams, and so on; UN, 2006a; WHO, 2002). Indeed, male perpetration of sexual violence against girls is rampant worldwide, and many women report that their first sexual experience at a young age was forced (24% of women in rural Peru, 28% in Tanzania, 30% in rural Bangladesh, and 40% in South Africa; WHO 2005). Clearly, girls of all social strata are sexually abused, yet it should be noted that those who live in extreme poverty worldwide, or girls whose families have been disrupted, appear to be especially targeted by males (Plummer & Njuguna, 2009; Robin, Chester, Rasmussen, Jaranson, & Goldman, 1997; WHO, 2002, 2005).

Because women and girls report such high numbers of sexual assault, it should not be surprising that they also report general sexual harassment by males within the community (including at school, at work, and other public spheres). Indeed, the UN (2006a) reports that in Malawi, up to 50% of schoolgirls reported they had been touched in an unwanted sexual manner by either male teachers or schoolboys, whereas in Ecuador, 22% of girls also reported sexual harassment by boys or adult males within school settings. Western countries have the same problems; for example, in the United States, up to 83% of girls in Grades 8 through 11 experienced some form of male-perpetrated harassment, and up to 60% of adult women have reported sexual harassment in the workplace (UN, 2006a).

CHARACTERISTICS OF MALE PERPETRATORS

Clearly, male violence against females spills out from the private sphere into the public and will conform to the unique cultural conditions of each specific location:

> Forms and manifestations of violence against women are shaped by social and cultural norms as well as the dynamics of each social, economic, and political system. Factors such as . . . race, ethnicity, caste, class, migrant or refugee status, age, religion, sexual orientation, marital status, disability or HIV status, will influence what forms of violence [females] suffer. (UN, 2006a, p. 46)

The same factors also influence the type of male perpetration supported by local conditions and the risk factors that support male violence. However, there appear to be three domains that increase risk for male perpetration that are common across the globe: (a) relatively young age, (b) relative poverty (and as a covariate of poverty, ethnic minority status as locally defined), and (c) endorsement of rigid masculine beliefs and male entitlement (and concomitant downplaying of personal responsibility for violent perpetration).

Male Perpetrator Age

Whether we examine lethal or nonlethal forms of violence, younger males seem to be more violent than older males across multinational locations (Catalano, 2007; CCJS, 2011; CDC, 2010; UN, 2006a, 2006b, 2008, 2010; USJD, 2005; WHO, 2002, 2005, 2010). Ages for male perpetration range from a low in the teenage years (approximately 12–15 years of age) in non-Western countries to a high during early middle age (approximately 30–39 years of age) within Western countries (e.g., Catalano, 2007; CDC, 2010; WHO, 2002, 2005, 2010); differences among various cultures seem to be driven by local definitions of the standard marriage age as well as expected length of the male lifespan. Nevertheless, males most at risk for perpetration appear to be located overall within the range of 19 to 39 years of age.

Male Ethnic Minority Status and Poverty

In terms of ethnicity, males most at risk for perpetration are those of minority ethnic status within any given locale. Regardless of geographic location, minority ethnic status also tends to covary with lower socioeconomic status (CCJS, 2011; CDC, 2010; UN 2008, 2010; USJD, 2005; WHO, 2005, 2010). For example, large sample studies within the United States show that ethnic minorities (African Americans and indigenous) tend to report higher rates of intimate partner violence per capita while at the same time are some of the poorest populations in the country (Amnesty International, 2008; CDC, 2010). Similar patterns can be seen in Canada (CCJS, 2011) and rural versus urban samples from multicountry studies (WHO, 2005, 2010). In other words, males living in relative poverty around the world (which tends to covary with minority ethnicity) seem more likely to be violent against females overall.

Male Entitlement, Denial of Violence, and Lack of Accountability

When male perpetrators of physical and sexual violence are directly queried about their behavior, it becomes clear that, in general, violent males believe they are entitled to obedience and ownership of the females in their lives, and that if they use violent tactics against others (including other men and children), it is only because they deserved it (Blacklock, 2001; Hamner et al., 2000; Khatun et al., 2010; Muchoki,

2011; Rothman, Butchart, & Cerda, 2003). Furthermore, violent males appear to take little or no responsibility for their actions and do not believe they should be held accountable for their own violence (see Table 11.2).

CONCLUSIONS: THE GLOBAL CULTURE OF MASCULINE SUPERIORITY AND VIOLENCE AGAINST FEMALES

As long as definitions of masculinity allow males to assault women (and other men and children) with impunity, such violence will continue. Male violence in all social spheres will decrease only when cultural and structural changes occur that challenge prevailing definitions of masculinity, and are changed in a way that holds violent males accountable. This concept is not new.

In 1998, Heise published a paper that used an embedded, socioecological framework that integrated a wide host of factors that creates, supports, and maintains male violence, including violence against women and children. Commenting on Heise's contribution, Sitaker (2009) wrote:

> her work was groundbreaking in that [it] organized existing research . . . according to their level of social influence [and] incorporated findings . . . on many types of interpersonal violence, including international and cross-cultural studies . . . she was able to find underlying factors at outer layers of the . . . model that have not traditionally been studied by North American [researchers]. (p. 168)

Heise's (1998) original model included four concentric circles, each embedded within the other. The innermost circle referred to the individual characteristics of violent men, the next outward circle referred to the immediate social context in which an individual male is embedded (family, intimate relationship, friendships, acquaintances, location where violence takes place, etc.), the third circle referred to local community structures (workplace, neighborhood, social networks, police and criminal justice system, etc.), and the fourth and outermost circle referred to the larger social and economic environment that permeate the culture at large. Since that time, others have either used her original four-layer model, or have expanded it to five to include another outer layer that represents the nation-state. Figure 11.1 represents a graphic example of an expanded socioecological model based on Heise's original work.

In order to reduce (and eventually eliminate) violence across the globe, interventions designed to reduce hegemonic masculinity within each of the five layers in Figure 11.1 must be brought to bear. Indeed, examples of masculine superiority within each of the five layers can be found

Table 11.2 *Male Entitlement, Denial of Violence, and Lack of Accountability*

Male entitlement within relationships (Blacklock, 2001; Hamner et al., 2000; Khatun et al., 2010; Rivet & Rees, 2004)	Denial of overall violent behavior (Blacklock, 2001; Fisher & Hall, 2011; Hamner et al., 2000; Muchoki, 2011; Polaschek, Calvert, & Gannon, 2009)
Citing male privilege as rationale for violence	Complete denial of own violent behavior
Policing partner (monitoring, stalking, etc.)	Selective inclusion–exclusion of own behaviors when recounting violent incidents
Male rule setting for "appropriate" relationship parameters (division of household duties, freedom to come and go, etc.)	Not knowing, forgetting, or blanking out when recalling own violent behavior
Punishing partner for violating male rules ("talking back" or "disrespect," failure to adhere to rules, and so on)	Minimization of own violent acts, especially in comparison to other's violent behavior
	Normalizing own violent acts as ordinary and having no great significance
	Denial and minimization of the effects of own violent behavior on others (other men, females, children, and so on)
Overall Lack of Accountability (Blacklock, 2001; Fisher & Hall, 2011; Hamner et al., 2000; Khatun et al., 2010; Muchoki, 2011; Polaschek et al., 2009; Rivet & Rees, 2004)	
Blaming others for causing own violent behavior ("unreasonable" resistance by others, challenge to male expectations, sexual "provocation," and so on)	
Blaming stress at work, in the family, or other outside influences (e.g., alcohol use, unemployment) as reasons for violent acts	
Citing "momentary insanity" that is out of normal character	
Blaming others for negative consequences of own violent acts (police, courts, social services, other men, intimate partner or partner's family, children, and so on)	

Figure 11.1 An expanded version of Heise's (1998) socioecological model.

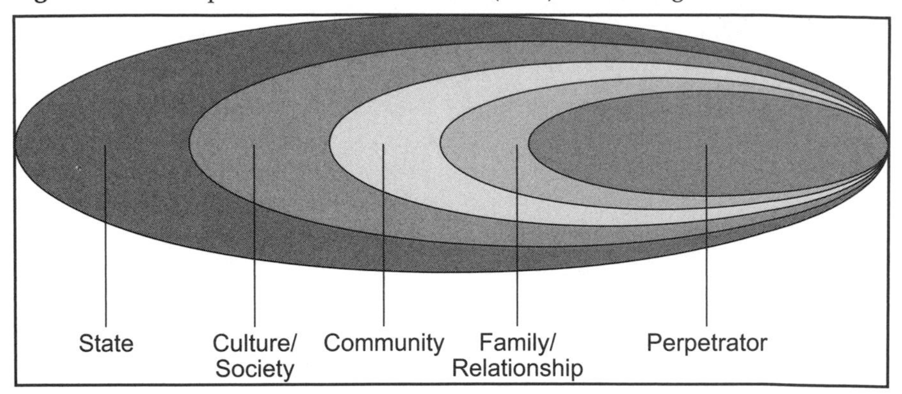

worldwide (Table 11.3). Understanding these different layers can only assist in designing interventions that can help curb male violence.

Creating interventions that specifically target each of the five layers noted in Figure 11.1 and Table 11.3 has proven to be especially challenging within multinational contexts; what might work in Denmark at the state and community level (Denmark National Institute of Public Health, 2007) may well fail in South Asia (Oxfam, 2004) because interventions must be tailored to the unique contexts and interpretations of male masculinity within different cultures. In addition, resources available to target the problem of masculinity are sorely lacking worldwide, and one size will definitely not fit all when translating effective interventions internationally. As Fontes and McCloskey (2011) noted:

> Prevention remains a relatively impoverished area . . . claiming but a miniscule amount of public funds as compared to criminal investigation and prosecutions . . . while committed activists throughout the world are working to reduce violence in their communities, a recent survey of the literature reveals a glaring lack of information on how to achieve cultural competence . . . and [men's violence] is often divided into subcategories such as sexual violence, sexual harassment, and domestic violence . . . we have not seen writings that pull these threads together into a larger whole to address the serious question: "How can we prevent violence against women from diverse cultures in diverse societies?" The answer undoubtedly involves many strategies aimed at all the levels where change can happen—in individual hearts and minds; in ethnic, geographic and religious communities; in local, state, national, and international law; and in the media that both normalize and glorify [men's] violence against women. (pp. 162–163)

Table 11.3 *Specific Forms of Masculinity within a Five-Layer Ecological Model*

Layer 5: State	Layer 4: Culture/society
Male-dominated militarism/ nationalism	General acceptance of religious beliefs that enshrine male superiority (male god[s], male religious leaders, etc.)
Male-dominated politics (officeholders, voting enfranchisement, etc.)	General acceptance of male honor, respect, control, and aggression
Male-dominated policies and resource allocation (education, employment, gender-equal pay, business policies/ protections, etc.)	General acceptance of male violence as conflict resolution
	General acceptance of male control of female behavior
Layer 3: Community	**Layer 2: Family/relationship**
Poverty levels and male control of community resources	Male-oriented hierarchic family structures (male children valued over female children, etc.)
General level of male violence within community	Male control of resources and decision making ("head of household")
Isolating females and other family members within community	Male-oriented policing/isolating of females and other family members
Male-oriented community policing of female behavior	Violence and conflict levels between intimate partners and other family members
Layer 1: Perpetrator	
Individual male acceptance of masculine gender role stereotypes (entitlement, lack of accountability, and denial of own violence)	
Highly variable individual male risk factors (young age, substance use, violent history, etc.)	

Note: Adapted and summarized from multinational findings obtained from each level: American College of Obstetricians and Gynecologists, 2007; Blacklock, 2001; Denmark National Institute of Public Health, 2007; Heise, Ellsberg, & Gottermoeller, 1999; Kimm, 2004; Michau, 2005; Montenegro Ministry of Justice, 2012; Oxfam 2004; Rothman, Butchart, & Cerda, 2003; Sitaker, 2009; Wright, 2009.

We clearly have our work cut out for us. Ending male violence against females is a huge undertaking and will take years of working at the national, social, community, family, and individual level to curb the underlying structures that bolster and maintain it—embodied and concretized definitions of superior masculinity.

REFERENCES

Abrahams, N., Jewkes, R., Hoffman, M., & Laubsher, R. (2004). Sexual violence against intimate partners in Cape Town: Prevalence and risk factors reported by men. *Bulletin of the World Health Organization, 82,* 330–337.

Adeleye, O. A., & Chiwuzie, J. (2007). "He does his own and walks away": Perceptions about male attitudes and practices regarding safe motherhood in Ekiadolor, Southern Nigeria. *African Journal of Reproductive Healt /La Revue Africaine de la Santé Reproductive, 11,* 76–89

Adinkrah, M., (2004). Witchcraft accusation and female homicide victimization in contemporary Ghana. *Violence Against Women, 10,* 325–356.

Adinkrah, M. (2008). Husbands who kill their wives: An analysis of uxoricides in contemporary Ghana. *International Journal of Offender Therapy and Comparative Criminology, 52,* 296–310.

Admon, Y. (2009). *The rising criticism of child bride marriages in Saudi Arabia* (Inquiry & Analysis Series Report No. 502). Washington, DC: The Middle East Media Research Institute. Retrieved from http://www.memri.org/report/en/0/0/0/0/0/141/3216.htm

Agathangelou, A. M., & Ling, L. H. M. (2004). Power, borders, security, wealth: Lessons of violence and desire. *International Studies Quarterly, 48,* 517–538.

Ahmed-Ghosh, H. (2004). Chattels of society: Domestic violence in India. *Violence Against Women, 10,* 94–118.

American College of Obstetricians and Gynecologists (ACOG) (2007). Vaginal "rejuvenation" and cosmetic vaginal procedures: ACOG Committee Opinion 378, *Obstetrics and Gynecology, 110,* 737–8.

American Psychological Association. (2007). *Report of the APA Task Force on the sexualization of girls.* Washington, DC: Author. Retrieved from www.apa.org/pi/wpo/sexualization.html

Amnesty International. (Spring 2008). *Maze of injustice: Failure to protect indigenous women from sexual violence in the USA—1 Year Report Update.* New York, NY: Author.

Association of Chief Police Officers. (2009). *Tackling perpetrators of violence against women and girls.* London, England: ACPO Review for the Home Secretary. Retrieved from http://www.acpo.police.uk/documents/crime/2009/200909CRIVAW01.pdf

Berns, N. (2001). Degendering the problem and gendering the blame: Political discourse on women and violence. *Gender and Society, 15,* 262–281.

Blacklock, N. (2001). Domestic violence: Working with perpetrators, the community, and its institutions. *Advances in Psychiatric Treatment, 7,* 65–72.

Borka, A. (2009, January 23). Pakistani newlyweds live in fear of honour killing. Reuters, India. Retrieved from http://www.reuters.com/article/worldNews/

idUSTRE50M0FI20090123?feedType=RSS&feedName=worldNews&rpc=22&sp=true

Brush, L. D. (2002). Changing the subject: Gender and welfare regime studies. *Social Politics, 9,* 161–186

Cáceres, C. F. (2005). Assessing young people's non-consensual sexual experiences: Lessons from Peru. In S. J. Jejeebhoy, I. Shah, & S. Thapa (Eds), *Sex without consent: Young people in developing countries* (pp. 127–138). New York, NY: Zed Books.

Canadian Centre for Justice Statistics. (2011). *Family violence in Canada: A statistical profile.* Ontario, Canada: Minister of Industry. Retrieved from http://www.statcan.gc.ca/pub/85-224-x/85-224-x2010000-eng.pdf

Catalano, S. (2007). *Intimate partner violence in the United States.* Washington, DC: US Department of Justice, Bureau of Justice Statistics. Retrieved from http://bjs.ojp.usdoj.gov/content/pub/pdf/ipvus.pdf

Centers for Disease Control and Prevention. (2010). *The National Intimate Partner and Sexual Violence Survey: 2010 summary report.* Atlanta, GA: Centers for Disease Control and Prevention, National Center for Injury Prevention. Retrieved from http://www.cdc.gov/ViolencePrevention/pdf/NISVS_Report2010-a.pdf

Chesney-Lind, M. & Pasko, L. (2004). *The female offender: Girls, women, and crime.* Thousand Oaks, CA: Sage.

Chopra, R. (2003). From violence to supportive practice: Family, gender and masculinities. *Economic and Political Weekly, 38,* 1650–1657.

Cossins, A. (2007). Men, masculinity, and child sexual abuse: A sex and gender question. In L. L. O'Toole, J. R. Schiffman, & M. Edwards (Eds.), *Gender violence: Interdisciplinary perspectives* (2nd ed., pp. 333–341). New York, NY: New York University Press.

Crowley, J. E. (2009). Fathers' rights groups, domestic violence and political countermobilization. *Social Forces, 88,* 723–755.

Das Gupta, M. (1987). Selective discrimination against female children in rural Punjab, India. *Population and Development Review, 13,* 90–95.

DeKeseredy, W. S. (1999). Tactics of the antifeminist backlash against Canadian National Women Abuse Surveys. *Violence Against Women, 5,* 1258–1276.

Denmark National Institute of Public Health. (2007). *Men's violence against women: Extent, characteristics, and measures against violence—2007.* Copenhagen, Denmark: Author. Retrieved from http://www.niph.dk/upload/english_summary.violence_003.pdf

Dobash, R. P., & Dobash, R. E. (1981). Community response to violence against wives: Charivari, abstract justice and patriarchy. *Social Problems, 28,* 563–581.

Fisher, S., & Hall, G. (2011). "If you show a bit of violence, they learn real quick": Measuring entitlement in violent offenders. *Psychiatry, Psychology, & Law, 18,* 588–598.

Fitzpatrick, L. (2008, November 19). Plastic surgery below the belt. *Time Magazine.* Retrieved from http://www.time.com/time/health/article/0,8599,1859937,00.html

Fontes, L., & McCloskey, K. (2011). A cultural perspective on violence against women. In C. Renzetti, J. L. Edelson, & R. K. Bergen (Eds.), *Sourcebook on violence against women,* (2nd ed., pp. 151–169). Thousand Oaks, CA: Sage.

Gavey, N. (2005). *Just sex? The cultural scaffolding of rape.* New York, NY: Routledge.

Guldi, M. (2008). Fertility effects of abortion and birth control pill access for minors. *Demography, 45,* 817–827.

Gurven, M., & Hill, K. (2009). Hunting as subsistence and mating effort? A re-evaluation of "Man the Hunter," the sexual division of labor and the evolution of the nuclear family. *Current Anthropology, 5,* 51–74.

Hamner, J., Itzin, C., Quiad, S., & Wigglesworth, D. (2000). *Home truths about domestic violence.* London, England: Routledge.

Heise, L. (1998). *Violence against women: An integrated ecological framework.* New York, NY: St. Martin's Press.

Heise, L., Ellsberg, M., & Gottermoeller, M. (1999). Ending violence against women. *Population Reports, 27,* 8–38.

Hill, K. (2010). Evolutionary biology, cognitive adaptations, and human culture. In S. W. Gangstead & J. A. Simpson (Eds.), *The evolution of mind: Fundamental questions and controversies* (pp. 348–356). New York, NY: Guilford Press.

Hollander, J. A. (2000). Fear journals: A strategy for teaching about the social consequences of gendered violence. *Teaching Sociology, 28,* 192–205.

Hsu, J. (2008, August 4). There are more boys than girls in China and India. *Scientific American.* Retrieved from http://www.scientificamerican.com/article.cfm?id=there-are-more-boys-than-girls

Hussain, A. (2001, August 10). Kashmir women face acid attacks. *BBC News.* Retrieved from http://news.bbc.co.uk/2/hi/south_asia/1484145.stm

Jewkes, R. (2005). Non-consensual sex among South African youth: Prevalence of coerced sex and discourses of control and desire. In S. J. Jejeebhoy, I. Shah, & S. Thapa (Eds.), *Sex without consent: Young people in developing countries* (pp. 86–95). New York, NY: Zed Books.

Jewkes, R., Penn-Kekanna, L., & Rose-Junius, H. (2005). "If they rape me, I can't blame them": Reflections on gender in the social context of child rape in South Africa and Namibia. *Social Science & Medicine, 61,* 1809–1820.

Jha, P., Kumar, R., Vasa, P., Dhingra, N., Thiruchelvam, D., & Moineddin, R., (2006). Low male-to-female sex ratio of children born in India: National survey of 1.1 million households. *The Lancet, 367,* 675–762. doi:10.1016/S0140-6736(06)67930-0

Kaighobadi, F., Shackelford, T. K., & Goetz, A. T. (2009). From mate retention to murder: Evolutionary psychological perspectives on men's partner-directed violence. *Review of General Psychology, 13,* 327–334.

Karkera, T. R. (2006). The gang rape of Mukhtar Mai and Pakistan's opportunity to regain its lost honor. *Journal of Gender, Social Policy and the Law, 14,* 163–176.

Kaur, R. (2008, July 26). Dispensable daughters and bachelor sons: Sex discrimination in northern India. *Economic & Political Weekly,* pp. 109–114. Retrieved from http://www.scribd.com/doc/4435246/Dispensable-Daughters-and-Bachelor-Sons-Sex-Discrimination-in-North-India

Khatun, M. N., Siddique, S. K., Das Roy, R., Deeba, F., Islam, N., & Siddiqi, S. S. (2010). *Exploring the experiences of male perpetrators: Violence against women in Bangladesh.* Naripokkho: Naripokkho Research Unit, Bangladesh [NGO Funded Research Project Report].

Kimm, J. (2004). *A fatal conjunction: Two laws, two cultures.* Sydney, Australia: Federation Press.

Levesque, R. J. R. (2001). *Culture and family violence: Fostering change through human rights law.* Washington, DC: American Psychological Association.

Liddle, J.R., Shackelford, T.K., & Weekes-Shackelford, V.A. (2012). Why can't we all just get along? Evolutionary perspectives on violence, homicide, and war. *Review of General Psychology, 16,* 24–36.

Lorber, J. (2002). Heroes, warriors, and "burqas": A feminist sociologist's reflections on September 11. *Sociological Forum, 17,* 377–396.

McCloskey, K., & Raphael, D. (2005). Adult perpetrator gender asymmetries in child sexual assault victim selection: Results from the 2000 National Incident-Based Reporting System. *Journal of Child Sexual Abuse, 14,* 1–24.

McCloskey, K. A., Sitaker, M., Grigsby, N., & Malloy, K. A. (2004). Characteristics of male batterers in treatment: An example of a localized program evaluation concerning attrition. *Journal of Aggression, Maltreatment, and Trauma, 8,* 67–95.

McFarlane, J., & Malecha, A. (2005). *Sexual assault among intimates: Frequency, consequences and treatments.* Washington, DC: U.S. Department of Justice. Retrieved from https://www.ncjrs.gov/pdffiles1/nij/grants/211678.pdf

McKibbin, W. F., Shackelford, T. K., Goetz, A. T., & Starratt, V. G. (2008). Why do men rape? An evolutionary psychological perspective. *Review of General Psychology, 12,* 86–97.

McMahon, P. M., & Puettl, R. C. (1999). Child sexual abuse as a public health issue: Recommendations from an expert panel. *Sexual Abuse, 11,* 257–266.

Meneley, A. (2000). Living hierarchy in Yemen. *Anthropologica, 42,* 61–73.

Meyers, C., & Woods, R. D. (1996). An obligation to provide abortion services. What happens when physicians refuse? *Journal of Medical Ethics, 22,* 115–120.

Michau, L. (2005). *Good practice in designing a community-based approach to prevent domestic violence.* Geneva, Switzerland: United Nations. Retrieved from http://www.un.org/womenwatch/daw/egm/vaw-gp-2005/docs/experts/michau.community.pdf

Miner, E. J., Shackelford, T. K., Block, C. R., Starratt, V. G., & Weekes-Shackelford, V. A. (2012). Risk of death or life-threatening injury for women with children not sired by the abuser. *Human Nature, 23,* 89–97.

Montenegro Ministry of Justice. (2012). *Study on family violence and violence against women in Montenegro.* Podgorica, Montenegro: Montenegro Ministry of Justice and Human Rights. Retrieved from http://www.gendermontenegro.me/wp-content/uploads/2012/07/Summary.pdf

Muchoki, S. (2011). Vocabulary used by sexual offenders: Meaning and implications. *Culture, Health, & Society, 13,* 101–113.

Oxfam. (2004). *Towards ending violence against women in South Asia.* Oxford, England: Author. Retrieved from http://www.oxfam.org/sites/www.oxfam.org/files/violence.pdf

Panchanadeswaran, S., Johnson, S. C., Go, V. F., Srikrishnan, A. K., Sivaram, S., Soloman, S., Bentley, M. E., & Celentano, D. (2009). Using the theory of gender and power to examine experiences of partner violence, sexual negotiation, and risk of HIV/AIDS among economically disadvantaged women in Southern India. In K. McCloskey & M. Sitaker (Eds.), *Backs against the wall: Battered women's resistance strategies* (pp. 143–165). London, England: Routledge.

Pinheiro, P. S. (2006). *World report on violence against children.* New York, NY: United Nations Secretary General. Retrieved from http://www.unviolencestudy.org/

Plummer, C. A., & Njuguna, W. (2009). Cultural protective and risk factors: Professional perspectives about child sexual abuse in Kenya. *Child Abuse and Neglect, 33,* 524–532.

Polaschek, D. L., Calvert, S. W., & Gannon, T. A. (2009). Linking violent thinking: Implicit theory-based research with violent offenders. *Journal of Interpersonal Violence, 24,* 75–96.

Posel, D. (2005). The scandal of manhood: "Baby rape" and the politicization of sexual violence in post-Apartheid South Africa. *Culture, Health & Sexuality, 7,* 239–252.

Rivet, M., & Rees, A. (2004). Dancing on a razor's edge: Systemic group work with batterers. *Journal of Family Therapy, 26,* 142–162.

Robin, R. W., Chester, B., Rasmussen, J. K., Jaranson, J. M., & Goldman, D. (1997). Prevalence, characteristics, and impact of childhood sexual abuse in a southwestern American Indian tribe. Child Abuse & Neglect, *21,* 769–787.

Rojanapithayakorn, W. (2006). The 100% condom use programme in Asia. *Reproductive Health Matters, 14,* 41–52.

Rosenthal, E. (2001, June 25). Harsh Chinese realities feed market in women. *New York Times.* Retrieved from http://www.nytimes.com/2001/06/25/world/harsh-chinese-realities-feed-market-in-women.html?scp=6&sq=bride%20shortage%20china&st=cse

Rothman, E. F., Butchart, A., & Cerda, M. (2003). *Intervening with perpetrators of intimate partner violence: A global perspective.* Geneva: World Health Organization, Violence and Injury Prevention Department. Retrieved from http://whqlibdoc.who.int/publications/2003/9241590491.pdf

Sanghavi, P., Bhalla, K., & Das, V. (2009). Fire-related deaths in India in 2001: A retrospective analysis of data. *The Lancet, 373,* 1282–1288. doi:10.1016/S0140-6736(09)60235-X

Santhya, K. G., & Jejeebhoy, S. J. (2005). Young women's experiences of forced sex within marriage: Evidence from India. In S. J. Jejeebhoy, I. Shah, & S. Thapa, (Eds), *Sex without consent: Young people in developing countries* (pp. 59–73). New York, NY: Zed Books.

Sidahmed, A. S. (2001). Problems in contemporary applications of Islamic criminal sanctions: The penalty for adultery in relation to women. *British Journal of Middle Eastern Studies, 28,* 187–204.

Sitaker, M. (2009). The ecology of intimate partner violence: Theorized impacts on women's use of violence. In K. McCloskey & M. Sitaker (Eds.), *Backs against the wall: Battered women's resistance strategies* (pp. 166–205). London, England: Routledge.

Skjelsbaek, I., & Smith, D. (Eds.) (2001). *Gender, peace, and conflict.* Thousand Oaks, CA: Sage.

Sokoloff, N. J. (Ed.). (2005). *Domestic violence at the margins: Readings on race, class, gender, and culture.* Piscataway, NJ: Rutgers University Press.

United Nations. (2002). *Integration of the human rights of women and the gender perspective: Cultural practices in the family that are violent towards women.* New York, NY: Author.

United Nations. (2008). *Unite to end violence against women fact sheet.* New York, NY: United Nations Secretary General's Campaign. Retrieved from http://www.un.org/en/women/endviolence/pdf/VAW.pdf

United Nations. (2006a). *In-depth study on all forms of violence against women.* New York, NY: Author. Retrieved from http://daccess-dds-ny.un.org/doc/UNDOC/GEN/N06/419/74/PDF/N0641974.pdf?OpenElement

United Nations. (2006b). *Report on violence against women, Secretary General.* New York, NY: Author.

United Nations. (2010). *The world's women 2010: Trends and statistics.* New York, NY: United Nations Department of Economic and Social Affairs. Retrieved from http://unstats.un.org/unsd/demographic/products/Worldswomen/WW_full%20report_color.pdf

United Nations Children's Fund. (2009). *Mali: Child marriage is a death sentence for many young girls.* New York, NY: Author. Retrieved from http://www.unicef.org/sowc09/docs/SOWC09-CountryExample-Mali.pdf

United Nations Population Fund. (2007). *A holistic approach to the abandonment of female genital mutilation/cutting.* New York, NY: Author. Retrieved from http://www.unfpa.org/public/global/pid/407

United States Justice Department. (2005). *Intimate partner violence risk assessment validation study.* Washington, DC: Author. Retrieved from https://www.ncjrs.gov/pdffiles1/nij/grants/209731.pdf

University of Melbourne (2000). *Eliminating sexual violence against women: Towards a global initiative—Report of the Consultation on Sexual Violence Against Women.* Melbourne, Australia: Author.

Vahdati, S. (2009, February 26). U.S. beheading is a crime, not an honor killing. *Women's eNews* [Electronic news organization article]. Retrieved from http://www.womensenews.org/article.cfm?aid=3932

Ward, J., & Marsh, M. (2006). *Sexual violence against women and girls in war and its aftermath: Realities, responses, and required resources—A briefing paper.* Brussels, Belgium: United Nations Population Fund.

Watts, C., & Zimmerman, C. (2002). Violence against women: Global scope and magnitude. *Lancet, 359,* 1232–1237.

Wilkinson, D. J., Bearup, L. S., & Soprach, T. (2005). Youth gang rape in Phnom Penh. In S. J. Jejeebhoy, I. Shah, & S. Thapa (Eds.), *Sex without consent: Young people in developing countries* (pp. 158–168). New York, NY: Zed Books.

World Health Organization. (2002). *World report on violence and health.* Geneva, Switzerland: Author.

World Health Organization. (2005). *WHO multi-country study on women's health and domestic violence against women: Summary report of initial results on prevalence, health outcomes, and women's responses.* Geneva, Switzerland: Author. Retrieved from http://www.who.int/gender/violence/who_multicountry_study/en/

World Health Organization. (2010). *Preventing intimate partner and sexual violence against women: Taking action and generating evidence.* Geneva, Switzerland: World Health Organization and the London School of Hygiene and Tropical Medicine.

Wright, R. G. (2009). The failure of sex offender policies. In R. G. Wright (Ed.), *Sex offender laws: Failed policies, new directions* (pp. 1–16). New York, NY: Springer Publishing Company.

Yang, J. A. (2004). Marriage by capture in the Hmong culture: The legal issue of cultural rights versus women's rights. *Law and Society Review at University of California, Santa Barbara, 3,* 38–49.

Yoon, Y. J. (2006). Gender imbalance: The male/female sex ratio determination. *Journal of Bioeconomics, 8,* 253–268.

Zorza, J., & Pines, S. (2007). *What a nice guy: Perfect relationship, secret abuse.* Indianapolis, IN: JIST.

Appendix

Resources for Researchers and Victims

Janet A. Sigal, Florence L. Denmark, Michele A. Paludi, Benjamin Freer, and Emily A. A. Dow

In this appendix, we have constructed a list of resources for researchers and victims related to some of the chapters in our two volumes. Both organizations that provide general information on important issues related to violence against girls and women, and specific websites and organizations that address topics including sex trafficking, domestic violence, and child abuse are included. These resources are selective in nature and not comprehensive. Despite the continuing violence against girls and women, it is encouraging to note the proliferation of national and international organizations dedicated to the prevention of violence and to helping victims worldwide.

GENERAL ORGANIZATIONS

Communities Against Violence Network: www.cavnet2.org
National Center for Victims of Crime: www.victimsofcrime.org
National Organization for Women: www.now.org
Nursing Network on Violence Against Women International: www.nnvawi.org

Office of Violence Against Women: U.S. Department of Justice: www.ovw.usdoj.gov

Partnerships Against Violence Network: www.padv.org

Tibet Justice Center: www.tibetjustice.org

UN Women: www.unwomen.org

U.S. Department of Justice's Victims of Crime: www.ojp.usdoj.gov/ovc/

Violence Against Women: www.vaw.umn.edu

Violence Against Women in American Indian/Native American and Alaska Native Communities: www.vawn.edu

Womenslaw: www.womenslaw.org

CHILD ABUSE

The International Society for the Prevention of Child Abuse and Neglect: www.ispcan.org

National Center for Missing and Exploited Children: www.missingkids.com

The National Children's Alliance: www.nationalchildrensalliance.org

The National Child Traumatic Stress Network: www.nctsn.org

COLLEGE VIOLENCE

The National Association of School Resource Officers (NASRO): www.nasro.org

Security on Campus: www.securityoncampus.org

Striving to Reduce Youth Violence Everywhere (STRYVE): www.vetoviolence.org/stryve

DOMESTIC VIOLENCE

American Domestic Violence Crisis Line: www.866uswomen.org

Asian and Pacific Islander Institute on Domestic Violence: www.apiahf.org/apidvinstitute

Battered Women's Justice Project: www.bwjp.org

Domestic Violence Clearinghouse and Legal Hotline: www.stoptheviolence.org

HPP Earth: International Domestic Violence Information: www.hotpeachpages.net

National Center on Domestic and Sexual Violence: www.ncdsv.org

National Coalition Against Domestic Violence: www.ncadv.org

National Domestic Violence Hotline: www.ndvh.org

National Latino Alliance for the Elimination of Domestic Violence: www.dvalianza.org

National Network to End Domestic Violence: www.nnedv.org

National Resource Center on Domestic Violence: www.nrcdv.org
New York Model for Batterer Programs: www.nymbp.org

ELDER ABUSE

Clearinghouse on Abuse and Neglect of the Elderly: www.ccrs.udel.edu/cane

International Network for the Prevention of Elder Abuse: www.inpea.net

The National Center on Elder Abuse (NCEA): www.ncea.aoa.gov/ncearoot/main_site/index.aspx

The National Committee for the Prevention of Elder Abuse (NCPEA): www.preventelderabuse.org

FAMILY VIOLENCE

British Columbia Institute Against Family Violence: www.bcifv.org
Family Violence Prevention Fund: www.endabuse.org
Stop Family Violence: www.stopfamilyviolence.org

REPRODUCTIVE JUSTICE

A Safe Passage: www.asafepassage.info
Center for Reproductive Rights: www.reproductiverights.org

SEX TRAFFICKING

Coalition Against Trafficking of Women: www.catwinternational.org
Polaris Project: www.polarisproject.org
Not For Sale: www.notforsalecampaign.org
Safe Horizon Anti-Trafficking Program: www.safehorizon.org/index/what-we-do-2/anti-trafficking-program-13.html

SEXUAL ASSAULT, SEXUAL VIOLENCE, AND SEXISM

Canadian Association of Sexual Assault Centres: www.casac.ca
Men Can Stop Rape: www.mencanstoprape.org
National Organization for Men Against Sexism: www.nomas.org
National Sexual Violence Resource Center: www.nsvrc.org
Rape, Abuse and Incest National Network: www.rainn.org

Index

About the Editors and the Contributors

JANET A. SIGAL, PhD, is Professor Emeritus of Psychology at Fairleigh Dickinson University. She received her PhD in social psychology from Northwestern University and taught courses in social psychology, experimental psychology, and cultural issues in clinical psychology. She is a past chair of the psychology department, and a past chair of the university institutional review board. She has more than 100 presentations, several articles, and many chapters in books primarily in the area of women's issues. Her recent 11-country research focused on cross-cultural perceptions of domestic violence. Dr. Sigal is a fellow of Divisions 1, 35 and 52 of the American Psychological Association and a fellow of the Eastern Psychological Association. She is president-elect of Division 1, a liaison of Division 35 to the United Nations, and a liaison of Division 52 to the Committee for Women in Psychology. Dr. Sigal is the main representative of the American Psychological Association at the United Nations, is co-chair of the NGO Committee on the Family, New York, vice chair of the NGO Committee of Ageing, New York, and is on the Sexual Assault Task Force of the NGO Committee on Migration, New York. She is active in the New York State Psychological Association in the Academic and Women's Issues Divisions, and in the psychology section of the New York Academy of Sciences.

FLORENCE L. DENMARK, PhD, is an internationally recognized scholar, researcher, and policy maker. She received her PhD from the University of Pennsylvania in social psychology and has six honorary degrees. Dr. Denmark is the Robert Scott Pace Distinguished Research professor of Psychology at Pace University in New York. Previously she was the Thomas

Hunter professor at Hunter College, and the executive officer of the doctoral program at City University. She is the International Council of Psychologists main NGO representative at the United Nations, a past president of the American Psychological Association (APA), Eastern Psychological Association, the International Council of Psychologists (ICP), and Psi Chi. She holds fellowship status in the APA EPA and the Association for Psychological Science. She is also a fellow of the Society for Experimental Social Psychology (SESP) and the New York Academy of Sciences. She has received numerous national and international awards for her contributions to psychology. She received the 2004 American Psychological Foundation Gold Medal for Lifetime Achievement for Psychology in the Public Interest. In 2005, she received the Ernest R. Hilgard Award for her Career Contribution to General Psychology. She is a recipient in 2007 of the Raymond Fowler Award for Outstanding Service to APA. Also in 2007, Dr. Denmark was elected to the National Academies of Practice as a distinguished scholar member. She received the Elder Award at the APA National Multicultural Conference in 2009. In 2011, she received the Award for Outstanding Lifetime Contributions to Psychology. Her most significant research and extensive publications have emphasized women's leadership and leadership styles, the interaction of status and gender, ageing women in cross-cultural perspectives and the history of women in psychology. Dr. Denmark has contributed numerous books to the field including: *The Praeger Handbook for Women Mentors: Transcending Barriers of Stereotype, Race and Ethnicity* (Praeger); *Victims of Sexual Assault and Abuse: Resources and Responses for Individuals and Families* (Praeger); and *Issues of Ageing and Disability: International Perspectives.*

KATHRYN BECKER-BLEASE, PhD, is an assistant professor in the School of Psychological Science at Oregon State University, where she researches child abuse and human development. She earned a PhD in developmental psychology from the University of Oregon in 2002. During her graduate training, she completed a predoctoral internship in Developmental Psychopathology. She then completed a 2-year postdoctoral internship at the Crimes Against Children Center/Family Research Lab at the University of New Hampshire. She is on the editorial boards for the *Journal of Trauma and Dissociation* and *Child Abuse and Neglect: An International Journal.*

EMILY BREITKOPF is a graduate student of psychology at the New School for Social Research. Working as a domestic child care provider while earning her women's studies degree inspired her to pursue research on the intersections of feminist psychology, queer theory, and childhood. She is a contributing writer for the New York City–based media literacy organization, *The Lamp,* where she has written on a wide range of social issues in media.

DONNA CASTANEDA, PhD, completed her doctorate in social psychology at the University of California, Davis, and after a two-year National Institute of Mental Health–funded postdoctoral position at the University of California, Los Angeles, she assumed her position in the psychology department at San Diego State University—Imperial Valley where she is currently a professor. Her scholarly work focuses on the role of gender and ethnicity in close relationships; health promotion in Latina/o communities; and how characteristics of service delivery systems influence the provision of health and mental health services. She has published work on the impact of close relationship factors in HIV sexual risk behavior, particularly among Latinas/os; the HIV/AIDS prevention needs of women factory workers in Mexico; the close relationship context and how it affects intimate partner violence; and health and mental health issues among Mexican American married couples. She has received funding for her work from various sources, including the National Institute of Mental Health and Agency for Health Care Research and Quality. At San Diego State University, she has received the Most Influential Faculty Award, Outstanding Faculty Award, and Quality of Life Leadership Award-Advocates for Women in Academia.

SUE-HUEI CHEN, PhD, is a professor of clinical psychology at National Taiwan University and a visiting adjunct professor at Emory University. Dr. Chen is a coinvestigator of the Project on Culture, Psychopathology, and Treatments, Excellence Research Project on Chinese Indigenous Psychology. She serves as the associate editor of *the Chinese Journal of Psychology*. Her research addresses the response to trauma following interpersonal violence and natural disasters.

JUNE F. CHISHOLM, PhD, is a licensed clinical psychologist who received her doctorate from the University of Massachusetts at Amherst. She has had a private practice in Manhattan, New York, for the past 30 years and is professor of psychology at Pace University where she has taught psychology courses at the undergraduate, master, and doctoral levels. She was a recipient of the Dr. Hilda A. Davis Award from the National Association of University Women. For many years, she was a senior psychologist in the Outpatient Psychiatric Department at Harlem Hospital Center, providing psychological services to an ethnically diverse, primarily poor, urban population. She has recently completed her second term serving on the New York State Board for Psychology. Her clinical, teaching, and research interests include: community psychology, cyberbullying, gender issues in the psychological treatment of women of color, multiculturalism as a perspective in psychology, prejudice in the theory/practice of psychology, psychological assessment of children and adults, parenting, and school violence.

JOAN C. CHRISLER, PhD, is the class of 1943 professor of psychology at Connecticut College where she teaches courses on health psychology and the psychology of women. She has published extensively on issues related to women's health and embodiment, especially on attitudes towards menstruation, premenstrual syndrome, body image, and weight. She edited *Sex Roles: A Journal of Research* from 2002 to 2006 and is editor or coeditor of 10 books including *Reproductive Justice: A Global Concern* (2012, Praeger), *Handbook of Gender Research in Psychology* (2010, Springer), *Women Over 50: Psychological Perspectives* (2007, Springer), and *From Menarche to Menopause: The Female Body in Feminist Therapy* (2004, Haworth).

EMILY A. A. DOW is a doctoral student in developmental psychology at the Graduate Center, City University of New York. She is interested in making connections between theoretical developmental psychology, education practices, and policy implications. Her research is focused on early childhood education, and teacher-student relationships.

BENJAMIN FREER, PhD, is an assistant professor of psychology at Fairleigh Dickinson University. Dr. Freer serves as a representative for Fairleigh Dickinson University to the United Nations, and is the recording secretary on the executive committee of the NGO Committee on the Family/New York. He served as the student representative for the Interdisciplinary Committee and on the Student and Early-Career Council at the Society for Research and Child Development. He maintains an interdisciplinary research program focused on the effects of traumatic stress on the cognitive development of children and adolescents.

JEANINE M. GALUSHA is a graduate student in the master's clinical neuropsychology program at the University of Texas at Tyler. Her academic goals include earning a doctorate in psychology and continuing research in dementia. She is a 2010 graduate of the University of Texas at Tyler where she earned a bachelor's in psychology and graduated Magna Cum Laude. While an undergraduate, she was accepted as a member of Psi Chi, the national honor society in psychology, and worked with several professors on various research projects. As a graduate student she is recognized as a member of the Honor Society of Phi Kappa Phi and has continued her research endeavors.

ADAM D. GARLAND is in the Ph.D. program at Brigham Young University. His academic goals include earning a doctorate in clinical psychology and pursuing research in childhood and adolescent disorders. His research interests include anxiety, depression, childhood disorders, and the psychological effects of childhood trauma on adult victims. During his undergraduate career, he volunteered at various local mental health organizations and was accepted as a member of Psi Chi, the national honor society in psychology.

AUDREY HOKODA, PhD, is an associate professor in the Child and Family Development Department at San Diego State University. She received her bachelor's in psychobiology from the University of California, Los Angeles, and her doctorate in clinical psychology at the University of Illinois, Urbana-Champaign. Funded by federal (e.g., National Institute of Mental Health, National Institutes of Health), state (San Diego County, Health and Human Services Agency, Sweetwater Union School District), and nonprofit health agencies (e.g., California Endowment, Alliance Health-care Foundation), she has been the principal investigator for more than 15 studies and community projects focused on developing, implementing and evaluating youth violence prevention programs. Her primary areas of research are peer abuse (bullying), teen relationship violence, and children exposed to domestic violence, particularly in Latino and Asian populations.

JAMIE KISSEE, MA, completed her master's in psychology at San Diego State University where she focused her studies on researching teen relationship violence (TRV), child maltreatment, and trajectories of intergenerational violence. She has published work on evidence-based interventions targeting risk factors such as drinking, to reduce violence on college campuses, and has presented studies about shame, harmful family dynamics, anxious attachment, peer norms, and other risk factors and consequences associated with TRV. She currently works at the Scripps Research Institute, broadening her understanding of alcohol and addiction, while simultaneously working for the Wellness and Restorative Practice Partnership aimed at reducing youth violence and improving overall community safety. She plans to apply to clinical PhD programs in the near future.

PAULA K. LUNDBERG-LOVE, PhD, is a professor of psychology at the University of Texas at Tyler (UTT) and was the Ben R. Fisch Endowed Professor in Humanitarian Affairs for 2001–2004. Her undergraduate degree was in chemistry, and her doctorate was in physiological psychology with an emphasis in psychopharmacology. After a 3-year postdoctoral fellowship in nutrition and behavior in the Department of Preventive Medicine at Washington University School of Medicine in St. Louis, she assumed her academic position at UTT where she teaches classes in psychopharmacology, behavioral neuroscience, physiological psychology, sexual victimization, and family violence. Subsequent to her academic appointment, Dr. Lundberg-Love pursued postgraduate training and is a licensed professional counselor. She is a member of the Tyler Counseling and Assessment Center, where she provides therapeutic services for victims of sexual assault, child sexual abuse and domestic violence. She has conducted a long-term research study on women who were victims of childhood incestuous abuse, constructed a therapeutic program for their recovery, and documented its effectiveness upon their recovery. She is the author of nearly 100 publications and presentations and is coeditor of *Violence and Sexual Abuse at Home: Current Issues in Spousal Battering and Child Maltreatment*. As a result of her training in psychopharmacology and child maltreatment, her expertise has been sought as a consultant on various death penalty appellate cases in the state of Texas.

JENNA MACKAY, MA, is a community activist, researcher, and writer. She has worked in the rape crisis movement for more than 10 years in multiple capacities in several Canadian provinces, including a recent project with the Ottawa Rape Crisis Centre. There she managed the development of a by-youth, for-youth sexual violence prevention campaign. Jenna earned her master of arts in the department of psychology at Carleton University where she documented the history of the Ontario antiviolence movement and its impact on hospital-based services for survivors of violence. She currently works in Toronto as a community-based researcher for Rainbow Health Ontario.

KATHY McCLOSKEY, PhD, CPE, PsyD, ABPP-CL, is a professor at the University of Hartford Graduate Institute of Professional Psychology in Hartford, CT. Her specialties include domestic violence, trauma, forensic populations, feminist psychology, multicultural and diversity issues, and the training of doctoral-level clinical psychologists. She is the coeditor of *Backs Against the Wall: Battered Women's Resistance Strategies,* and coauthor of *A Sexuality and Gender Diversity Training Program: Increasing the Competency of Mental Health Professionals.* She has been a past member of the Committee for Women in Psychology of the American Psychological Association and is currently a member of the implementing Committee of the Association for Women in Psychology. In 2006, she was the recipient of the Psychotherapy With Women Award conferred by the Society for the Psychology of Women (Division 35) of the American Psychological Association for an article she coauthored concerning intimate partner violence.

MEAGAN A. PAGITT is a graduate student in the master's in clinical neuropsychology program at the University of Texas at Tyler. She is a 2009 graduate of the University of Texas at Tyler where she earned a B.B.A. in management and graduated Summa Cum Laude. She spent 2011 in Lima, Peru, serving as a rotary ambassadorial scholar. Her academic and professional goals include earning a doctorate in clinical psychology, working in private practice, and joining annual psychological missions that serve people in areas without access to mental health care.

MICHELE A. PALUDI, PhD, is the author or editor of 48 college textbooks and more than 180 scholarly articles and conference presentations on sexual harassment, campus violence, psychology of women, gender, and sexual harassment and victimization. Her book *Ivory Power: Sexual Harassment on Campus* (1990, SUNY Press) received the 1992 Myers Center Award for Outstanding Book on Human Rights in the United States. Dr. Paludi served as chair of the U.S. Department of Education's Subpanel on the Prevention of Violence, Sexual Harassment and Alcohol and Other Drug Problems in Higher Education. She was one of six scholars to be selected for this subpanel. She also was a consultant to and a member of former New York State Governor Mario Cuomo's Task Force on Sexual Harassment. Dr. Paludi serves as an expert witness for court proceedings and administrative hearings on sexual harassment. She has had extensive experience in conducting training programs and investigations of sexual harassment and other equal employment opportunity issues for businesses and educational institutions.

YVONNE RAFFERTY, PhD, is a professor of psychology at Pace University, New York. She teaches courses in both the psychology department (e.g., Social Psychology, Community Psychology), and women's and gender studies (e.g., The Girl Child: A Global Perspective; Gender, Race and Class). She also teaches a number of service learning interdisciplinary courses (e.g., International Issues in Child Protection; The Impact of War on Women and Children). At the United Nations, she is a representative of the Society for the Psychological Study of Social Issues (SPSSI), where she is particularly active with the Working Group on Girls (WGG). Dr. Rafferty is a member of the WGG Steering Committee, and chairs the WGG Research and Writing Group. Throughout her career, she has conducted research on a range of topics including child trafficking, commercial sexual exploitation, homelessness, aids and adolescents, children with disabilities, and early childhood education.

ROSWITH ROTH, PhD, Professor Emerita of Psychology, University of Graz, Austria, received her PhD in 1980 from the University of Graz. She received a license in client-centered psychotherapy and behavior therapy. She was an associate professor in the department from 1994 to 1999, and chair of the interuniversity coordination center for gender studies. From 1994 to 2006, she was chair of the working group for equal opportunities, for the entire University of Graz. In 1999, she was a visiting professor at the University at Little Rock, Arkansa and in 2001–2002 was president of the International Council of Psychologists. She was a university professor at the University of Graz in 2004 and a visiting professor at Hiroshima

University in Japan in 2005. From 2000 to 2009, she was chair of the health and gender section at the Department of Psychology, University of Graz. In 2011–2012, Dr. Roth was the chair of the NGO Committee on the Family at the UN in Vienna. Her research interests and publications were in gender research, gender issues in higher education, women's health, chronic diseases in children and adolescents (Type 1 diabetes), psychological and ethical issues, and prediction and prevention of Type 1 diabetes.

LISA RUBIN, PhD, is an assistant professor of psychology at the New School for Social Research and a practicing clinical psychologist in New York City. She chairs the Reproductive Issues Committee of the Society for the Psychology of Women. Her research and clinical interests concern the interface of objectification and medicalization processes in women's health care, particularly in relation to body image and obesity, reproductive health and assisted reproductive technologies, and psycho-oncology. She is particularly interested in how processes of objectification and medicalization are enacted, how they intersect with gender and racialized ideologies and how they are resisted or otherwise negotiated across individuals and within social groups.

NANCY FELIPE RUSSO, PhD, is a regents professor of psychology and gender studies—Emeritus, Arizona State University. She has worked on international issues related to gender violence and women's rights as a researcher and policy advocate for more than four decades. An author or editor of more than 200 publications related to the psychology of women and gender, she is a former editor of the *Psychology of Women Quarterly* and *American Journal of Orthopsychiatry*. Her many awards and honors include the Distinguished International Psychologist Award from APA's Division of International Psychology and the Denmark-Gunvald Award for significant contributions to the psychology of women and gender from the International Council of Psychologists.

ALEXANDRA RUTHERFORD, PhD, C. Psych, is an associate professor in the history and theory of psychology graduate program, Department of Psychology, York University, Toronto. She received her PhD in history/theory of psychology and clinical psychology from York University. Her research focuses on the relationship between feminism and psychology from the late 1800s through the second wave of the women's movement. She coedited the *Handbook of International Feminism: Perspectives on Psychology, Women, Culture, and Rights* (Springer, 2011) and was the winner of the 2012 Distinguished Publication Award from the Association for Women in Psychology. She directs the Psychology's Feminist Voices oral history and digital archive project (www.feministvoices.com) and is a Fellow of the Society for the Psychology of Women.

STEPHEN P. SHEWMAKE received his BS in psychology from the University of Texas at Tyler in 2011. He is currently pursuing his BS degree in Biochemistry at Texas State University and hopes to pursue a career in medicine.

GINNY SPRANG, PhD, is the buckhorn professor of child welfare and children's mental health at the University of Kentucky. Dr. Sprang is principal investigator and executive director of the Center on Trauma and Children, a center whose mission is dedicated to the enhancement of the health and well-being of children and their families through research, service, and dissemination of information about child trauma. She served as a member of the National Steering Committee for the National Child Traumatic Stress Network (NCTSN), is the current co-chair of the Secondary Traumatic Stress Committee for the NCTSN, and is the chair of the Terrorism and Disaster Special Interest Group of the International Society for Traumatic Stress Studies. Her scholarship focuses on the clinical, forensic, and empirical aspects of traumatic stress and the efficacy and effectiveness of treatments to address the biopsychosocial impact of violence against children. Dr. Sprang has published extensively in the leading journals focusing on trauma, maltreatment, and treatment efficacy in adults and children.

EMILIO C. ULLOA, PhD, earned his doctoral degree in social psychology from Arizona State University. He is an associate professor and has served as the director of undergraduate advising and programs in the department of psychology at San Diego State University since 2003. He has published research articles and book chapters on the topics of youth violence, dating violence, bullying, and intimate partner abuse, some exploring the link between violence and alcohol and, in many examples, with Latino populations. His research aims to understand the etiology of youth violence and victimization from a socioecological and feminist perspective. In particular, much of his work aims to identify the mechanisms that link risk factors to violence and aggression. Dr. Ulloa has been involved with research and student support programs focused on psychology student success, particularly for underrepresented students, and has also served as faculty adviser for the SDSU chapter of Psi Chi, the national honor society in psychology. Dr. Ulloa has received awards for his teaching and mentoring and was recognized in 2009 for his advising by The National Academic Advising Association.

DEBORAH A. WILLIAMS is a graduate of Barnard College and currently a doctoral student in Pace University's School-Clinical Psychology Program. She will be completing her clinical internship at the Superior Court's Child Guidance Center in Washington, D.C.